Modern Comparative Politics Series
edited by
Peter H. Merkl
University of California,
Santa Barbara

D1565387

Comparative Federalism
The territorial dimension
of politics

Drahé Helence (mám rád její dimence)
bez jejíhož přerušování
by byla tato kniha
napsána daleko dříve

3/21 1970   Ivoňák

COMPARATIVE FEDERALISM
The territorial dimension of politics

Ivo D. Duchacek
The City College of
the City University of New York

HOLT, RINEHART AND WINSTON, INC.
New York   Chicago   San Francisco   Atlanta
Dallas   Montreal   Toronto   London   Sydney

To Dr. Harry Gold

The selection on p. 46 from "The Death of the Hired Man" is from *Complete Poems of Robert Frost*. Copyright 1930, 1939 by Holt, Rinehart and Winston, Inc. Copyright © 1958 by Robert Frost. Copyright © 1967 by Lesley Frost Ballantine. Reprinted by permission of Holt, Rinehart and Winston, Inc.

Printed in the United States of America

9 8 7 6 5 4 3 2 1

FOREWORD
TO THE SERIES

This new series in comparative politics was undertaken in response to the special needs of students, teachers, and scholars that have arisen in the last few years, needs that are no longer being satisfied by most of the materials now available. In an age when our students seem to be getting brighter and more politically aware, the teaching of comparative politics should present a greater challenge than ever before. We have seen the field come of age with numerous comparative monographs and case studies breaking new ground, and the Committee on Comparative Politics of the Social Science Research Council can look back proudly on nearly a decade of important spade work. But teaching materials have lagged behind these changing approaches to the field. Most comparative government series are either too little coordinated to make systematic use of any common methodology or too conventional in approach. Others are so restricted in scope and space as to make little more than a programmatic statement about what should be studied, thus suggesting a new scholasticism of systems theory that omits the idiosyncratic richness of the material available and tends to ignore important elements of a system for fear of being regarded too traditional in approach.

In contrast to these two extremes, the Modern Comparative Politics Series attempts to find a happy combination of rigorous, systematic methodology and the rich sources of data available to area and country specialists. The series consists of a core volume, *Modern Comparative Politics,* by Peter H. Merkl, country volumes covering one or more nations, and comparative topical volumes.

Rather than narrowing the approach to only one "right" method, the core volume leaves it to the teacher to choose any of several approaches he may prefer. The authors of the country volumes are partly bound by a framework common to these volumes and the core volume, and are partly free to tailor their approaches to the idiosyncrasies of their respective countries. The emphasis in the common framework is on achieving a balance between such elements as theory and application, as well as among developmental perspectives, sociocultural aspects, the group processes, and the decision-making processes of government. It is hoped that the resulting tension between comparative approaches and politicocultural realities will enrich the teaching of comparative politics and provoke discussion at all levels from undergraduate to graduate.

The group of country volumes is supplemented by a group of analytical comparative studies. Each of these comparative volumes takes an important topic and explores it cross-nationally. Some of these topics are covered in a more limited way in the country volumes, but many find their first expanded treatment in the comparative volumes—and all can be expected to break new scholarly ground.

The ideas embodied in the series owe much to the many ume. Although they are far too numerous to mention here, a persons whose names are cited in the footnotes of the core vol-special debt of spiritual paternity is acknowledged to Harry Eckstein, Gabriel A. Almond, Carl J. Friedrich, Sidney Verba, Lucian W. Pye, Erik H. Erikson, Eric C. Bellquist, R. Taylor Cole, Otto Kirchheimer, Seymour M. Lipset, Joseph La Palombara, Samuel P. Huntington, Cyril E. Black, and many others, most of whom are probably quite unaware of their contribution.

P. H. M.

Santa Barbara, California

PREFACE

This book is a comparative analysis of the reasons for the different patterns of territorial distribution of political authority in the contemporary world. The territorial delineation of power in terms of delegation, division, or subdivision is usually inevitable and is often wise. Rather than classifying political systems in rigid unitary, federal, or confederal categories, this book instead focuses on the fluidity of the process of territorial distribution of authority under the impact of wars and international tension, technology, new communications, welfare planning, and new aspirations.

The central concept of the book is that of the territorial community or the territorial interest group—an aggregate of individuals and groups who share not only common experiences, values, fears, and purposes but also an awareness of the territorial dimensions of their collective interests and actions. Political systems in Europe, North America, South America, Australia, Asia, and Africa that are considered to be or that claim to be federal in nature are subject to a comparative analysis that challenges the traditional yardsticks of federalism. The study also points to the gap between the federal, or unitary, myth and reality.

The book is primarily meant for use in courses on comparative politics. Its systematic references to the American federal theories and practices make the book particularly suitable for advanced courses in American government and politics. It may also be found useful in courses that deal with international politics or the history of nationalism.

The intellectual debts of an author of a book such as this are numerous and heavy. I have tried to identify and acknowledge them in the text. A deliberate effort has been made to refer to or incorporate the major, although frequently contradictory, findings on the subject of federalism that are reflected in the work of such scholars as Carl J. Friedrich, William H. Riker, K. C. Wheare, William S. Livingston, Morton Grodzins, and Arthur W. Macmahon. References have also been made to almost all papers presented at the impressive gathering of scholars at the Sixth World Congress on "New Trends and Practice of Federalism," organized by the International Political Science Association in 1964 in Geneva. The author would like particularly to acknowledge the inspiring influence of the new analyses presented in Geneva by Professors C. J. Hughes, R. L. Watts, Richard L. Merritt, and S. A. H. Haqqi.

As to the more direct contributions to my study, I should like, first of all, to express my grateful appreciation for the many constructive criticisms and creative suggestions concerning both the structure and the substance of my manuscript made by the General Editor of the series, Peter H. Merkl. In a subject as controversial as comparative federalism, I can hardly imagine a smoother and more productive cooperation than I have experienced with Professor Merkl, whose examination of my first and then the penultimate draft was not only systematic and thorough but also imaginative and stimulating.

In addition, several friends and scholars in the Political Science Department at The City College of the City University of New York, have contributed to my work with advice and encouragement: John A. Davis is initially responsible for the shift of my teaching and research orientation toward comparative politics and its links with international relations. Harry Lazer, Thomas G. Karis, and Hillman M. Bishop have given me advice and encouragement as well as criticism in the initial stages of my project. And John H. Herz, whose generous advice has significantly marked most of my research and writing, has again given me his helping hand in preparing and organizing this book. In completing my research and then the manuscript I had the diligent and able cooperation of my research assistant Joel Wachs. All involved deserve my warm thanks.

I. D. D.

New York City
December 1969

CONTENTS

INTRODUCTION
POLITICAL MAN:
A TERRITORIAL
ANIMAL

Every difference is apt to create a division. The greatest division is perhaps between virtue and vice; then there is the division between wealth and poverty; and there are also other divisions, some greater and some smaller, arising from other differences. Among the last we may count the division caused by difference of territory. . . . Heterogeneity of territory is also an occasion of sedition. This happens in states with a territory not naturally adapted to political unity.

ARISTOTLE (*Politics*)

Territoriality—the drive to gain, maintain, and defend the exclusive right to a piece of property—is an animal instinct approximately as ancient and powerful as sex.

ROBERT ARDREY (*African Genesis*)

One aspect of every nation's self-image is the equation of national identity with possession of a certain piece of territory; a nation's self-image has been identical with the territory occupied, directly or as colonies.

JEROME D. FRANK (*Sanity and Survival*)

1

The main concern of this comparative study is the territorial aspect of politics. Political organization of the whole world remains primarily based on territorial divisions and subdivisions. They reflect and represent territorial interests. Some territorial divisions have been created by the central authority (from "above") in order to improve the administrative efficiency on the local level. The territorial subdivisions of France, the *départements*,[1] were created in this way. Other territorial divisions, although also created by delegation of power (from "above"), represent responses of the central authority to pressures of territorial groups seeking self-government. The delegation of authority in both cases characterizes *unitary* systems as they have developed in England, Japan, or within the fifty states composing the American federal union. There is also the frequent case of self-ruling territorial communities that have decided to form a higher supranational union from "below," delegating power to a central authority for some purposes while retaining local self-rule for other purposes. These are usually called *confederal* or *federal* systems.

Territorial communities are in contact, cooperation, competition, or conflict with each other. They are also in cooperation or in conflict with organized nonterritorial interest groups, such as those based on special skills, with the resulting division of labor and wealth, or on a creed or ideology.

Today the human race is compartmentalized into some 140 territorial nation-states despite the contrary pulls that represent the growing awareness of worldwide interdependence in an era whose advanced technology makes both mass destruction and mass construction possible. Political authority everywhere is clearly territory-bound. Well-protected national boundaries indicate the limits of each national government's territorial control and coercive power. Within the nation-states, internal territorial boundaries determine the extent of administration and control exercised by the subnational units of government, provincial and local. Political parties, even when committed to transterritorial creeds, are usually organized to reflect or manipulate the interests of electoral (territorial) districts. Functional

[1] In order to avoid confusion with the English term "department" reserved for the designation of executive departments, the French spelling for the basic unit of French local government will be used.

interest groups, although dedicated to the promotion or defense of nonterritorial interests, cannot escape the territorial dimension of any political organization; the interest groups are bound to be organized into local cells or chapters.

Dividing and subdividing the world according to the territorial principle is probably as old as humanity. It seems inescapable. It may have begun with the first delineation of boundaries between two clusters of inhabited caves and their respective hunting reservations. Peace and order, based on such mutual recognition of territoriality, followed. So did conflicts over the extent of territorial control. Unlike animals, men often desire more territory than they need. Unlike animals, they also can merge their territories into higher unions. Nations, governments, and political movements derive considerable strength from being based on and mirroring a territorial interest. As a political animal, man seems to be also a territorial one.

It is an observable fact that people identify with territorial institutions, whether they are created from "above" or from "below." (In Chap. 1 a few of the fundamental reasons for such identification will be examined.) Of course, the intensity of their identification with the different territorial communities to which they simultaneously belong varies greatly. Usually, the rational and emotional identification of individuals and groups with their territorial nation-state takes precedence over loyalty to communities beyond and within the national boundaries. Identification with subnational communities, such as provinces or villages, is aptly called *local patriotism.* Its potentially secessionist tendencies should never be discounted. When viewed from the national or imperial center, the revolutionary quest for territorial self-determination often appears to be parochialism posing as nationalism. Neglect or oppression may have endowed what originally was localism with all the explosive ingredients of fierce nationalism.

DELEGATION AND DIVISION OF AUTHORITY

In order to make a political system effective, it is usually wise and often imperative to either divide or delegate authority on a functional or territorial basis or on both. This imposes a difficult task: to differentiate, however flexibly and approximately, between general and collective issues to be handled by the central authority, and special or local ones to be taken care of by local government or functional agencies. No system, democratic or authoritarian, can do without the division of tasks that is bound to be accompanied by some dispersion of the decision-making authority. This happens and must happen even in modern totalitarian systems. The reason is simple enough: political rulers can focus on some problems some of the time but cannot focus on all the problems all of the time and in all localities.

Perhaps only some tribal territories or some of the modern microstates could conceivably be administered by a ruler as a personal fief on account of his Godlike omnipotence and omnipresence. When a territorial state is of some size, its leader and his immediate aides must organize power territorially; for even modern detection and communication devices, coupled with extreme mobility of enforcing agents, necessitate some delegation of power, at least to those who manipulate the devices and transports and command their immediate and local uses. Hitler, who had condemned the federal territorial diffusion of power under the democratic Weimar system, introduced another, albeit a much more tightly controlled, system. The Third Reich was divided into new territorial units, *Gaue*,[2] each headed by one of Hitler's trusted lieutenants,[3] a *Gauleiter*. They proved loyal to the bitter end. Yet, one can perhaps speculate as to what would have been, for instance, the loyalty of an Austrian *Gauleiter* had the Allied policy been that of *conditional* surrender and had he been appropriately approached by the Allies following their invasion of the southern underbelly of Europe instead of Normandy.

In Communist China, the only serious leadership crisis

---

[2] There were 32 *Gaue* in Germany proper, 7 in annexed Austria, and 1 in the Sudetenland, which was detached from Czechoslovakia in 1938. Ultimately the Nazi Reich was divided into 43 *Gaue*. These were further subdivided into 920 districts (*Kreise*, under the control of a *Kreisleiter*). These, in turn, were territorially subdivided into about 30,000 communal groups (*Ortsgruppen*), which were broken down into blocks (*Blocke*) in urban areas and some 110,000 cells (*Zellen*) in rural areas. Harold Zink, *Modern Governments*. Princeton, N.J.: Van Nostrand, 1958, pp. 427–428.

[3] *Lieutenant* is, of course, another territorial term. A person holds a place—*tient un lieu*—in behalf of somebody else.

within the Chinese party prior to the so-called Socialist Cultural Revolution of the late 1960s developed around the ambitions of two party secretaries, Jao Shu-shih and Kao Kang, who were accused of having built personal *territorial* bases of power in Shanghai and Manchuria, respectively, for the alleged purpose of plotting against the heart of the system and party, Peking.[4]

The history of all great empires is full of examples of crises precipitated by provincial lords who used their territorial power for the purpose of capturing the central imperial authority or of successfully seceding from it. Often, ancient empire builders who had personally, with sword in hand, conquered distant provinces had finally no choice but to transfer their administration to proconsuls and viceroys, usually relatives, friends, or trusted chieftains. And ever so often the empire builders were made to regret their choice, because the men who had the organizational skill and political talent necessary to rule over the newly taken territory (that is, to command local garrisons, legions, or police and to collect taxes) were quite capable of a rebellious bid for independent power.

The extent of territorial or functional dispersion of any central authority and the resulting responsibility and autonomy of territorial or functional agencies vary, evidently, not only from system to system, but within the same system from time to time, from technology to technology, and from personality to personality. The spectrum of variations on the subject of power dispersion presents such extreme opposites as a totalitarian system on the one hand and a loose confederation on the other; the difference in degree seems qualitative rather than quantitative, just as the difference between oil afire and oil frozen—a matter measurable in degrees Fahrenheit—appears to us as a difference in kind.

[4] In 1967, a Red Guard wall poster announced the purge of Ulanfu, a party leader, governor and military commander of the Inner Mongolian province of China. The poster accused him of plotting to transform Inner Mongolia into an "independent kingdom."

In 1968 Wang En-mao, the Communist leader of the strategic Chinese province of Sinkiang (Chinese Turkestan, inhabited by a Moslem people, the Uighurs), was purged. On December 22, the Sinkiang Revolutionary Committee, carrying out Mao's Cultural Revolution in Sinkiang, accused Wang of "mountain stronghold mentality" and of attempts to preserve "his independent kingdom."

In all systems the problem is to find the boundary at which general and central problems end and special or local problems begin. At best the boundary is blurred.

First, power eludes any precise measurement. When one says that political power has been divided fifty-fifty or delegated on a ninety-ten basis, the terms are at best allegorical expressions of intent rather than factual descriptions of reality. Even though James Madison spoke of "sums" or "quantities" of power, we cannot really quantify "all those activities which are or may become the subject of governmental control, we cannot presume that these activities are finite or infinite, and we cannot employ the idea of ratio except metaphorically." [5]

Second, in a world of constant economic, technological, social, and political changes, no division of labor, responsibility, and power can be considered immune to alteration, erosion, or explosion as a result of environmental or political changes. New inventions, discoveries of new sources of raw materials, new means of transportation, and other technological innovations may catapult a backward, sleepy province into a position with an energetic basis of power in a political system. Also, what has been delegated to institutions, groups, or men on the assumption of its marginal or purely local nature may be subsequently maneuvered into a decisive area of power. Many rulers, when suddenly deposed by their inferiors and awaiting execution in prison, have realized, much to their surprise, that their fall stemmed from having delegated too much of their power. "We have kiss'd away kingdoms and provinces" is a famous melancholic statement made by Antony's friend Scarus in Shakespeare's *Antony and Cleopatra*.

On the other hand, many a ruler, dreading a dangerous dilution of his power, has tried to concentrate authority in his own hands so excessively that his rule was undermined by the inefficiency of overcentralization. While choking all initiative, he probably contributed to the assertion of the only remaining initiative, rebellion. The art of politics in many instances consists of maintaining an appropriately flexible compound of centralized and decentralized power.

[5] Rufus Davis, "The 'Federal Principle' Reconsidered," *Australian Journal of Politics and History*, Vol. 1, No. 2 (May 1956), 227.

A delegation or division of political authority may be either functional or territorial. Such a distribution of power may be caused by concern for a rational division of labor or administrative expediency or both; or it may be a response to pressures as exercised by either functional interests or territorial interests.

FUNCTIONAL INTERESTS AND INSTITUTIONS

By *functional* (nonterritorial) distribution of authority in the present context we mean assignment of specialized roles to men or institutions whose present or future expertise is assumed. Examples of such specialized agencies or agents in the broadest sense are administrators, lawmakers, judges, economists, and managers. Functional institutions are further subdivided into more and more narrowly specialized compartments. The executive branch of government, for instance, contains departments that specialize in foreign affairs, defense, treasury, internal affairs, private or nationalized industries, commerce, labor, agriculture, technology, education, welfare, health. And, here again, further functional subdivisions permit administrative focusing on, and contact with, very narrow areas of functional interest. The legislative assemblies are also functionally subdivided into committees that largely correspond to the executive functional compartments (such as congressional standing committees on foreign affairs, armed services, appropriations, ways and means, and internal trade). In many countries even the judicial branch is subdivided into courts specializing in criminal, civil, patent, labor, administrative, family, divorce, and inheritance (surrogate) cases.

The need for a functional specialization and use of expert and skilled personnel is obvious: the very principle of effective administration requires it. Even a charismatic dictator who necessarily considers any dilution of his personal power as a curse is bound to discover that he cannot decide everything by intuition only and then implement every decision personally. He needs, first of all, information about his external and internal foes and friends, and must therefore organize his espionage, investigation, and police establishments, and then rely not only on their skills and techniques but also on their loyalty. No dictator has ever had the guarantee—and this has always been his nightmare—that all the information that may be decisive for his political as well as his physical survival has been channeled to him loyally, in time and in full. A dictator also needs, and therefore must rely on, the expert knowledge, organizational skill, talents—and loyalty—of his generals, party organizers, bureaucrats, managers, scientists, educators, and even poets and artists. Reliance on them for the purpose of implementation of his decisions endows the persons or agencies with a share in power. A less dependent or totally independent source of power may emerge. In modern dictatorships, mutually permeating party and police controls are supposed to prevent persons and agencies that have access to instruments of coercive control or mass influence (army officers, police officials, and journalists or poets) from using the instruments against the central authority in order to weaken it, make it dependent, or replace it. A classic example of a rise of an independent *functional* authority is the attempt of the Soviet police chief Lavrenti Beria to replace the party and army leadership. Following Stalin's death, Beria, relying on the organizational skill and loyalty of his police establishment, had the Kremlin encircled by tanks in an attempt to solve the Soviet succession crisis in his favor. The attempt failed, and Beria was executed. An example of a successful replacement of one functional sector of government by another sector was the military *coup d'état* in Indonesia. Sukarno, the fiery orator and charismatic leader of the liberation struggle against Dutch colonialism, had ruled his country by carefully balancing the power and organization of the Communist party with the power and organization of the armed forces. In October 1965 the Communist party allegedly attempted to seize power by a coup, which was, however, frustrated by a military countercoup, led by the defense minister, General Abdul Haris Nasution. Subsequently, the military eliminated both the Communist party and President Sukarno from the political scene. Partly organized and partly spontaneous, the purge of the Indonesian Communists resulted in an officially admitted 84,000 dead (about the same number killed in Hiroshima by the atomic bomb); unofficial estimates were 300,000 to 500,000 dead. The fall of the Indonesian dictator confirms the general experience that no ruler, however shrewd or respected by the masses, can rule without delegating some power to others and without relying on their skill and loyalty. But even a partial delegation of power may result in a challenge to or a rebellion against the original source of authority.

In democracies, functional divisions of authority have been not only institutionalized but also appropriately glorified. Terms such as *separation of power* (legislative, executive, and judiciary), *checks and balances,* and *collective responsibility* of the cabinet to the legislative assembly from which the cabinet issues represent different forms of division of labor and function-specialization; they may be amply justified by the requirement of efficiency based on a rational distribution of specific tasks. In addition, since Montesquieu such divisions of power have been viewed as guarantees against a dangerous concentration of power and, therefore, as conditions for constitutional (that is, limited) government. The French Declaration of the Rights of Man and Citizen of 1789 proclaimed: "Any society in which the guarantee of the rights is not secured, or the separation of powers not determined, has no constitution [that is, constitutional limited government] at all."

Furthermore, the democratic creed and practice encourage functional interests to get organized and, as groups, to articulate their demands, which a responsive government promises to aggregate and convert into binding rules, usually in the form of laws. In the past, functional interest groups such as those of labor, agriculture, business, and industry or professional associations such as those of doctors, teachers, or craftsmen were created, and they established their channels of contact and communication with political authorities *extraconstitutionally;* only later were their activities subject to regulation by law (lobbying in legislative bodies of the United States, for instance).

In democratic countries that are engaged in economic and social planning for the purpose of stability and growth, groups representing the interests of labor, agriculture, and consumers increasingly participate in the preparation as well as the implementation of national plans (Britain, for instance). "Planning means that the enterprises and people that carry out plans must be brought in on their formulation . . . as planning develops, functional representation will likewise develop." [6] Preliminary consultations with functional groups on the subject of national planning may include such issues as competitive prices and quality of national products, export and import problems, balance of payments, incomes, new inventions and materials, and other matters well beyond the traditional meaning of collective bargaining, which was limited to bargaining over wages, working hours and working conditions, and fringe benefits. In this way, the trend toward further centralization of political and economic power into the hands of the national authority as a manager of national economy is challenged, although not reversed, by the need to consult, and therefore cooperate, with functional interest groups. The participation of functional groups and experts in the formulation of policies and plans allows the authority to adopt feasible (that is, acceptable) measures.

Modern constitutions, especially those that have been proclaimed since World War II, recognize the existence and the role of functional interest groups, although some constitutional texts do so in a somewhat laconic or peremptory way. Some constitutions include interest groups simply among those who have the right to exist and participate in political processes. Other constitutions are more elaborate. Several countries have experimented with an institutionalized representation of functional interests on the legislative level, frequently in the form of a third chamber to be added to a bicameral parliament—a "House of Lobby Representatives" of sorts. Weimar Germany, Ireland, a few Latin-American countries, France under the Fourth and Fifth Republics, and under French influence several French-oriented African states established a parliamentary body whose role and composition were based on nonterritorial functional subdivisions of the national society. In France and Africa today, such third chambers are called economic and social councils; they consist of partly elected and partly appointed representatives of labor unions, agricultural cooperatives, chambers of commerce, private and nationalized industries, business groups, professionals, and nationwide associations of consumers. What

[6] Samuel H. Beer, "The Comparative Method and the Study of British Politics," *Comparative Politics,* Vol. 1, No. 1 (October 1968), 34. Also see Samuel H. Beer, *British Politics in the Collectivist Age.* New York: Knopf, 1966, p. 390.

initially had been a brave attempt to move toward a tricameral system, with one chamber being added to a territorially determined bicameral system, has, however, proved a failure, mostly because the new functionally based institutions have been endowed only with a consulting, hardly audible whisper. In 1968 President de Gaulle proposed a merger of the French functional chamber and the Senate into a new Economic and Social Senate, which was to contain representatives of both functional and territorial (regional) interests. (More will be said about it in Chap. 9.) Again, the territorial principle, when challenged by the functional principle, has prevailed. This may perhaps be deplored, as Karl Lowenstein thinks:

> It may seem regrettable that corporativism [representation of organized functional interests], though discredited by totalitarian abuses [fascist Italy and its Chamber of Corporations] . . . has not been given a democratic trial . . . the powerful combines of labor, cooperative, management, agriculture, civil servants, professional and other interest groups, deprived of legitimate participation in the formation of public policies, are forced to operate through political parties or to exert power outside the constitution itself.[7]

Territorial and functional interests may seem to complement or overlap each other, but they may also be in competition or in hostile conflict with each other. In all political systems there has always been a problem—and a controversy—as to which is the best principle of organizing authority: should it be based on territorial divisions or on functional divisions? So far the practice seems to indicate a trend toward a combination of both; the formula is to base parties and governments primarily on territorial divisions with functional specialization within, allowing or encouraging functional interests to exercise their pressures on the territorial units of authority.

The problem of balance between transterritorial functional and territory-bound interests is also present in the field of international relations. Foreign offices, for example, are usually

[7] Karl Lowenstein, "Reflections on the Value of Constitutions in Our Revolutionary Age," in Arnold J. Zurcher (ed.), *Constitutions and Constitutional Trends since World War II*. New York: New York University Press, 1951, pp. 191–224.

organized in such a fashion as to reflect both the functional and the territorial concerns; there are divisions dealing with legal and economic problems on a global scale, and there are divisions dealing with regions (such as Central America or Western Europe), and within them are divisions concentrating on individual countries. In the United Nations, the Security Council is based on the territorial principle, while the Economic and Social Council is supposed to reflect, in addition to its territorial composition, a horizontal, functional approach that is expected to cut across vertical national boundaries and unite territorial nations in a common functional approach to the problems they have in common (see Chap. 6). International nongovernmental pressure groups, such as international labor organizations (WFTU and ICFTU), international chambers of commerce, and churches, are associated with the work of the Economic and Social Council.

TERRITORIAL DISTRIBUTION OF POWER

By *territorial distribution of authority,* which is the subject of our book, we mean a recognition or creation of geographically delineated authority to deal with matters of territorial import. From the standpoint of a central authority, such a territorial division or delegation of authority fulfills four useful purposes, regardless of the existence or nonexistence of territorial demands for autonomy:

1. It unburdens the central authority and makes it more effective by transferring the day-to-day concern with, and handling of, local territorial matters to subnational units of rule making, such as villages, municipalities, counties, districts, or provinces. This allows the central authority to focus on problems of vital national importance such as economic and welfare planning, defense, and foreign policy. Even if there were no natural or preexisting elements of territorial identity, a rational distribution of the burden of rule making in itself would cause and justify the creation of units of territorial self-rule.

2. A territorial distribution of authority also contributes to the mobilization of local initiative and responsibility on the

assumption that people usually care more about what is familiar and immediate in space and in time than about abstract distant concepts and goals. This, of course, is generally but not always true. In the early 1960s, several Communist systems experimented with unburdening the central government and with a partial revival of local initiative and responsibility. One of their hopes was to compensate for the lack of the healthy effects of free competition by stimulation of interterritorial competitiveness, of local responsibility, and of local initiative consistent with a broadly defined framework of national socialist planning. Some Communist leaders may have considered territorial pluralism a lesser challenge to a one-party rule than political pluralism (for instance, a multiparty system). It may be true that territorial pluralism is less of a challenge. However, in polyethnic Communist systems, territorial pluralism may open another Pandora's box, because it may revive old ethnic-territorial cleavages and stimulate serious centrifugal or outrightly secessionist tendencies. Both Yugoslavia (with regard to Croatia) and Czechoslovakia (with regard to Slovakia) have run into such problems since the mid-1960s. More about this will be said in Chapter 10, which deals with polyethnic federal systems.

3. Any rule-making agency, whether national, local, or functional, because it exists and functions, unavoidably becomes a target for corresponding demands for satisfaction of what men consider their interest. In the case of satisfactory performance, such an institution may also become an object of gratitude and emotional identification on the part of satisfied citizens. More about this will be said in Chapter 2.

4. A unit of local territorial authority should also be viewed as an important channel for transmission of political will and information in two directions: from the central authority to the local authority and from the local authority to the cenral authority. In democracies, especially the federal type, the traffic from the local authority to the central (national) authority may be heavy. But even in these systems where local units of authority were created from "above" by a dictator to serve as docile transmission belts in one direction only (from the central authority to the local authority) there is also a thin stream of messages in the opposite direction. This often is a mere trickle of political signals

from "below"; they are usually contained in confidential reports of local representatives whose role it is to be not only the mouth but also the *ears* and *eyes* of the central authority in their assigned territories. Whether we have in mind local Communist party secretaries, local commanders in military systems in Asia, in Africa, or in Latin America, or local Falangist chapters in Franco Spain, they all cautiously and discreetly inform the central authority as to where the national shoe locally pinches.

Unburdening the central authority, mobilizing local initiative, responsibility, and supports, learning about local needs and discontent, and translating national goals and policies into local terms are the main reasons all governments, even the most centralist of dictatorships, find it both inevitable and useful to distribute authority on a territorial basis. Even though dictators see to it that the degree of local autonomy is minimal and remains subject to rigid control and manipulation from the central authority, they are right in their suspicion that any territorial unit of authority may become a focus of independent and hostile power.

Participation and pluralism, which dictators dread, is usually welcomed and extolled by democracies. Territorial division of authority is but a geographic expression of the core creed of a free society: to make the authority responsive and responsible to the will of the people, the people must be able to participate. And in order to participate meaningfully, political, functional, and territorial groups must enjoy the freedom of expression, initiative, and self-rule. If democratic politics are primarily described as a process of conversion of freely expressed demands into enforceable compromises and rules, then, clearly, free articulation, aggregation, organization, and communication of territorial interests must compete with, or complement, the articulation and communication of functional and ideological interests.[8]

The preceding analysis of the reasons for territorial distribution of power leads to the preliminary conclusion that territorial identity, interest, and authority result from an interplay

[8] The terminology is that of Gabriel A. Almond and G. Bingham Powell, Jr., *Comparative Politics.* Boston: Little, Brown, 1966, p. 29.

of two demands that sometimes, but certainly not always, tend to meet halfway: the desire of territorial interest groups to obtain or preserve their autonomy and the need of central authorities to rely on territorial units for local initiative, responsibility, and self-rule.

PART ONE
THE BIRTH AND GROWTH OF TERRITORIAL IDENTITY

ONE
TERRITORIAL
IDENTITY

I only regret I have but one life to lose for my
country.
NATHAN HALE (Speech from the gallows)

They wrote in the old days that it is sweet and fitting
to die for one's country. But in modern war there
is nothing sweet nor fitting in your dying. You will die
like a dog for no good reason.
ERNEST HEMINGWAY (Notes on the Next War)

Ask not what your country can do for you; ask what
you can do for your country.
JOHN F. KENNEDY (Inaugural Address)

You'll never have a quiet world till you knock the
patriotism out of the human race.
G. B. SHAW (O'Flaherty, V.C.)

The central concept in our study is a territorial interest group
or a territorial community. By *territorial interest groups* we
mean aggregates of individuals and groups who are aware of
their bonds of identification with each other as well as with the
past, present, and future of their territory. Such territorial com-

munities are present in all political systems. Sometimes the territorial communities have emerged before the political systems; at other times the territorial communities have emerged after the political systems. In a federation, territorial communities are its basic components.

The spatial two-dimensionality of the territory is of cardinal importance. Speaking of the national state, Kenneth E. Boulding noted that the dimension of simple geographical space is perhaps "the most striking characteristic of the national state as an organization, by contrast with organizations such as firms or churches, that it thinks of itself as occupying, in a 'dense' and exclusive fashion, a certain area of the globe." [1]

It should be recognized that men identify not only with a territory as such but also (if not primarily) with its political and economic system, its methods and goals, and with its history and its destiny. This is what makes inhabitants of a given area a "community of complementary habits and facilities of communications [that] permits a common history to be experienced in common," [2] into a unit aware of "common sharing of values, purposes, interests and fears." [3]

If we view a territorial community as primarily a geographically delineated *social communication system,* its decisive boundary is represented by a relative discontinuity in the frequency of communication.[4] People do not communicate as frequently across a border as they do within a territorial community. Some of the reasons are language, habit, and the fact that usually the boundaries of communicative efficiency and administrative coercion coincide. The coercive apparatus sets limits to communications in the form of frontier guards, customs officers, passport requirements, censorship, or the jamming of foreign broadcasts and television programs.

A territorial nation-state represents today the most exten-

[1] Kenneth E. Boulding, "National Images and International Systems," *The Journal of Conflict Resolution,* 3 (1959), 123.

[2] Karl W. Deutsch, *National and Social Communication.* Cambridge, Mass.: M.I.T. Press, 1966, p. 96.

[3] Peter H. Merkl, "Federalism and Social Structure," paper read at the Sixth Congress of the International Political Science Association, Geneva, 1964, p. 4.

[4] Merkl, "Federalism and Social Structure," p. 7.

sive territorial interest group to which individuals and groups give their *effective* allegiance and with which they most intensely and most unconditionally identify themselves.[5] Despite the unifying compulsion of modern technology and global mass movement of goods, persons, and ideas, men primarily feel and act as members of their national communities. A territorial nation-state is still considered a more efficient instrument than any alternative for coping with men's collective problems: it protects them against external dangers (or so they believe), maintains internal order, and, taking up the collective challenges of modern economy and technology, provides people with economic security, social progress, cultural advancement, and group identity. The claim of internal decentralization and participation partly erodes territorial communities from within but also partly strengthens their cohesion vis-à-vis other territorial communities. A territorial state may still, in John H. Herz's words,

> salvage one feature of humanity which seems ever more threatened by the ongoing rush of mankind into the techno-logical conformity of a synthetic planetary environment: diversity of life and culture, of traditions and civilizations. If the nation can preserve these values, it would at long last have emerged as that which the philosophers of early nationalism had expected it to be: the custodian of cultural diversity, among groups mutually granting each other their peculiar worth.[6]

Devotion to one's geographically determined area, its values and inhabitants, is called *nationalism,* and on a subnational level, *local patriotism.* If territorial nation-states are considered to be fully emerging only in the wake of religious wars of the seventeenth century, local patriotism (devotion to one's city or province) may be considered an older brother of modern nationalism anchored in a fully organized territorial state. People's allegiance to subnational communities, territorial or functional, is usually less intensive and less unconditional than their devotion to the national community. A lesser intensity also characterizes men's

[5] Rupert Emerson, *From Empire to Nation,* Cambridge, Mass.: Harvard University Press, 1960, p. 95. (Italics added.)

[6] John H. Herz, "The Territorial State Revisited," *Polity,* Vol. 1, No. 1 (1968), 34.

relations to supranational territorial communities such as regional alliances or common markets, or supranational movements and creeds such as communism or Christianity. However it may be deplored, the weakest of all is man's identification with the abstract notion of the human race. The problem of conflicting loyalties will be discussed more in detail in Chapter 2.

The question now is what causes the birth and the growth of any degree of territorial awareness, that is, how and why men identify, rationally or emotionally or both, with a given territory and its values and goals. Several explanations will be suggested. Although they will be discussed in separate categories, it should be kept in mind that they are intimately interconnected, each conditioning, causing, or reinforcing the other. All of them perhaps could be called *political and cultural socialization.*

DUTY AND HABIT TO OBEY

Men often identify with a territory and with each other because they must. A territorial authority that asks for and enforces obedience within its boundaries is sometimes based on both past and present consensus and at other times it is based on the results of a successful *coup d'état* or conquest. In either case, "the existence of a political boundary is itself a major contribution to a sense of solidarity. . . . Among the most important experiences that can unite a group is that they share the same unit of government." [7] This is clearly so when the authority represents a territorial consensus. Our point is that a certain degree of solidarity—a solidarity based on collaboration due to fear—may also result from sharing the same unit of government that has been artificially or forcibly imposed, that is intensely disliked, but that within its boundaries must be obeyed.

Usually only an activist minority chooses to oppose an illegitimate government or chooses to emigrate. Both decisions have territorial implications, because in the first case the rebellion occurs within the territory whose control is at stake, and because in the second case those who have chosen exile have placed themselves under a different territorial authority whose

[7] Leslie Lipson, *The Great Issues of Politics.* Englewood Cliffs, N.J.: Prentice-Hall, 1965, pp. 288–289.

goals and methods they deem preferable. And what about the majority that neither rebels nor emigrates? Evidently it is not composed of millions of Joans of Arc or Ché Guevaras. The majority chooses to live as best as it can, recognizing its own powerlessness and the territorial authority's awesome power to coerce and, under totalitarian socialism or fascism, to determine and distribute education and jobs (in short, to distribute the life itself). To the majority perhaps applies Sidney Hook's admonishment that life itself should not be viewed as a value:

> What gives life value is not mere existence but its quality. Whoever proclaims that life is worth living under any circumstances has already written for himself an epitaph of infamy. For there is no principle or human being he will not betray; there is no indignity he will not suffer or compound.[8]

In order physically to survive, the majority may not see any rational choice other than to address its demands for order, services, and means of survival to that authority—thus cooperating with it—which, however artificial, illegitimate, and therefore resented it may be, is now in charge of territorial tranquillity and welfare.

Such a dilemma [9] between resistance against insuperable odds (and possible death) and partial collaboration with the illegitimate territorial authority confronted (life) was met by the majority of Frenchmen after the defeat of their armed forces by Nazi Germany in June 1940. The French territory was then divided into two zones to suit the defense and security requirement of the occupying Nazi forces. Northern France (one of the two zones of divided France) was administered by the German military government that was also in charge of Paris, and the Atlantic Coast. Southern France and central France (both of which constituted the other zone of divided France) were administered by a French puppet government in Vichy, presided over by Marshal Pétain. However, some Frenchmen

[8] Sidney Hook, "Foreign Policy for Survival," *The New Leader* (April 7, 1958), p. 10.

[9] A similar dilemma confronted the Hungarians in 1956 and the Czechoslovaks in 1968 following the Soviet invasion and occupation of their respective national territories.

went into exile and formed the Free French movement under General de Gaulle. Other Frenchmen submerged and formed an underground resistance movement, operating behind the German lines and disregarding all territorial boundaries. And very few Frenchmen actively collaborated with the territorial authorities and their concept of a divided France. The majority of Frenchmen considered the imposed and entirely artificial division of their country a crime, treason, folly, and a very temporary arrangement. But having chosen to live as best or as honorably as they could under the circumstances, they had to obey the territorial authorities and even respect the new territorial boundaries. From those authorities, and only from them, were the French able to obtain their food rations, working permits, and permissions to travel between the two zones of divided France.

This entirely artificial division of France, imposed by a superior force as a temporary measure, was of such short duration that no real habit or significant vested interests in the division had time to develop. But had the Nazi Reich lasted for a thousand years (as Hitler had predicted) it is conceivable that the initial reluctant acceptance of the temporary would have been transformed into an unenthusiastic habit, tempered, of course, with a hope that in the future some external events or the decay of the ruling authority would restore the French territorial unity.

That the duty to obey may change into habit and acceptance may be further illustrated in the following three contexts: (1) when homogeneous nations are internally subdivided by external forces over a long period of time, (2) when heterogeneous polyethnic or polytribal societies are forced into unity from "above," and (3) when artificial units of territorial self-rule are created by the central authority for its own administrative convenience.

Homogeneous nations subdivided by external forces

After World War II, four nations very much against their will were subdivided into Communist and non-Communist sectors: Germany (West Germany and East Germany and the West Berlin enclave); Korea (North Korea and South Korea); China (mainland China and Taiwan); and Vietnam (North Vietnam and South Vietnam). (Divided Austria was reunited and neutralized in 1955.) Although the divisions have been imposed and maintained for a quarter of a century by the balancing needs of the United States and the Soviet Union, an emergence of real separate territorial identities is certainly no longer beyond imagination, even though all concerned insist that the divisions are temporary. If the divisions are made to last for several generations, the duty to recognize the externally imposed divisions may change into acceptance. It would not be the first time in history that the temporary became permanent. Nor would it be the first time that political antagonism gave birth to separate territorial nation-states whose inhabitants originally shared the same language, culture, and political authority but later developed their own political identities and cultures. The United States and its secession from England is one example. Another possible example (which, however, would be imposed by external forces) may one day be two separate Chinese states, China-mainland and China-Taiwan. It is conceivable that the German culture, language, and people will remain forever divided into four territorial units (or five, if West Berlin were to become a separate unit as, at one point, Moscow suggested): East Germany, West Germany, the long-established Austria, and Switzerland.

Heterogeneous societies forced into unity

Our example of the imposition of unity on heterogeneity is taken from Africa, where territorial units have been created without much regard for such factors as language, tribal, transportation, and geographic boundaries. When the British, French, Spanish, Italian, Portuguese, German, and Belgian states were in the process of establishing their colonial empires in Africa, they subdivided the whole continent arbitrarily among themselves, usually proceeding from the coast and its natural harbors into the interior, cutting across all traditional boundaries. Africa was divided in such a way as to translate the European balance of power into African territorial terms. The resulting units, created to accommodate competing colonial imperialists, were administered as territorial units by colonial officers and began to be viewed as units to be captured by the revolutionary elites. The administrative center of colonial oppression was to be the capital of the liberated territorial nation-state. Although the African and Asian independence movements had been conducted in the name of the self-determination of nations, often understood in its ethnic or lingual sense, "they were, in fact, demands for political independence not in accord with ethnic distributions, but along the essentially happenstance borders that delimited either the sovereignty or the administrative zones of the former colonial powers." [10] Territories that initially were artificial creations are now in a painful, not always successful process of becoming nation-states in the real sense of the word. Even though, at least at the outset, an awareness of national territorial identity of countries such as Gambia, Sierra Leone, or Upper Volta might have been limited to a thin top layer of the ruling elites, it is conceivable that in due time the territorial authority based on the glory of liberation from an alien rule and based on the subsequent power to coerce will be able to transform the habit to obey into positive, rational (as well as emotional) supports. The problem of creating a community— that is, an aggregate of "people who have learned to communicate with each other and to understand each other well beyond the mere interchange of goods and services" [11]—has been called the primary crisis of developing nation-states, the identity crisis. It requires time before the people in a new state recognize their territory as being a true homeland and before they feel "as individuals that their own personal identities are in part defined by their territorially delimited country. In most of the new states traditional forms of identity [some nonterritorial] ranging from tribe to ethnic and linguistic groups compete with the sense of larger national identity." [12] The cases of Congo and Nigeria demonstrate that the tribal and linguistic competition with the new territorial identity may be deadly. In other cases, however, there are indications that what initially was artificial may in due time become natural.

The conflict between the European-imposed territorial division and the African-desired fragmentation was well-illustrated in a paper that the Nigerian statesman Chief S. O. Adebo presented to the United Nations Institute of the City University of New York (May 26, 1969), in which he stated:

[10] Walker Connor, "Self-Determination," *World Politics,* Vol. 22, No. 1 (October 1967), 31.

[11] Deutsch, *National and Social Communication,* p. 91.

[12] Lucian W. Pye, *Aspects of Political Development.* Boston: Little, Brown, 1966, p. 63.

It is fashionable to lay the responsibility for Africa's fragmentation at the door of the European politicians who in 1885 partitioned the bulk of the continent into national shares for their respective countries. That that act was reprehensible there can of course be no question. But, considering Africa as it was before that partitioning, and Africa as it has developed at and since independence, supposing it had been left to its own resources and there had been no Treaty of Berlin, would the continent have been less divided today than it actually is? I wonder. . . . Certainly in British West Africa there were fewer independent units at the end of colonialism than at its beginning. . . . What I know of the African colonies of the other European powers makes me feel able to submit, without an intention to excuse the fact of colonialism, that if it had not happened, there might in fact be more rather than fewer separate countries in Africa today.

Artificial units of self-rule created by the central authority for its own administrative convenience

Another context in which the possibility of transforming the duty to obey into habit and acceptance may be examined is the creation of territorial units of self-rule by a central authority, not in response to corresponding territorial pressures but in order to satisfy the administrative needs of a central authority. In these cases, too, habit and acceptance may follow the initial arbitrariness and result in a birth and growth of a genuine territorial identity.

Decentralization in modern France may serve here as a good example. Feudal and royal France was originally a composite of more or less self-administered provinces such as Burgundy, Normandy, Anjou, Poitou, Provence, and Brittany. Until the French Revolution of 1789, the awareness of provincial identity was strong. In order to build the French nation so that it would coincide with the boundaries of the French territorial state and eliminate local patriotism anchored in the various provinces, first the Jacobins and then their heir, Napoleon, decided to replace the original revolutionary hope for decentralization and participatory democracy (a natural reaction against the former royal absolutist centralism) with a new tight centralization of all power in Paris. Local implementation of national policies and programs, as determined by the capital, was delegated from the national center to eighty-three (now ninety-five) carefully supervised units of local authority, called *départements*.[13] The *départements* were superimposed on the pre-existing provinces of feudal and royal France.

One of the purposes of the *départements* was to eliminate [14] the former territorial loyalties and the provincial patriotism that could conceivably conflict with the French national interest. The *départements* were small enough to permit their inhabitants to reach the seat of the higher territorial authority (that is, higher than the mayor of a city or a commune), attend to their affairs, and return home (presumably after a five-course luncheon in the restaurant of a *chef-lieu,* the seat of the prefecture)—all this in one day. Each *département* was to be, and still is, presided over by a prefect, an experienced civil servant appointed by and responsible to the central authorities in Paris for ensuring the predominance of national policies over the narrow parochial interests, budgetary irresponsibility, and, where warranted, centrifugal tendencies. By raising the walls of sovereignty and national consciousness with regard to neighboring nations while breaking down the former provincial loyalties and interests, France became a relatively homogeneous nation; the side effect was a near end of local participation,[15] responsibility, and self-rule.

With the advent of national economic planning and rapid transportation, the Napeolonic division into now excessively

[13] The *départements* represent an intermediate level of authority between the national government in Paris and the local units of self-rule such as communes, municipalities, *arrondissements,* or cantons.

[14] A French administrative expert, Conseiller d'État Hervé Detton, noted that the old royal provinces "had not been so fully broken up as some think. They had remained, to say the least, under the surface (*sous-jacentes*)." Hervé Detton, *L'Administration Régionale et Locale en France*. Paris: Presses Universitaires de France, 1964, p. 14.

[15] Detton, *L'Administration,* p. 16: "All that had been marked by confusion in, the administration of the Ancien Régime (Royal France) disappeared. But the former royal paternal contralization was replaced by an iron hand. This system of the postrevolutionary Year VIII which had contributed to give France an internal peace, suffocated all local political initiative. . . . The spirit of the Year VIII still persists. It had been softened to a great extent during the last 150 years; local territorial authorities now have some independence, yet the administrative system of France basically remains the same as it had been organized by Napoleon."

small *départements* has proved less useful and practical than it used to be. Under General de Gaulle, a new administrative reform (again from "above" rather than in response to local interests voiced from "below") was enacted; its purpose was to regroup the Napeolonic *départements* into much larger Gaullist *régions* for the purpose of planning; as nobody in Paris seems to be preoccupied with the potentiality of a resurgence of pre-republican provincial patriotism, the new territorial groupings have been made to correspond roughly to the traditional internal boundaries of prerepublican France. In Figure 1–1 is reproduced

Figure 1–1   Map of France showing the twenty-one new regions of political activity and the ninety-five *departements*

a map of France that shows the superimposition of twenty-one new regions over the ninety-five *départements*.

The twenty-one regions are presided over by regional super-prefects, appointed by and responsible to Paris. When in 1968 President de Gaulle proposed the creation of a new upper house, the Economic and Social Senate, by merging the old Senate with the Economic and Social Council, the twenty-one regions were to be endowed with some independent tax resources, legislative assemblies, and direct regional representation in the Senate. This was viewed as a limited concession to the demands for decentralization and participatory democracy, a development containing ingredients of potential federalism. Several observers of the French political scene expressed regret when in June 1969 the authoritarian President de Gaulle was swept by a popular vote from power and with him also his plan for decentralization and reform of local government, which, unlike other de Gaulle policies, seemed to have a considerable merit.

Yet, and this is our reason for discussing the highly centralized system of local government in France, the *départements* that had been artificial under Napoleon had over the past 150 years become units reflecting not only the geographic limits of local administration but also corresponding economic activities, transportation networks, and a modest degree of vested interests. The new administrative regions, grouping three to five *départements* into one unit, are now being criticized mostly on the grounds that they destroy what has become natural (although this was originally artificial). The arbitrariness of some of the new regions was attacked by one of the most influential French newspapers, *Le Monde* (August 29, 1966), as follows:

> Several of the new regions correspond to economic and social realities; regions such as *North, Brittany* and *Alsace* constitute coherent entities. On the other hand, we find true magmas of artificially aggregated *départements* that really have nothing in common, such as the region of *Rhone Alps, Midi-Pyrénées, Loire,* and *Center.*

The author of the study, André Passeron, pointed out that in other cases such as *Champagne, Burgundy, Provence,* and *Languedoc* some of the component *départements* are more attracted to the neighboring regions than to their own region.

The United States offers a different, yet related example of a transformation of arbitrarily delineated territories into bases of vested interests and loyalty. The original thirteen colonies grew into the present union of fifty states by successive additions of territories made into states. The immigrant population moved into the frontier states *after* their identity had been established, and while those states were still almost empty and while their boundaries could be drawn geometrically without much regard to natural or economic realities. Morton Grodzins, who called these boundaries "the worst inanities," adds, however, the following:

> The strong constitutional position of the states—for example, the assignment of two senators to each state, the role given the states in administering even national elections, and the relatively few limitations on their law making powers—[establishes] the geographical units as natural centers of administrative and political strength.[16]

The artificial origins of North Dakota and South Dakota are often used as good examples of the transformation of a synthetic creation into a natural one. Although it is indeed doubtful "that the two Dakotas warranted the dignity of separate statehood at the time of their entry into the union . . . who can deny now that, having lived as states for a number of years, they would look with disfavor upon any proposal to deprive them of their individuality by merging them into one?" [17]

SATISFACTORY PERFORMANCE

People usually support, and identify with, persons and institutions that largely satisfy their fundamental demands for identity, internal order, external security, progress, welfare, and culture. Gratitude for benefits received and expectation of more to come constitute the foundations of political loyalty. Hans Kohn defines nationalism as the state of mind in which the

---

[16] Morton Grodzins, "The Federal System," in the American Assembly, Columbia University (ed.), *Goals for Americans.* Englewood Cliffs, N.J.: Prentice-Hall, 1960, p. 271.

[17] William S. Livingston, "A Note on the Nature of Federalism," *Political Science Quarterly,* Vol. 67, No. 1 (March 1952), 95.

supreme loyalty of the individual is due the territorial state that is recognized as the ideal form of political organization. This nationalism may be viewed as a result of two interacting factors: the binding rules that come from the authority (and that people have the duty and habit to obey) and supports that come from the people (that are based on its satisfaction with the authority's performance). The same combination of the authority's and people's supports also accounts for patriotism on a subnational level (that is, provincial or local awareness of separate territorial identity). Graphically, the political two-way traffic may be expressed as shown in Figure 1–2.

Emotional identification with the territorial authority, be it a king or an abstraction such as a province, canton, nation or state, has often had an artificial beginning. The authority and

Figure 1–2   Rules and supports—political two-way traffic

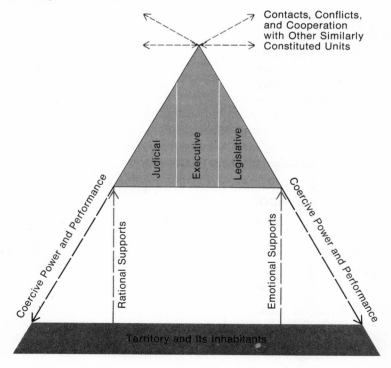

the duty and habit to abide by its rules came first; later, in response to the authority's satisfactory performance, rational and emotional consent followed. When in 1648 the Peace of Westphalia pacified Europe by breaking it into hundreds of dynastic territorial states (which replaced the previous fundamental division of Europe between the Catholics and the Protestants), people were not consulted as to their territorial preferences. They began, however, to identify with the new authorities partly because they had no other choice and partly because these authorities gave them what they had desired (that is, internal order and external security) after they had suffered and bled for many decades under the blows of the intra-European religious strife. Understandably, the initial identification with the territorial authority centered around the sovereign ruler and his court and administration; later, the inhabitants of a royal or princely territory proved able to transfer their allegiance and loyalty from their sovereign (Louis XIV allegedly said, "The State is I"—*L'État c'est moi*) to the institutions and symbols of the territory. After Louis XVI was beheaded, the majority of Frenchmen began to identify with his abstract successor, the French Republic, *la France*. In the process of reidentification, the new abstraction was endowed with familiar human features. The symbol of the French Republic, as we find it on the French stamps, or in the forms of busts displayed in many town halls is now a young woman, Marianne, with the revolutionary Phrygian cap on her head. The national territory—land—is combined in many languages with mother or father images (motherland, fatherland).

TERRITORIAL INDOCTRINATION

Men become attached rationally and emotionally to their territory, its way of life, its institutions, and its culture by a complex process that, in our present context, we may call *territorial socialization*. Our term only emphasizes the geographical aspect of the general process of political socialization.[18] From ten-

[18] Compare Herbert Hyman, *Political Socialization*. New York: Free Press, 1959. Also David Easton, *A Systems Analysis of Political Life*. New York: Wiley, 1965 (in particular, pp. 278–343); Gabriel A. Almond and G. Bingham Powell, Jr., *Comparative Politics: A Develop-*

der age, men learn about values and goals, political authority and political culture, folk arts and entertainment, the existence of rewards and punishments, as well as the existence of geographic boundaries between their own territory and the external alien world. The schoolroom maps that divide the world into colored shapes that are identified as nations are an important part of what we have called territorial socialization.[19]

Political socialization, by which information about, and values and feelings toward, the territorial community are transmitted, is so gradual and often so imperceptible that some aspects of it seem latent. In contrast, there is also a manifest indoctrination that addresses itself to man's reason and heart openly and that does not conceal its aim to create a territorial man.

All territorial authorities engage in verbal, visual, and symbolic propaganda to make the identity with the territory separate from that with the rest of the world. From cradle to grave, a continuous display and manipulation of territorial symbols— flags, flowers, trees, birds, uniforms, emblems, slogans, and anthems—are meant to enhance local pride (and prejudice) and a sense of belonging forever to a given territory, be it a nation-state, a province, or a city.

All nation-states have not only their territorial symbols but also their subnational divisions—cities, provinces, cantons, or states in federal unions. Most of the fifty states in the United States have and display their own flags, mottos, and other symbols expressing a common territorial past and destiny. The fiftieth state, Hawaii, for instance, adopted "The Life of the Land Is Perpetuated in Righteousness" as its state motto, the hibiscus as its state flower, the nene (Hawaiian goose) as its state bird, the kukui (candlenut) as its state tree, and "Hawaii Ponoi" as its state song. Nevada's state song is "Home Means Nevada." In the 1950s the states of Vermon and New York mildly disputed whether the state tree of Vermont, the sugar maple, could or could not be also adopted as a state symbol by New York. It was. The reason, however, was unemotional and eminently

---

mental Approach. Boston: Little, Brown, 1966, pp. 50–72; and Richard E. Dawson and Kenneth Prewitt, *Political Socialization.* Boston: Little, Brown, 1968 (in particular, pp. 143–180 on education and schooling).

[19] Kenneth E. Boulding, "National Images and International Systems," *The Journal of Conflict Resolution,* 3 (1959), 123.

practical because New York's aim was to promote the sales of its maple syrup in competition with Vermont.

It is a familiar practice to enhance positive identification with one's own territorial community by inducing hostile emotions and attitudes toward some or all outside groups. Feuds between regional and ethnic groups within nation-states often parallel in intense hatred those among nation-states. In biethnic or polyethnic states, an intramural hatred may be fanned into an all-devouring fire if the component units of such states are or have been made aware of their intimate links with their blood relatives abroad who administer their own territorial states. International enmity between nation-states is thus transferred to the domestic scene; and domestic tensions, in turn, contaminate the international arena. Examples of such reciprocal contagion are numerous: the German minorities in Eastern Europe before World War II, the Chinese minorities in Southeast Asia, the Arabs in Israel, or the Turks and the Greeks on Cyprus. Within the biethnic state of Cyprus, for instance, people are being taught (indoctrinated) from childhood to extol the glory of their community and to debase the history and characteristics of the other national group. A text for Greek sixth-graders describes the Turkish massacres of the Greeks on Easter Sunday in 1821 as follows: "Turks with madness depicted on their faces seized, tortured and hanged the patriarch and left his remains hanging for three days." Throughout the Greek texts the Turks are depicted as "barbarians," "heathens," "ignorant," "avaricious," "mad," and "merciless." On the other hand, the Turkish textbooks extol the Ottoman Empire. A history text for Turkish sixth-graders concludes: "Our ancestors never attacked others unless they themselves had met with wrong and aggression. The sole reason why they won great wars was because they had right on their side."

Indoctrination by history textbooks is not, of course, a Greek or Turkish speciality. All communities engage in it. While Western Europe attempts to create a higher community, the French and German history texts still condition the children in the old framework of French-German enmity (see Fig. 1–3). Bilateral agreements between the two countries have enjoined the respective governments to promote a correct understanding of the other country by means of more objective text-

Figure 1–3   Cartoon indicating first Western Europe's criticism of history texts that transform German and French children into enemies and then hope for friendship through texts stressing a common destiny

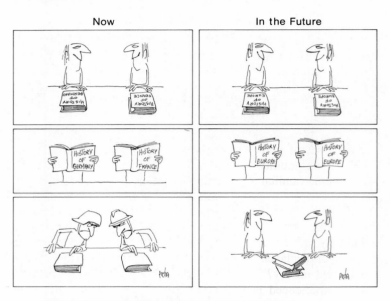

Source: *European Community*, 117 (October 1968), 8.

books. So far, few revisions of the texts have actually been made. In addition, the Council of Europe and other institutions encourage rewriting history in European terms rather than in French, British, German, or Italian terms.

A recent study of ethnic biases in the American and English textbooks showed that their authors

write unabashedly as Americans or Englishmen, standing squarely with feet planted in Boston or Washington or London. The result is distortion, often subconscious, but nonetheless dangerous. . . . Readers emerge from such accounts with the impression that the patriots (itself a biased word) lost only the Battle of Bunker Hill, and that because they ran out of powder. English writers dwell with equal affection on the triumphs of their generals, leaving the student bewildered that such a series of victories could have lost a war. . . . Not a single junior high school textbook used in the United States fails to describe the burning of Washington by the British troops during the war, and not one tells of the American burning of the Canadian city of York that led to England's retaliation.[20]

Commenting on his task of transforming immigrant children into patriotic Americans, a school superintendent described how the children "catch the school spirit. . . . American heroes become their own, American history wins their loyalty, the Stars and Stripes, always before their eyes in the school room, receives their daily salute." [21]

Thus, through indoctrination and direct experience, men acquire a set of perceptions about, and attitudes toward, their territorial community and its values; the territory and its ways have become familiar, comforting, and personal. In contrast, the rest of the world seems distant, exotic, and potentially hostile. The world is physically and psychologically walled off by boundaries, passports, visas, often unintelligible scripts and languages, and unfamiliar currency; "ugly Americans" abroad, asking about the price of displayed goods, are sometimes heard to say: "What is it in *real* money?" *Real* is to them only what could be previously experienced in life, however parochial such a life may have been.

School, siblings, parents, work groups, clubs, professional voluntary associations, and political movements all contribute to the never-ending process of socialization but sometimes also to that of desocialization. Information about, and feelings toward, the territory and its political and nonpolitical cultures that have been learned and accepted may subsequently be unlearned and rejected. An early attachment to the territorial community and its values may be later replaced by a total rejection and a decision to identify with, or immigrate into, an alien country and an attempt to make that alien country one's own by a new socialization process. Although such cases are frequent, for the

[20] Ray Allen Billington, "History Is a Dangerous Subject," *Saturday Review* (January 15, 1966), pp. 60–61.

[21] Quoted in Robert Dahl, *Who Governs?* New Haven, Conn.: Yale University Press, 1961, p. 317.

majority the early conditioning (with modification) of one's native country usually lasts a lifetime and remains very intensive.

A succinct but tragic example of an unsuccessful search for identification with a community is a statement made by Sirhan Bishara Sirhan, the assassin of Robert F. Kennedy. During his trial in Los Angeles (March 4, 1969) he spoke about his unassimilated life in the United States:

> I was sick and tired of being a foreigner, of being alone. I wanted a *place* of my own, where they speak my own language, where they eat my own food, share my own politics. I wanted to have something I could identify with as a Palestinian and an Arab. I wanted my own *country,* my own *city,* my own business. I wanted my own everything, sir. [Italics added.]

In the set of territorial values, as absorbed through the process of socialization, the territory itself—the spatial area—appears as an important element by itself because of its assumed durability. Willa Cather spoke of the universal human yearning for something permanent, enduring, without shadow of change; a slice of the surface of our planet seems indeed so much more permanent than everything else; men, institutions, beliefs, values, and laws change, but the territory undergoes changes only perceptible to geologists studying millennia of evolution. Defining a *nation,* Abraham Lincoln identified its main ingredients—its territory, its people, and its laws—and then added, "The territory is the only part which is of certain durability." [22] An area, of course, may be lost, divided, conquered, and, now, also transformed into a heap of radioactive dust. Yet, by comparison, everything else is even more perishable.

INSTINCT

Ethologists [23] stress instinct as a possible explanation of man's observable drive to possess, defend, and politically organize a

[22] Second Annual Message to Congress, December 1, 1862.

[23] Ethology, a study of patterns of animal behavior with possible insights into human behavior, was pioneered by Austria's Konrad Lorenz

delineated geographic area. The ethologists argue that possession of, and identification with, a territory represents a prerequisite for the fulfillment of man's basic needs such as security (as opposed to anxiety), stimulation of border quarrels (as opposed to boredom), and, above all, identity (as opposed to anonymity). Robert Ardrey expresses the concept of personal identity derived from territorial identity as follows:

> "This place is mine; I am of this place," says the albatross, the patas monkey, the green sunfish, the Spaniard, the great horned owl, the wolf, the Venetian, the prairie dog, the three-spined stickleback, the Scotsman, the skua, the man from La Crosse, Wisconsin, the Alsatian, the little-ringed plover, the Argentine, the lungfish, the lion, the Chinook salmon, the Parisian. I am of this place which is different from and superior to all other places of earth and I partake of its identity so that I too am both different and superior, and it is something that you cannot take away from me despite all afflictions which I may suffer or where I may go and where I may die. I shall remain always and uniquely of this place.[24]

Accordingly, all the following result from our innate (genetically determined) behavior: chasing trespassers from our private property, defending our province against the national central authority, or defending our nation against an external threat. Local patriotism and nationalism are viewed by the ethologists as nothing more and nothing less than a human expression of the animal drive to maintain and defend a territory. Robert Ardrey's book *The Territorial Imperative* has as a subtitle: *A Personal Inquiry into the Animal Origins of Property and Nations.*

The explanation of group identification with a territory on the basis of genetic inheritance inevitably challenges the effect

---

and Holland's Niko Tinbergen in the 1930s. A comparative study of animal and human behavior was popularized in the United States by Robert Ardrey in his two books, *The Territorial Imperative* and *African Genesis,* quoted in this section.

[24] Robert Ardrey, *The Territorial Imperative.* New York: Dell Publishing Co., Delta Books, 1968, p. 337. A critique of ethology as a guide to human behavior is contained in M. F. Ashley Montagu (ed.), *Man and Aggression.* New York: Oxford, 1968, p. 178. It attacks in particular the concept of instinctive, inescapable human tendency to aggressive inhumanity.

of such environmental factors as the duty to obey a hated government, socialization, and man's rational and emotional responses to new challenges and opportunities. Some men, for instance, often migrate and identify successively with different territories and environments, whereas a few are true cosmopolitans who, like Gypsies, feel everywhere and nowhere at home. Men have also often conquered territories they really did not need for survival in order to fulfill some messianic dream, realize some ideological goal, or obtain an absolute security (that is, a world in which all actual or potential rivals would be destroyed).

(Apparently, the question of food supply cannot by itself explain animals' attachment to a given territory. According to the ethologists, many animals need a certain amount of territory regardless of food supply; a wren, for instance, always seeks possession of two and a half acres. On the other hand, among men the territorial food supply may affect his attachment to the territory although trade and technology may solve the problem for man even if he lives in a smaller and food-deficient area.)

Evidently, man's instincts, which we do not intend to deny, are in competition with his empirical experiences and rationality. His rational estimate of risks involved may lead to a surrender of part of or the whole of national territory. In 1918 at Brest Litovsk, Lenin decided to sign a humiliating peace treaty with imperial Germany. He had reached a conclusion that the preservation of a territorial basis, however limited (a major portion of the national territory and its major resources had to be surrendered to the Germans), was more important for the future of communism than the whole of the Ukraine and Russia's western provinces. We suspect that animals cannot voluntarily reason in such a fashion, although they can be forcibly deprived of their territory and transferred to a cage.

In addition, when Robert Ardrey compares territorial nationalism of men with animal territorial urges (which are not so general; our closest relatives, gorillas and chimpanzees, do not defend territories), he adds that nationalism differs from the social territoriality of the primates only by the degree of "man's capacity to form coalitions." In our context, we would add: "and federations." [25] But this is an important qualification. Unlike the

[25] Robert Ardrey, *African Genesis.* New York: Dell Publishing Co., Laurel Edition, 1967, p. 178.

lion, the lungfish, or the little-ringed plover, who do not seem to have any rational choice in the matter, human groups may select either to establish or not to establish broader territorial coalitions such as alliances, confederations, common markets, and federal unions, all based on an agreement to engage in a cooperative territorial venture; the nation-state itself represents an aggregate and a coalition of many subnational territorial communities and institutions.

It may be concluded that, in contrast with animals (which are guided primarily by instincts), men are both worse off and better off than other primates in the matter of territorial behavior. This is so because men's instincts have to compete not only with their capacity to reason, which is good, but also with their irrationality and complex emotions, which is often quite bad.

LANGUAGE AND TERRITORIALITY

Unlike animals, men learn complex patterns of social behavior by means of verbal communication. The language barrier usually raises the walls separating territorial states to considerable heights. The reality of territorial identity is then obvious at the first sound, even though political and lingual boundaries often overlap. True enough, there are many territorial communities that lack the additional dimension of a separate territorial language. Examples are the United States and all the English-speaking members of the Commonwealth; West Germany and East Germany, Austria and a portion of Switzerland; France and portions of Belgium, Switzerland, and Canada; and Spain, Portugal, and Latin America. But in many other parts of the world the territorial boundaries coincide with the lingual ones; the language appears then not only as one of the most important ingredients in one's awareness of territorial identity, but also as the most effective instrument of territorial socialization and the most treasured heritage of the common past. Often, after a long sojourn abroad, hearing one's mother tongue again—or hearing the home accent again, as is the case of territories that share the same literary language—represents a high degree of personal gratification and an upsurge of emotional identification with one's own nation's culture, way of life, and history. Svetlana Alliluyeva, a Russian-educated daughter of a Georgian father,

Stalin, after having read Boris Pasternak's *Doctor Zhivago* in the original while she was in exile, wrote, "This encounter with the Russian tongue at its most powerful went through me like a shock, like a great surge of electricity." [26]

Within nation-states, territorial "linguism" may prove one of the most disruptive and centrifugal forces leading to demands of complete separation. In India, for instance, territorial and linguistic differences had been for centuries submerged under the unifying lid of the common Hindu culture. This was the period of dominantly face-to-face relations; the problem of what language or languages to use in the mass media had not yet arisen. Furthermore, the common struggle against the British rule added another unifying element to Indian nationalism. Today, the situation is different. Secularism weakened the religious Hindu bonds. The unifying enmity against the British has only been partly replaced by a common fear of China and a common anger at Pakistan. The national struggle against illiteracy has increased the role of local vernaculars that are used in primary and secondary schools; furthermore, local vernaculars have become important instruments of political communication and participation on a local level and in the assertion of local and regional interests vis-à-vis the federal central authority in New Delhi. It has become almost irresistible for a local politician, a product of postliberation education in local written language, not to utilize linguistic territorialism in his struggle for power and status. Writing with noticeable melancholy, a former nationalist delegate at the two round table conferences in 1926 and 1932 defines Indian linguism as "a claim that Indians speaking the same language should have a state: *one language, one state*." He adds, "Linguism has come to occupy the center of the stage. . . . The fissiparous linguistic communalism of today, when there is no British overlord to stoke it, is somewhat disillusioning to the ardent Indian nationalist." [27]

The Linguistic Provinces Commission, appointed by the Indian Constituent Assembly in 1948, reported with melancholy:

[26] Svetlana Alliluyeva, "To Boris Pasternak," *The Atlantic Monthly* (1967), p. 133.

[27] P. Kodanda Rao, "Communalism in India," *Current History* (February 1956), p. 84.

> Some of the ablest men in the country came before us and confidently and emphatically stated that language in this country stood for and represented culture, race, history, individuality, and finally sub-nation. . . . We were simply horrified to see how thin was the ice upon which we were skating.

There are 845 languages and dialects in India, 14 of which, in addition to English, are recognized by the Constitution (Eighth Schedule) as major and official. More about the effects of linguism on federations will be said in Chapter 9.

TERRITORIALITY[n]

One factor can raise the intensity of territorial awareness to the nth power (if we use mathematical terminology): contact with an alien group, especially if it is a hostile one. In his classic study of international law and relations, Charles de Visscher, a former justice of the International Court of Justice, wrote:

> It is in contact with the world outside that any social group differentiates and becomes conscious itself. . . . Only against the stranger does its solidarity fully assert itself. National solidarities have triumphed over internal tensions, even the most deep-rooted such as between class and class.[28]

Like two men who, when engaged in a street fight, readily gang up against a policeman or a would-be arbiter and, following the removal of the outsider, either make peace or resume fighting, groups and individuals are often able to discover harmony only when they become aware of a common danger that originates outside them (either in external groups or in nature). External threat has often proved capable of aggregating internal concerns, however normally divisive they may be, into one overriding interest in the preservation of the community as such. As one depressing but nonetheless truthful comment on human nature expresses it, "The brotherhood of man finds much of its working expression within the nation, though its other face is hostility to those outside." [29] Similarly, Nehru defined nationalism

[28] Charles de Visscher, *Theory and Reality in Public International Law*. Princeton, N.J.: Princeton University Press, 1957, p. 89.
[29] Emerson, *From Empire to Nation,* p. 108.

as fundamentally an "anti-feeling—which feeds and fattens on hatred and anger against other national groups." In his *Principles of Ethics,* Herbert Spencer described how tribal as well as civilized societies carried on constantly *external* self-defense and *internal* cooperation and amity. "An amiable xenophobic whole," a term coined by Robert Ardrey with reference to his observation of rhesus monkeys and their instinctive tendency to establish proper hostility to neighboring groups, largely applies to human territorial group behavior. Somewhat facetiously, he expressed the amity-enmity relationship in a mathematical formula:

$$A = E + h$$

Amity (A) is equal to the sum of the forces of enmity (E) that originate in men and the forces of hazard $(h,$ natural and supernatural dangers).[30]

It would, however, be wrong to exaggerate the monolithic response of a community to an external threat. The exact meaning of the collective interest to be protected may be a matter of controversy. Should the people sacrifice their lives for the protection of their territorial integrity or should the people sacrifice their territorial integrity for the protection of their lives? There may also be controversy as to the method of protection of territorial values, ranging from capitulation to atomic retaliation. Furthermore, individuals and groups may disagree as to their perceptions and estimates of the gravity and imminence of an external menace.

In addition, not all threats are or are perceived as aimed at the territorial community as a whole. There are sometimes highly selective threats; the aim of these threats is to prevent a nation-state from achieving unity and to contribute to that nation's dissolution. External groups have often offered paradise to some groups—ethnic minorities or workers—while promising hell to others. Previous injustice or neglect may endow subnational groups with reasons to listen to external lures attentively. This is what external interference in the domestic affairs of territorial nation-states is made of. Our focus on territorial

---

[30] Ardrey, *The Territorial Imperative,* p. 270.

communities should not make us forget that men and groups are simultaneously members of different communities—territorial ones (national, subnational, and supranational) as well as functional ones (workers, employers, peasants, owners). Interests and goals of these different communities sometimes complement and reinforce each other, but more often they are in conflict— and internal conflict, especially if on a collision course, has always been a magnet for external intervention. Conflicting interests among different communities will be discussed in the following chapter.

TWO

CONFLICTS OF TERRITORIAL ALLEGIANCES

Who is here so vile that will not love his country?

SHAKESPEARE (*Julius Caesar*)

The workingman has no fatherland. . . . Proletarians of all countries unite!

KARL MARX AND FRIEDRICH ENGELS (*The
Communist Manifesto*)

'Home is the place when, you have to go there,
They have to take you in.'

'I should have called it
Something you somehow haven't to deserve.

ROBERT FROST ("The Death of the Hired
Man")

I should like to be able to love my country and still
love justice.

ALBERT CAMUS (*The Rebel*)

Men are simultaneously members of and feel loyalty to several
interest groups and communities such as family, school, work
group, ethnic or racial community, church, professional association, club, political movement, or territorial interest group.
Men's attachment to any of these groups varies in intensity and

in time; rarely can we speak of perfect compatibility between men's loyalties to different communities. There is bound to be conflict; a territorial community that is the main subject of our study competes with all nonterritorial ones. Furthermore, a territorial community is in itself a composite of competing geographically delineated interest groups, ranging from a street block or hamlet to districts, counties, cities, provinces, nations, and supranational, regional, continental, or global communities.

For the purpose of our analysis, six communities that compete for people's effective allegiance can be identified: (1) the nation-state (whose effectiveness as a source of political socialization and as an object of identification and loyalty has already been discussed); (2) supranational movements; (3) political parties; (4) functional interest groups; (5) dispersed ethnic, linguistic, or religious groups; and (6) subnational territorial interest groups.

SUPRANATIONAL MOVEMENTS

Supranational movements and institutions seek to gain support by their opposition to the present national divisions among men. They profess supranational creeds such as Christianity, Islam, communism, and pacifism. As determinants of political loyalty and action they have, however, so far proven weaker than national loyalties. Supranational beliefs such as communism or Islam have been grafted on nation-states and become corrupted by territorial nationalism in the process. Perhaps a more serious challenge to the existing territorial national division has come from movements and institutions that express supranational *regionalism*. Their aim, however, is not to do away with territorial divisions but to amalgamate several national territories into a higher territorial union. The success of attempts at supranational regionalism depends on many factors, geographic proximity [1] being only one of them—similarity in political culture,

---

[1] Bruce M. Russett demonstrated with the use of rigorously classified data that proximity is too simple an indicator of international groupings and the probability of their future political integration. See his "Delineating International Regions," in J. David Singer (ed.), *Quantitative International Politics—Insights and Evidence*. New York: Free Press, 1968, pp. 317–352.

economic development, interdependence, and formal institutions supporting integration play an equally if not more, important role. A recent study suggested a low-to-high ordering for spillover effects associated with various kinds of supranational institutions: (1) narrowly functional organizations, (2) tariff unions, (3) military organizations, (4) economic unions (common markets), and (5) political unions.[2] In observing the slow progress and very often rapid decline of supranational regionalism, we cannot omit the possible effect of the enmity as a spring and fuel of the rise of cooperative solidarity.[3] Regional unions frequently are being established not only in distinction from, but mainly in *opposition* to, other national or regional territorial communities; for instance, Western Europe seems united when pitted against Russia, America, or both and seems much less united if the external danger or competitive pressure is removed; the Arab unity is successfully asserted only against Israel, Pan-Americanism against Europe or communism, Pan-Slavism against Germany, Pan-Africanism against former or new colonialism. Movements advocating world government or world federation have not yet moved away from the level of daydreaming to the level of an even distant reality; one of the reasons for the lack of success is certainly that, unlike any other project of territorial amalgamation, world unity cannot yet be convincingly promoted *against* the "territorial interests" of other planets.

POLITICAL PARTIES AND FUNCTIONAL INTEREST GROUPS

As a rule, *political parties,* even those with international links and supranational creeds, are groups of leaders and followers that compete with other such groups for the political control of a given *territory.* If a party is in opposition to the incumbent party, its goal is to capture the territorial control; if the party is in control, then its goal is to maintain its power. In their activities, parties compete on the basis of who can run a given territory better. Parties and movements that aim at the control of

[2] Amitai Etzioni, "Atlantic Union, the Southern Continents, and the United Nations," in Roger Fisher (ed.), *International Conflict and Behavioral Science.* New York: Basic Books, 1964.

[3] Chap. 6 returns to this in more detail.

only a portion of the national territory (*separatist parties*) will be discussed in connection with subnational territorial interest groups, because such parties represent the political arm of these interests.

Functional interest groups reflect the specialization and division of labor that usually results in unequal sharing of wealth. Labor unions, professional associations, farmers' organizations, and business groups belong to this category. The line between functional interest groups and political parties is often blurred because in many countries political parties and functional interest groups merge into one group or represent a mutually controlling relationship (labor parties in Europe that originally aimed at political mobilization of industrial labor only, and agrarian or peasant parties in Southern or Eastern Europe, and so on). Such political-functional groups may respond to oppression and exploitation by occasionally detaching themselves from their territorial bases; in so doing they may acquire a powerful supranational ideology, loyalty, and organization. So far, however, such a functional or social (class) internationalism has not succeeded in eliminating the territory-bound loyalties. Proletarian internationalism, which under the Comintern (1919–1943) was the best organized of all supranational movements, was originally an article of a very fervent faith and a source of strong loyalty. In 1914, when both the French and the German socialist workers gave full support to their respective countries' wars, the collapse of the international working-class solidarity efforts was the first indication that Karl Marx's call "Proletarians of all countries unite!" was to become an almost inaudible whisper when the trumpets of nationalism signaled the beginning of a defensive or offensive war. By the second half of the twentieth century, proletarian internationalism was eroded beyond recognition first by the territorial-national interest of Russia and second by the national Communist opposition to the Russian dominance (Yugoslavia, Hungary, Albania, China, Rumania, and Czechoslovakia). Karl Marx apparently believed that the awareness of a common functional destiny was bound not only to unite the exploited workers in their struggle against oppression within their national boundaries but also to transform them into one transnational phalanx. The national class struggle was only to be the first step; the Communist Manifesto of 1848 could not help taking into account the inescapable facts of territorial organization and fragmentation of the world: "In form, the struggle of the proletariat with the bourgeoisie is at first a *national* struggle. The proletariat of each *country* must, of course, first of all settle matters with *its own* bourgeoisie." (Italics added.)

What according to Marx and Engels was to be only the first national step on the way to global class brotherhood has so far proved also to be the last one; proletarian loyalty to class did not prove stronger than that to a territorial state, administered by the workers' class enemies, the capitalists. Marx and his followers evidently underestimated [4] the force of nationalist emotions that may make the workers prefer a bearable situation at home to a vague promise of *foreign* enlightenment. Nor did Marxism-Leninism anticipate the emergence of a non-Communist welfare state that may be changed from a one-class instrument of political organization and coercion into a multiclass one, mostly by universal suffrage, power of the labor unions, economic and welfare planning, and progressive taxation. In the words of Edward Hallett Carr,

> The democratization of the nation . . . meant the assertion of the political claims of the dominant middle class. The socialization of the nation for the first time brings the economic claims of the masses into the forefront of the picture. The defence of wages and employment becomes a concern of national policy and must be asserted, if necessary, against the national policies of other countries; and this in turn gives the worker an intimate practical interest in the policy and power of his nation. The socialization of the na-

[4] The Socialist President of Senegal, Leopold Senghor, wrote: "Marx underestimated political and national idealism, which, born in France upon the ruins of provincial fatherlands with the Revolution of 1789, won over the world. . . . If the creator of scientific socialism returned to this earth, he would perceive with amazement that . . . the concept of Nation [and humanity, liberty, equality, fraternity, and independence] are living realities in the twentieth century. . . . [Marx also demonstrated] a blind confidence in proletarian generosity and conscience. . . . The European proletariat has profited from the colonial system; therefore, it has never really—I mean effectively—opposed it." Leopold Sedar Senghor, *African Socialism*. New York: Praeger, 1964, p. 47.

tion has as its natural corollary the nationalization of socialism.[5]

Two qualifications should be added to our effort to differentiate functional and political groups from the territorial ones: first, as we have already noted, functional or political groups have to act within the existing territorial, national, and subnational boundaries. Even if their ideology is nonterritorial and their goals and links are supranational, their pressures are directed at territorial authorities and institutions. The links between functional interests and political territorial organizations (government and parties) vary greatly; they include functional parliamentary chambers, coadministration of economic and welfare programs in the socialist states, and traditional forms of pressure such as agitation, propaganda, lobby, pledges of electoral support, pickets, strikes, and violence.

Our second qualification concerns the territorial organization of the functional groups themselves; in order to be effective, all-national or supranational functional interest groups have to match the territorial organization of political power. The line between functional and territorial interests becomes blurred. Some authors actually call a territorial aggregation of functional interests a variety of *functionalism;* others call it *functional federalism* (although the term *federalism* has a dominant territorial connotation) when pluralism and institutionalized cooperation among functional groups are actually meant.

DISPERSED GROUPS

Other types of subnational groups are linguistic, racial, ethnic, or religious communities (usually called *minorities*) that live *dispersed* over territories organized and dominated by other groups. They do not desire assimilation but, on the contrary, they aim at maintaining and developing further their separate identity; they are, however, unable (because they do not live in sufficiently compact settlements) or unwilling (as orthodox Jews, for instance) to translate their separate destiny into territorial terms, such as a separate territorial state. In many ways, when

[5] E. H. Carr, *Nationalism and After.* New York: St. Martin's, 1945, p. 27.

organized, they resemble functional groups because, like labor, agriculture, business, and the professions, they lack any *clear* territorial interest. Their forms of political pressure are usually similar to those adopted by functional interest groups, such as propaganda, lobby, pledges of electoral support, or violence. In developing countries they often articulate their interests informally and intermittently through individuals, cliques, family, or religious heads.[6]

There are, however, some important differences in the degree of group solidarity as felt by a functional interest group, on the one hand, and a minority, on the other. There is first of all a high potential of a successful emotional aggregation of all conflicting class interests and professional interests into one linguistic, racial, or ethnic whole. A dispersed group of this type may be actually viewed as a *territoryless potential nation.* It cannot realistically entertain a hope for a self-ruling territory —except ghettolike portions of cities. Such dispersed groups usually hope and press for different forms of recognition and guarantees of their separate identity and interests, such as communal representation, protection against undesirable integration, permission to use their language in official, educational, and entertainment media, and financial and other support for their separate cultural development. Chapter 4 will deal with such demands in greater detail.

Furthermore, such dispersed groups, although in our sense of the word they are *nonterritorial,* retain and sometimes newly acquire an awareness of common territorial roots from the past. Groups that feel they are different from the culture of the dominant group and that now live in dispersion are either the aborigines of the territory (for example, the American Indians— however, long ago they did come from somewhere else) who were crowded out by subsequent immigration and forced into dispersion or onto ghetto-reservations; or they are immigrant settlers who came to the territory more or less voluntarily. We say, "more or less voluntarily" because groups rarely move from one area to another unless they must. They usually try to escape

---

[6] Groups based on kinship, ethnic, religious, or lineage bonds are called *nonassociational* interest groups by Gabriel A. Almond and James E. Coleman, *The Politics of Developing Areas.* Princeton, N.J.: Princeton University Press, 1960, p. 33.

a threat originated by fellowmen or by nature, with the hope for a better life in what at a distance appears to them a heaven but what under the impact of subsequent discrimination may prove to be only another version of hell in the old country. Some Chinese groups apparently so miscalculated when they moved to Southeast Asia.

Many dispersed ethnic, racial, or linguistic groups preserve very strong bonds between themselves and their blood relatives who have maintained or newly established their own territorial nation-states. Often the achievements and glory of their relatives help the isolated and dispersed group to maintain itself in an unfriendly environment. The existence and glory of France stimulates the French Canadians to a high degree. The Chinese minorities in Southeast Asia remain not only unassimilated but primarily loyal to China as their homeland.[7] Their Indonesian or Filipino citizenship does not prevent them from sharing with the Chinese who live on the mainland or on Taiwan an interest and involvement in such questions as who and what system should prevail over their original home territory. This split interest applies, of course, to all groups that have settled outside their home territory, like the Cubans, Scandinavians, Poles, or Czechs in the United States; with passion they follow and try to influence the political destinies of their former home territories. It was once said about Chicago that no man could run there for Congress unless he was able to say something either nice or nasty about Poland and Czechoslovakia, depending on the situation in these two countries. Chicago used to be described as the second largest Polish or Czechoslovak city after Warsaw and Prague.

In the case of the dispersed Jewish community, the memory of the past territorial community has played an important role for millennia ("If I forget thee, O Jerusalem, let my right hand forget her cunning"—Psalm 137). The link with the ancestral home has been greatly increased since Zionism translated the dream into territorial reality in the form of the state of Israel. In 1960 Ben Gurion, then prime minister of Israel, argued, "There is nothing that has united the entire Jewish people of all parties, views and sections, so much as the state of Israel.

[7] A. Doak Barnet, *Communist China and Asia.* New York: Knopf, 1961, p. 172.

There is no doubt that the state has straightened the backs of Jews in every country." Here is an example of a dispersed ethnic-religious group that at least partly has become territorial; of course, orthodox and assimilated Jews and even some Zionists have a different opinion on the matter and strongly object to Ben Gurion's view that Jews who remain outside the territorial state of Israel violate the basic precept of Judaism every day they remain away from the Israeli territory. According to this concept, commitment to living in the territory of Israel is the only true distinction of a Zionist and Jew.[8] Without such commitment Jews living in free and prosperous countries, according to Ben Gurion, face "a slow and imperceptible decline into the abyss of assimilation."[9]

The black communities in the Americas represent dispersed and potentially territorial groups and also fully territorial groups (for instance, those of Jamaica, Haiti, and other Caribbean Islands; and, in a way, ghettos in North American cities). Whether dispersed or territorial, the black groups do not represent immigrant settlers in the usual sense of the word. They did not come more or less voluntarily; in the slave trade there was no element of free choice. Such a forcible migration may be actually viewed as a conquest; instead of territory, its labor force was conquered, annexed, and denationalized. "We are a people who were captured and brought to a strange land," wrote Barbara Ann Teer. She added:

> We were stripped of our language, robbed of our names, our family ties, we were completely naked psychologically. Our bodies were clothed, but our minds were filled with nega-

[8] At Hadassah's winter conference in Jerusalem in 1968, Mrs. Mortimer Jacobson, president of the group, rejected the view held by Israeli leaders that "a Zionist is only one who is committed to living in Israel." *The New York Times* (February 11, 1968).

[9] The author of the congressional resolution in favor of a homeland in Palestine for the persecuted Jews, passed in 1923, Hamilton Fish, protested in a letter to *The New York Times* (January 14, 1961) against Ben Gurion's statement, which he labeled "intolerant" and, recording his own shock and distress, added: "This is carrying Jewish nationalism to absurd and disastrous extremes. It is such willful, deplorable and exaggerated policies that create misunderstanding, distrust and enmity. It has no place in America."

tive, hateful, and demeaning images of ourselves by those who had everything to gain by suppressing the truthful images.[10]

For many decades the memory of a common territorial past, unlike the Jewish case, was apparently dim. It was forgotten by the new generations or sometimes pretended to be forgotten. When in the nineteenth century free American slaves, with the help of white charities, created Liberia by remigration and settlement, the emergence of a free black territory had no electrifying effect on the black community in the United States in any way similar to that of Israel on the Jews. The postcolonial emergence of new African states in the 1950s, however, had a more profound impact. Since the later 1950s some of the leaders and groups among the black communities in the United States have added a territorial dimension to black nationalism. A few of these leaders and groups glorify the territorial isolation of ghettos; others promote the idea of a black territorial state to be carved from the United States, either from the South (Mississippi, Louisiana, Alabama, Georgia, and South Carolina)[11] or from the West (California and Oregon). As in the case of Israel, the concept of a territorial state is controversial within the black community for many reasons. Some view it as totally unrealistic or as a development that the white racists could welcome as a cheap way out. "We do not intend to let white people off the hook that easy," said Whitney M. Young, Jr., director of the National Urban League, while embracing the concept of black power at a conference at Columbus, Ohio.[12] Others who view a carving of a black state out of the United States as a possibility in the future refuse to consider any commitment on their part to settle in such a state, especially if it were formed in the most underdeveloped part of the United States, the Deep South. Many speak in ill-defined terms of a territorial dimension of the solution of the black-white problem

[10] *The New York Times* (July 7, 1968).
[11] A convention sponsored by Detroit's Malcolm X Society, held in March, 1968, proposed the establishment of such a Southern black state in combination with "reparations" (a form of "white" developmental aid) for damages sustained over the past 150 years. In 1969 a black leader, James Farmer, presented a multimillion-dollar reparations bill to all American churches.
[12] *The New York Times* (July 7, 1968).

or "geographic control" by black power (Roy Innis, June 21, 1969), terms vaguely suggestive of some black-and-white federal territorial formula. Finally, many still refuse to abandon the dream of biethnic harmony and ultimate integration.

German settlements in Eastern Europe represent another case of dispersed ethnic groups whose territorial memories continue to play an important political role. German settlers began their move eastward before the tenth century when, apparently, linguistic nationalism had not yet reached the present-day high degree of mutual suspicion. In 1325, however, a Czech pamphlet blamed the princes for encouraging the German immigration into Bohemia: "The normal and proper thing is for the bear to stay in the forest, the wolf in his cave, the fish in the sea and the German in Germany. In that way the world would have some peace." More than six centuries later, at the Potsdam Conference (August 1945) concluding World War II in Europe, the victorious allies (the Soviet Union, the United States, and Great Britain) authorized Poland and Czechoslovakia to reverse the move of the German settlers and expel all their German-speaking citizens westward into the American- and the Soviet-administered zones of defeated Germany. About ten million Germans were in this fashion uprooted and resettled in their original homeland. It may be assumed that for the past several centuries the German minorities in Eastern Europe had preserved a very strong sentimental, cultural, and political link with Germany; they did not assimilate the language and culture of the majority (Czech, Polish, Hungarian) among whom they had chosen to live but whom they had probably considered inferior. Now, however, it seems that the German expellees who have not yet been fully absorbed into the German life retain a vivid memory of and a hope for a return to their settlements in Poland and Czechoslovakia; they form a powerful pressure group in this respect in West Germany. It is, however, possible that the memory of their settlements outside Germany, probably quite strong with the older generation, will become increasingly dimmer with the younger generation, with every additional year of residence in Germany, and with every new intermarriage between the Germans from Germany and those from Eastern Europe.

Can any ethnic, racial, or linguistic minority be really free of any territorial memory or hope for territorial self-expression?

Hardly. Even nomadic groups such as Gypsies [13] or Bedouins are usually attached to the broad concept of a territory that allows them to continue their otherwise nonterritorial way of life. (If one were to stretch the definition of an *ethnic* group to include also the totally alienated or truly cosmopolitan groups [whose home territory is the whole world], one could consider the groups in search of a never-never land as purely nonterritorial—however, that never-never *land* has strong territorial implications too.) There seems to be no case of an ethnic, racial, or linguistic group that would be entirely free of some territorial memory or territorial hope.

SUBNATIONAL TERRITORIAL INTEREST GROUPS

The focus of our study is on subnational territorial communities; they were defined as aggregates of individuals aware of their common bonds as well as the history and the future of their territorial organization. Their contacts, coalitions, cooperation, and conflicts are our central concern.

Intensive identification with a nation-state, the most extensive as well as effective territorial interest group, does not exclude, as we have already indicated, a simultaneous allegiance to supranational and subnational communities. The intensity of such loyalties varies a great deal. This may perhaps be best illustrated by a series of concentric circles extending from one's own person, family, and home to the city, the province, and, finally, the nation (see Fig. 2–1). In between there may be loyalties to dispersed ethnic, religious, racial, and also functional and professional groups (marked in the figure by an undulated line). Beyond the national circumference (marked by a dark circle) there are increasingly lighter circles representing first the immediate international neighborhood (for instance, Canada and Mexico in the case of the United States), second the continent, and last (the ill-defined, nebulous circle) the global community of the human race. Seen from the point of view of practical, concrete, personal interests, the human race appears amorphous,

---

[13] In Communist Eastern Europe, Gypsies represent a constant problem for the socialist-planned economy. They keep on resisting the authorities' efforts to socialize them into permanent occupations and residence.

Figure 2–1   Gradation of loyalties

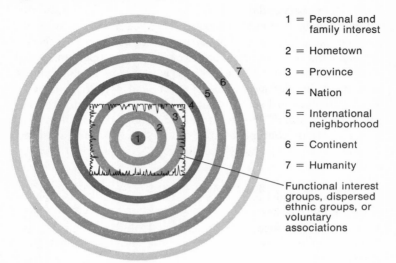

1 = Personal and
    family interest

2 = Hometown

3 = Province

4 = Nation

5 = International
    neighborhood

6 = Continent

7 = Humanity

Functional interest
groups, dispersed
ethnic groups, or
voluntary
associations

vague, distant—basically a mass consisting of more or less hostile
aliens living I-don't-much-care-where beyond the national boundaries. In contrast, the territorial state and its benefits and coercive
power seem immediate, tangible, and in many ways comforting.

Passing over the national circumference, the intensity of
effective (not merely verbal) people's identification with communities lying beyond individual and national experience tends
to decline sharply. The intensity gradually increases when one
approaches his home from a distance. An American, for instance,
who returns home from Nepal or Mongolia via Europe, experiences a gradation of emotional identification while passing from
one concentric circle of familiarity to another. An American's
first contact with European civilization makes him feel at least
partly at home in comparison with his feelings of exotic thrill or
discomfort experienced in Katmandu or Ulan Bator. Then comes
the flight over the Atlantic Ocean in an efficient American jet; a
tasteless cold chicken aspic has just beeen served by a stewardess
with an impeccable make-up—and all that is home, too. And
then comes the sight of the Statue of Liberty or New York harbor
(the beginning of his national territory). These are tangible
and familiar sights, and because they are familiar, they are both

comforting and irritating (for instance, a customs officer). He hears an understandable language everywhere, he sees the familiar flag, he is caught in the familiar traffic jam, and he notes the familiar road signs and advertisements—in Deutsch's terms, the "boundary of social communicative efficiency" is, so to speak, visible at first sight. And then the traveler arrives even closer to his home, at his city and street—"Oh dream of joy, is this indeed/ The lighthouse top I see/Is this the hill? Is this the kirk?/Is this mine own countree?" [14]

The set of concentric circles in Figure 2–1 represents an attempt to express visually the different communities to which men feel different degrees of loyalty (expressed by different shades of gray and black). Arranged to form a Chinese puzzle of a sort, our model could not indicate possible competition or irreconcilable clashes either between functional and territorial interests (for instance, all-national labor interests against territorial provincial ones) or between different territorial loyalties (a city or a region against the national center, for instance). The model implies compatibility, and this often may be the case; individual, provincial, national, and supranational interests and the loyalties associated with them may indeed point in the same direction.

The opposite situation—incompatibility and conflict—is, however, equally, if not more, frequent. Interests that have been deemed for a long time complementary may be found in a mild or wild conflict. If the interests of different communities are perceived as pointing in diametrically opposed directions, a choice must be made. It may mean neglect or outright sacrifice of the interests of one community in favor of the interests of another community. Caught in such a loyalty and support dilemma, individuals and groups have to determine their priorities. An individual in the United States may find, for example, that, when the chips are down, he is really black first, Muslim second, and American third—or he may reverse the order. In France one may be Parisian first, French second, and European third, if at all. Writing on the subject of patriotism in 1843, Joseph de Maistre observed that in his time he had seen Frenchmen, Italians, and Russians—and thanks to Montesquieu also a

[14] Samuel T. Coleridge, *The Rime of the Ancient Mariner,* Part VI.

Parisian—but "as for man, I declare that I have never met him in my life—if he exists, it is without my knowledge."

The nature and intensity of competition or conflict between different types of territorial loyalties and other loyalties, including that to one's own ego, vary greatly. Evidently, our simple model of concentric circles of loyalties is in need of further qualification to indicate variations in either determined attachment to or rejection of conflicting values.

In Figure 2–2 are reproduced ten different combinations of attachment to or rejection of personal egoistic, provincial, national, and supranational interests. In the ten columns (there could be many more) the letter A refers to attachment and the letter R to rejection; the different priorities indicate the most usual decisions in which some of the conflicting values are sacrificed (R) while others are maximized (A). They range from treason or secession to patriotism or supranational idealism. (The model should be considered a mere visual, somewhat facetious, illustration of the problems discussed.)

The columns may be interpreted as follows:

1. (A-R-R-R): This represents a traitor or a spy who places his sordid or pathological personal interests above everything else—his province, his nation, and humanity. He would transform the model of concentric circles of different loyalties into one amorphous nebulous whole with only one clear black point in the middle: his expectation of rewards and fear of punishment. Nothing else counts.

2. (R-R-R-A): This represents a selfless person or group whose only overriding commitment is to a supranational creed,

Figure 2–2   Attachment to or rejection of interests

Interest	Spy	Saint	Egoist or Rationalizer				Fool	Nihilist	Selfless or Selfish Secessionist	
Personal	A	R	A	A	A	A	A	R	R	A
Provincial	R	R	R	R	R	A	A	R	A	A
National	R	R	R	A	A	A	A	R	R	R
Supranational	R	A	A	R	A	R	A	R	R	R

mankind, peace, or justice. This category may include conscientious objectors, pacifists, dedicated members of ideological supranational movements, missionaries, and saints. It also may include spies or traitors (such as atomic scientists who betray their nation for other than egoistic reasons). Harold A. R. Philby, an Englishman who spied for Russia within the British intelligence system and the CIA, expressed his system of priorities as follows: "To betray you must first belong. I never belonged. . . . The fight against fascism [in the 1930s] and the fight against imperialism [in the 1950s, meaning the United States and Britain] were fundamentally the same fight." [15]

3–6. $(A$-R-R-$A)$, $(A$-R-A-$R)$, $(A$-R-A-$A)$, and $(A$-A-A-$R)$: These represent varieties of the frequent assumption— sometimes sincere self-deception, more often a mere rationalization—of harmony between, on the one hand, the interests of humanity, the nation, and a subnational group and, on the other hand, selfish personal or group interests. Statements such as "What's good for General Motors is good for the country," "What's good for the AFL, is good for the United States" or "What's good for Russia is good for world Communism" belong to this category of rationalization or self-deception. The Soviet spy Kim Philby saw himself in this category too when he equated his own interests, Soviet interests, and British interests: "I felt, and I still feel, that by doing this work [spying for Russia] I also served my English people."

7. $(A$-A-A-$A)$: This is a person or group that perceives all interests and all communities in perfect harmony. This is probably a fool.

8. $(R$-R-R-$R)$: This person rejects everything. He is probably a candidate for suicide.

9–10. $(R$-A-R-$R)$ and $(A$-A-R-$R)$: These represent a selfless or a selfish *secessionist* (leader of an anticolonial struggle or a promoter of territorial self-determination), respectively. A territorial interest group in search of autonomy or sovereign independence rejects all consideration other than its interest in a separate future destiny. If the group were to redraw our figure of concentric circles, it would reduce the black circle indicating the national community and its interests to a pale gray or a

[15] *Izvestia* (Moscow, December 18, 1967).

white, whereas the previously gray circle expressing its sub-national community and its interests would appear in glossy black. A territorial interest group that has been so far considered and treated by the central authority as a subordinate sector of the national or imperial whole may solve its perception of an irreconcilable conflict of interests and loyalties by a demand for a partial or full territorial self-rule.

Not all interest and loyalty conflicts need to lead to full separation. There are gentle and there are explosive types of discontent. Both satisfaction and dissatisfaction are very relative concepts; they may shade from one to another. There has perhaps never been, nor could there be, an unqualified, total satisfaction of any man or group with anything political or territorial.

When men are dissatisfied, the intensity of their determination to do something about it partly depends on the intensity of their dissatisfaction and partly on other variables, such as the capacity or incapacity and will power or weakness of their own leaders and their opponents. Some groups when dissatisfied write to their congressman or party secretary; others organize a labor union, professional association, club, or party; still others build a barricade, occupy a building, chain a college dean, or start a revolution. Many steps separate remedial action from actual discontent. The Russian revolutionary leader Trotsky once wisely noted that the mere existence of privations—and the resulting conflict of interests and discontent—was "not enough to cause insurrection; if it were, the masses would be always in revolt."

If we tried to list all the reasons for which men object to their government, it would be a multivolume encyclopedia containing several million entries. Many of the reasons would be formulated by average citizens, and probably many more by the intellectuals who differ from the rest of the people by their capacity of independent insight and critical judgment. In his analysis of the prerevolutionary alienation of the intellectuals, Crane Brinton rightly points out that

> after all one of the great functions of the intellectuals in Western society has always been to shake ordinary mortals out of their unthinking optimism, and Cassandra has perhaps as

much claim as Plato to be the founder of a great academic tradition.[16]

Our concern here is primarily with the types of conflict and discontent that are expressed in territorial terms, and therefore may be resolved along a new, more satisfactory delineation or distribution of the territorial authority. The following chapter will deal with a wide spectrum of solutions, ranging from territorial secession to assimilation.

Depending on the groups' perception of either irreconcilability or a possibility for conciliation of its diverging interests and loyalties, the following measures have been adopted:

1. *Secession*. This measure transfers what has been internal pluralism—territorial or ethnic—to the international level; a formerly subnational territorial interest group emerges as a new territorial nation-state to be recognized by and to have diplomatic relations with other nation-states, including the one of which it used to be a part. Territorial secession from a colonial empire or from an oppressive national state are only two variations of an identical solution of hostile incompatibility.

2. Internal *elimination* of territorial and ethnic pluralism by genocide, expulsion, or assimilation. These measures are connected with the "right" to ethnic homogeneity (see Chap. 4).

3. *Preservation* of territorial or ethnic pluralism by institutional or political guarantees from "above" or by agreements from "below," as is the case in many federal or confederal systems.

[16] Crane Brinton, *The Anatomy of Revolution*. New York: Vintage Books (Knopf and Random House), 1965, p. 66.

THREE
TERRITORIAL
DISINTEGRATION

The right to rise up and shake off the existing government . . . a most valuable, a most sacred right
. . . [is not] confined to cases in which the whole
people of an existing government may choose to
exercise it. Any portion of such people that can may
revolutionize and make their own so much of the
territory as they inhabit.

> ABRAHAM LINCOLN (1848, in reference
> to the Mexican War)

Plainly, the central idea of secession is the essence
of anarchy.

> ABRAHAM LINCOLN (First Inaugural Ad-
> dress, in reference to the South)

Self-determination . . . is an imperative principle
of action, which statesmen will henceforth ignore
at their peril. . .

> WOODROW WILSON (February 11, 1918)

A study that focuses on issues that divide territorial communities
within nation-states seems to differ very substantially from the
study of international politics, which deals with conflict and
cooperation *among* nations. Nation-states maintain themselves
in separation from, competition with, and often hostility to other

nation-states; if they cooperate among themselves, it is usually *against* others. They do not conceive of themselves as members of a global community, based on consensus and dedicated to a worldwide cooperative order. Occasionally, at best, there is a sense of an incipient community—usually that of a shared fear. In the nineteenth century, for instance, the aristocratic Great Powers in general, and the Holy Alliance in particular, seemed to have a common fear of revolutionary republicanism. In the second half of the twentieth century the atomic superpowers occasionally admit of their common interest in avoiding mutual nuclear destruction. Their consensus is a tacit, nonsuicide pact of sorts. But can a community based on only such negative common interest become a positively cooperative one?

In contrast, a nation as a self-contained unit is assumed to have a positive common will and common determination to develop its territorial political and legal organization, economy, and culture and to develop its own way of life. This is in addition to its fear of external enemies. This image is correct only when we think of some well-ordered and long-established nation-states; but even they can experience a collapse of consensus. In the developing countries such a collapse or, rather, absence of consensus and lack of awareness of national identity, is quite frequent.

Under the conditions of a civil war or a revolution, the definitional line between the presence of consensus within the nation-states and its absence among the nation-states becomes quite blurred. Actually, a nation that two rival groups have split asunder in a revolution tends to surpass in hatred and ferociousness of fratricidal fighting an armed conflict between two nation-states. A psychologist, Jerome D. Frank, noted on this subject:

> Combatants in fratricidal wars mobilize special sources of bitterness springing from their initial membership in the same group. . . . By the time organized violence breaks out, each side has seceded, in effect, from the society defended by the other, so that to this extent they are no longer subject to inhibitions against killing their own kind. . . . The enemy is dehumanized . . . he becomes a statistic, an abstraction, and a beast . . . and like an animal he is impervious to reason and will respond only to punishment.[1]

[1] Jerome D. Frank, *Sanity and Survival*. New York: Vintage Books (Knopf and Random House), 1968, p. 185.

Peace within a nation seems based on no more solid foundation than peace among nations. Is this another depressing comment on human nature? It is.

In his carefully researched study of international and civil wars, Quincy Wright found that out of a total of 278 wars fought between 1480 and 1941, 78 (28 percent) were civil wars. For the period between 1800 and 1941, the ratio was one civil war to three international ones.[2]

It has always been difficult to distinguish internal from international wars. Some civil wars are international wars by proxy; great powers fight each other by supplying arms and advice to their respective sympathetic elites. To a large extent, the Spanish Civil War in 1936, the Korean War in 1950, and the long war in Vietnam belong to this category. Presently the atomic superpowers, dreading a direct nuclear confrontation, may try to affect the global balance of power by interference in the domestic affairs of other countries, ranging from foreign aid and technical assistance to infiltration, subversion, or open military action. Some civil wars are planned, instigated, and manipulated from without; others attract external support in the process of their success or failure. Foreign support may be directed to either the incumbents or the insurgents. "When people have taken up arms against the government," as Machiavelli wisely noted, "there will never be lacking a foreigner to assist them."

If an originally genuine civil conflict can be internationalized, so can an international conflict be transformed into internal upheavals within the territories of the fighting parties. The Bolshevik revolution and the subsequent revolutionary attempts in Germany and in Hungary after World War I are examples. In some cases, groups within a nation anticipate such support although it has been neither promised nor contemplated; yet even such a "phantom intervention" may act as a trigger of insurrection or have a decisive effect upon its outcome; a "phantom intervention"[3] may increase the self-confidence of the rebels and produce a state of despair and feeling of international iso-

[2] Quincy Wright, *A Study of War*. Chicago: University of Chicago Press, 1942, p. 651. It now exists in an abridged paperback edition, issued by the University of Chicago Press (Phoenix Books), 1965.

[3] The term is used in the author's study and research on the role of perception in revolutionary situations.

lation on the part of the incumbents. One variety of "phantom intervention" is the unintended magnetism of successful revolution or secession elsewhere. This is especially so now when mass media transmit all news around the globe in a matter of seconds.

Despite the intense hostility that characterizes civil wars, both the insurgents and the incumbents, paradoxically, retain something solid in common: their attachment to the national territory over the possession and control of which they fight and kill each other. The insurgents have seceded from the national community only ideologically, not geographically.

But there are other internal conflicts in which the issue really is not which and whose policy should prevail in the nation; the very concept of the territorial community is actually at stake. The nation has already split into two or more groups, one of which desires to go it alone or at least achieve a high degree of territorial autonomy. Here, the secession is both ideological and *territorial*. The urge for a territorial self-rule or full independence usually contains all the emotional ingredients of nationalism.

Although any separatist movement represents by definition an erosive force directed at the existing territorial order, it is highly aggregative in another direction: it increases the territorial solidarity and cohesion of the subnational group in a similar way as external enmity raises the national unity to nth power. The separatist movement enhances the unity of the territorial group in the period of its struggle against the present and for a different territorial future. For the separatist movement, hand in hand with its present discontent goes its expectation of satisfaction in a new territorial community (an autonomous province or a sovereign state) that grants the people what the present territorial authority has refused or has proved unable to do.

There are many reasons for a territorial group's discontent and quest for a new territorial arrangement. The most usual and obvious reasons are its sense of oppression, injustice, neglect (deliberate, unwitting, or due to the ineptness of the central government) or simply a growing divergence of interests between the central government and the territorial groups. This is particularly so in colonial empires where all the previous reasons for discontent and search for autonomy or independence are underscored by the memory of conquest, racial, and lingual differences, cultural antagonism, color discrimination, and blatant exploitation by a distant colonial central government. Clearly, the same elements may exist also in oppressive polyethnic states.

The process of the territorial disintegration of empires or nation-states is usually accelerated—as all revolutions are—by the emergence of a feasible alternative, as promoted by the separatist elites and supported by an organized movement. And then there is the prevailing international context or mood; if favorable to the idea of territorial self-determination, it may considerably enhance the chances of the separatists and contribute to the loss of confidence or sense of legitimacy on the part of the ruling groups. There were periods in history when empire building was accepted by a great many persons as a fact of life; other periods of history are marked by dissolution of empires. We are in such a period now—this is an era of national self-determination. This era is partly the aftermath of the general reaction against Western European colonialism in Asia and Africa. Some view the era partly as a phenomenon related to the individual identity crisis. As individuals react against their feeling of insignificance and anonymity in a world dominated by modern technology, mass media, and mass organizations, so territorial groups react against the world dominated by superpowers and their technologies. Nationalism would then appear to be on a group level what individual self-assertion is on the personal level. The call for decentralization and participation heard within nations has its echo on the international level.

SECESSION IS THE MESSAGE

When a territorial group finds it impossible to coexist with another group within the same framework, it may decide, in the words of the American Declaration of Independence of 1776, to "dissolve the political bonds which have connected them with another, and to assume among the powers of the earth, the separate and equal status to which the Laws of Nature and the Nature's God entitle them." [4] The authority to which such a

[4] Compare the Norwegian declaration of secession from Sweden, June 7, 1905. It reads in part as follows: "Whereas his Majesty the King has declared himself unable to procure for the country a new Government; and whereas the constitutional Royal power has thus ceased to be

message is directed—be it George III, Abraham Lincoln, the Hapsburgs, or General de Gaulle—usually calls it *secession,* endowing the term with a highly derogatory connotation. The separatists—the thirteen American colonies, the Southern Confederacy, the Czechs (in 1918), or Algeria—call it the right of national self-determination and crown the term with an aura of sanctity. Actually, territorial self-determination is always secession because no group lives in a vacuum and, therefore, in order to exercise its right to independence, it always has to secede from some territorial framework, be it a province, a nation-state, a federation, or a colonial empire.

The late 1960s were the years not only of miniskirts but also of ministates. The temptation to secede and form an independent territorial unit has assumed epidemic proportions; it has affected even microscopic islands—leftovers of the colonial empires—and coral atolls. In 1967, for instance, the fifteen-mile-long Caribbean island of Anguilla (5000 inhabitants) decided to form an independent state instead of joining the projected federation of Saint Kitts-Nevis-Anguilla. The vote for national self-determination was indeed overwhelming: 1815 votes against 5. On February 7, 1969, Anguilla decided to become a republic—the smallest in the Caribbean—and break all ties with Britain: the vote was 1739 against 4. On March 19, 1969, Britain used air, land, and sea power to seize control of the island again. The purpose allegedly was to prevent the rule of an armed minority that had developed intimate relations not only with several American businessmen but also with the American underworld. In the House of Commons the British foreign secretary, Michael Stewart, justified the invasion as one of Britain's continuing responsibilities for the former colony's external affairs and for stability in the Caribbean. The British-installed government was planned to remain on the island for "a number of years." In the Pacific another example of a truly microscopic nation is Nauru Island, which proclaimed its independent statehood in 1967; it

---

in function, the Storting [Parliament] authorizes the members of the ministry resigning today . . . to exercise the authority vested in the King in accordance . . . with the Laws in force, with such modifications as are made necessary by the fact that the Union with Sweden under one King has been dissolved, in consequence of the King's having ceased to function as Norwegian King."

has 3100 inhabitants and a means of livelihood (phosphates) calculated to last for only a few more decades. In Micronesia the United States has been searching for a formula to end its administration of the 2141-island Pacific Trust Territory, consisting of the Marshall Islands, the Mariana Islands, and the Caroline Islands (German colonies until the end of World War I, when they were transformed into Japanese mandates; after World War II they became a United States trust territory). While some islanders claim full independence, others proposed (in July 1969) a federation with the American territory of Guam in order to form a commonwealth and be associated with the United States after the model of Puerto Rico. The United Nations mission that went to evaluate the American administration of the trust territory recorded the following observations concerning insular and often intolerant "nationalism," or tribalism, in the area:

> There exists great insularity among the majority of the inhabitants and . . . in some instances there is to be found a degree of cultural hostility between the different island groups. An instance of this . . . is to be found in a petition . . . which the U.N. Mission received in the Marshall Islands and which protests against the activities of a Ponapean trading company. A passage in this petition may be cited as follows: "We understand and appreciate the American ideal of 'One People,' but we are a separate country from Ponape with our own separate customs and culture and language and have no more desire to be classed with or merged with the Ponapeans than France has desire to merge with Germany or China with Japan. We feel that it is unfair to us as a people to be lumped together with other groups of Micronesian peoples as one people. We are proud of our race and our heritage and fear any attempt to merge us culturally or otherwise with the resultant loss of our own culture and individuality." [5]

In 1965 another group of islands, the Maldives, obtained its independence and became the 125th member of the United Nations; it now has a vote in the General Assembly equal to that of 500 million Indians, 200 million Russians, or 200 million

[5] U.N. document, a report of the U.N. Mission submitted to the General Assembly in 1953.

Americans. The Maldive Islands consist of 2000 atolls, covering a total area of 112 square miles (slightly more than Manhattan and Brooklyn put together); the total population of 104,000 (1968 figures) is composed of Indians, Arabs, and Chinese. In 1959 the southern part of the Maldive Islands, Suvadivian atolls, attempted secession, claiming a right to a separate Sinhalese "manifest destiny." The principle of territorial self-determination is evidently highly contagious.

In his 1967 *Annual Report,* the United Nations Secretary-General, U Thant, raised the issue of the microstates and their membership in the world organization and warned that "while universality of membership [that is, all nations should be members] is most desirable, like all concepts it has its limitations and the line must be drawn somewhere." The question is where. Before World War II, London would have drawn the line in such a way as to keep U Thant's native country, Burma, within the British Empire. Where will Burma now draw its line with regard, for instance, to attempts at secession on the part of its non-Burmese territorial groups such as Chins, Shans, or Karens?

In U Thant's understandable concern over the future consequences of the expected rise in the number of ministates, we find an echo of Lazare Carnot (1753–1823), who in 1793 addressed the French National Assembly to warn against the excesses of the revolutionary idea of decentralization and participatory self-rule: "If . . . any community whatever had the right to proclaim its will and separate from the main body under the influence of rebels, every county, every town, every village, every farmstead might declare itself independent."

And this is the real issue when territorial secession is applied as a solution of interethnic or interterritorial tension. If we accept the right of territorial self-determination in blanket fashion, warns Rupert Emerson in his classical study on nationalism, we "endow social entities which cannot be identified in advance with a right of revolution against constitutional authority of the state, and even oblige the state to yield to the demands of the revolutionaries." [6] The state yields only when it is forced to.

[6] Rupert Emerson, *From Empire to Nation.* Cambridge, Mass.: Harvard University Press, 1960, pp. 297–298. Now also available in paperback. Compare the American writer and Pulitzer Prize winner Norman Mailer, who, in 1969, competed in the Democratic party mayoral

Although the insurgents view the right of national self-determination as absolute—and superior to any other consideration—the incumbents consider it as merely a very relative principle, coordinate with or subordinate to other values, such as unity and internal order as conditions of progress, territorial integrity, and the authority's right to punish high treason, a crime that may consist of an attempt at secession with foreign help; such was the case of the American revolutionaries who had sought and received help from England's enemy, royal France.

Even if the ruling group finds some demands for secession more justifiable than others, it will tend to resist them all because it fears a chain reaction—a kind of domino theory of self-determination. "If the Union with Ireland is to be dissolved," warned the British Prime Minister Sir Robert Peel in the period of Anglo-Irish tension, "why may not Scotland and Wales demand the same? Why should not the empire be broken up altogether?" It finally was, and even the United Kingdom, by chain reaction and contagion, has not been protected against the secessionist fever. In the 1960s Welsh and Scottish nationalisms began significantly to assert themselves. In the 1968 municipal elections, the Scottish Nationalist party more than doubled its gains of 1967 and won nearly one hundred seats on city councils in Scotland. The party's main complaints seem economic, namely, that the Scots are being shortchanged by London (whether the government is run by the Conservative party or by the Labour party); allegedly, little of the taxes paid by Scotland is returned to benefit Scotland; and not enough industry is being directed there by the English administrators of economic and social planning. Mrs. Winifred Ewing, the first Nationalist member of Parliament from Scotland after twenty years, com-

---

primary. The chief plank in his political platform was to make New York City the nation's 51st state. Secession from the New York State is "an idea neither wholly absurd nor wholly new," commented *The New York Times* (May 5, 1969) and added: "As Caesar had his Brutus, Charles the First his Cromwell, and George the Third his Patrick Henry, so now Governor Rockefeller and the New York State Legislature have their Norman Mailer." The argument for secession was the usual one: economy. New York City contributes more taxes to the state than it receives back from it in revenues.

mented on the victory of her anti-English party: "The wind of nationalism is blowing on the London parties, and they will have to make concessions to it or face political suicide." The Scottish Nationalists ultimately aim at their own parliament, thus in effect ending the terms of the 1707 English-Scottish union.

Wales, too, has a Nationalist party (*Plaid Cymru*); its leader, Gwynfor Evans, was elected as member of Parliament. The aim of the party is to obtain the majority of votes in Wales and thus give a "clear and unequivocal mandate for its MPs for the setting up of a Welsh Parliament and a Welsh Government in Wales immediately." The Welsh Nationalist party is opposed to the use of violence and is committed to the use of constitutional means only. In its 1968 public statement it refused to associate itself in any manner with all the events being planned in Wales for the investiture of the heir to the British throne, Charles, as the prince of Wales. However, it called on its members to "exercise the sort of discipline and responsibility that the Czechoslovaks have so eminently demonstrated in the recent crisis [the Soviet invasion]." [7]

On July 17, 1967, the British Parliament agreed to end a legal prohibition on the use of the Welsh language in the public administration of Wales. The original restriction dated from the time of Henry VIII, who made the prohibition of the Welsh language a part of his efforts to integrate Wales into Tudor England. As the events indicate, he was not successful.

In her 1968 "Speech from the Throne," as drafted by the Labour Cabinet, Queen Elizabeth announced a formation of a "Commission on the Constitution" to consider the ties that have so far bound "several countries, nations and the United Kingdom" and to suggest a reform that would also include the relationship of the Channel Islands (Jersey and Guernsey) and the Isle of Man, which are not part of the United Kingdom and are not represented in the British Parliament. The title of the Commission on the Constitution is curious because Britain has no constitution at all in the usual sense of a single written document; the result of the work of the commission might very well be a proposal for a written constitution that would express some

[7] *The Guardian* (London, September 3, 1968).

federal formula for the varied relationships between England and the Celtic areas, including the largely autonomous Northern Ireland, which has its own Parliament and Cabinet.

The Celtic nationalist movement in Britain—for a long time an eccentric irrelevancy rather than a real problem—has even established some contacts with fellow Celtic nationalists in French Brittany. At an International Celtic Congress, held in Fougères, Brittany, on August 25, 1968, a representative of the Isle of Man explained to the Congress the island's opposition to Britain and announced that from then on the official buildings would display only the Manx flag and no longer the British flag.

In French Brittany, Celtic nationalism has been grafted onto farmers' unrest and resentment against Parisian economic policies. Since the 1960s the rallying motto of separatism *BZH* (*Breizh*—the Celtic name for the province of Brittany) may be seen displayed on many roads, walls, and cars of Brittany's local patriots. When challenged by the centralist authorities from Paris, the people of Brittany interpret *BZH,* with tongue in cheek, as meaning *Bretagne Zone Heureuse*—Britanny, a Happy Zone in federated Western Europe. It is not taken too seriously by Paris—except perhaps when the *BZH* separatism also implied criticism of de Gaulle's foreign policy. This was so when de Gaulle's excessive preoccupation with the French province of Quebec in Canada (de Gaulle's slogan was "Vive le Québec libre!" at the time of his visit to the World Exhibition in Montreal in 1967) was countered in Brittany by "Brittany first, Quebec after."

Other long-established polyethnic countries have not been spared either, as tensions in bilingual Belgium and Canada and in Spain indicate. In Spain, for instance, there is a noticeable revival of regionalism in Catalonia (from Barcelona to Valencia) underscored by a lingual difference, and in Guipúzcoa Province (the Basque country), neither of which areas has ever quite reconciled itself with centralism as practiced by Madrid.

In Turkey, Iran, and Iraq the Kurdish tribesmen have been asking and often fighting for their own nation-state for decades. In 1969 the new Revolutionary Command Council, the highest executive organ of the Iraqi government, proposed a "peaceful and just solution" to the Kurdish problem in the form of territorial autonomy for the one and a half million Iraqi Kurds.

Similar interethnic, intertribal, or interlingual tensions character-ize most newly established states in which the new national iden-tity must compete with traditional tribal and other territorial communities.

There are also problems in the Communist countries that have pretended for a long time that they have solved their inter-ethnic problems by the application of the Marxist-Leninist federal formula ("nationalism in form, socialism in content"). Incipient crises may be noted in biethnic Czechoslovakia; in Yugoslavia, composed of four major ethnic groups; and in the Soviet Union, consisting of fifteen major ethnic territories, known as Union Republics (more on this in Chap. 6).

In a period of territorial-ethnic claims it would be more than astonishing if dreams of territorial self-determination were not shared at least by some of the 40 million Ukrainians, who have always questioned the Great Russian domination of the Tsarist empire and its successor, the Soviet Union. On February 19, 1968, for instance, *Pravda* published an article by the Ukrainian Communist party secretary, Pyotr Y. Shelest.[8] It said in part that

> drivel about the so-called independence, about a sort of degra-dation of [Ukrainian] culture and language, is rotten bait that will be taken only by a person who is politically blind, a nar-row-minded and embittered man, demagogues and degenerates, or by people who oppose everything our people do.

Pravda also condemned the United States and West Ger-many for their alleged intelligence activities and interference, that is, the use of "Ukrainian counterrevolutionary traitors" to subvert the Ukrainian people and promote secession. Clearly such a vigorous attack against the allegedly "embittered" and "politically blind" Ukrainians would be unnecessary if they did not exist in numbers and did not try to act.

Some scholars deny the virulence of centrifugal tendencies

---

[8]Pyotr Y. Shelest allegedly was the most energetic advocate of the use of force against Czechoslovakia in August 1968. Apparently he was motivated by the fear that the Czechoslovak assertion of democ-racy and independence might significantly affect the interethnic tensions in the Soviet Union.

among the non-Russian nationalities of the Soviet Union. They consider that the program of Russification, extended over a long period of time, has had its profound impact. At a conference on the "State of Ethnic Minorities in the Soviet Union," held in 1965 at Brandeis University, the Ukrainians, the Byelorussians, and the Jews in particular were deemed to be "scheduled" for Russification. It was also argued that under the Soviet system the Russification is not primarily motivated by Russian ethnocentrism as such but by the need to centralize Communist economic and political controls and, concomittantly, foster a unified national culture. Given the numerical and historical predominance of Russians, this Soviet culture is bound to be Russian.[9]

In China the non-Chinese (non-Han) minorities [10] represent only about 6 percent of the total population of about 700 million but inhabit half the national territory (42 percent). It is the inhospitable, arid, or mountainous part of China. These groups, which indeed fully deserve the term *territorial-ethnic,* live in boundary areas contiguous to other Asian states. In most cases, their non-Chinese blood relatives live on the other side of the Chinese state frontiers. The possibility of secession is not unrealistic and is hence a matter of great concern for any regime in Peking. In 1958, on the eve of the Chinese conflict with the Soviet Union, Hsinhua, the official agency, reported (January 17, 1958) on the speeches of several vice-chairmen of the Na-

[9] This was the thesis developed by John A. Armstrong, director of the Russian studies program at the University of Wisconsin at the 1965 conference. Compare the Soviet magazine *Bolshevik* (No. 18, 1947), which defined Soviet patriotism as follows: "Soviet patriotism and national pride are based on the realization of the world-historic significance of the successes of socialism and of the leading part of this country and her people in the world history of mankind. The feeling of Soviet national pride is based on the understanding of the great and unequalled superiority of Soviet culture, ideology, science, and morals." From a different angle the Soviet case of territorial expansion is also discussed in the concluding portion of Chap. 6.

[10] In the order of numerical importance the five major non-Chinese minorities, all in theory endowed with territorial autonomy, are Chuangs in the province of Kwangsi (south), Uighurs in Sinkiang (west), Moslem Huis in Kansu (northwest), Tibetans (southwest), and Mongols in Inner Mongolia (center), separated by the Gobi Desert from the People's Republic of Mongolia, an ally of the Soviet Union.

tionality Affairs Committee of the Chinese People's Congress (Parliament). One of them, Liu Chen, told the committee that "mounting regional nationalism" had emerged and had become "a danger that must be taken seriously." Another vice-chairman, Wang Feng, declared at a meeting in Lanchow that the Hui group (a Moslem minority of about 4 million people— as many people as in Lebanon and Libya) had separatist ideas "derived from capitalism." He termed as highly erroneous the idea among the Huis that China was not their motherland as well as the Hui concept that Arabic was their original mother tongue. Still, another spokesman, Liu Ke-ping, chairman of the committee, announced a rectification campaign among the minority peoples in view of "the dangerous nature and seriousness of separatist activities." In particular he scored the minorities for their resentment toward Han (Chinese) officials, peasants, and workers who, on the order from Peking, have begun moving into the minority areas with the obvious aim of sinicizing them. Liu also stressed that the separatist ideas were harbored mainly by young intellectuals among the Mongols (they may dream about reunification of all Mongols, now divided into three sectors, the Chinese province of Inner Mongolia, the People's Republic of Mongolia, and the Buryat Mongol provinces in the USSR), the Uighurs in Sinkiang, and the Korean minority in Manchuria. Their ideas allegedly were inspired by a desire to restore the old rule by capitalists, federal lords, and slaveowners.

The reader may wonder what proof there is to confirm the allegation that the minorities in China really wish for a return of slaveowners—unless, of course, *slaveowners* is an "imaginative" Chinese translation of the right of territorial self-determination.

The separatist ferment in all corners of the world has different intensities, and very different chances of eventual success, either in the form of independence or broader territorial autonomy. It would be unrealistic to compare, for instance, separatism in French Brittany or Spanish Catalonia with that of the Soviet Ukraine, inhabited by almost 40 million people who, as the French saying puts it, cannot all be wrong.

Whatever their final choice of goals and means of action may be, it is obvious that some territorial communities which are now parts of polyethnic federal or unitary systems are more justified candidates for independent statehood than a great many members of the United Nations, the microscopic states of doubtful national identity and doubtful economic viability.

It should be also recognized that territorial secession, although a frequent and extreme solution, is not the only way of solving interethnic conflicts within a territorial nation-state. Territorial interest groups have at their disposal and employ all types of pressure techniques that other interest groups use: lobby, agitation, propaganda, pledges of electoral support, and politics of confrontation or violence. Although theoretically a dissatisfied territorial group could use the secessionist blackmail all the time, this is not the case. Dissatisfaction is one thing, and secession another. A larger degree of local autonomy or a more generous channeling of funds from the central authority down to the territorial groups often proves more advantageous than secession or independent nationhood. Dissatisfied provinces or cities are not constantly on their way out from the existing territorial framework in an effort to transfer their grievances from the domestic to the international scene; most of the time they are on their way, literally, to the national capital to plead their case within the established framework. In some situations the ethnic territorial emotions, a matter of the heart, may call for secession, whereas economic pragmatism, a matter of reason, points to a continued membership in a larger economic unit. Economic advantages to be derived from such an association certainly play their role in the case of Quebec in Canada, non-Russian republics in the Soviet Union, Brittany in France, or Scotland and Wales in Britain.

For another reason a dissatisfied territorial group may not press for, or even threaten with, secession: its estimate of the efficacy of the central coercive power may, rightly or wrongly, point to the conclusion that what is desirable is not feasible because of risks involved. An alert and powerful national center has nipped in the bud many a quixotic attempt at secession. Other secessions, however, have been crushed after a protracted civil war that, at a high cost, restored the previous territorial unity. The secession of the Southern Confederacy from the United States was, for instance, crushed at an estimated cost of 500,000 soldiers' lives, which, in terms of the present United

States population would roughly correspond to 3 million soldiers killed (nine times the United States casualties in World War II). Thus, many potential secessions smolder under a seemingly quiet surface for decades and centuries, hoping and waiting for a realistic opportunity to shake off an alien rule. Such was the case of Slavic territorial communities within the Austro-Hungarian Empire before its coercive power was weakened by defeats in World War I; similarly, the claim of national self-determination in Asia and Africa fully surfaced only during World War II, partly at least also as a result of difficulties or defeats that the Western European colonial powers (France, England, Holland, and Belgium) had on the European battlefields. It is possible that, in addition to economic reasons (discussed earlier), their estimate of the unfeasibility of the enterprise is the cause of the relative calm on the part of the non-Russian communities within the Soviet Union and on the part of the non-Chinese minorities, including Tibet, in China.

Although we observe today an increased emphasis on the need for planning and working in a broader cooperative framework in our interdependent world, national self-determination and the concomitant territorial disintegration are high and certainly will remain so for some time on the agenda of the last third of the twentieth century. Both the integrative (federalizing) and disintegrative principles compete and conflict with each other. And the principles of national and individual freedoms also compete and conflict. The glory of liberating territorial collectivities from an oppressive rule is but rarely coupled with the glory of liberating men as individuals. Just as socialism may be distorted in slavery, so can nationalism and its call for liberty. Both nationalism and socialism, which were strongly associated with the concept of humanism and individual liberty in the nineteenth century, have changed. Both are now marked by a shift

> from the emphasis on the dignity of the individual to that on the power of collectivities . . . from open outstretched arms to clenched fists; nationalism centered around barracks, socialism around factories, each a symbol and model of teamwork and discipline.[11]

[11] Hans Kohn, *The Twentieth Century*. New York: Crowell-Collier-Macmillan, 1949, p. 64.

TERRITORIAL ALIENATION

So far in our discussion of the causes of territorial disintegration the emphasis was on conflicts of interests underlined by differences in language, race, religion, or ethnic origins. There are, however, cases when alienation and finally secession take place, although the tension and conflict cannot be referred to as inter-ethnic or interracial. "Even if the same language, culture and basic institutions were shared originally through the entire territory," notes Karl W. Deutsch, "individuals and groups may cease to identify themselves with the territorial authority if it proves persistently incapable or unresponsive." [12] There are territorial alienations and secessions without any ethnic connotation, at least not initially.

Although Deutsch's observation was meant to apply mostly to the present problems in the underdeveloped world, it rightly points to the fact that territorial alienation and the demand for secession need not be expressed in different language or be based on a different race or religion. There are many examples of territorial secessions from relatively homogeneous linguistic, religious, racial, and cultural communities: the nucleus of future Switzerland, the three German cantons of Uri, Schwyz, and Unterwalden, separated from the German Empire. Linguistic differences played a very minor or no part in the decision of Ireland to secede from Britain, the Netherlands to secede from the German Empire, and the South-African and Rhodesian white governments to secede from the Commonwealth. Spanish-speaking Roman Catholic Central America and South America separated from Spain, and Brazil separated from Portugal. Whereas under the Spanish colonial empire Central America and South America were divided into only eight administrative units, the process of further secessions resulted in almost three times the original colonial number. Today, the ruling elites in eighteen Spanish-speaking republics and the Commonwealth of Puerto Rico act and challenge each other in terms of territorial nationalism and have difficulties in overcoming regional jealousies and in creating cooperative ventures such as common markets, although they all share a common history, culture, religion, language, and tradition.

[12] Karl W. Deutsch, "Social Mobilization and Political Development," *The American Political Science Review* (September 1961), p. 498.

And then, of course, there are the cases of the United States and its secession from England in 1776 and of the Southern Confederacy's secession from the North in 1861. As in the previous cases, the territorial groups perceived the existing territorial authority as either inept or tyrannical, following its own interests, different from, or opposed to, the interests of the territorial group. If a territorial group has such a perception, whether correct or false, the solidarity of the territorial group in the struggle against the central rule grows and may translate its discontent into a demand for secession. When this happens and the degree of alienation and hostility is high, within the same ethnic and language group and within the same institutional framework the strident voice of territorial *nationalism* will be heard. "We are enemies as if we were a hostile State," said Georgia's Senator Alfred Iverson, speaking in the Congress in 1860. "The Northern people hate the South worse than ever the English people hated France." Then he added, "And I can tell my brethren over there that there is no love lost upon the part of the South." [13]

Eighty-six years before, the South spoke in unison with the North—again in English to another English-speaking audience. In the Declaration of Independence, authored by Thomas Jefferson from the South (and signed, among others, by Button Gwinnet—first name in the left column—born in England, on behalf of Georgia) admitted that governments long established should not be changed for a light or transient reason.

> All experience hath shewn, that mankind are more disposed to suffer, while evils are sufferable, than to right themselves by abolishing the forms to which they are accustomed. But when a long train of abuses and usurpations, pursuing invariably the same Object, evinces a design to reduce them under absolute Despotism, it is their right, it is their duty to throw off such Government, and to provide new Guards for their future security. . . . We, Therefore, . . . declare, That these United Colonies are, and of Right ought to be, Free and Independent States, . . . and that all political connections between them and the State of Great Britain, is and ought to be totally dissolved.

[13] Quoted by Kenneth M. Stampp (ed.), *Causes of Civil War.* Englewood Cliffs, N.J.: Prentice-Hall, 1959, p. 181.

THE RIGHT TO ETHNIC HOMOGENEITY

When World War I was concluded by an Allied victory, the Versailles Peace Conference was called to implement the Allied war aims. One of the most universally recognized aims was the right of national self-determination, the suppression of which was considered to be one of the major causes of the world war. President Woodrow Wilson, on February 11, 1918, stated, "This war had its roots in the disregard of small nations and nationalities that lacked the union and the force to make good their claim to determine their own allegiance and their own form of political life."

The result of the victory and the peace conference should have been "a worldwide scheme of political organization in which each nation is also a state and each state is also a nation." [14] The boundaries of territorial authority and homogeneous nationality were to be coextensive. This, however, was not the case. The principle was not intended to have a universal application. First, it was applied so as to punish, not favor, the defeated enemies. Second, it was not applied against the territorial integrity of the French, British, and Italian colonial empires. It was for whites only. The right of national self-determination was mainly applied against Turkey in the Middle East, and against Germany and Austria in Eastern Europe. And even there, additional considerations were found to be superior to the concept of national self-determination. From a universal right it was reduced to a very relative principle, to be applied in balancing it with other principles and considerations of equal or superior value. In order to establish new territorial states such as Poland, Rumania, Czechoslovakia, and Yugoslavia, frankly nonethnic reasons for the delineation of their boundaries were invoked: *defensibility* of the boundaries, *economic viability* (Should, for instance, raw materials be separated from industry and transport systems be disrupted for the sake of ethnic or linguistic purity?), and considerations of *geography, history,* and *political traditions.* The result was a creation of many new states in the name of the right of national self-determination which, however, in violation of that right, contained many minorities. These minorities' dissatisfaction under the new, not always democratic or tolerant, territorial

[14] Ernest Baker, *National Character.* London: Methuen, 1927, p. 15.

authorities or their disloyalty and subversive links with the outside racially related powers were bound to cause new interethnic tensions and possibly further territorial disintegration. This was characteristically so after World War I and again after World War II, during the process of decolonization.

Those who have caused the disintegration of former polyethnic structures can be expected to desire—in this sense they are not dissimilar to their former masters—to protect their creations, the new states, against the erosive effects of their own cure. The right of national self-determination, so passionately applied against the former masters, is now to be denied or its cause (polyethnicity) eliminated in one way or another. As both a consequence of and a reaction against the disintegrative effects of the principle of self-determination, the new right to ethnic homogeneity will be invoked by the new elites of the new states.

To achieve such ethnic homogeneity, five measures, ranging from barbaric cruelty to mild inhumanity, have so far been used to remove the possible cause of future territorial disintegration or disloyalty: (1) genocide, (2) mass expulsion, (3) boundary changes, (4) prevention of incipient heterogeneity by biased immigration laws, and (5) forcible assimilation. The concluding portion of this chapter will also examine *voluntary* assimilation in the process of attaining ethnic homogeneity.

Genocide

Mass killing has been used either to assure ethnic or racial homogeneity or to punish groups for an alleged collective guilt of collusion with the enemy. An International Convention on the Prevention and Punishment of the Crime of Genocide, accepted by the United Nations General Assembly in 1946 and subsequently ratified by most nations, proclaims genocide, whether committed in time of peace or war, a crime under international law (Article 1). By *genocide* is meant any of the following acts committed with the intent to destroy, in whole or in part, a national, ethnical, racial or religious group as such (political groups are not so protected):

1. Killing members of the group
2. Causing serious bodily or mental harm to members of the group

3. Deliberately inflicting on the group the conditions of life calculated to bring about its physical destruction

4. Sterilization or transfer of children (measure aimed at annihilating the group's future)

Examples are Hitler's "final solution" of the Jewish question and Stalin's forcible removal of the Volga German, Crimean Tatars, and Chechens to deadly conditions of life and work in Siberia during World War II. Unofficial spontaneous communal and racial riots, if their goal is physical *elimination* of undesirable groups from the community, should also be included in this category. For instance, in Malay Indonesia the Chinese, whom at one time the Dutch colonial rulers used as intermediary colonial supervisors, have been a target for Malay hatred and extermination outbursts. It was said that in 1945 the Indonesians celebrated their independence by looting Chinese shops and killing their owners. Twenty years later, in the wake of the anti-Communist military *coup d'état* (1967), which in the Indonesian context was also anti-Chinese, primitive Dyak tribes in Borneo engaged in beheadings, cannibalism, and plunder; they drove well over 30,000 Chinese from their homes. The immediate pretext seemed to be an increase of Chinese Communist guerrilla activities in West Borneo.

Mass expulsions

The goal of ethnic homogeneity has also been achieved by organized mass expulsion; in some cases unorganized spontaneous self-expulsion (for example, the Arabs of Palestine) took care of some of the interethnic problems. Whether organized or unorganized, politically justifiable or not, all such mass movements represent violent uprooting from native territories. History has recorded several cases:

After World War I, Greece and Turkey agreed on mutual expulsion (exchange) of the Greek minority from Turkish Asia Minor and the Turkish minority from Greece. Although a clearly inhumane measure, the political argument was that one of the major sources of friction between Turkey and Greece was thus removed. A similar agreement was concluded between Greece and Bulgaria.

After World War II, Poland, Czechoslovakia, and Hungary

were authorized by the Big Three Conference at Potsdam to expel all their German-speaking citizens into the Western and Soviet zones of occupied Germany. Hungary did not avail herself of this opportunity. Poland and Czechoslovakia expelled about 10 million people (three times the population of Norway) from their old or newly acquired territories. A relatively homogeneous slavic Poland and Czechoslovakia are now the result.

A somewhat spontaneous exchange (self-expulsion) of population followed the partition of the Indian subcontinent between independent India and independent Pakistan. Millions tried, many successfully, to escape cruel intercommunal strife. They found refuge in their respective religious communities, now territorial states. The result, however, was neither a homogeneous India nor a homogeneous Pakistan. Both countries still contain minorities whose allegiance to the territory in which they reside is often questioned. There are about 10 million Hindus in East Pakistan and over 55 million Moslems in India.

Another example of a partly voluntary migration of an ethnic group was the departure of freed American slaves back to Africa, to settle a portion of the western coast of Africa and to establish the territorial state of Liberia. This attempt at a territorial solution of interracial tension in America has solved little. It was resented by native African tribes, whom the American black settlers not only displaced but also have continued to dominate.

The idea of national self-determination combined with the right to expel seems as old as territorial nationalism. It made its appearance in the wake of the French Revolution of 1789, when the revolutionary national party, the Jacobins, suggested that the German-speaking citizens of Alsatia should be expelled and replaced by "good Frenchmen." E. H. Carr condemned such solutions when he wrote:

> Perhaps the apex of nationalism is reached when it comes to be regarded as an enlightened policy to remove men, women, and children forcibly in order to create homogeneous national units. . . . Today annexations of territory are regarded as more, not less, respectable if they are accompanied by wholesale deportation of the existing population—not perhaps the most callous act reported in history, but surely the most explicit exaltation of the nation over the individual as an

end in itself, the mass sacrifice of human beings to the idol of nationalism.[15]

Boundary changes

In some minor cases the coincidence of territorial and ethnic boundaries was achieved by exchanging or shifting territories rather than by pushing people around. Homogeneity obtained by redrafting boundaries may be viewed as a form of territorial secession and accession, based on an international agreement between two neighboring states whose ethnic communities have overlapped. The relative infrequency of these boundary rearrangements indicates again that strategic, economic, historical, and emotional prestige considerations complicate a solution, even in the cases in which areas of equal square mileage could be exchanged.

Prevention of heterogeneity

Restrictive immigration laws represent an effort to prevent possible future interethnic or even interterritorial tensions (in the case of immigration and settlement in compact areas) by preserving and protecting the present relative homogeneity. The former United States immigration quota system belongs to this category because it discriminated against colored races and the inhabitants of Southern and Eastern Europe, while favoring those of Western and Northern Europe. Similar is the effort of Australia and New Zealand to maintain their Caucasian composition by barring immigrants from Asia and Africa and offering various kinds of inducements to European immigrants. After World War II, Australia and New Zealand engaged in active recruitment of immigrant labor from among the inmates in the refugee and displaced persons camps that had to be established all over Western Europe, mostly in Germany, Austria, and Italy, in order to accommodate provisionally the many thousands who had to leave their homes in the period of Stalinist communism and then during the Hungarian revolution in 1956 and the Soviet occupation of Czechoslovakia in 1968. Another example

[15] Edward H. Carr, *Nationalism and After.* New York: St. Martin's, 1945, pp. 34–35.

of an official effort to preserve relative homogeneity is the immigration laws and constitutions that try to lure immigrants from Spain or Portugal (or also from other Latin American republics or Italy) into Central America and South America by grants of special favors.

The new *Commonwealth Immigration Acts* of March 2, 1968, accepted by the British House of Commons after a dramatic debate, established new controls, especially over the rate of Asian immigration from the newly established states of East Africa, Tanzania, Kenya, and Uganda.

The vote of the House of Commons, on February 27, 1968, was 372 to 62. Of the negative votes, 35 were Labour, 15 Conservative, 10 Liberal, and, significantly, 1 Scottish and 1 Welsh Nationalist. The majority's main argument was that the sudden influx of Asians into Britain would arouse color prejudice in the communities in which they would settle. Compact settlement seemed to be particularly feared. An official publication of the British Labour Government (*Factel No. 552, British Nationality and Immigration,* March 1968) estimated that at least

> 200,000 Asians living in East Africa have retained citizenship of the United Kingdom notwithstanding the attainment of independence of Tanzania, Uganda and Kenya. . . . The Kenya Independence Constitution of 1963 provided for a two-year period in which [immigrant settlers from Asia, mostly India] could acquire Kenya citizenship; whether or not they did so, they retained their United Kingdom citizenship and were entitled [apply] . . . to the British High Commission [Commonwealth Embassy] for a passport . . . which . . . carried with it exemption of immigration control.

The new law now establishes such controls. In addition there are about one million persons, mainly Chinese, in Malaysia who also have dual nationality and, therefore, according to the old law, are entitled to enter England without any immigration controls. The *Factel* noted that the rate of immigration in January 1968 was eight times that of January 1967 and added, "Given their understandable tendency to live near other people from their home country, the flow of these immigrants was giving rise to problems of assimilation which were serious in certain cases." [16] The British understated term *serious* actually meant a flare-up of racial riots.

In France a somewhat similar situation developed in the summer of 1968, when the French government reduced the average rate of 3000 Algerian immigrants per month to 1000 as a first step to a total ban. Although the reasons for the ban seem primarily economic (unemployment in France itself), there are indications of some discrimination and tension between native Frenchmen and the Arab immigrants from Algeria.

Assimilation

Many nations that today appear to us as relatively homogeneous have actually been formed by successful assimilation of different territorial and ethnic groups. Nations such as France, Germany, Italy, and Spain are results of such gradual integration. The facts of territorial contiguity, similar political culture, linguistic or racial affinity, and common territorial authority played a role. In many cases an effective government and its satisfactory performance sped up the process, if accompanied by tolerance and economic opportunity for all.

In developing nations the assimilative qualities of big cities, industry, and the national army should be emphasized. Millions rush to the cities and factories, which, as seen from the point of view of rural communities and their languages, are indeed foreign. Migrants learn the new national language in the army and through mass media as well as the new modes of life, manners, and values.

Assimilation here appears as only partly voluntary; conscription into the Indian or Nigerian army, for example, which forces upon the recruit a new command language, can hardly qualify as a voluntary step. Most forms of assimilation represent a mixture of lures and irresistible pressure. People may be encouraged to "denationalize" themselves by adopting the ruling group's culture and language while, at the same time, groups scheduled for assimilation may be deprived of their right to use

[16] The net result of it all was that the Asians, fleeing black racial discrimination, saw the doors of Britain (which had brought them to the African continent in the first place and whose citizenship they had retained) shut on them.

their language in schools, official communications, and higher careers. There are limits to what a territorial authority can do in this respect: it can remove the language of the group from the official scene, "rewrite history books and public inscriptions, including those on monuments and tombstones of the dead," [17] but unless equipped with an omnipresent or omniscient Orwellian Big Brother it cannot totally control private communications, a mother speaking to her child, or a lover's whisper.

Modern African constitutions try to help the process of ethnic and territorial integration by strictly forbidding any "regionalist propaganda" (Constitution of Senegal, 1963, Article 51), or "particularist propaganda of racial or ethnic nature" (Constitution of Ivory Coast, Article 6), or "all manifestations of propaganda of ethnic nature" (Preamble to Constitution of Chad).

It should be noted that similarity of culture, contiguity, and linguistic or racial affinity, if not combined with an integrative effort on the part of the authority, cannot by themselves assure the success of integrative processes. For instance, the two Latin sisters, France and Italy, have not merged and cannot be in the foreseeable future expected to merge into some form of higher Roman unity. On the contrary, like many other sisters, France and Italy went through several periods of extreme jealousy and hostile territorial claims. In the 1930s, for example, Mussolini claimed three *départements* of France, Corsica, Savoy, and the Maritime Alps (that is, the French Riviera), for Italy. In Eastern Europe no parallel evolution toward large nations such as they developed in Western Europe has taken place since the Middle Ages. Eastern Europe still remains an area of small nations and interethnic tensions.

The American nation, composed of many European groups that could not integrate in their home territories, seems to stand as a contrasting record of success. Many authors have pointed to the presence of several amalgamating factors that are absent

[17] Compare Karl W. Deutsch and Richard L. Merritt, "Effects of Events on National and International Images," in Herbert C. Kelman (ed.), *International Behavior*. New York: Holt, Rinehart and Winston, Inc., 1965, pp. 138–139, where shifts in policy of governments and communication elites as managers of public messages about events are discussed.

in Europe. The pattern of early settlement created a dominant Anglo-Saxon culture, and it was upon this firmly established cultural basis that ethnic groups, on their own initiative and usually bidding a definitive good-bye to Europe, were added in relatively small numbers in successive immigration waves. As a result, ethnic problems in the United States, unlike those in Europe or Asia, "have not been primarily characterized by minorities resisting assimilation, but rather by the unwillingness of the dominant group to permit assimilation at the tempo desired by the minorities." [18] Another observer, O. I. Janowsky, noted that especially the second generation of immigrants moved quickly into the mainstream of American life, spreading in all directions over the vast land, although initially the immigrants from Europe tended to huddle in their groups of common language and social habits. This was so on account of three environmental factors: (1) the absence of sustained persecution; (2) agencies of Americanization, especially the public school, which fostered a child's identification with the American language and culture; and (3) the dynamic character of the American environment, especially the economic system, offering so many opportunities in the period of its expansion and conquest of a thinly populated, yet rich continent. Furthermore, the immigrants from Europe came to the United States not as an ethnic unit but as individuals or heads of families—"only individuals can be assimilated and not conscious national communities." [19] In the 1960s John Steinbeck, traveling with his French poodle Charley, could report,

> From start to finish I found no strangers. . . . For all of our enormous geographic range, for all of our sectionalism, for all of our interwoven breeds drawn from every part of the ethnic world, we are a nation, a new breed. Americans are much more American than they are Northerners, Southerners, Westerners, or Easterners. And descendants of English, Irish, Italian, Jewish, German, Polish are essentially American. This is not patriotic whoop-de-do; it is a carefully observable fact. California Chinese, Boston Irish, Wisconsin German, yes, and

[18] Walker Connor, "Self-Determination," *World Politics,* Vol. 22, No. 15 (October 1967), 49.

[19] O. I. Janowsky, *Nationalities and National Minorities.* New York: Crowell-Collier-Macmillan, 1945, pp. 4–5.

Alabama Negroes, have more in common than they have apart. . . . It is astonishing that this has happened in less than two hundred years and most of it in the last fifty. The American identity is an exact and provable thing.[20]

Steinbeck's optimism should be, of course, qualified. When, for instance, measured by the individual and collective experiences of some communities, especially the black one, the melting-pot saga is not only unimpressive but also quite depressing. Recent studies of ethnic voting behavior and political attitudes also indicate a persistency in ethnic identification that is fundamentally affected by neither middle-class jobs, neighborhoods, ideas, associates, and styles of life nor increases in education, geographic dispersion, intermarriage, and intergroup contacts. Although in his study of New Haven politics Robert Dahl expected that ethnic ties were to recede in local politics, he had to note that "in spite of growing assimilation, ethnic factors continued to make themselves felt with astonishing tenacity." [21] It is conceivable that the dynamic assertion of black and Puerto Rican ethnic identity may speed up the emergence of an all-white identity; but we cannot exclude the possibility that the result may be also a simultaneous maintenance of unassimilated ethnic values among the whites.

A recent study by Michael Parenti clearly indicates that residual ethnic cultural valuations and attitudes persist, showing that acculturation is far from complete; the pluralistic parallel system of ethnic institutions shows impressive viability and support; and feelings of minority group identity remain also deeply internalized. It is possible that ethnic values will in the future disappear from the American scene altogether, but Parenti warns, "Before relegating them to the history of tomorrow, the unassimilated ethnics [in the United States] should be seen as very much alive and with us today." [22]

---

[20] John Steinbeck, *Travels with Charley*. New York: Viking, 1962, pp. 184–185.

[21] Robert Dahl, *Who Governs*. New Haven, Conn.: Yale University Press, 1961, p. 59.

[22] Michael Parenti, "Ethnic Politics and the Persistence of Ethnic Identification," *The American Political Science Review*, Vol. 61, No. 3 (September 1967), 724–726.

FOUR

MINORITY AND MAJORITY: DIVERSITY AND UNITY

Now suppose that all the English . . . were to leave
India. . . . Is it possible that under these circumstances two
nations—the Mohammedan and Hindu—could sit on
the same throne and remain equal in power? Most
certainly not.

> SAYYID AHMAD KHAN (Speech made in
> 1890)

It is in general a necessary condition of free institutions that the boundaries of government should coincide in the main with those of nationality.

> JOHN STUART MILL (*Considerations on
> Representative Government*)

There is the country of the white—relatively prosperous . . . and free to shape its own destiny. And,
then there is the country of the Negroes—a country
whose capital is ghetto, whose constitution states:
"All men are created equal, but Whitey comes first."

> *The New York Times* (July 16, 1967)

The coexistence of several nations under the same
state is a test as well as the best security of freedom.

> LORD ACTON (*History of Freedom*)

The principle of national self-determination is closely related to the revolutionary theory of democracy: a people that has the right to formulate its own constitution and choose freely its own government has also the right "to decide whether to attach itself to one state or another, or constitute an independent state by itself." [1] If our interpretation of democracy also includes the principle of decision by a majority combined with the guarantees of minority right to become a majority, only in a few interethnic conflicts the majoritarian formula could offer a solution: three hundred million Indians could by electoral processes shake off the rule by a few thousand English civil servants who used to represent about forty million Englishmen; the same could be done by the black majority in South Africa or Rhodesia. "The instances in which a government has permitted a democratic process to decide a question of self-determination within its own territory are rare indeed," notes a recent study and adds: "It seems clear that governments believe the questions involving the political allegiance of groups residing within the sovereign territory are much too important to be left to popular opinion." [2]

In many other interethnic conflicts the problem is that the dissatisfied territorial group is a minority in the broader polyethnic framework (and a *permanent* numerical minority with no chance of becoming a majority at the next election) but on its home territory a 51 percent to a 99 percent majority. There arises the possibility of a local majority being oppressed by the national majority. In such a case, the simple mathematical formula of democracy does not and cannot offer a solution. A permanent minority cannot change its inferior status or ask for independence by using the usual form of democratic decision making. The majority-minority formula could not free Ireland from Britain, Biafra from Nigeria, Katanga from the Congo, Poland from Prussia and Russia, Guinea from France, or underdeveloped and underpopulated America from England. Only *negotiations* aiming at an agreement on separation or *violence* can offer a solution in such situations. Regardless of their numerical strength or weakness, territorial groups get what they want

---

[1] Alfred Cobban, *National Self-Determination*. New York: Oxford, 1944, p. 5.
[2] Walker Connor, "Self-Determination," *World Politics*, Vol. 22, No. 15 (October 1967), 21.

if they are skillful or violent enough to make the ruling majority yield.

RECOGNITION OF DIVERSITY—DISPERSED GROUPS

If ethnic or territorial groups cannot be assimilated, fully integrated, or eliminated by one of the methods discussed previously, ranging from secession or mass expulsion to mass murder, the opposite principle may be applied: that of recognition of diversity. Ethnic or territorial communities may be granted effective political, institutional, and constitutional protection. One of the reasons for this solution is often the belief on the part of the ruling elites in the principle of unity and diversity as an integral part of the democratic theory. Territorial or ethnic pluralism is viewed by them as a special—geographic, racial, or linguistic—expression of the democratic right of all groups to exist, organize, compete, and formulate their demands and in this manner to share in the democratic decision-making processes. It is indeed consistent with the democratic creed to protect ethnic and territorial minorities against a potential tyranny by a permanent majority. Another reason why recognition instead of elimination is sometimes adopted with reference to ethnic or territorial heterogeneity is simply that elimination, although perhaps desired by the majority, is not feasible. For instance, the number of people or the number of square miles involved may militate against any radical solution. In some cases, on the contrary, the number of people involved is too insignificant to bother; diversity is, so to speak, tacitly accepted.

Institutional recognition of territorial communities by means of decentralization or federalism will be the subject of Part II of this book (Chaps. 5–10); Chapter 6 will deal with the inferior status of territorial communities as may be found in imperial structures or in the mandate and trusteeship systems. Here, our focus will be on *dispersed* ethnic, racial, lingual, or religious minorities which may be treated individually as separate and equal or whose separate status as a group may be expressed and institutionalized according to three different principles: (1) separate but inferior; (2) equal with special privileges; (3) communal representation.

Separate but inferior

Dispersed ethnic groups have often been reduced by law or practice or by both to the level of second- or third-class citizens. They are separate, sometimes by choice and sometimes not by choice, and inferior despite their opposition to such a status.

In contrast, a separate-but-equal status that is possible only within a framework of proclaimed and practiced tolerance—a very rare occurrence among men indeed—means the right to remain separate and to develop the group's identity (African "negritude," for instance), culture, institutions, and political as well as economic power while enjoying equality in all respects. If the separate-but-equal status does not include also the right of the group to change its aspirations and to abandon its separation in favor of assimilation, then such a status in reality implies separate inferiority because the separation has been imposed or is being maintained by the decisive will of the majority.

Groups that find themselves in the position of separate inferiority are usually referred to as ethnic, racial, religious, or national *minorities*. The term implies a numerical ratio; in fact, in most cases the numerical minority is also inferior in the political sense, that is, in terms of political and economic power. The use of the term *minority* becomes, however, quite confusing in the few cases when a racial minority oppresses a group of second-class citizens who may constitute an overwhelming racial majority, as is the case in South Africa and Rhodesia.

A United Nations study [3] on the problem of national minorities and their collective rights defines a *minority* as a

[3] Memorandum submitted by the U.N. Secretary-General to the Subcommission on Prevention of Discrimination and Protection of Minorities "in order to facilitate discussion of this item." *Definition and Classification of Minorities,* publication No. E/C 4/Sub 2/85, 1950, p. 26. The United Nations Charter does not mention the problem of minorities; the problem of human rights is referred to seven times. One of these references provides for a permanent Commission on Human Rights (Article 68). In 1949 a solemn, although not legally binding, Universal Declaration of Human Rights spelled out in detail what the different individual and group rights are. It was adopted by forty-eight votes. For different reasons eight nations abstained: Saudi Arabia, South Africa, and six Communist countries, the only Communist members of the United Nations at the time.

"more or less distinct group, living within a State, which is dominated by other groups." Inferior status is essential in the United Nations definition. The document then analyzes the problem and lists the most usual collective rights that minorities demand in order to emerge from their inferior status:

A fundamental distinction may be drawn between (a) minorities whose members desire equality with dominant groups in the sense of nondiscrimination alone [their goal is then assimilation or integration], and (b) those whose members desire equality with dominant groups in the sense of nondiscrimination *plus* the recognition of certain special rights and the rendering of certain positive services.

The minorities in category (b) . . . feel . . . that even full realization of the principle of nondiscrimination would not place their group in a position of real equality—but only of formal equality—with respect to the dominant group.

The "positive services" and "special rights" . . . usually include one or more of the following provisions: . . .

a.   adequate primary and secondary education [4] for the minority in its own language and its cultural traditions;

b.   maintenance of the culture of the minority through the establishment and operation of schools, libraries, museums, media of information, and other cultural and educational institutions;

c.   adequate facilities to the minority for the use of its language, either orally or in writing, in the legislature, before the courts, and in administration, and the granting of the right to use that language in private intercourse [in some countries even private use of the minority language was often forbidden . . . ;

d.   respect of family law and personal status of the minority and their religious practices and interests; and

e.   a certain degree of autonomy.

[4] The United Nations Subcommission on Prevention of Discrimination and Protection of Minorities in a further study (1958) set the following three criteria that should be met by separate but equal schools: (1) course and program of study must be of the same standard as those in majority schools; (2) ability and training of the teachers must be comparable to those in majority schools; and (3) if students are not able to complete their studies (secondary or college) in their local language they must be provided with instruction in the language used in majority schools.

The rendering of "positive services" may take either of two forms:

a.   provisions effected at the expense of the minority; or
b.   provisions effected out of public funds and facilities.

Groups in inferior positions naturally seek remedies that would guarantee them equality whether coupled with integration or, on the contrary, with separation if so desired by the minority. Usually, equality cannot be achieved unless the minority is guaranteed special rights and services that help it to emerge from its inferior status.

Equality and special privileges

Equality and special privileges do not seem to rhyme. They may even appear mutually exclusive. Furthermore, special privileges may actually perpetuate separation and interests vested in it when and if assimilation is the minority group goal. In a political system that not only preaches but also practices respect for individual rights and equality, the question may be also asked why should men, if individually free and equal, ask for additional guarantees of *collective* rights and *collective* equality? There are three interrelated answers to this question.

First, men desire to be free and equal not only as individuals but also as groups. The right to identify with, and promote the interests of, a subnational group belongs to the list of fundamental individual rights. Men derive satisfaction from their identification with a group—its rights and status—particularly if they have been born into it rather than if they have only joined it by paying membership dues.[5]

"Ethnocentrism, the overevaluation of one's own group in comparison with other groups, especially those perceived as rivals," writes Jerome D. Frank, is virtually universal.

Membership in a group is an integral part of an individual's concept of himself. The group's success is his success and its failures damage his self-confidence; its friends and enemies

[5] In the United States the black community demanded radical rewriting of the American history textbooks, which almost entirely neglected the American black history, development, and contributions to the American culture, economy, and politics.

are also his. Many peoples' group identification is so much part of their personal identity that they would rather die than be absorbed into an alien group.[6]

This dual—individual and collective—aspect of rights and liberties is clearly reflected in the Universal Declaration of Human Rights, whose Article 1 proclaims that "all human beings are born free and equal in dignity and rights" and whose Article 2 amplifies, "Everyone is entitled to all the rights and freedoms set forth in this Declaration, without distinction of any kind such as race, color, sex, language, religion, political or other opinion, national or social origin, property, birth, or other states." Article 15 adds the individual and group right to integrate or not to integrate: "No one shall be arbitrarily deprived of his nationality (for instance, by forcible assimilation) nor denied the right to change his nationality (for instance, by voluntary assimilation)." [7]

In many areas of the world, forced integration, that is, denationalization, is resented as bitterly as a refusal of integration in some other countries.

Second, right or wrong, men consider the satisfaction of their group interests as a precondition for the fulfillment of their individual goals and liberties. The Ghanaian nationalist leader, Kwame Nkrumah's often quoted statement "Seek ye first the political kingdom and all things shall be added unto you" correctly expresses not only the nationalist desire for statehood but also the basic goal of the groups that are dispersed, that live within the framework of another community, and that want to survive as a community, conscious of its separate past, present, and future.

Third, even in a community of free and equal individuals, a majority could conspire to deny a minority and its members

[6] Jerome D. Frank, *Sanity and Survival.* New York: Vintage Books (Knopf and Random House), 1968, p. 104. Frank also shows that many cultures (Javanese, for example) use the same word for "human" and members of their own group.

[7] Article 26 adds this new unusual right: "Everyone is entitled to a social and international order in which the rights and freedoms set in this Declaration can be fully realized." How this article could be invoked in practice and then enforced is beyond the most poetic imagination.

their individual and collective rights. Such a danger is particularly present in any community that consists of groups whose majority-minority relationship does not reflect their changing political preferences but is, as it were, preordained by the fact of birth into an ethnic, racial, religious, or linguistic group. A political or ideological minority can hope for a reversal of the numerical relationship at the next election; its present defeat (that is, minority status) is temporary. In contrast, a racial, linguistic, ethnic, or religious minority is a permanent one; it cannot hope to do better the next time. Unlike a territorial minority that, as discussed previously, can claim, and often succeeds in obtaining, territorial autonomy or independent statehood, practical options left to a *dispersed* minority are severely limited. Mostly they can only pray and hope for the majority's self-restraint, tolerance, and wisdom—rare commodities among men; or if the situation permits, they can resort to pressure techniques, including violence.

Is there any institution or device that could guarantee political participation and political equality of nonterritorial, dispersed minority groups? There is relatively little that can be done when a minority cannot press for territorial autonomy because it does not live in a compact area and when the majority and minority do not form a consensual community in which issues are decided on merit and not on the basis of a majority-minority ratio. There is always the possibility that the minority, oppressed by the majority, may seize power and subject the majority to oppression. However, there is no device that could transform a permanent minority into a dominant majority—except an increased birthrate, which, as some Zionists fear, could alter the present numerical relation between Jewish majority and Arab minority in the extended territory of Israel. In India some Hindu extremists began accusing the Moslem minority (a minority of fifty-five million people) of avoiding the government-sponsored birth control clinics as a part of a plot to challenge the Hindu control of India. The fact is that the rate of increase among the Indian Moslems is noticeably higher than that of the rest of the non-Moslem population. One of the constant worries in Malaysia is that the birthrate of the Chinese minority soon will make it a majority. This is one of the reasons for the relief with which the Malaysian rulers accepted the secession of Singapore, a city of two million people, now independent and a member of the United Nations. Eighty percent of its population are Chinese, and the addition of Singapore to Malaysia would have added too many Chinese to its delicate Malay-Chinese balance.

The rights of minorities are usually protected by constitutional prohibition of either discrimination or forced assimilation. After World War I an attempt was made to add international guarantees to the pledges of the ruling majority.[8] This was done by means of special *Minority Treaties,* concluded between the Principal Allied and Associated Powers, on the one hand, and Czechoslovakia, Greece, Poland, Rumania, and Yugoslavia, on the other. Provisions on the rights of minorities were included in the peace treaties with the defeated enemies, Austria, Bulgaria, Hungary, and Turkey. Special declarations on the subject of minority rights were made before the Council of the League by Albania, Estonia, Finland (for the Aaland Islands), Iraq, Latvia, and Lithuania at the time of their admission to the League. Special minority provisions were also made part of international treaties concerning the territories of Upper Silesia (Poland and Germany) and Memel.[9]

Whether minority rights are protected by a national constitution or an international treaty, much depends on the actual practice; sometimes a minority may freely use its own language, run its own mass media, and glorify its own separate culture and heritage and yet be effectively barred by the majority from any real share in the political decision-making processes; as a result, living in a ghetto-like situation, such a group may permanently trail behind the political, social, and economic evolution of the rest of the country. Enjoyment of cultural and educational equality may be viewed as a precondition for all political and economic rights; but also, political rights may be considered to be the only keys to economic opportunity and cultural and spiritual development.

[8] International protection of territorial communities of an inferior status (mandates and trusteeship territories) is discussed in Chap. 6.

[9] For a more detailed treatment of international protection of individual and group rights see James Frederick Green, *The United Nations and Human Rights.* Washington, D.C.: Brookings, 1956 (in particular, pp. 3–26).

A Turkish scholar writes, "Minority guarantees aim to provide protection only in the field of human rights, leaving the participation of the minority group in the government of the country quite open." He adds, "No legal guarantee of human rights can be effective unless the minority group has its share in the political fate and the government of the country. . . . It is necessary to recognize to the minority national groups a *proportional* possibility of having their word in the destiny of the country. [Italics added.]" [10] Clearly, the particular problem of the Turkish minority among the Greek majority on Cyprus echoes through these words.

Communal representation

One device has been tried in India and elsewhere: communal proportional representation (sometimes called "quota system"); its aim is to prevent the majority from depriving a minority of its proportional share in the legislative, administrative, and judicial bodies. This does not, of course, protect the minority against being constantly outvoted, but at least it guarantees the minority's presence at different levels of decision making.

The Indian experiment began in 1909 when the so-called Morley-Minto reforms were enacted for the purpose of associating "the people of India to a greater extent with the Government in the decisions on public questions." [11] Indians were to be given places in provincial councils and in the Central Legislative Council by means of direct and indirect elections. The problem, however, was that India was not one community but was an aggregate of a great many groups, territorial as well as dispersed, some of which were extremely hostile to each other. The British introduction of majoritarian devices of democracy, however impartial it was supposed to be, was bound to be viewed with fear and distrust by several minorities. The Moslem spokesman, the Aga Khan, addressed the Viceroy, Lord Minto, at Simla, and asked for a separate electorate for the Moslems of India:

[10] Tahsin Bekir Balta, "Some Considerations on Federalism," paper presented at the Sixth World Congress of the International Political Science Association, Geneva, 1964, p. 5.

[11] The secretary of state for India, Lord Morley, and the viceroy, Lord Minto, were both reluctant to consider India ready for a British type of parliamentary democracy.

> The position accorded to the Mohammedan community in any kind of representation, direct or indirect, and in all other ways affecting their status and influence, should be commensurate not only with their numerical strength, but also with their practical importance and the value of the contribution which they make to the defence of the Empire [here, the martial qualities of the Moslems were contrasted with the nonviolent aspects of the Hindu culture] . . . and with the position they occupied in India a little more than a hundred years ago.[12]

The last sentence reflects the Moslem fear of a Hindu revenge against the minority that, under the Mogul empire, ruled over the Hindu majority.

Partly in response to this request, the people of India were then not enfranchised as members of a single national territorial community but as members of their respective, often quite dispersed, religious or racial groups (Anglo-Indians, for instance). "Separation of the electorates along the communal lines was in one sense a forward step," notes an authority on Indian history and politics, "as the very existence of electorates was a novelty in India." He then adds, "On the other hand, it implied the abrogation of all responsibility by the Hindu politician for the Muslim voter and by the Muslim politician for the Hindu voter—even though they inhabited the same village. Thus the seeds of partition were in one sense planted by the first British 'liberal' reforms." [13]

Although criticized by Indian nationalists who saw in the communal system another gimmick of British imperialist tactics of "divide-and-rule," the communal system did not leave the Indian scene when independence and statehood were attained. In order to protect minorities against intolerant majorities, the new Constitution of independent India assured underdeveloped tribes and castes (*Scheduled Tribes and Castes,* in the Indian-English terminology) a quota of seats in the Indian Parliament if the Hindu and upper-caste majorities were to lack tolerance

---

[12] Quoted by Norman Palmer, *The Indian Political System.* Boston: Houghton Mifflin, 1961, p. 67.

[13] Norman D. Palmer, "India," in George McTurnan Kahin (ed.), *Major Governments of Asia.* Ithaca, N.Y.: Cornell University Press, 1963, p. 284.

and wisdom to elect representatives of such minority groups. Seventy-five seats out of the total 500 are reserved for the representatives of the 65 million Untouchables [14] in the Indian Parliament. This was deemed a temporary measure, first for ten years, later extended (1959, Eighth Amendment to the Constitution) for another decade. Enlightenment takes longer than two decades to overcome a millennia-long prejudice. As to the Anglo-Indian community, the Indian Constitution (Article 331) provided for the president to nominate two members of Parliament "if he is of the opinion that the Anglo-Indian community is not adequately represented in the House of the People."

A communal system does protect a group against some aspects of the majority's intolerance; but it also perpetuates the separate status even when the communal system is adopted as a temporary measure of equalization for the purpose of ultimate assimilation. As one study noted, a special aid to Untouchables in India

> tends to perpetuate the caste system by establishing new vested interests. The Harijan [Untouchable] is not encouraged to forget his untouchable caste background, for it is precisely because of it that he receives special benefits from the state. For him to surrender his membership in one of the Scheduled Castes would mean the loss of his children's free tuition in school, his opportunity of acquiring free land, etc. [for instance, reserved quota in the civil service].

The same study also noted that Indian and Moslem converts whose respective religions reject the caste system "were nevertheless trying to revive their former caste identities with the hope of obtaining governmental aid." [15]

In the United States the advocates of Black Power came very near to advocating the principle of such a quota system:

> When black people lack majority, Black Power means proper representation and sharing of control. . . . The goal

[14] In the first elections, three additional Untouchables were elected to the unreserved seats, a modest beginning of a more enlightened attitude of higher castes toward those whom the Indian religious system had originally placed beyond the pale.

[15] Donald Eugene Smith, *India as a Secular State*. Princeton, N.J.: Princeton University Press, 1963, p. 518.

of black self-determination and black self-identity—Black Power—is full participation in the decision making processes affecting the lives of black people. . . .[16]

If a communal system were adopted in the United States, the black community would be entitled to 11 percent representation on the national level: eleven black senators and forty-eight representatives in the Congress; 11 percent in the Cabinet, armed forces, and civil service; about fifteen ambassadors (would an ambassadorial post in Paris weigh the same as one in Sierra Leone?); one in the Supreme Court (but many more in the rest of the federal judiciary); and so on. Although the quota would change only from census to census, the variations from election to election would be in the political orientation of the black minority legislative representation (Democratic, Republican, Conservative, radical, Communist, fascist, Moslem). As noted previously, such an arrangement would assure the presence of the black community but would not protect it against being outvoted unless the minority would be endowed with a veto power.

In Indonesia the non-Malay communities, namely, the Chinese, the Europeans (Dutch), and the Arabs, were constitutionally assured of communal representation by having assigned to them nine, six, and three deputies in the national Parliament, respectively. If they were not elected, the President had the right to appoint them and so, if necessary, increase the total membership of the national legislature. A similar quota guarantee may be found in other countries; for instance, in New Zealand the aboriginal Maoris are assured of four seats in the national Parliament; in Pakistan the minority which requires a particular protection are women. The Constitution of 1962, for instance, contained a provision that in the National Legislature 6 seats of the total of 156 "shall be reserved exclusively for

---

[16] Stokely Carmichael and Charles V. Hamilton, *Black Power: The Politics of Liberation in America.* New York: Random House, 1967, pp. 46, 47. Compare the six-point program of the W. E. B. Du Bois Club at the City College of New York (*The Master Plan,* October 1968, mimeographed) Point 1 read "That the racial composition of all future entering classes reflect that of the high school graduating classes in New York City."

women, but this clause shall not be construed as making a woman ineligible for election to any other seat [of the remaining 150] in the National Assembly."

A combination of proportional communal representation with a partial veto was tried on Cyprus, where the numerical relation between the Greek majority and the Turkish minority is roughly seven to three. In 1959, the short-lived Constitution of independent Cyprus provided for a presidential system with a Greek President and a Turkish vice-president, each having a veto power over any law concerning foreign affairs, defense, and —a somewhat vague category—security. A six-to-four ratio between the Greeks and the Turks was to be reflected in the composition of the Cypriote army; whereas a seven-to-three ratio was to be maintained in the police force, in Parliament, and in the Cabinet, in which also one of the key ministries (Defense, Finance, or Foreign Affairs) was always to be held by a Turk. A Supreme Court composed of Greek and Turkish judges was presided over by a neutral (a Canadian took the office for a short time).

The Cypriote system collapsed. In 1963, instead of inter-communal cooperation, intercommunal fighting broke out when President Makarios proposed a change of the Constitution that was interpreted by the Turkish community as a threat to their communal rights and the scope of their veto. In 1964 the United Nations Security Council approved a resolution that provided for an international peace-keeping force to be sent to Cyprus. Periodic crises have frequently occurred despite the stationing of United Nations troops on the island. In 1967 the plight of the Turkish minority brought about the threat of Turkish invasion. In 1968 a new effort was made to find a formula for cooperation between the two communities, which, in the meantime, almost walled each other into their respective territorial enclaves by barricades. One of the problems raised in connection with a demand for a new constitution was whether the two communities would police themselves, whether there would be mixed police patrols (a seven-to-three ratio?), or whether an all-Cypriote police force could be established. When two hostile communities face each other, it is almost impossible to find an institutional formula that will initiate a process toward mutual trust when there is nothing but mistrust. An extrainstitutional and informal beginning of conciliation and consensus must antedate the institutional formula.

In Lebanon, on the basis of a relatively smoothly working consensus, the religious communal representation is reflected in both the executive and the legislative branches of the government. The President is always a Maronite Christian, the prime minister a Suli Moslem, the minister of foreign affairs a Greek Orthodox Christian. And the legislative seats are distributed proportionately among fourteen different Christian and Moslem sects.

Theoretically, the proportional communal formula seems logical and basically sound. The practice, however, has proved disappointing for several reasons. First, even in an underdeveloped, dominantly rural, or relatively uncomplicated economic system (such as in Cyprus) communal separation adds another barrier to progress and modernization in all communities. This may be even more true of developed systems that cannot be subdivided according to the communal lines because these systems are based on an intricate web of intertwined economic relations and usually require all-national planning. Second, if a veto power is added to communal representation, it must be all-embracing to assure an all-embracing protection; but then it can paralyze the government and bring it to a standstill as happened on Cyprus, where the Turkish minority was endowed with a veto in matters vaguely defined as security. Yet, without such a veto, even a six-to-five ratio of representation of two communities on all levels may not guarantee a minority against a tyranny by majority if the mutual hostility and suspicious separation between them continue. If, on the other hand, hostility and suspicion are removed and a consensus emerges, then the proportional communal representation may no longer be necessary.

In any communal system there is the additional problem of the qualitative aspects of simple quantitative measurements. A seven-to-three ratio applied to Cabinet posts would still mean little unless also the power of the Department of Defense or the Treasury is computerized and compared with that of the Interior or Health. And the prime minister or President, if almost all power is in his hands, cannot be compartmentalized on the communal lines. Furthermore, any ratio agreed upon would also have to be applied to the whole hierarchy of positions and ranks in the administrative and economic systems, ranging from an army general to NCOs and from a director of an industrial enterprise (nationalized or not) to a cleaning woman.

A warning concerning the ultimate consequences of a proportional representation of different ethnic groups at all echelons of administration and economy was issued by a Czech Communist Trade Union publication that seemed to be equally concerned with both the need for ethnic justice and the requirement of modern efficiency based on skills, not on ethnic or racial origins:

> Modern society in an industrial state cannot be . . . mutually isolated. . . . A chemically pure distribution of leading posts, according to a strictly defined key, is not possible. . . . However, in general, personnel policies must express the equality [of all ethnic components]. Wherever the relationship of a larger and a smaller nation is involved, guarantees must be established preventing the smaller nation from being overwhelmed by the larger nation. . . . All citizens [must] have the opportunity to assert themselves . . . if this state is to be regarded by all the citizens as their own territorial state.[17]

Finally, we should mention the problem of people of mixed origins. Theirs may not be a major problem in communities that have been fully segregated by law or mutual hatred. Yet it is evident that the quota system cannot be applied to children of mixed Chinese-Malay, Hindu-Moslem, black-white, or Turkish-Greek parentage, unless a special communal representation is given to such mixed groups (this was done in the case of the Anglo-Indians under the British in India and then again after Indian independence).

It should be recognized that communal representation is often opposed by many members of the underprivileged com-

---

[17] M. Hubl, "Community of Czechs and Slovaks," *Práce* (Prague, January 28, 1968).

munity itself because they consider cooperative integration as the only way to lose the sense and status of inferiority. Their argument is that communal representation tends to codify and perpetuate not only the separation that may be desirable but also the numerical ratio and with it also the superior-inferior relationship, with undesirable political and psychological implications.

PART TWO
TERRITORIAL DISTRIBUTION OF AUTHORITY

FIVE
DECENTRALIZATION IN UNITARY STATES

The axis of the earth sticks out visibly through the
centre of each and every town or city. . . . Boston
State-house is the hub of the solar system.

> OLIVER WENDELL HOLMES (*The Auto-
> crat of the Breakfast Table*)

In the *Départements* and the Territories,
the Delegate of the [central] Government shall be
responsible for the national interests, for administrative
supervision and for seeing that the laws are respected.

> CONSTITUTION OF FRANCE (1958, Article
> 72)

We find . . . the confidence of the [American]
society in its citizens—in the authority delegated
to local government to administer everyday aspects
of life and to make decisions in the fields of city
planning, health, and education—decision-making
powers our central government would be terrified
to put into the hands of [locally] elected officials.

> J. J. SERVAN-SCHREIBER (*The American
> Challenge*)

111

Territorial distribution of authority may issue from two distinct processes, each starting from an opposite pole. One process is the movement from diversity to *unity;* the result is an association of territorial communities based on either compulsion or consent. The absence of consent distinguishes a forcible territorial association, usually called *empire,* from a voluntary association whose forms and cohesion range from an alliance, customs union, commonwealth, and confederation to a federal nation-state (which will be discussed in Chaps. 7 to 10). The process of unification and centralization may reach a point at which territorial communities (of which, in a sense, every nation-state consists) have not an infinitely small particle of authority left to it. In practice, as indicated previously, this is rare.

The other (and opposite) process is *decentralization*—the subject of this chapter. It is a movement from the pole of centralized unity to that of diversity. The term *decentralization* presupposes the existence of a central authority whose leaders deem it useful—or inevitable—to delegate a portion of their centrally held power to subnational centers, for the sake of administrative expediency or in response to subnational pressures. Such a decentralization may occur within nation-states and may result in different forms and degrees of local self-rule; it may also occur within empires and result in replacement of the former forcible imperial unity by a voluntary association of territorial communities. Under some circumstances the momentum of decentralization may reach the ultimate point of secession from the national state or multinational empire.

The delegated portion of central power may be substantial (as certainly is the degree of self-rule enjoyed by countries and cities in the fifty states of the American union) or may be marginal (as is the central authorization to determine locally only the day and the hour of local fiestas or weekly markets in the light of local traditions and needs). Decentralization reflects the central authority's conclusion that its commitment to unity does not exclude some degree of local autonomy within limits as determined by the central authority. Whether such a conclusion represents a response to local pressures, represents the authority's need for greater flexibility by means of decentralization, represents the central authority's ideological commitment to pluralism, or represents a combination of all three of these reasons, *in principle* a delegation of authority by the central authority and from the central authority is always amendable or revocable. The movement from unity to diversity may be stopped or reversed.

The process of decentralization and that of territorial association by consent or force may be expressed graphically as is shown in Figure 5–1. It will be noted that at a certain point both movements, although proceeding in opposite directions and

Figure 5–1   Decentralization and territorial association

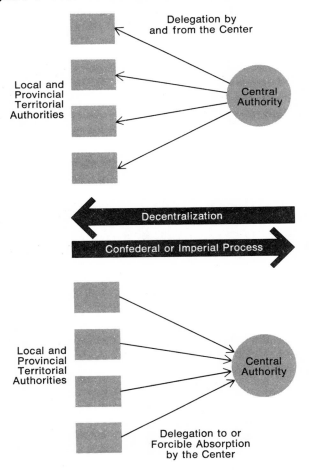

although differently motivated, may result in an identical pattern. Except for its origin, a significantly decentralized unitary system does not differ from an institutionalized association of states. In the first case, the once delegated and, in principle, revocable delegation of power from the central authority to local units may have become in fact irrevocable. And, in the associations of territorial communities, the once revocable membership and, in principle, revocable delegation of power from the communities to a common center may have in fact become permanent. Our illustration represents a point reached, and cannot adequately express the constant movement and changes that necessarily occur within any structure or system designed by men.

DELEGATION OF POWER

When power is delegated from the central authority to territorial units of self-rule (as seen on the upper part of Fig. 5–1), such a system of territorial distribution of authority is called a *unitary* system. Most nation-states have adopted the system nationally, for instance, Britain, France, Communist China, Japan, Poland, Spain, Belgium, Holland, Scandinavian democracies, Rumania, Bulgaria, and the majority of African and Latin-American countries; in federal systems, the unitary form of power delegation prevails within the subnational components, such as states or provinces; this is so in the United States, which has a federal system on the national level but a unitary system in each of its fifty states.

The list of unitary systems suggests that unitary systems have been adopted by democratic, authoritarian, imperial, and fully totalitarian systems. *Unitary* itself means no more than the principle of territorial decentralization that may or may not produce real local autonomy. In a unitary system, it is then the central government, authoritarian or democratic, that determines how much or how little of its power may be delegated to subcenters.

There is a great variety in the processes, structures, and institutions by the means of which power delegated by the central authority may be exercised locally. Four very broad categories of territorial self-rule under a unitary system may be distinguished:

1. Agencies and officials are *appointed* by the central authority to run territorial subdivisions, take into account the local problems, solve them, and report on the challenging ones back to the center. This was so under imperial structures or in Nazi Germany. Rarely, however, is this done so blatantly; some appearances of local participation are usually added. The result is the second category:

2. Agencies and officials are appointed by the central authority but the appointment is confirmed by a plebiscitary ceremonial called "elections" although there is no choice because only one slate of candidates is presented by the party or by the leader. This is so in Communist countries where all subnational levels of authority are in principle elected but are in reality appointed by the party and confirmed by an electoral ceremonial. Such units of local government are called *soviets* (councils) *of working people's deputies* in the Soviet Union, *people's committees* or *people's councils,* in Eastern Europe, and *people's congresses* in China.

The fact of their appointment and the fake nature of their election do not necessarily mean that these officials or agencies cannot also be responsive to local pressures, even though they primarily serve as channels for transmitting orders from the central authority to subnational groups.

3. In many countries we find a combination of centrally appointed officials in charge of local government with locally elected councils. Although the centrally appointed official is responsible to the center, the locally elected bodies are responsible and accountable to their local electorates. This is so in France and in a great many other countries that have followed its (Napoleonic) formula. The French Constitution of 1958 prescribes in Article 72 that

> the territorial units of the Republic are the Communes, the *Départements,* the Overseas Territories. Other territorial units may be created by law.—These units shall be free to govern themselves through elected council and under conditions stipulated by law.

This is fully so only on the commune level. On the immediate level below the national one, in the *départements,* a prefect, appointed by Paris, is responsible "for the national interests, for administrative supervision, and for seeing that the laws are respected." Besides the prefects as appointed heads of the 95 *départements,* there is also a network of subprefects (*sous-préfet*) in charge of *départemental* subdivisions, called *arrondissements* (280); the subprefects are also appointed by Paris. A French prefect has a dual role: he is the local agent of the central government and executive head of a *départemental* government. Although the French Constitution seems to guarantee territorial autonomy, it actually places the civil servant above the locally elected representatives who form the *Départemental* Council (*Conseil Général*). The prefect appoints numerous members of the civil service—local tax collectors, school teachers, postmasters, postal clerks, sanitary officers. He supervises most of the national as well as the local services. In relation to the elected council, the prefect exercises a review and administrative supervisory function, a so-called administrative guardianship (*tutelle administrative*). In situations of disorder, his independent power to act is decisive; his responsibility is to the Ministry of Interior in Paris. The whole arrangement illustrates the traditional French mistrust of locally elected representatives and the implied confidence in highly professionally trained civil servants.

Similar provisions that combine territorial self-rule with strict supervision by central appointees has been adopted by most systems in Latin America and in Africa, all evidently inspired by the French model. Haiti, for instance, identically provides for centrally appointed prefects in its *départements* and subprefects in its *arrondissements* (Article 127). The French-oriented African states commit themselves in general terms, to the principle of local autonomy leaving all the essential details of central supervision to laws or decrees. The Republic of Chad, the Ivory Coast, and many others limit themselves to the following laconic constitutional provision for a unitary distribution of power:

> Territorial collectivities will be instituted by a law and established by a decree. The Law will determine the fundamental principle of a free administration of territorial collectivities, their powers and their resources. [Chad, Article 56, Ivory Coast, Article 68—identical wording]

The Constitution of Morocco (Article 93) states: "Local authority divisions of the Kingdom shall be prefectures, provinces and communes. They shall be established by law."

4. Some countries have rejected any form of central appointment in connection with provincial or local autonomy and prescribe an electoral basis for all subnational and national levels of government. This is so, for instance (under American influence and pressure), in the case of unitary Japan. Its Constitution proclaims the principle that there shall be territorial autonomy and that local officials must be elected by direct popular vote, although before World War II they used to be appointed by Tokyo, like the prefects in France. The Constitution further stipulates (Article 93) that local authorities have the right to manage their property affairs and administration, and prescribes (Article 93) that "local public entities . . . establish assemblies as their deliberative organs." A special law, applicable only to one territorial unit, "cannot be enacted by the Diet without the consent of the majority of the voters of the local public entity concerned" (Article 95). This represents a constitutional prohibition of territorial discrimination by the national center.

A fear lest alliances, coalitions, or subnational federations upset the internal balance seems to be reflected in constitutional limitations of interterritorial associations that perhaps could combine against the national center and upset a delicate internal balance. The Constitution of Belgium (Article 108), for instance, proclaims:

> Provincial and municipal institutions are regulated by laws. These laws consecrate the application of the following principles:
>
> *1.* Direct election. . . .
>
> *2.* The attribution to the provincial and municipal councils of all matters of provincial or municipal interest. . . .
>
> Several provinces or several boroughs may reach an agreement or enter into an association under conditions and in the manner to be laid down by the law, in order to regulate and manage on a joint basis those matters which are of provincial or municipal interest. However, it is not permissible for several provincial councils or several municipal councils to debate in joint meetings.

The preceding few selected examples can only suggest but cannot describe the extraordinary variety of territorial distribution of authority that we may find in the some 100 unitary national systems existing in the world today. They vary from country to country and sometimes also from region to region within the same country, as to their source of power (election or appointment), scope of authority, and accountability. This has always posed problems when it comes to translation of terms assigned to the hierarchy of subnational units of government; identical terms, such as *commune* in France or China or *county* in England or in an American state, may represent a contrasting distribution of authority. In France, as we have seen, local units of government are called in the descending order of importance *départements* (they number 95), *arrondissements* (280), *cantons* (3000—insignificant in terms of local autonomy, certainly not to be compared with Swiss cantons, the constituent units of the Swiss federation), and *communes* (38,000). Britain is subdivided into administrative counties (61 and London), county boroughs (83), noncounty boroughs (318), urban districts (564), rural districts (474), and parishes (7500). On June 12, 1969, a royal commission proposed a complete overhaul of local government, including the abolition of thirty-nine counties in England as well as their subdivisions, such as county boroughs and rural districts. The argument was that the nineteenth-century governmental division between town and country has been invalidated by suburban living and present-day high mobility. According to the proposal, a single authority should plan and administer larger sizable cohesive areas, even if they were to mean some sacrifice of intimacy with the electorate. At the same time, these larger units of territorial self-government are expected to represent a new counterweight against the centralizing tendencies of London. In Japan, the basic division imitates the French prefecture—*département* (*ken*). In China, there are three special municipalities (Peking, Shanghai, and Tientsin), autonomous ethnic regions (5), provinces (21), and within them autonomous-ethnic areas (*chou*), rural counties (*hsien*), municipalities (*shih*), and, on the lowest level, towns, urban districts, and rural districts (*hsiang*). The Chinese experiment in functional-territorial *communes* in the countryside and also in the cities was to juxtapose the new revolutionary units to the existing constitutional territorial subdivisions. In the United States, whose fifty states have adopted a unitary system of territorial decentralization, the state governments have delegated power to counties with the exception of Alaska, Rhode Island, and, since 1960, Connecticut, which transferred to the state the already severely restricted powers of its eight counties. The Soviet levels of local government are identified by the Soviet Constitution (Articles 94 and 95): "The organs of State power in Territories, Regions, Autonomous Regions, Areas, Districts, cities, and rural localities (stanitsas, villages, hamlets, kishlaks, auls) are the Soviet of Working People's Deputies . . . elected . . . for a term of two years."

ADVANTAGES OF UNITARY SYSTEMS

A unitary system with its strong emphasis on centralized national direction that does not exclude a flexible delegation of authority to somewhat closely supervised units of territorial self-rule appears suitable for communities that either are or try to be markedly homogeneous.

A note of the government of Ghana that accompanied the draft Constitution, submitted to the people of Ghana in March 1960, read in part as follows:

> Ghana to be a Unitary State.—The Government asks the people, by voting for the draft Constitution, to show that they believe in the unity of Ghana and reject any form of federalism. The Government will consider a vote in favour of the draft Constitution as a mandate to maintain the unity of Ghana. . . . The Government realises that the present frontiers of Ghana, like so many other frontiers on the African continent, were drawn merely to suit the convenience of the Colonial Powers who divided Africa between them during the last century. The object of the draft Constitution is to provide firm, stable and popular Government in Ghana . . . and [facilitate] the entry of Ghana into a union of African states.[1]

[1] Quoted in Egyptian Society of International Law, *Constitutions of the New African States—A Critical Survey,* Alexandria, March 1962, p. 65.

Although in some cases at the cost of local initiative and participation, a unitary system fits the era of national planning and of the welfare state because it aims at assuring a *uniform* development and progress, not hindered by local shortsightedness but perhaps assisted by local flexibility and responsibility within the framework of a national plan. If, however, no appropriate powers have been delegated to local subcenters, an excessively contralized unitary system may suffer from overburdening the national center with problems that could have been dealt with better locally. This was the case of many Communist systems and was, therefore, the reason for their experimentation with local autonomy in the early 1960s; one of their hopes was that local responsibility, flexibility, pride, and competitiveness within a firm framework of socialist planning may compensate for the absence of competitiveness, which, in capitalism, has some very good effects besides the bad ones.

There is also a danger of excessive or unwise decentralization that may compartmentalize a national community into feuding, intolerant, and egoistic local communities, totally disregarding the interest of the collective whole. In some situations a grant of local autonomy is viewed only as a first concession by tribes or movements whose hearts are set, not on local self-rule, but on secession. This is often a distinct possibility in newly established states and, therefore, is a favorite argument on the part of the national leadership for tightly centralized authoritarian rule. In another context, in the unitary democratic system of prewar Czechoslovakia, the Sudeten German ethnic group began its pressures by a demand for minority rights that later changed into a demand for territorial autonomy or federation and finally, in 1938, after the Munich Conference, led to secession from Czechoslovakia and accession to Hitler's Germany.

"INDESTRUCTIBLE" UNITS IN UNITARY SYSTEMS

A delegation of authority in a unitary system has so far been presented as amendable and revocable by the center. This has now to be qualified in two ways.

First, what is revocable in theory, law, or constitution may not be so in political practice. Although the central authority in a unitary system may curb local self-rule at will and, acting quite legally but perhaps quite unwisely, reduce it to zero, it rarely does so. Why? No central government is really so blind as to totally disregard either the reality of territorial interests or the advisability of local participation. Central authorities do not operate in a weightless nonpolitical atmosphere. Local centers of political gravity, as the experience shows, exercise their magnetic pull whatever the constitutional arrangement may be. A good example is the unitary United Kingdom. Parliament is seemingly omnipotent. Theoretically, Parliament could tomorrow replace monarchy by a people's democracy and abrogate not only all local government in England but also the very divisions of the United Kingdom into North Ireland, Scotland, Wales, and England and could change all this into a tightly London-dominated nation-state. It will not do so, being prevented from it not by a constitution but by history and political conventions. Not only the self-rule of Northern Ireland, Scotland, and Wales is quite safe but it is also even in the process of being further broadened. Northern Ireland has its own Parliament and Cabinet and has a modified form of nationalization of gas and electricity; Scotland, which has its own church and legal system, is represented in the Parliament by its elected representatives, forming a Committee on Scottish Bills,[2] and is represented in the Cabinet by a secretary of state for Scotland, assisted by a minister of state for Scotland. The Scottish Nationalists now ask for their own Parliament and Cabinet. Wales is represented in the Cabinet by a secretary of state for Welsh Affairs, assisted by a minister of state who resides in Wales.

The territorial distribution of authority in the United Kingdom, so solidly guaranteed by a constitutional consensus without a written constitution and generally implemented in practice, has led many close observers of the British political practice to conclude that the unitary system of British government is in fact federal.

Second, many constitutions that proclaim their systems to

[2] Compare William S. Livingston, who analyzed the evolution of the Scottish Committee of the British House of Commons from a mere instrumentality into an institution that has become a thing of value in itself—"an essential part of the *federal* relation between England and Scotland [italics added]." See his "A Note on the Nature of Federalism," *Political Science Quarterly,* Vol. 67, No. 1 (March 1952), 93.

be unitary also proclaim the principle of territorial division of authority, describe and guarantee the formation and powers of territorial autonomous units, and often enumerate such units by categories or names, especially in the case of territorial-ethnic or linguistic communities.

The People's Republic of China, a unitary state, provides for a combination of territorial autonomy with central supervision as follows:

> *Article 3*   The People's Republic of China is a unitary multi-national state. . . . Regional autonomy applies in areas where a minority nationality live in a compact community. All the national autonomous areas are inseparable parts of the People's Republic of China.

As noted before (page 75), five such regions were established: Mongolia (to be distinguished from the Soviet-protected People's Republic of Mongolia, separated from the Chinese Mongolia by the Gobi Desert), Sinkiang-Uighur region (the Chinese Turkestan), Ningsia (inhabited by the Moslem Hui people), Kwangsi (inhabited by Chuangs), and Tibet. There are other subdivisions for minor non-Chinese groups (such as Tais, related to the Thais, Koreans in Manchuria, Miaos in Kwangsi, and Szechuan or Lolos in Szechuan and Yunnan)—altogether about fifty national autonomous areas on the county level and above.

The constitutional provisions for such subdivisions, found in Article 53, read as follows:

> *1.*   The country is divided into provinces, autonomous regions, and cities directly under the central authority.
> *2.*   Provinces and autonomous regions are divided into autonomous *chou* [subregions], counties, autonomous counties, and cities.
> *3.*   Counties and autonomous counties are divided into *hsiang* [districts], nationality *hsiang,* and towns. . . . Autonomous *chou* [subregions] are divided into counties, autonomous counties, and cities.
>
> Autonomous regions, autonomous *chou,* and autonomous counties are all national autonomous areas.

In all these units, people's congresses (legislative assemblies) and people's councils (executive organs) represent local authority. Article 67 adds that the form of each organ of self-government "may be determined in accordance with the wishes of the majority of the people of the nationality or nationalities enjoying regional autonomy in a given area."

Other articles stipulate that the organs of self-government exercise autonomy within the limits of their authority as prescribed by the Constitution, administer the finances of their areas, and organize the public security forces (Article 70); in performing these functions the spoken and written language or languages commonly used in the locality will be employed (Article 71). And the whole section on local and ethnic autonomy ends with the following Article 72:

> The higher organs of state should fully safeguard the exercise of autonomy by organs of self-government of autonomous regions, autonomous *chou* and autonomous counties, and should assist all the minority nationalities in their political, economic, and cultural development.

In China's Parliament (the National People's Congress), there is a Nationalities Committee provided for by the Constitution; it is a permanent committee that remains in session even when the National People's Congress is not.

The constitutional provisions for territorial autonomy in unitary China are, as may be seen, quite elaborate and detailed. The Nationalities Committee somewhat reminds us of the Scottish Committee in England, and a foreign observer could also reach the conclusion that the Chinese Constitution contains very significant federal features. Of course, this would be denied by official Chinese spokesmen. The chairman of the Nationalities Committee, Liu Ke-ping, emphasized that China was "not a federation of republics but a unitary republic in which all ethnic groups have equal standing." [3] And any illusion of federalism and pluralism in China has been denied by actual practice, which means not only a highly centralized unitary system but also a deliberate effort to sinicize the whole country under conditions of an all-permeating totalitarian dictatorship.

[3] Hsinhua (New China News Agency), January 17, 1958.

The gap between a constitutional promise and manifest lack of its implementation is not a feature characteristic only of authoritarian or totalitarian systems. Even a democratic country may not come around to implementing fully what it has promised in its constitution. The postwar Constitution of the Italian Republic, for instance, provided for regionalism in a detailed way. The names [4] of all regions, their financial autonomy, legislative councils, and executive organs (*giunta*) are described in the Constitution (1947). In all regions, the representative of the central authority (*commissario*) supervises the working of local self-rule. Special conditions of broader autonomy were assigned to—and implemented in—five regions: Sardinia, Sicily, Trentino-Alto Adige (where there is a problem of German-speaking Italian citizens), Friuli-Venezia Giulia (a sensitive area contiguous with Yugoslavia; Trieste is part of that region), and Valle d'Aosta (neighboring France). The Italian political leaders representing the dominant force of Christian Democracy in different combinations with democratic socialists have hesitated for the past twenty-two years to implement the constitutional provisions for the establishment of the other fourteen autonomous regions. In 1968, the parliamentary majority passed another bill concerning the establishment of the regions and their organs, but there is no reason to believe that the process will now be any quicker than it was in the past. The experience with the existing five regions is not too encouraging; under the umbrella of local autonomy they have proved quite scandal-ridden. Furthermore, the ruling majority dreads that the autonomous regions may become too convenient bases of power—and blackmail—for the Communist party, which in some cases could transform such regions into "soviet autonomous republics" of sorts.[5]

[4] Piemonte, Valle d'Aosta, Lombardia, Trentino-Alto Adige, Veneto, Friuli-Venezia Giulia, Liguria, Emilia-Romagna, Toscana, Umbria, Marche, Lazio, Abruzzi e Molise, Campania, Puglia, Basilicata, Calabria, Sicily, Sardinia (Article 131). Chap. 5, which deals with regional autonomy, divides the national and regional powers and describes regional autonomy in great detail (Articles 114–133).

[5] This was also one of the reasons why, after World War II, France did not experiment with real autonomy for her *départements;* the emergence of several "soviet" republics, administered by local Communists in charge of the then still fully armed Communist resistance groups, seemed a real possibility—and a nightmare—to de Gaulle's Paris.

Whatever the past and present fears may be, the Constitution seems to be, however, very clear on the subject:

> *Article 114*   The Republic is divided into Regions, Provinces, and Communes.
>
> *Article 115*   The Regions are constituted as autonomous bodies with their own powers and functions according to the principles fixed by the Constitution.
>
> *Article 118*   The administrative functions pertaining to the subjects listed in the preceding article [such as organization of the administrative bodies dependent on the Region, urban and rural police, vocational training, town planning, roads, lake navigation and ports, agriculture, artisanship, mineral and thermal waters, hunting, surface transport of regional interest, museums, libraries, health assistance, and tourist trade and industry] reside in the Regions.

In Communist Eastern Europe, where the problems of linguistic territorial or dispersed communities have traditionally been sensitive issues, the unitary systems guarantee their autonomous development in their constitutions. The Socialist Republic of Rumania, for instance, assures (Article 22) its "co-inhabiting nationalities" of the free use of their native language as well as "books, papers, magazines, theatres and education at all levels in their own language." Where a non-Rumanian group lives in a compact area, "all the bodies and institutions use the language of the respective nationality in speech and in writing and appoint officials from its ranks or from the ranks of other citizens who know the language and the way of life of the local population." The question may be asked how satisfied the Hungarians of Rumania are if, according to the Constitution, not a Hungarian but a Rumanian expert on the Hungarian language and way of life is appointed in a dominantly Hungarian area. Curious is the case of Czechoslovakia. Until 1968 that country proclaimed it was not and did not want to be a federation. Article 1 of its Constitution proclaimed that "the Czechoslovak Socialist Republic is a *unitary* State of two fraternal nations, possessing equal rights, the Czechs and the Slovaks" (italics added). The second half of the constitutional text (Articles 73–85) spelled out the autonomy and reserved powers of Slovakia in some detail. There was a

Slovak legislative chamber that, at a certain time, appointed a quasi cabinet for Slovakia. Curiously, the Constitution did not provide for corresponding organs of autonomy for the Czechs; the common Czechoslovak organs were to serve the western Czech half of the country, while the eastern Slovak portion had its own political and administrative framework. At first sight it appeared to be a federal system heavily tilted to the advantage of the Slovaks. In reality, it was the opposite. The more advanced and industrial as well as the more populous Czech portion of the state has always played the decisive role in the direction of the republic. The Czechs dominated the leading organs of the Czechoslovak Communist party and the Prague government. The Slovak resentment against this state of affairs was one of the triggers of the short-lived attempt to combine Czechoslovak socialism with pluralism in terms of both a multiparty system and federalism. The other triggers were the opposition of the youth and the intellectuals against the inhumanity of communism and the resentment of the workers and the consumers against the demonstrated gross inefficiency of the Communist economy. Although among the Czechs the revolutionary ferment had dominantly liberal overtones—the central issue being the freedom of expression—among the Slovaks nationalist self-assertion represented a decisive ingredient. A new constitutional change—commitment to true federalism—was announced on the fiftieth anniversary of the republic (October 28, 1968), two months and seven days after the Soviet occupation—a very strange framework indeed for an attempt at federal (territorial) pluralism.

Besides the problem of the Slovak-Czech relationship, the Czechoslovak system must also solve the problem of other minorities whose members are citizens but are not viewed as constituent territorial communities in the same way as the Slovaks and the Czechs. Article 25 of the 1960 Constitution said:

> The State shall ensure citizens of Hungarian, Ukrainian, and Polish nationality every opportunity and all means for education in their mother tongue and for their cultural development.[6]

[6] There are over 560,000 Hungarians in Czechoslovakia. Mostly they live among the 3 million Slovaks. So does the Ukrainian minority. This is why the 1960 Czechoslovak Constitution repeated the constitu-

Figure 5–2   Delegation of authority

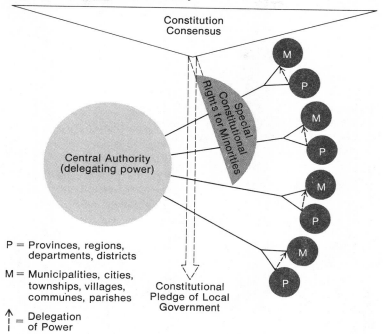

No similar assurance has been given the German minority, the Sudeten Germans, who were not included in the mass expulsions in 1945–1947 mostly because of their special skills or because they were members of the Communist or Socialist party; a Communist minister of interior was in charge of the mass expulsions.

Figure 5–2 presents a summary of the preceding analysis. It demonstrates the delegation of authority, from the central authority to provinces, regions, counties, districts, or cities; initially we have said that it is an amendable or revocable grant. This has now been qualified. A constitution may commit the

tional guarantee of the Hungarian (and Ukrainian) identity once more in the title dealing with the Slovak autonomy: "The Slovak National Council shall have the competence to . . . ensure in the spirit of equality the full development of the life of citizens of Hungarian and Ukrainian nationality."

central authority to establishing and maintaining local government. The central authority in principle may enlarge or narrow local autonomy, but it cannot reduce it to nothing (the dotted vertical line on our model). Furthermore, a constitution (or consensus and tradition, as in constitutionless Britain) often guarantees special forms of protection to ethnic and territorial groups: territorial autonomy or collective rights. This, on our model, is marked by the black shield, derived from the constitution, and directed against the potential centralistic ambitions of the central authority. The dotted lines between *P* (province) and *M* (municipality) suggest that the central authority may delegate the supervision over townships, rural districts, or parishes from itself to the provincial government.

DECENTRALIZATION OF EMPIRES

Whatever their origins and causes (discussed in Chap. 6), imperial unions of conquered territorial communities were bound to be, sooner or later, like any other forcible and oppressive structure, subject to erosion, sometimes violent explosion, and often also deliberate transformation by decentralization. For the sake of administrative expediency, all empires (the ancient as well as the modern ones) could not avoid delegating some authority from the imperial center, first to colonial viceroys or governors, and later (reluctantly and usually belatedly) to the native elites. After World War II, when the metropolitan heads of colonial empires were weakened by war and economic exhaustion, the imperial builders and managers tried to prevent a total dissolution of colonial empires by means of what they had hoped to be a timely offer of territorial autonomy within a new confederal or federal framework. The secession from a *forcible* imperial association was to be combined with *voluntary* accession to the new union. Necessity, rather than dedication to the ideal of democratic pluralism and decentralization, characterized these attempts that aimed at the preservation of the former economic and strategic advantages of the empires (and perhaps also the prestige of their builders). The rationale and the process of imperial decentralization by means of reluctant grants of territorial autonomy did not fundamentally differ from that in unitary nation-states.

One obstacle to a successful transformation of an imperial into a confederal union was the memory of having been conquered, deprived of self-rule, and annexed by an alien group; we have already mentioned the political importance of collective territorial memories—the past glories and tragedies are powerful factors in a group's awareness of territorial identity. Memories of having been conquered contain very painful ingredients of regret, defeat, humiliation, injustice, discrimination, and exploitation. "If we are sometimes exasperated by officialdom even at home," writes the British historian Herbert Butterfield, "can we imagine what must be the reaction of awakening minds in regions where the officialdom represents the foreigner, and the foreigner is in the country also to exploit it?" [7] Memories of conquest with their concomitant mistrust of the imperial ruler are bound to last for a considerable length of time and therefore play an important political role; even if half forgotten by the subsequent generations, memories of defeat and hope for a better future may be easily revived by internal agitation and external interference.

Some territorial communities may finally forget or may have already forgotten. History cannot any longer be transmuted into a trigger for political explosion. In Western Europe, for instance, many territorial communities and ethnic groups, albeit conquered in some distant past, have been so successfully integrated that their ancient annexations represent but a few lines in the history books. With the partial exceptions of Brittany, Alsace, and the Basque country, France is now a very homogeneous community, although originally a composite of distinct conquering and conquered Germanic, Latin, and Celtic tribes. An attempt at a revival of ancient divisions was made during France's turbulent spring of 1968, when the striking students in the south of France, at the University of Toulouse, presented also a demand that the language of Oc (*langue d'oc* or Occitan) be introduced into primary education. This language that the medieval troubadours used in their ballads was forbidden by the French kings in the north in the sixteenth century, but its different local variations, such as Provençal (used by the great poet Mistral) or Gascon, are still spoken in the rural south. The

[7] Herbert Butterfield, *Christianity, Diplomacy, and War*. Nashville, Tenn.: Abingdon, n.d., p. 114.

assertion of the southern French territorial and linguistic identity has not been taken too seriously by Paris. The students' emphasis on the idiom of the troubadours was viewed as only a local expression of the general revolt of the guitar generation.

Western European colonial empires in Asia and Africa, which had lasted for a relatively short period of time, were too exploitative and too discriminatory to allow any degree of integration. Bitter memories of conquest could not be forgotten; the forcible aspects of the imperial union could not be accepted. Only in the case of Britain a partial success accompanied the effort to transform the empire into a commonwealth. Other cases were less successful. For instance, Holland, which after World War II tried to reimpose its colonial rule on Indonesia by violent means, finally offered its colonies a two-level federal formula: a federated Indonesia (initially divided into three and later into sixteen territorial units to break up the political power of nationalist Java) was to be associated with unitary Holland. It was a short-lived experiment that finally broke down and led to the severance of all bonds, including the diplomatic and consular ones, between Holland and Indonesia. The leaders of now fully independent Indonesia immediately suspended the federal constitution of the United States of Indonesia, adopted a unitary system, and from then on tended to view with suspicion any indigenous claim for decentralization or federalism as a Dutch intrigue—the colonial "divide-and-rule" gimmick—although perhaps a federal or confederal formula could have been appropriate for the geographic and polyethnic characteristics of the vast Indonesian Archipelago.

Only somewhat more successful was de Gaulle's effort to transform the French colonial empire in Africa into an aggregate of states associated with France as the political and economic center of the whole system. The text of the new French Constitution adopted in 1958 (Title XII—"On the Community") described the new plan as follows:

> *Article 77*   In the Community instituted by the present Constitution, the States shall enjoy autonomy; they shall administer themselves and manage their own affairs democratically and freely.
> *Article 78*   The Community's jurisdiction shall extend over

foreign policy, defense, currency, common economic and financial policy, as well as over policy on strategic raw materials.—It shall include . . . the supervision of tribunals, higher education, the general organization of external transportation . . . as well as telecommunication.

Article 80   The President of the [French] Republic shall preside over and represent the Community. . . .

Article 82   The Executive Council of the Community shall be presided over by the President of the Community. It shall consist of the Premier of the Republic, the heads of Government of each of the member States of the Community and the ministers responsible for the common affairs of the Community.

The French colonies were expected to accept by a referendum the proposed association with France. With the exception of Guinea, which voted No, the colonies did so. In 1959 the organization of the Community began in Africa. In France, several organic laws implemented the general provisions of the Constitution. It became clear that all three main organs of the Community would be dependent on the French president: the Executive Council, whose agenda was to be established by the president; the Court of Arbitration, which was to be composed of "seven judges named for six years by the president"; and the Senate of the Community only consultative at any rate, which was to be composed of 284 members, of which the majority, 186, were to represent France and only the minority of 98 French Africa.[8]

One year later, in 1960, the Community was a thing of the past. One by one the African states proclaimed their independence, became members of the United Nations, and yet at the same time asked for cooperative agreement (that is, economic aid) with France. The 1958 Constitution had to be amended, for it allowed only two alternatives: either to be with France within the Community or to leave the Community and look out

---

[8] According to a decision reached on February 9, 1959, the following apportionment of senatorial seats was enacted: Madagascar, 17; Sudan (later Mali), 13; Upper Volta, 12; Ivory Coast, 11; Chad, 9; Niger, 9; Senegal, 8; Dahomey, 6; Central African Republic, 4; Congo (Brazzaville), 3; Gabon, 3; and Mauritania, 3.

for itself as best it could. This led Guinea into temporarily intimate cooperation with the USSR and the Eastern European Communist states. Article 86 was amended as follows:

> *Article 86, 1958* . . . a member State of the Community may become independent. It shall thereby cease to belong to the Community.
> *Article 86, 1960* . . . a member State of the Community can likewise become independent through a special agreement, *without ceasing to belong to the Community.* [Italics added.]

Even so loosened, the French Community was plagued by the same problems that are perhaps inevitable in all asymmetric territorial associations, especially those that combine a highly developed nation with weak and underdeveloped ones. The smaller units tend to criticize the leading member for his lack of generosity, foresight, and wisdom; he is accused of egocentric misuses of the association for the promotion of his own narrow national interest at the expense of the rest; and sometimes the dominant power is simply resented for being dominant—the imbalance itself is the cause of suspicion and resentment. In the case of the African states there was, in addition, the understandable suspicion that the new federal or confederal formula was to preserve French colonialism under a new garb.

Furthermore, in French Africa the atmosphere of exuberant, triumphant nationalism made it difficult for the national leaders to assert cooperation with the former master without exposing themselves to the domestic accusation of being more Francophile than patriotic. Unlike the British Commonwealth, the French *Communauté* also suffered from extreme racial imbalance. On one side, there stood prosperous France, European, Western, and white; on the other side, there stood an Arab or black block of developing African states whose continental solidarity was bound to prove stronger than their attachment to France. If the composition and operations of common French-African institutions were to be tilted in favor of France, as they were, they were bound to prove unacceptable to the African nationalists; and France, on the other hand, could not accept what would amount to taxation of France's wealth by an African majority. Finally, the very symbol of the Community, President de Gaulle, a controversial personality, yet respected by many Africans, was necessarily a very temporary cement of the new unity. A French observer rightly pointed out:

> De Gaulle's prestige . . . with the African leaders is a powerful factor of cohesion. Nevertheless this is a factor narrowly connected with the person of the general and his successors will not probably enjoy it any more. The British crown is no more than a symbol of the Commonwealth but abstract symbols often resist better the test of time than the popularity and the prestige of one man.[9]

The British Commonwealth

The transformation of the British Empire dominated by Britain into a Commonwealth dominated by white dominions and finally into a Commonwealth in which the white dominions are in minority [10] and the territorial association is dominated by none has been extended over a long period of time; unlike the French effort to express political changes in constitutional or definitional formulas, the British Empire moved to the commonwealth-confederal status by pragmatic steps. It began with Lord Durham's report in 1839 on the causes of discontent in Canada; there was then a fear in Britain that Canada might follow the secessionist example of the United States in 1776. Lord Durham proposed a transformation of the colonial rule toward a government locally formed and locally responsible. By 1847, the system of locally accountable authority was in operation in Canada and was soon extended to Australia, New Zealand, and the whites in South Africa. The Act of Westminster of 1931 gave the dominions a status of component units in a confederation, including presumably the right of secession, which so far only Ireland (Eire) and South Africa have exercised. The Act of Westminster stated:

> Now, therefore, be it enacted by the King's most Excellent Majesty, by and with the advice and consent of the Lords

[9] Marcel Merle, "Fédéralisme et Problèmes d'Outre Mer en France," paper presented at the Sixth World Congress of the International Political Science Association, Geneva, 1964, p. 15.

[10] This evolution was further hastened by the secession of the white-dominated government of the South African Republic precisely over the racial question.

Spiritual and Temporal, and Commons, in the present Parliament assembled, and by the authority of the same, as follows:—

1. In this Act the expression "Dominion" means any of the following Dominions, that is to say, the Dominion of Canada, the Commonwealth of Australia, the Dominion of New Zealand, the Union of South Africa, the Irish Free State and Newfoundland.

2. . . . No law and no provision of any law made after the commencement of this Act by the Parliament of a Dominion shall be void or inoperative on the ground that it is repugnant to the law of England, or to the provisions of any existing or future Act of Parliament of the United Kingdom, or to any order, rule or regulation made under any such Act, and the powers of the Parliament of a Dominion shall include the power to repeal or amend any such Act, order, rule or regulation insofar as the same is part of the law of the Dominion.

3. It is hereby declared and enacted that the Parliament of a Dominion has full power to make laws having extraterritorial operation.

4. No Act of Parliament of the United Kingdom passed after the commencement of this Act shall extend or be deemed to extend to a Dominion as part of the law of that Dominion, unless it is expressly declared in that Act that that Dominion has requested, and consented to, the enactment thereof. . . .

At present there are twenty-five members of the Commonwealth,[11] with their forty dependencies [12] and some units with an unclear status, such as Rhodesia and several islands in the Caribbean (for example, Saint Kitts, Anguilla, and Nevis).

All countries of the Commonwealth recognize the Queen as the head of the Commonwealth. Britain, Canada, New Zea-

[11] Britain, Canada, Australia, New Zealand, India, Pakistan, Ceylon, Ghana, Malaysia, Nigeria, Cyprus, Sierra Leone, Tanzania, Jamaica, Trinidad and Tobago, Uganda, Kenya, Malawi, Malta, Zambia, Gambia, Lesotho, Botswana, Barbados, and Guyana.

The descriptive and factual material on pp. 134–136 was supplied by the Reference Division, Central Office of Information, London.

[12] Most of the dependencies are those of Britain; some are administered by Australia and New Zealand. These are mostly small islands or sparsely populated territories.

land, Ceylon, Sierra Leone, Jamaica, Trinidad and Tobago, Malawi, Malta, Gambia, Barbados, and Guyana are monarchies in which (except in Britain) the Queen is represented by a governor-general; India, Pakistan, Ghana, Cyprus, Nigeria, Tanzania, Kenya, Zambia, and Botswana are republics; Malaysia and Lesotho have their own sovereigns, and Uganda (since 1966) has a prime minister who is head of state.

The very nature of the present-day Commonwealth precludes the possibility of the formulation of a central policy on, say, economic or foreign affairs. On the other hand, it is vital for the continuance and development of the relationship that there should be the greatest possible measure of consultation and of cooperation to achieve common ends where they exist.

Commonwealth governments are represented in the capitals of other Commonwealth countries by *high commissioners* who are *equal in status with ambassadors,* taking precedence with them according to the date of taking up duty. For the Commonwealth members who acknowledge the Queen as head of state, high commissioners are *appointed from government to government,* not, as is the case of ambassadors, by head of state to head of state. As for Commonwealth members who have a head of state other than the Queen, high commissioners are accredited from head of state to head of state.

In the countries other than Britain where the Queen is head of state, she is represented by a *governor-general* appointed on the *recommendation of the government of the country concerned.* He acts in accordance with the constitutional practice of that country and is, of course, wholly independent of the British government.

From 1944 onward, the prewar Imperial Conferences have been replaced by less formal Prime Ministers' Meetings held at intervals of about eighteen months. No formal agenda is published and proceedings are in private, permitting a frank exchange of views.

In addition to the Prime Ministers' Meetings, since World War II there have been meetings of the Commonwealth foreign ministers, supply ministers, and finance ministers.

Proposals for the establishment of a Commonwealth secretariat were made at the Commonwealth Ministers' Meeting in 1964. The 1965 conference agreed on its terms of reference and initial arrangements to bring it into being. . . . Its functions include disseminating factual information to member countries on matters of common concern; promoting wide-ranging studies to supplement the work of existing agencies; advancing development projects and technical assistance on a multilateral Commonwealth basis; reviewing existing intra-Commonwealth organizations dealing with economic and related affairs; and servicing Commonwealth meetings.

The somewhat general acceptance of the English common law is another unifying element in the Commonwealth, in particular the English law of precedent, the English manner of interpreting statutes, the English law of evidence, and the English public law. There are, of course, exceptions. The provinces of Quebec and Mauritius have legal systems based on the French law; Ceylon and Rhodesia on the Dutch Roman law. In India and Pakistan the private law, as opposed to the English public law, is based on a completely different legal tradition or religious codes.

In the past the Judicial Committee of the Privy Council in London was also the final court of appeal on some legal issues arising in any Commonwealth country except Britain. Many countries have now ended the right of appeal from the courts to the Judicial Committee.

The British case illustrates the possibility of a process of secession from the empire coupled with accession to the Commonwealth; thus, the formerly forcible territorial association has been replaced by a voluntary association. By this secession-accession process, the Commonwealth has impressively grown in number since World War II; almost all the British colonies (Burma is one exception) have chosen to remain in the Commonwealth, despite some domestic opposition to the new association with a distant and weakened old colonial master. It is debatable whether the growth in Commonwealth membership has been accompanied by a similar growth in cohesion, especially in view of the steady decline of the British political and economic power, epitomized by the uncertainties concerning the British pound, which used to be one of the most important links in the Commonwealth. It seems that the memory of a common imperial past, especially among the now-aging English-speaking leaders of the Commonwealth nations in Asia and Africa and the continuing use of common symbols are more significant elements of unity than any real agreement as to what to do in common now and in the future. At present it is impossible to foretell whether the challenges of the Common Market in Europe and the American economic power in the Pacific will result in the strengthening of or the weakening of the existing bonds of what once was the British Empire and what now is a loose association of independent states or, as the English sometimes call it, the world's oddest, most ill-assorted club, whose membership depends on nothing more than an accident in history.

The Soviet case [13]

The Soviet federal union represents another case of a simultaneous secession-accession or decentralization-centralization process. Like all the other colonial empires, the Tsarist Empire began to be challenged from both without and within by the end of World War I. The Bolshevik and socialist leaders attacked the empire as a "prison house of nations"; for the purpose of its destruction and replacement by a better, unoppressive order, the Communists joined their forces with those of the peasants, desirous of the private ownership of land, and with those of dissatisfied non-Russian ethnic communities that had for a long time resented their oppression by imperial Russia. Whereas in the British Empire color bar and racial discrimination in both official and interpersonal private relations were usually the issue, in the Russian Empire, forcible assimilation (Russification) was the major source of nationalistic agitation and opposition. The alliance between the Russian Communists and anti-Russian nationalists was quite unholy: the Communists were dedicated to their concept of proletarian internationalism with its emphasis on supranational class struggle, the non-Russian nationalist leaders were guided by their supraclass nationalist emotions. Their enemy was not a social class but a nation, Russia. However artificial and temporary such an alliance was, it did not lack in collective vigor so long as the Communist hatred against a class rule and the nationalist anger at the Great Russian domination pointed to the same targets: Petrograd and Moscow.

[13] Compare Ivo D. Duchacek, *Nations and Men*. New York: Holt, Rinehart and Winston, Inc., 1960, pp. 128–133.

The control over these two centers of the Russian Empire was seized by the Bolsheviks on November 7, 1917. Their task was then to reorganize and reform according to their revolutionary doctrine not only Russia but also Russia's imperialistic relationship to the Ukraine and other conquered territorial ethnic communities in the Baltic Sea (Estonia, Latvia, Lithuania, and Finland), in the Caucasus (Georgia, Armenia, and Azerbaijan), and in Central Asia (Kazakhstan, Kirghizia, Turkmenistan, Tadzhikistan, and Uzbekistan). Between 1500, when the Russian territorial conquests had begun, and 1900 the Russian polyethnic empire grew by fifty square miles a day; corresponding "Cold War" statistics indicate that between 1789 and 1960, the United States grew by fifty-two square miles a day.

For a short time after the Bolshevik Revolution, its leaders repeated their former commitment to the concept of the liquidation of the empire and the principle of national self-determination. On November 15, 1917, the new Soviet government, the Council of People's Commissars, issued its proclamation on the right of the ethnic groups in Russia to secede and form their independent states. The concluding portion of that manifesto reads in part as follows:

> The Congress of the Soviets held in June this year proclaimed the right of the nations of Russia to free self-determination.
>
> The Second Congress of the Soviets in October this year confirmed this inalienable right of the nations inhabiting Russia in an even firmer and clearer manner.
>
> Fulfilling the will of these congresses, the Council of People's Commissars decided to base its actions in the ethnic question of Russia on the following principles:
>
> 1. Equality and sovereignty of the nations of Russia
> 2. The right of the nations in Russia to free self-determination, including the right of secession and formation of an independent state. . . .
>
> People's Commissar for Nationalities Questions: JOSEPH DZHUGASHVILI [STALIN]
>
> Chairman of the Council of People's Commissars: V. ULYANOV [LENIN]

This Manifesto of 1917 was reproduced in full again in a Prague weekly on November 7, 1968.[14] The intended message was clear: the Soviet occupation of Czechoslovakia in August 1968 denied its people the right of national self-determination that Lenin had promised to all nationalities in the Tsarist prison house of nations. The Czech editors evidently hoped that on November 7, the anniversary day of the October Revolution, the censors—reintroduced after the Soviet occupation—would not dare to censor Lenin. They did not.

It is true that in 1917 the right of secession from a Socialist state was already significantly qualified. In his report to the party in 1917, Stalin had stressed that the exercise of the right of self-determination depended on circumstances:

> The recognition of the right to secede must not be confused with the expedience of secession in any given circumstances. . . . Thus we are at liberty to agitate for or against secession, according to the interests of the proletariat, of the proletarian revolution.

Similarly, Trotsky argued that the Communists must give

> full support to the principle of self-determination, whenever it is directed against feudal, capitalist, and imperialist states. But whenever the fiction of self-determination, in the hands of the bourgeoisie, becomes a weapon directed against the proletarian revolution, we have no occasion to treat this fiction differently from the other "principle" of democracy perverted by capitalism.

Before 1917 Lenin, Trotsky, and Stalin were primarily concerned with the problem of seizing and then preserving power. After the October Revolution the preservation of the

[14] *Listy* (Prague, November 7, 1968), No. 1, p. 16. Compare the warning which in the early twenties a German Communist leader, Rosa Luxemburg, addressed to the Russian leaders on the subject of the danger involved in their playing with the nationalist fire: "Instead of defending the integrity of the Russian state, the Bolshevists, with their nationalist phraseology of the right of self-determination including separation, have provided the bourgeoisie of all the border territories with the idea, pretext, or even a banner for their counterrevolutionary strivings."

revolutionary territory (which happened to be a multinational empire) against the hostile world became the dominant preoccupation of the new regime. Although the mobilization of the anti-Russian ferment was useful in the process of achieving power, it was found quite harmful in the process of consolidating power. According to the theory, nations were, first, to liberate themselves from capitalist oppression and, second, to amalgamate into a higher proletarian supranational union. In the critical period of the first five years of communism, the non-Russian nationalities, inhabiting the border regions of what was to become the USSR, were to exercise their right of national liberation from Tsarist oppression, so to speak, simultaneously with their proletarian duty of amalgamation.

This "duty" of association was furthermore placed into the framework of the postwar international situation that was perceived by the Soviet leaders as an extreme polarization between two hostile worlds, permitting no nation to occupy a neutral and independent position in between. Under such circumstances secession from Communist Russia could only lead to accession to the camp of Russia's enemies. Stalin expressed this as follows:

> When a life-and-death struggle is being waged, and is spreading, between Proletarian Russia and the imperialist Entente, only two alternatives confront the border regions: either they join forces with Russia, and the toiling masses of the border regions will be emancipated from imperialist oppression; or they join forces with the Entente, and the yoke of imperialism is inevitable. There is no third solution. So-called independence of so-called independent Georgia, Armenia, Poland, Finland, and so forth, is only an illusion.

Despite these and similar warnings that had followed the initial appeal to exercise the right of national self-determination, several non-Russian nationalities attempted to go it alone. Some, like the Ukrainians, desired full independence; others, like the Moslems, hoped for a national autonomy. Whatever their concepts of the future were, one by one all were brought by force into a "fraternal union" with Great Russia: the Ukrainians, Georgians, and Moslems first and the Estonians, Latvians, and Lithuanians last (in 1940).

It is interesting to note that it was Stalin, the Georgian,

rather than Lenin, the Great Russian, who issued the severe warnings to the non-Russian nationalities of the Soviet Union. According to Louis Fischer,

> Stalin, the Georgian, and Felix Djerzhinsky, the Soviet leader of Polish origin, thought they knew better than Lenin, the Great Russian, how the minorities felt; both were convinced that concession to the wishes of the Ukrainians, Georgians, and many more constituted a mortal peril to the Moscow dictatorship. The appetite of the national minorities would only be whetted by partial home rule: they might demand more, indeed they might ask fulfillment of the promise of the Soviet Constitution: self-determination. . . . Who was right, Lenin or Stalin . . . who believed Lenin underestimated [nationalism's] dangers? One could contend cogently that Stalin was a better Leninist than Lenin. I think it more fruitful to suggest that Lenin left his heirs no clear guidance on how to deal with our present nationalistic world.[15]

The revolutionary pledge of decentralization and self-determination, including the right of secession, was very quickly replaced by the opposite process of imperial centralization. The result is the polyethnic, multilevel Soviet federalism that gives a constitutional recognition to the cultural and linguistic heterogeneity of the Soviet Union but, at the same time, sees to it that the linguistic and cultural autonomy does not interfere with the monolithic unity of the party and the state, both dominated by the Russians. (The institutional features of the Soviet formula will be discussed further in Chaps. 8 and 9.)

For a long time the Soviet Union has enjoyed a relative immunity against the accusation that her federal system, denying political self-determination, was, in fact, colonialism, only tempered by a federal recognition of linguistic and cultural autonomy. There were several reasons for this immunity: (1) Comparatively speaking, the non-Russian territorial groups in the Soviet Union experienced a more significant economic and educational advancement than did most Western colonies in Asia and Africa. (2) The Russian imperial conquests were less conspicuous (as they had been directed against contiguous areas)

[15] Louis Fischer, "Lenin's Legacy," *Columbia University Forum,* Vol. 7, No. 4 (Fall 1964), 6.

than the French and British imperialistic expeditions carrying the colonial rule over many seas and oceans into distant lands. The spectacular aspect of the distance between England and India or France and Indochina cannot be underestimated. Furthermore, the British and French overlord could be, so to speak, distinguished from the subjugated race at first sight. The Russian imperial thrusts were directed against peoples of white or near-white skins. The Russian domination over the Baltic, Caucasian, or Central Asian Turkic peoples is, as it were, less "visible" indeed This is certainly one of the reasons for which the Asians and Africans refuse to see or label conquests, exploitation, and oppression within the white race as "colonialism" or "imperialism." Another reason is the skillful Soviet presentation of the polyethnic federal formula as *the* solution of the problem of harmonizing political and economic unity with ethnic and cultural diversity. The effect of the Soviet propaganda has been considerably increased by the inaccessibility of the Soviet Union, especially its border areas. For a long time a travel ban based on a plausible security argument (because the Soviet non-Russian territories are mostly on the Union's periphery) has prevented research and verification of the Soviet federal myth and the reality of authoritarian centralization.

Yet, even before World War II and throughout it, some disturbing facts did come to surface and did begin to challenge the Soviet image of political unity and ethnic diversity. During Stalin's bloody purges of 1936 many non-Russian Communists were executed following their "confessions" of anti-Soviet agitation for the right of the Ukrainians, Georgians, and Armenians to exercise national self-determination. During the war the German Volga autonomous republic was liquidated and its German-speaking population was sent to Siberian camps. Cities bearing the German names of the founding fathers of proletarian internationalism, such as Karl Marx-Stadt and Friedrich Engels-Stadt, became Russian, though ghost towns. Stalin provided a final and paradoxical postscript to his theory and concept of national self-determination: During the war two of the national groups that were promised the right of secession in 1917 in the previously quoted manifesto by Lenin and Stalin, the Chechens and the Crimean Tatars, were partly liquidated and partly re-settled for the alleged collective guilt of unreliability and collaboration with the enemy.

While colonialism persisted in Asia and Africa—and while the persecution of nationalist sentiment within the Soviet Union was limited to the wartime period—the Soviet immunity against any suspicion of colonialism continued for some time even after World War II. Only an occasional specialist studied the fate and the aspirations of the non-Russian peoples of the USSR.

With the end of Western colonialism in Asia and Africa and with an increased knowledge about the internal situation in the USSR, the Soviet solution, or lack of one, of the national question was bound to come under closer scrutiny.

In the United Nations General Assembly in 1962 the Permanent Representative of the United Kingdom, Sir Patrick Dean, protested against Britain's being called a colonial power by the Soviet Union, whose own colonialism did not entitle it to assume the pose of a champion of the rights of dependent peoples; specifically, Sir Patrick Dean then made the following comparisons:

> In 1815 the whole of Ceylon came under British rule at the same time as Azerbaijan was being occupied by Russia. Ceylon achieved its independence in 1947; when, may we ask, can we hope to see Azerbaijan independent? Nigeria and Ghana came under British influence in the middle of the 19th century. . . . The same period saw the Russian conquest of the independent states of Central Asia with their ancient civilization; the last independent Kazakh State submitted in 1854, the conquest of the three Uzbek states of Turkestan was completed by 1876, and the whole of Turkmenia was finally subjugated and annexed in the early 1880s. After nearly a century of British rule Ghana became independent in 1957 and Nigeria in 1960; what is the target date for the independence of the Soviet Central Asian territories?
>
> After some years of British occupation, Cyprus was formally annexed by Great Britain in 1914; some three years previously, in 1911, Tannu Tuva was occupied by the Russians and declared a protectorate. Cyprus became independent in 1960; we trust that Soviet plans for the independence of Tannu Tuva [16] will soon be made.

[16] Since 1961 Tannu Tuva has had the status of an Autonomous Soviet Socialist Republic. It is located on the northern boundary of the People's Republic of Mongolia and is part of the Russian Soviet Federated Socialist Republic (RSFSR).

Territories occupied by the British Government in the course of the 1914/1918 war were placed under the League of Nations mandate after that war, and after the Second World War those that had not achieved independence [like Iraq, Syria, Lebanon, and Palestine] were placed under United Nations Trusteeship.[17] Tanganyika, the last of these, became independent in 1961. What of the territories acquired by the Soviet Union during and since World War II, notably Estonia, Latvia, Lithuania, South Sakhalin and the Kuriles [former Japanese possessions]?

The British criticism of the Soviet domestic record was certainly not a result of a tender concern for the fate of the non-Russian minorities in the Soviet Union. The Cold War played here, as in everything else, its role. This does not mean that Sir Patrick's comparative questions were without substance, and, which is perhaps even more important, without an important echo inside the Soviet Union herself. In a period of increased contact with the outside world, of liberalization, and of ferment among the Russian youth, questions similar to those of Sir Patrick were bound to be asked by the younger generation examining Russian history, both before Bolshevism and after it. A significant trace of such an echo may be found in the novel *The Trial Begins* by Abraham Tertz (that is, Andrei B. Sinavsky, condemned to imprisonment in 1967 for having had his novels published abroad).

The novel begins with a discussion between Seryozha, a young student who had difficulties with his history teacher, and the student's father, Globov, who is the City Public Prosecutor:

Seryozha ran into his own room and brought back several notebooks covered with his minute writing.

"So what I couldn't understand was [the history teacher's] saying that Yermak's [18] conquest of Siberia was just, and so was the crushing of Shamyl's [19] rebellion. . . ."

[17] The mandate and trusteeship systems as special types of territorial associations are discussed in Chap. 6.

[18] In 1581 cossack Yermak Timofeyevich stormed the capital of the Tatar state Sibir on the river Irtysh. From that area, brought under the control of Ivan the Terrible, the Russian "manifest destiny," the conquest of the northern third of Asia, began.

[19] Shamyl: last leader of the anti-Russian resistance in the Caucasian region in the nineteenth century.

"Yes," said Globov thoughtfully, "we can't do without Siberia. Not without the Caucasus. Oil. Manganese. You know the folk-song? 'Upon the peaceful bank of Irtysh, Yermak sat deep in thought.' Remember?"

"And when the English conquered India, they also . . ."

"You stop making such comparisons," cried Globov in alarm. "What have the English got to do with it? Where do you think we're living? in England?"

"But historically speaking . . ."

"Historically speaking my foot! Study your history but don't forget the present day. Think of what we're building!" [20]

This dialogue illustrates much more than a generation gap: it points to the inevitability of comparison between imperial decentralization and liquidation in the West and the continuation of imperial controls in the Soviet Union. It would, indeed, be astonishing if the storm of nonclass nationalism that so irresistibly swept through Africa and Asia and affected also such old, established multiethnic states as Belgium, Canada, and even Switzerland (separatism in the canton of Bern) were to stop so very conveniently at the gates of Soviet Russia.

The polyethnic character of the Soviet federation confronts its Russian leaders with a painful dilemma: they cannot disregard the eruptive strength of partly recognized and partly suppressed ethnic emotions, especially in the era in which we live, and yet they cannot overlook the fact that the present ethnic sub-divisions conflict not only with the desired goal of political unity but also, perhaps more importantly, with the requirement of broader superethnic regional economic planning. In October, 1963, a conference in Frunze, capital of the Kirghiz Republic in Central Asia, concluded by recommending the establishment of scholarly study groups in Central Asia, Transcaucasia, and the Baltic region to devise ways of replacing the old federal divisions by lumping together into three broader regional confederations, first, the five Central Asian republics, second, the three Caucasian republics, and third, the three Baltic republics. According to *Sovetskaya Kirghizia* (October 18, 1963) the conference con-demned the "pseudoscientific theory" of linguistic purity, hailed the importance of the Russian language as a means of communi-

[20] Abram Tertz, *The Trial Begins*. New York: Vintage Books (Knopf and Random House), 1960, pp. 16–17.

cation among the Soviet non-Russian groups, and demanded an investigation of nationalistic bourgeois ideology that might oppose the intended mergers of ethnic territorial communities. *The New York Times* correspondent in Moscow (October 20, 1963) added the following comment:

> The Soviet Union is quietly pressing a far-reaching plan to convert the present structure of national republics into a system of regional federation that would de-emphasize the distinctiveness of non-Russian ethnic groups.[21]

The internal record of the Soviet polyethnic formula is bound to be placed into a much sharper focus also in the light of the Soviet behavior in Eastern Europe, especially the two Soviet armed interventions in the domestic affairs of the allied Communist states of Hungary (1956) and Czechoslovakia (1968). Two non-Russian nations outside the state boundaries of Soviet Russia proper were denied the right of political self-determination and the right of secession from an alliance. If the right of self-determination is not respected by the Soviet Union *outside* its borders, how real indeed can be the autonomy of its thirty to forty ethnic territorial groups *within* its borders? The official explanation of the Soviet right of intervention, deemed superior to the right of self-determination and subsequently known as the "Brezhnev Doctrine," is worth quoting:

> We cannot ignore the assertions made in some places that the actions of the five socialist countries [that is, invasion of Czechoslovakia] run counter to the Marxist-Leninist principle of sovereignty and the rights of self-determination. . . .
>
> As a social system, world socialism . . . is indivisible and its defense is the common cause of all Communists. . . .
>
> The demand for . . . Czechoslovakia's withdrawal from the socialist community . . . would have come into conflict

[21] Compare Moscow's criticism of the performance of the Central Asian Moslem Soviet Republic, Tadzhikistan. On January 13, 1969, the party journal *Partiinaya Zhizn* (*Party Life*) published a sharp attack of the alleged Tadzhik toleration of nationalism, Moslem customs such as child marriages, relegation of women to a secondary position in society, corruption, and falsified production reports. The Tadzhiks were given one year to put their house in order.

with its own vital interests and would have been detrimental to the other socialist states. . . .

Discharging their internationalist duty toward the fraternal peoples of Czechoslovakia and defending their own socialist gains, the USSR and the other socialist states had to act decisively and they did act against the antisocialist forces in Czechoslovakia.[22]

One may find here almost an echo of Winston Churchill's famous statement, made in London in 1942: "I have not become the King's Prime Minister in order to preside over the liquidation of the British empire." Leonid Brezhnev's present version would be, "I have not become the Party's First Secretary in order to preside over the erosion of the Socialist Commonwealth." Somehow, Kipling's imperialistic slogan of the "white man's burden" has become the "Soviet man's burden."

A final note on the Western and Soviet attempts at simultaneous secession-accession within their respective imperial systems suggests itself. Paradoxically, Britain, France, Holland, and Belgium were parliamentary democracies at home while they oppressed and exploited their colonial possessions overseas. In the "mother country" free press and free opposition were able to carry the colonial protest right to the very heart of the colonial system. No such possibility of domestic criticism of the nation's colonial behavior has ever existed in Russia, where the authoritarian methods of silencing all criticism have been applied not only to the subjugated non-Russian groups but also to the "imperial" Russian nation itself. Similarly, authoritarianism at the home base at least partly explains the durability of the Portuguese imperial structure and the delay in the liquidation of the leftovers of the Spanish colonial empire in Africa. When, belatedly, Spanish Equatorial Guinea became an independent state and the 126th member of the United Nations, it was noted that the right of political self-determination granted by Franco to Africans was actually greater than that enjoyed by Spaniards, Catalans, and Basques in Spain.

[22] "Sovereignty and International Duties of Socialist Countries," *Pravda* (Moscow, September 25, 1968).

SIX
UNIONS
AND ASSOCIATIONS
OF STATES

We must all hang together, or assuredly we shall all
hang separately.

BENJAMIN FRANKLIN (July 4 1776)

The Contracting Parties declare that they will act
in a spirit of friendship and cooperation with a view
to further developing and fostering economic
and cultural intercourse with one another.

THE WARSAW PACT (Articles 4, 5, and 8)

It shall be the aim of the [European] Community,
by establishing a Common Market and progressively
approximating the economic politics of Member
States, to promote throughout the Community
a harmonious development of economic activities
. . . an accelerated raising of the standard of living
and closer relations between its Member States.

THE TREATY OF ROME (1957—Article 2)

When bad men combine, all good must associate,
else they will fall, one by one, an unpitied sacrifice
in a contemptible struggle.

EDMUND BURKE (*Thoughts on the Cause
of the Present Discontent*)

Movement from diversity to unity may result in either a loose or a tightly structured association of territorial communities. Such a process of aggregation may be based on compulsion or consent; often it is a mixture of both, as is usually the case in politics.

Forcible aggregation of territorial communities against their will is called *imperialism.*[1] The term is, however, controversial for many reasons. One of the reasons is that *imperialism* describes the process of territorial conquests by military force or by indirect political or economic controls as well as describes the result of the process, the empire and its preservation or defense. Imperialism as a dynamic process and imperialism as a defense of the status quo represent two different situations, usually occurring in different historical periods and differently affecting the rest of the world. Building the Roman Empire, for instance, extended from the period of the Republic (from the Punic Wars to the Republic's overthrow by Julius Caesar). When Augustus gave Rome and its domination over conquered territories the constitution of an empire, the imperialistic expansion of Rome essentially came to an end.[2]

REASONS FOR IMPERIALISM

Another controversy concerns the reasons for the imperialist flow of nationalism over its natural banks and the imperialist absorption of the "near or distant territory of reluctant and unassimilable people."[3]

According to Lenin, empire building and struggles between competing empires are the unavoidable results of the insoluble contradictions in capitalism; monopoly capitalism, a very high stage in capitalist evolution, was the quintessence of imperialism. "Monopolies, oligarchy, the striving for domination instead of striving for liberty, the exploitation of an increasing number of

[1] *Imperialism* is defined by the *Encyclopaedia Britannica* (1960, Vol. 12, p. 121) as "a policy of a state aiming at establishing control beyond its borders over people unwilling to accept such controls."

[2] Hans J. Morgenthau, *Politics among Nations.* New York: Knopf, 1967, p. 43.

[3] J. A. Hobson, *Imperialism: A Study.* London: Constable, 1905, p. 4.

small or weak nations by an extremely small group of the richest or most powerful nations—all these have given birth to those distinctive features of imperialism which compel us to define it as parasitic or decaying capitalism." [4] In Lenin's economic interpretation of imperialism, capitalism appears as a monster that inevitably grows and moves toward its equally inevitable doom. It is a moribund, all-evil monster that nothing can save, but its final doom may be sped up by revolutionary action.

Lenin, in his polemics with the social democratic leader Karl Kautsky, whom Lenin called "the principal Marxian theoretician of the epoch of the so-called Second International (1889–1914)," [5] opposed any departure from his theory of capitalist determinism. Especially venomous were Lenin's attacks against Kautsky's arguments that imperialism was not an inescapable but only a preferred policy of capitalist states.

According to Kautsky, adoption of an imperialist policy of annexations by the capitalist systems is a matter of choice, not of iron inevitability. Kautsky opposed Lenin's equation "capitalism = imperialism = wars" and spoke of a possibility of peace among imperialist nations (that is, a cooperative global union of world imperialism) based on an agreement "jointly to exploit the world." Kautsky labeled such an interimperialist union "ultra-imperialism"; Lenin called it "ultra-nonsense" and insisted that a "general alliance embracing *all* the imperialist powers [is] *inevitably* nothing more than a 'truce' in periods between wars." [6] Accusing Kautsky of sentimental attitudes, he called his theory admitting of interimperialist cooperation and peace "the most reactionary method of consoling the masses with hopes of permanent peace being possible under capitalism, distracting their attention from sharp antagonisms and acute problems of the present era, and directing it along illusory perspectives of an imaginary 'ultra-imperialism' of the future." [7]

In contrast with both Lenin and Kautsky, many authors tended to view imperialism, not as a highest stage of economic

[4] V. I. Lenin, *Selected Works: Imperialism and Imperialist War* (*1914–1917*). New York: International Publishers (printed in the Soviet Union), n.d., p. 115.

[5] Lenin, *Imperialism,* p. 82.

[6] Lenin, *Imperialism,* p. 110.

[7] Lenin, *Imperialism,* p. 109.

development, but as an antiquated leftover from "early centuries of animal struggle for existence . . . a depraved choice of national life, imposed by self-seeking interests which appeal to the lust of quantitative acquisitiveness and of forceful domination." [8] Joseph A. Schumpeter, in particular, insisted that imperialism was an atavistic, precapitalist "psychological disposition acquired in the dim past" that under capitalism "will wither and die." Trained in economic rationalism, people under capitalism "left no sphere of life unrationalized, questioning everywhere about themselves, the social structure, the state, the ruling class. . . . Everything that is purely instinctual, everything insofar as it is purely instinctual, is driven into the background by this development. . . . *It is a basic fallacy to describe imperialism as a necessary phase of capitalism.*" [9]

Other authors preferred to explain causes of imperialistic drives by a mixture of motives such as wrongly or rightly perceived needs of defense, ideological messianism, including "white man's burden" or "communist man's burden," search for glory, or profit, which in an era of nationalist egocentrism may attract any system, capitalist, socialist, or communist.

Not all forcible imperial unions were established by sword and fire. A milder method of conquest is the transfer of territorial communities from one rule to another without asking their inhabitants for their opinion or preferences in the matter. A territorial community has sometimes been annexed in the form of a royal wedding gift. The Austrian Empire, for instance, grew mostly by dynastic agreement and marriages: *Bella gerunt alii; tu, felix Austria, nube*—a Latin sentence, ascribed to King Mathias Corvinus, that may be translated "While others wage wars, thou, lucky Austria, shouldst expand through marriages." Territorial and ethnic groups so annexed were bound to claim their territorial and national due when democratization of political life, defeats in wars, and examples of successful secessionism elsewhere began to challenge the authority of the kings as well as their territorial agreements. The Austro-Hungarian Empire finally split into its territorial-ethnic units at the end of World War I; the international mood of the era and the

[8] Hobson, *Imperialism,* p. 324.

[9] Joseph A. Schumpeter, *Imperialism and Social Classes.* New York: August M. Kelley, 1951, pp. 84–130 (*passim*).

military defeat of the empire on the European battlefields assured victory for the claim of self-determination on the part of Poland, Czechoslovakia, Rumania, and Yugoslavia.

Former interdynastic territorial agreements have modern parallels of sorts, summit meetings at which great powers divide and subdivide other nations' territories to suit their political or strategic conveniences. One such example was the Munich Conference in 1938, which handed a portion of Czechoslovakia to Nazi Germany. The decision was that of Germany, Italy, France, and England; Czechoslovakia was neither consulted nor admitted to the deliberation of the conference. Another example was the Moscow Conference in 1939 between the Nazi and Communist leaders, which resulted in erasing the whole of Poland from the map of Europe by halving it between the two expansionist systems. A third example was the Yalta Conference in 1945, when the United States, England, and Soviet Russia decided on the future territorial destinies of Poland and China. The official text of the Yalta Protocol says about the Polish territory that the "eastern frontier of Poland should follow the Curzon line with digressions from it in some regions to five to eight kilometres in favor of Poland. They recognize that Poland must receive [for this territorial loss] substantial accessions of territory on the North and West [at the expense of Germany]." As to China, the Yalta agreement provided for the Soviet take-over of former Japanese (extraterritorial) railroads in China (Manchuria) and the Chinese ports of Dairen and Port Arthur, and for the continuation of the separate status of Outer Mongolia (formerly, a part of imperial China) under Soviet tutelage. In the case of both Poland and China, the Yalta Protocol promised that the Polish and Chinese authorities should be consulted about the territorial changes in due course. With reference to China, however, the Protocol says with brutal frankness, "The Heads of the three Great Powers have agreed that these claims of the Soviet Union (with regard to China and Japan) shall be *unquestionably* fulfilled after Japan has been defeated [italics added]."

REASONS FOR VOLUNTARY UNIONS

In contrast with imperial unions, *voluntary* associations or unions of states are based on consent, that is, on a decision reached by two or more independent territorial communities, usually nation-states, to express their awareness of interdependence and their will to cooperate by explicitly agreeing to some common goals and some common procedures or machinery.

When nations beome aware of their community of interests or their interdependence, they usually find ways and means to cooperate. However, "not every community of interests, calling for common policies and common action, also calls for legal codification in an explicit alliance," [10] commonwealth, community or confederation. Because of an informal understanding, territorial communities act as if they were allies or confederates. This has been partly so in the case of Great Britain and the United States, from the proclamation of the Monroe Doctrine in 1823 to their first fully formalized alliance in NATO in 1949. Their cohesion and cooperative intimacy has often been superior to many other publicly proclaimed and celebrated alliances or confederations.

Why and under what conditions do some nations consider it useful to proceed one step beyond their informal cooperation and attempt a formal association (functional, economic, military, or political) or integration? "We still know little enough about the necessary prerequisites for successful integration [of territorial communities] and in what sequence they need to occur," concludes one recent study on regionalism and suggests that

> the necessary prerequisites for successful . . . political integration at the international level, particularly the union of formerly independent states . . . include a degree of cultural homogeneity, interdependence and the existence of formal institutions with substantial "spill-over." [11]

Geographic contiguity seems to be a powerful element in many territorial associations but certainly not in all. Many territorial states contain territorial units more or less widely separated by intervening bodies of water (the United States and Hawaii;

[10] Hans J. Morgenthau, "Alliances in Theory and Practice," in Arnold Wolfers, *Alliance Policy in the Cold War*. Baltimore: The Johns Hopkins Press, 1959, p. 184.

[11] Bruce M. Russett, "Delineating International Regions," in J. David Singer (ed.), *Quantitative International Politics*. New York: Free Press, 1968, p. 321.

Italy, Sardinia, and Sicily; France and Corsica; Australia and Tasmania; England and Northern Ireland) or by intervening land masses (the United States and Alaska; West Pakistan and East Pakistan; Germany and East Prussia [1919–1945]). If noncontiguity did not prevent political unity in the past, it is even less of a hindrance in the age of the jet and rapid communications. Much more important than geographic noncontiguity, as a recent study shows, are the political, ethnic, linguistic, or religious noncontiguities. The study also demonstrates how external pressures may unify widely separated communities, as, for instance, East Pakistan and West Pakistan against India.[12]

An external challenge seems to us the most frequent and effective catalyst for transforming the awareness of interdependence into concrete action and institutions.

By *external challenge* we mean environmental pressures, such as new economic, technological, or climatic problems or political events (for instance, the emergence of a nation whose goals and policies are perceived as a collective threat to a set of nations). Rather than a sudden outburst of humane and brotherly feelings among nations, such an external challenge makes it manifest to several territorial communities that they are indeed interdependent and their interests more compatible than they have thought and that they might be better off by combining their efforts and resources rather than by keeping their separate ways. When Benjamin Franklin described the choice confronting the revolutionaries gathered on July 4, 1776, to sign the Declaration of Independence as being one between hanging together or hanging separately, he rightly pointed to the most productive cause of fraternal unions: an external danger.

The dominantly defensive tone is clearly expressed in the Articles of Confederation. When listing the reasons for confederation in Article 3; "defense" is named first and the possibility of "attacks" last: "The said States hereby severally enter into a firm league of friendship with each other, for their common defense, the security of their liberties, and their mutual and general welfare, binding themselves to assist each other, against all force offered to, or attacks made upon them, or any of them,

[12] Richard L. Merritt, "Noncontiguity and Political Integration," paper presented to the American Political Science Association, New York, 1966, pp. 1–26.

on account of religion, sovereignty, trade, or any other pretence whatever." Numerous variations of Franklin's basic sentence have always been present in the minds of statesmen who are about to decide to limit their freedom of action in order more effectively to meet collectively a common challenge.

The effects of the aggregation of communities on others who have been left out have recently been analyzed in connection with the European Community, a magnet but at the same time a cause of counterintegrative reaction on the part of the nation-states on its periphery, especially the British-Scandinavian Free Trade Association. Being limited to only six nations (Germany, France, Italy, Belgium, Holland, and Luxembourg), it has also stimulated "the self-awareness and distinctiveness" of the Outer Seven (Free Trade Association). "In this sense economic confinement reflects and might ultimately contribute to political integration" [13] within the initial association and then, as a reflex, among the outsiders.

In examining associations or unions of states, the stress was on either their forcible beginnings (empires) or their voluntary beginnings (confederations or alliances). The voluntary aspect of territorial associations should now also be projected into their subsequent development. One can indeed, at least theoretically, imagine a component unit that initially surrenders its freedom of action with a knowledge that the new structure will be a rigid authoritarian order; all components agree they will have to merge and obey for their own good. The result will be a tightly knit system. Or, on the contrary, a very loose system may develop around the initial compact if it is so vague as to necessitate constant renegotiations of additional, more specific agreements for the purpose of implementation. The existence and continuation of such a union will be a "daily plebiscite" (a term used by Ernest Renan in reference to the existence of a nation). Only consent by all will guarantee implementation by all; or as Alexander Hamilton had put it in the *Federalist* (No. 15),

> In our case the concurrence of thirteen distinct sovereign wills is requisite, under the Confederation, to the com-

[13] Hayward Alker, Jr., and Donald Puchala, "Trends in Economic Partnership: The North Atlantic Area, 1928–1963," in Singer, *Quantitative International Politics*, pp. 315–316.

plete execution of every important measure that proceeds from the Union.

Whatever the original delegation of authority from the territorial components to the central authority has been, it may undergo subsequent formal or informal changes. The distribution of authority may remain stabilized at the originally agreed-on level, but it may be, by common accord, expanded further from the existing diversity toward a tighter unity or, on the contrary, contracted from unity to greater diversity. What has been integrated by agreement may also—by agreement or otherwise—disintegrate. In most territorial associations, the delegation of power to the central authority remains, *in principle,* not only amendable but also often entirely revocable. We say "in principle" because in reality asymmetric territorial associations that combine powerful units with very weak ones may distort the principle beyond recognition. The weak members of an asymmetric association may subsequently desire to but may no longer dare to oppose the dominant group. This group may be in the process of successfully transforming an initially voluntary and highly decentralized association into a close parallel with a forcible and tightly centralized imperial union. This was so, for instance, in the German Confederation (*Der Deutsche Bund*) of 1815, when a few decades after its birth it fell under the domination of Prussia and Austria.

In territorial associations, conditional membership and conditional participation of the component units usually manifest themselves in three ways:

1. The right of secession is often retained by the member units. This is so in many alliances, international organizations such as the League of Nations or the United Nations, and some confederations.

2. The principle of unanimity in all major questions is made part of the basic agreement, thus assuring all the member units of their right to veto such decisions. Secession is not necessary because the component units are bound by a common decision insofar as they have individually and severally consented to them. This is the usual principle present in most alliance treaties, with the exception of the Organization of American States, which will be analyzed later.

3. The principle of unanimity is limited only to the fundamental agreement on the delegation of power to the central authority; and amendment of the original compact is subject to consent by all. This was so, for instance, in the United States under its first Constitution, the Articles of Confederation of 1777. The right of secession was implicitly ruled out. The very title of the document spoke of a *perpetual* union: "Articles of Confederation and Perpetual Union between the States of New-hampshire, Massachusetts-Bay, Rhode Island and Providence Plantations, Connecticut, New-York, New-Jersey, Pennsylvania, Delaware, Maryland, Virginia, North Carolina, South Carolina and Georgia."

And Article 13 repeats: "The Union shall be perpetual." On important matters a decision by nine states was to bind all; in lesser matters a simple majority was sufficient. Article 9 expressed the principle as follows:

> The United States in Congress assembled shall never engage in a war, nor grant letters of marque and reprisal in time of peace, nor enter into any treaties or alliances, nor coin money, nor regulate the value thereof, nor ascertain the sums and expenses necessary for the defense and welfare of the United States, or any of them, nor emit bills, nor borrow money on the credit of the United States, nor appropriate money, nor agree upon the number of vessels of war, to be built or purchased, or the number of land or sea forces to be raised, nor appoint a commander in chief of the army or navy, unless nine States assent to the same: nor shall a question on any other point, except for adjourning from day to day be determined, unless by the votes of a majority of the United States in Congress assembled.

Any amendment of the Articles was, however, to be first accepted by "a Congress of the United States, and be afterwards confirmed by the Legislature of *every* State [Article 13; italics added]."

TYPES OF ASSOCIATIONS

A voluntary territorial association (the term as used in this study) represents an aggregate of territorial communities that have established some machinery in common while agreeing to some limitations on their freedom of action, be it only as little as, for example, a duty to consult with others prior to taking an important action, or as much as a duty to abide by a majority decision of the component units. The thirteen American states, for instance, accepted such an important limitation on their freedom of action while retaining their "sovereignty, freedom and independence, and every power, jurisdiction and right which is not by this confederation expressly delegated to the United States, in Congress assembled [Article 2]."

The agreement on delegation of power as well as its limitation does not, however, include (at least not at the present time) a commitment of the territorial communities to a merger into one supraterritorial nation. This is the line by which many authors distinguish a close alliance or a confederation, on the one hand, from a federal union, on the other. A union of states (which is an approximate translation of the quite convenient German term *Staatenbund*) differs from a federation (*Bundesstaat*) precisely because the latter creates a new (federal) nation and its state. Some alliances or confederations in the past finally led to federations. The Swiss federal union began as a defensive alliance, the Treaty of Everlasting Alliance of 1291; its present constitutional order was preceded by a confederation (1813–1848). The interdynastic association of German kings and princes, the German Confederation (*Der Deutsche Bund,* 1815–1866) was ultimately followed by the Weimar and now the Bonn federal unions. The United States Confederation (1777–1789) was transformed into a federation at the Philadelphia Convention. Other confederations or alliances, on the contrary, dissolved. Confederation (or an alliance) is sometimes the first step, at other times the last step, in formalized cooperation among nation-states. Western European associations of nation-states, some African trade or political associations, and new efforts of regional cooperation in Central America and South America contain the elements of hope that they may be but the first steps on the way to a confederation and ultimately perhaps federation.

Much will depend on the benefits derived from the common endeavor. The component units of any territorial association can never avoid asking themselves the question whether even a partial limitation of their freedom of action is commensurate with the benefits expected or obtained from their association with the other units that are (but should they be?) deemed to be identically interested, equally threatened, and similarily incapable of handling the new environmental challenges or opportunities by themselves. The uncertainty as to the measurement of sacrifice offered and benefits expected is part of the explanation for the retention by the territorial communities of a veto power or right of secession or of both. Rarely can an association of groups avoid also the suspicion that some member groups, like individual persons, may try to get out of the contract (*foedus,* the Latin term for "compact," from which the terms *federal* and *confederal* have been derived) more than they are ready to give. As in the animal kingdom, in territorial associations lions may also be members. And any "lion" may claim "I carry off the chief share because I am called the Lion [Phaedrus, A.D. 8]."

When and if a territorial association establishes some permanent machinery and a common authority, they are bound to reflect the composite nature of the union—usually in the form of a council, a congress, and an assembly, consisting of the representatives of the territorial communities. They may be either delegates of the executive branch of their states and serve therefore as ambassadors, mostly to transmit messages and suggestions from their governments to the common assembly; or they may be delegations of men who, in their respective communities, participate in the decision-making processes. The difference between delegates-ambassadors and delegates–policy makers is often blurred. In the United Nations, for instance, member nations are sometimes represented by the diplomatic civil servants, at other times by the policy makers (prime ministers, presidents, Communist party first secretaries, and foreign ministers). The representatives of the thirteen states in the Congress of the American Confederation seemed to have belonged to the policy makers' category rather than to the civil servants' category.

If the territorial association also establishes a military force for the purpose of common defense, it is usually a mosaic body rather than a unified body. If, however, a unified command is added, the composite armed force, equipped and trained under order, may undergo a significant transmutation and become a source of integrative, spill-over effects.

One recent study suggested a low-to-high ordering of spill-over effects of interterritorial institutions (armies, markets, parliamentary assemblies) established by territorial communities that have moved beyond the limits of informal cooperation or only occasional cooperation:

1. narrowly functional organizations
2. tariff unions
3. military alliances
4. economic unions such as common markets
5. political unions [14]

In a union of states a permanent common machinery is not endowed with any significant central coercive and tax-collecting powers. This is what distinguishes a nonfederal territorial association from a federal union. If such a common machinery acts upon the citizens of the component units directly, it does so only in minor matters. Generally, common decisions are implemented by each territorial member within its area and with regard to its citizens only.

Following is a list of some of the better-known voluntary associations or unions of states whose members have *not* decided to create a new federal nation-state; the component units have retained a greater or lesser portion of their freedom of action while voluntarily joining the association and agreeing on some common goals and some delegation of authority to a common machinery.

Their haphazard listing (in terms of both chronology and the nature of association) is deliberate; its purpose is to illustrate the sharp contrasts that we feel exist between their respective goals, institutions, cohesion, duration, size, and progress toward higher unity or dissolution. For various reasons the reader will feel uncertain about, resolutely deny, or unhesitantly apply the adjective *confederal* to them. When confronted with the great variety in form and goals of these territorial associations, the reader may resort to the time-honored device, saving all vague

---

[14] Amitai Etzioni, "Atlantic Union, the Southern Continents, and the United Nations," in Roger Fisher (ed.), *International Conflict and Behavioral Science*. New York: Basic Books, 1964.

definitions and refer to many of them (including perhaps the United Nations or the Cominform) as confederations *sui generis* and be thus neither wrong nor right. The following is a partial list of associations of states:

1. The French Community (1958)
2. The British Commonwealth (1931); (both examples of imperial decentralization and, therefore, a subject of analysis in Chap. 5)
3. The Andean Development Corporation (1968—Bolivia, Chile, Colombia, Ecuador, Peru, and Venezuela)
4. The German Confederacy (1815–1866)
5. Union of Central African States (1968—Chad, Central African Republic, and Congo-Brazzaville)
6. The Arab League (1945)
7. The "Confederation" of South Arabian sheikdoms [15]
8. The League of Nations (1919)
9. The East African Common Market (1968—Kenya, Uganda, and Tanzania)
10. The Southeast Asia Treaty Organization (1954—the United States, Great Britain, France, Australia, New Zealand, Thailand, Pakistan, and the Philippines)
11. The United States Confederacy (1777–1789)
12. The European Community (1952, 1958–1968—France, West Germany, Italy, Belgium, Holland, and Luxembourg)
13. The United Nations (1945)
14. Puerto Rico's association with the United States

[15] In 1968 nine sheikdoms, bordering on the Persian Gulf and the Arabian Sea, decided on their first steps leading toward a federation. The nine rulers established a Federal Council to act as both the Cabinet and legislature of this new interdynastic association. Its immediate tasks were described as being to prepare a new constitution, develop common currency and a postal system, and decide on a common national flag, anthem, and emblem.

Previous attempts at Arab federal unions proved failures: the federal union of Egypt, Syria, and Yemen, announced in 1958, was supposed to later include also Iraq and ultimately perhaps all the Arab states. In 1958 in a countermove, however, Iraq, then under King Faisal, and Jordan announced their federal union with the hope that Saudi Arabia might later join their federal state. None of these Arab federal attempts have succeeded so far because of dynastic and personal rivalries.

15. The Organization of American States (1947—Twenty-one American republics) [16]
16. The Comintern (1919–1943) and the Cominform (1947–1956)
17. The Warsaw Pact (1955) and the North Atlantic Treaty Organization (1949)
18. The mandate and trust systems (1919 and 1945)

THE EUROPEAN COMMUNITIES

Three territorial associations, interlocked and overlapping, today form what is usually referred to as the Western European Community, the first step, according to some, to the United States of Western Europe. They are the European Coal and Steel Community (1952), the European Economic Community (Common Market, 1958), and the European Atomic Energy Community (Euratom, 1958). Their membership is identical: Belgium, France, Holland, Italy, Luxembourg, and West Germany. Their structures are similar with some institutions in common; the spirit is also similar: *functionalism,* marked by its hope that cooperation in specific critical economic areas will spread to all and by habit in common workshop transfer cooperation to the political level to such an extent that a supranational Western European state may emerge. Not all participants share such a hope, but all are in basic agreement as to the present benefits of the structure, even if further steps are never to be taken. France, in particular, insists on the loose associational features of the whole arrangement. President de Gaulle expressed this succinctly when he referred to the unity of Europe as that of fatherlands, a unity combined with emphasis on separate nationalisms—*l'Europe des patries.* As noted previously, all associations of states may be plagued by suspicions with regard to the numerically or economically most powerful component. This is also so in Western Europe. Germany often resents the French tendency to use the Community for the promotion of the

[16] "The ideal of restoration of union is persistent in Central American thought. . . . Four of the Central American Constitutions include rather dramatic references to the aspiration for union . . . business correspondence is addressed accordingly: San Salvador, El Salvador, C.A." James L. Busey, *Western Political Quarterly.* 1961.

French economic, diplomatic, and military ambitions. This was particularly noticeable when the French opposed British entry into the Community and when de Gaulle insisted on his *force de frappe;* West Germany seemed to imply that its prosperity is indirectly taxed to pay for de Gaulle's atomic toys. On the other hand, France seems still to dread the German dominance, partly because of Germany's superiority in industrial and technological power, partly in view of the French memories of the Nazi conquests. These memories may nearly completely fade away as Germany today has nearly forgotten the French imperialistic expansion under Napoleon, an expansion that today is a matter of interest only for students of history. But the natural superiority of Germany in economy and population is and will remain a problem. Since the 1870s, France has tried to counterbalance Germany by a system of alliances with the European East and England. In this diplomatic effort to make up for its own relative weakness, France has, however, failed to prevent being conquered by Germany. In this connection, the Western European Community is seen by some as an entirely new pattern of taming the natural superiority of Germany, which France and some other European nations are reluctant to accept. In Morgenthau's words, "the other nations of Western Europe are trying to draw, as it were, Germany into their arms in order to disarm it and to make the superior strength of Germany innocuous. The European communities are, in other words, an attempt of fusing a superior power with an inferior one for the purpose of creating a common control of their pooled strength." [17]

The official illustration of the European institutions is reproduced in Figures 6–1 and 6–2.

The confederal features of the European Community are an agreement among the participants (the Treaties of Rome, 1957, in particular); common goals, common machinery (or machineries, as just shown); and the principle of sovereignty retained by its members, who have the right to leave the Community and have made the decisions of some of the Community's organs dependent on their unanimous consent. The European Community cannot by itself "revise its own constitution, nor be a

[17] Hans J. Morgenthau, *Politics among Nations.* 4th ed. New York: Knopf, 1967, p. 512.

Figure 6–1   The institutions of the European Community—1962

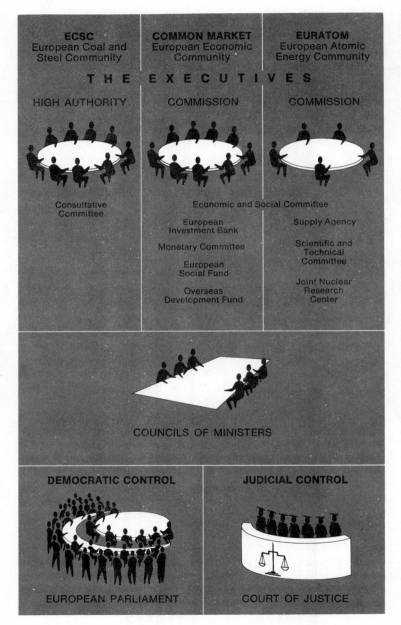

Source: The European Community Information Service.

**Figure 6–2   The institutions of the European
Community—since 1967**

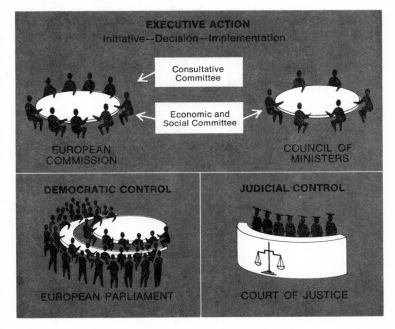

Source: The European Community Information Service.

substitute to its members unto the external world except in the
field of trade policy; and, above all, it is not based on a political
consciousness and a political will." [18]

There are some features, however, that go beyond our
definition of a confederal system. In particular, the executive
organ of the *Coal and Steel Community* approximates a supranational (federal) agency. It is supposed to act "in complete
independence, in the general interest of the Community," without instructions from any government. The nine members of the
High Authority resemble a cabinet that is collectively "responsible for assuring the achievement of the purposes stated in the

[18] Dusan Sidjanski, "Aspects Fédératifs de la Communauté Eu-
ropéenne," paper presented at the Sixth World Congress of the International Political Science Association, Geneva, 1964, p. 32. The author
speaks of federal features where our study refers to the confederal ones.

Treaty" (Article 8). The High Authority acts by vote of a majority of its members (Article 13). Here the confederal principle of unanimity has been abandoned. The veto power was retained by the member nations only for the first appointments; eight of the nine members are appointed by the six member nations by agreement among themselves; the appointment is for six years. The elected eight elect the ninth.

The sphere of activities for the High Authority in the Coal and Steel Community is broad indeed: for the purpose of creating a common market for coal and steel, the High Authority must be

> a management consultant, an investment banker, a policeman, and a research agency. It must also make sure that coal and steel producers produce, that consumers buy their products on equal terms and at equitable prices, that living and working conditions of the labor force are improved, that international trade in coal and steel is fostered, plants modernized, quality improved, efficiency raised, and natural resources developed and used rationally. For motivation the governments rely on private enterprise.[19]

The *European Economic Community* was established by the Treaty of Rome in 1958. The purpose was to create a customs union by installments within a period of twelve years, that is, by providing in 1968 for a free movement of goods, labor, service, and capital within the community (a fact as of July 1, 1968). It also aimed at coordination of agricultural policies (which has proved difficult) and transport systems. A social fund was established to compensate for national losses resulting from the application of freer trading policies and affecting both the labor force and industries. In all associations of states, the problem of the cost of the union must be considered, because in many cases tariff barriers have protected employment and production, which without such protective barriers or government incentives would succumb in free competition. One observer noted that in the Western European communities not only goods, services, and capital but also

[19] Donald C. Blaisdell, *International Organization*. New York: Ronald, 1966, p. 229.

several undesirable, negative elements have moved freely among their members; for instance, "one can even speak of the importation of inflation into Germany." [20] Thus the Western European Community affects the citizens of constituent states directly. This represents another departure from the confederal system and movement toward the federal system.

The *European Atomic Community,* which was expected to replace the dwindling resources of coal and supplies of oil by a rapid development of atomic plants and atomic fuels has not proved successful; the progress has been slow, evidently complicated by the military aspects of any atomic development, however nonmilitary in theory it may be. Furthermore, new supplies of oil and natural gas made cooperation in the atomic field less urgent than seemed to be the case in 1958.

Nevertheless, it should be said that the total progress of the Western European communities was remarkable. The combined GNP of the six Community members has grown 52 percent (to $253 billion), whereas trade among them has risen by 238 percent (to an estimated $23 billion in 1967). We speak here, of course, of economic achievements.

Political integration has made little progress, mostly because of France's objections. In the economic sphere there are some complaints that were clearly not anticipated by the founding fathers of a United Europe (Jean Monnet and Robert Schuman in particular). These European complaints concern the fact that the broad perspectives and opportunities that the European Community offers seem to be better understood and used by the American industries and corporations, who are more accustomed to flexible planning in vast territorial dimensions than are the more conservative and often parochial Western European enterprises. In the influential Western European best seller 1967–1968) *The American Challenge,* the author, Jean-Jacques Servan-Schreiber, points to the fact that "nine tenths of American investment in Europe is financed from European sources. In other words, *we pay them to buy us.*" [21] This statement is supported by the figures taken from the *Survey of Current Busi-*

---

[20] Sidjanski, "Aspects Fédératifs," p. 1.

[21] Jean-Jacques Servan-Schreiber, *The American Challenge* (*Le Défi Américain*). New York: Atheneum, 1968, p. 14.

ness, which indicates that the American investment of $4 billion in Europe in 1965 came mostly from loans from the European capital market (Euro-issues, 55 percent), subsidies from European governments and internal financing from local earnings (35 percent), and direct dollar transfers from the United States (10 percent). In 1968, under the headline "The American Rush on the Euro-Market," the Paris daily *Le Monde* (August 27) reported that in the first six months of 1968 the American enterprises further borrowed from the European capital market (Euro-issues) $1,097,000,000; in contrast was the borrowing of only $72 million by Europe and $538 million by the rest of the world. The American share in European loans was then 64 percent.

These are facts that made Servan-Schreiber say in 1967 with both admiration and bitterness:

> Already, in the ninth year of the Common Market, this European Market is basically American in organization. . . . While French, German, or Italian firms are still groping around in the new open spaces provided by the Treaty of Rome, afraid to emerge from the dilapidated shelter of their old habits, American industry has gauged the terrain and is now rolling from Naples to Amsterdam with the ease and the speed of Israeli tanks in the Sinai desert. . . . While Common Market officials are still looking for a law which will permit the creation of European-wide business, American firms, with their own headquarters, already form the framework of a real "Europeanization." [22]

Concluding our examination of the confederal features of the European communities and of their American dimensions, we should note that in addition to some elements that seem to go beyond the usual definition of confederation (such as the majoritarian decisions and collective responsibility of the High Authority in the Coal and Steel Community), there are also some other ones that are below the level of very loose confederations or alliances: all the Community members have retained and exercise their freedom of action in foreign affairs and even in defense matters. France insisted for a long time not only on her

[22] Servan-Schreiber, *The American Challenge,* pp. 3, 6, 29.

independent *force de frappe* and her right to block the British application for membership in the Common Market, but also on her special relations with China, Eastern Europe, and French Canada and on her somewhat strained relations with the United States.

THE UNITED NATIONS

This is not the place to explore in detail the Charter, structure, and working of the United Nations organization. Often, the United Nations is defined as the loosest possible association of territorial states that does not even deserve the label of *organization* (and much less *confederation*) because one basic ingredient is clearly missing: any semblance of a common goal. There is not even a real community of fear because there is no external threat to the security and well-being of member nations. The threat is internal. Some would argue, however, that there is at least a basic agreement as to the desirability of creating and maintaining an international debating and negotiating forum with a near-universal membership; there is also a common and permanently working machinery, the Security Council, the Secretariat, the International Court of Justice, the specialized functional agencies incorporated into the United Nations system, and the regularly meeting Economic and Social Council, the Trusteeship Council, and the United Nations General Assembly with its standing and *ad hoc* committees. There are also police contingents, created *ad hoc,* for the purpose of peace-keeping operations (the Middle East, the Congo, Cyprus); as in confederations, they are composite rather than integrated armed forces. The United Nations decisions affect the citizens of the component units only through their national sovereign intermediaries. And there is the right of secession, which so far has been invoked only once, by Indonesia in 1965; two years later Indonesia joined the United Nations again.

The United Nations has adopted two different formulas for voting in its two main organs, the general Assembly and the Security Council. A two-thirds majority decides on important matters in the General Assembly. This seemingly qualified majority principle has been, however, largely emptied of its significance by the provision that the General Assembly's decisions are never binding; they are resolutions or recommendations that leave it to the addressees whether to abide by them or not. At most, such resolutions contain some elements of moral persuasion, which in our world means depressingly little.

In contrast, the decisions of the Security Council are binding. The Security Council has fifteen members: five Great Powers (that is, the powers that in 1945 recognized each other as Great), who are the Security Council's *permanent* members; ten *nonpermanent* members (small and medium powers) that are elected by the General Assembly for a term of two years. The voting formula in the Security Council is a combination of the unanimity and majority principles. To be binding upon all member nations, the decision must be based on a unanimous consent of the five permanent members (a negative vote constitutes the famous veto) to which any four votes from among the ten nonpermanent members must be added. Such a decision by the majority of nine out of fifteen members of the Security Council is binding upon all because all member nations have agreed "to accept and carry out the decisions of the Security Council in accordance with the present Charter [Article 25]." Such a binding decision made by nine nations in behalf of all could, for instance, order all the members to penalize an aggressor and to discriminate in favor of his victim—this could possibly make a neutral country violate its own neutrality. This possibility, however theoretical it may appear, has caused traditionally neutral Switzerland to refuse membership in the United Nations. Switzerland, however, was a member of the League of Nations, because that association of sovereign states was ruled by the principle of unanimity. Switzerland is also a member of the specialized functional agencies (see page 11) of the United Nations, whose decisions can never be considered legally binding.

If and when the five Great Powers, representing the maximum capability to punish or reward (that is, to enforce the Security Council's decisions), were to agree among themselves (and assuming that these powers could always easily find four other nations to agree with them among the other ten nonpermanent members), the Security Council would then become a World Cabinet and could, conceivably, rule over and dictate to the world. The member nations that by their adherence to the Charter have indeed accepted a limitation of their independence might live in peace but also in total subordination to the Big Five Brothers and their four fellow travelers—possibly a nightmare for some. A member nation could secede from the world organization, but there would be nowhere to go in a world dominated by the joint dictate of five atomic superpowers. Our image assumes that mainland China has replaced the symbolic one on Taiwan as a permanent member of the Security Council. For the time being, Taiwan has the Great Power veto, whereas the People's Republic of China is not a member but has the power ingredients, the hydrogen bomb and missiles, that in our world determine Great Power status.

Because such a situation of total or permanent agreement among the Big Five seems highly improbable, the member nations have to accept another type of international nightmare, the Great Powers' constant mutual mistrust and hostility and, therefore, their collective incapacity to dictate or to do anything at all. The result is collective insecurity under the aegis of the United Nations.

Originally, there was a plan to provide the Security Council with a permanent police force; it was to be built around the nucleus of the five Great Powers' armed forces (Article 43). The continual animosity and distrust among the Big Five amply demonstrated that this confederal feature was, to say the least, premature. When occasional peace-keeping operations in the Middle East, the Congo, or Cyprus were agreed upon, one of the essential conditions was that the troops of the Great Powers would not participate; only small and generally uncommitted nations were to send their contingents to compose the *ad hoc* security forces. Seemingly taken out of the Great Powers' context, these operations could not, however, escape the adverse effects of the Great Powers' disagreements as to the scope and goals of such operations and the resulting unwillingness on their part to finance them.

The political discord among great and small powers necessarily also affects the allegedly nonpolitical functional activities of the United Nations, which are directed or coordinated by the Economic and Social Council and the specialized functional agencies affiliated with it. The United Nations' specialized functional agencies may be divided into two broad categories: [23] (1) the agencies whose major purpose is to facilitate communications among nations, such as the Universal Postal Union (UPU), the International Telecommunication Union (ITU), the International Civil Aviation Organization (ICAO), the World Meteorological Organization (WMO), and the Inter-Governmental Maritime Consultative Organization (IMCO); and (2) the agencies that specialize in specific economic, social, humanitarian, health, or educational activities with the hope that cooperation among nations in these fields will stimulate their cooperation in political fields. We may find in this latter category the following: the International Labor Organization (ILO), the United Nations Educational, Scientific, and Cultural Organization (UNESCO), the World Health Organization (WHO), the Food and Agriculture Organization (FAO), the International Atomic Energy Agency (IAEA, which deals with peaceful uses of atomic energy), the International Bank for Reconstruction and Development (IBRD or World Bank), and the International Monetary Fund (IMF).

The Economic and Social Council and the specialized functional agencies represent what is called the "functional approach to peace." They are based on the proposition that international cooperation in nonpolitical humanitarian, economic, and other functional fields is a prerequisite for the ultimate solution of political conflicts and for the elimination of international violence. The theory is appealing because it seems indeed possible to separate a group of international social or economic ills and to subject them to treatment in an international operation room that the nations enter after having washed political viruses off their hands and having donned politically sterilized overalls. There, in the Economic and Social Council (UNESCO), they can hopefully concentrate on issues that do not divide the nations but that bind them, as it were, horizontally, cutting across their vertical national division. In practice it is debatable "whether states can in fact be induced to join hands in functional endeavor before they have settled the outstanding political and security

[23] John G. Stoessinger, *The Might of Nations*. New York: Random House, 1965, pp. 253–254.

issues which divide them." So concludes a study on functionalism by Inis L. Claude. He adds,

> Functionalism's insistence upon putting first things first does not settle the matter of what things are first. . . . The dilemma of functionalism is that its ultimate impact upon politics may never be tested because of the immediate impact of politics upon functionalism. . . . Functional activity is, at least in the short run, more dependent upon the political weather than determinative of the political weather.[24]

THE MANDATE AND TRUSTEESHIP SYSTEMS [25]

The mandate and trusteeship systems are other very special types of territorial associations that contain more elements of forcible accession than of voluntary decision. The mandate system in the League of Nations and the trusteeship system under the United Nations represent a three-layer asymmetric relationship among unequal territorial units. At the very bottom and clearly inferior position, we find a mandate or a trust territory; in the middle we find the administering national state; and at the top we find the seemingly superior supervising international agency, the League or the United Nations.

At the end of World War I there arose the problem of what exactly to do with the Arab provinces under the Turkish rule and the German colonies in Africa and in the Pacific.[26] It was decided that they should not be left in the hands of defeated Germany and Turkey. On the other hand, national self-determination was not envisioned because it could have had an undesirable,

[24] Inis L. Claude, Jr., *Swords into Plowshares.* New York: Random House, 1959, pp. 373–402.

[25] Compare Ivo D. Duchacek, *Nations and Men.* New York: Holt, Rinehart and Winston, Inc., 1966, pp. 98–100.

[26] Under the mandate system the former Turkish dependencies of Iraq and Palestine (Jordan and Israel) were administered by Britain, and Syria and Lebanon were administered by France. The German colonies in Africa and the Pacific were Togo and Cameroons (divided between Britain and France); Ruanda-Urundi (administered by Belgium); Tanganyika (by Britain); South-West Africa (by the South African Union); the Marshall Islands, the Marianas, and Caroline Islands (by Japan); New Guinea and Nauru Island (by Australia); and Western Samoa (by New Zealand).

contagious effect on the colonial possessions of the victorious Allies; and yet, in view of the wartime pledge of the Allies not to seek any annexation of foreign territories, the territories could not be just simply added to the colonial empires of the Allies. How, then, to annex without saying so was the question. The mandate formula gave the answer; it justified and allowed the transfer of the former German and Turkish territories in the Middle East, Africa, and the Pacific under the administration of a few selected members of the League (England, France, Belgium, Japan, Australia, New Zealand, and South Africa). Article 22 of the Covenant of the League of Nations explained the main principle:

> To those colonies and territories which as a consequence of the late war have ceased to be under the sovereignty of the States which formerly governed them and which are inhabited by peoples not yet able to stand by themselves under the strenuous conditions of the modern world, there should be applied the principle that the well-being and development of such peoples form a sacred trust of civilisation. . . . The best method of giving practical effect to this principle is that the tutelage of such people should be entrusted to advanced nations who, by reason of their resources, their experience or their geographical position, can best undertake this responsibility . . . as Mandatories on behalf of the League.

By the end of World War II some of the mandates became independent nation-states (Iraq, Syria, and Lebanon); after World War II Palestine was split into Israel and Jordan, and the remaining mandates were transferred under a new trusteeship system established by the United Nations Charter. It mainly differed from the former mandate system by a much stricter international supervision of the administering powers (such territories were granted the right of direct complaint to the United Nations, against their administrators and were also to be visited by U.N. inspection teams every two years) and by the trustee's independence or self-government being made one of the basic objectives of the trusteeship system. By now, with only two exceptions, all the former mandates of the League and later trust territories have already become self-governing or independent nation-states or parts of newly independent nations or self-governing territories: Cameroun, Rwanda, Burundi, Tanganyika, Togo, Western Samoa, Nauru, and New Guinea. The first exception is the former German colony of South-West Africa, which the South African Union received as a mandate from the League, subsequently annexed, and now claims, although illegally, as an integral part of the South African Republic. The other exceptions are the former German colonies in the Pacific, the Marianas, the Marshall Islands, the Caroline Islands, Japanese-held mandates as of 1920 and taken over by the United States after World War II.

In 1967 President Johnson proposed that the islands under United States administration (which, in turn, is supervised by the United Nations) hold a plebiscite in 1972 to determine their political future. Many Micronesian leaders consider such a date as premature in view of the extreme backwardness of some areas (the "grass-skirt age") and important cultural differences, suspicions, and feuds among the 2141 islands composing the trust "territory." The national consciousness on the part of the population (about 90,000) is almost nil. Four different nations ruled the islands throughout Micronesia's known history: first, the Spaniards; then, the Germans; after World War I, the Japanese; and now, the Americans. In 1967 Micronesia's leading body, the Congress, appointed a commission to study different possible forms of the islands' future: becoming independent, becoming a state in the United States (favored by many leaders), becoming a commonwealth (like Puerto Rico), becoming a Federal territory of the United States (like Guam and American Samoa), gaining semi-independent status (as the Cook Islands have in relation to New Zealand). These were all complex questions to answer, even for very sophisticated students of comparative politics and comparative federalism. In 1969 the Micronesian commission favored a federation with Guam and a free association of such a federal commonwealth with the United States.

As is evident, the association of territorial communities under the mandate and trust systems was (and in the Pacific still is) of a very peculiar kind. This association had many ingredients of imperial involuntary association because the people of the mandate and trust territories were not originally asked under what foreign authority they wanted to be placed. The Covenant of the League of Nations spoke with fake tenderness of these territories' inability "to stand by themselves under the strenuous conditions of the modern world." On the other hand, under the United Nations there was a relatively efficient and searching supranational supervision of the administering powers. According to the Charter of the United Nations (Article 76b), these powers were to promote (as one of the basic objectives of the trusteeship system) the development of these territories "towards self-government or independence as may be appropriate to the particular circumstances of each territory and its people and the freely expressed wishes of the peoples concerned."

This strange combination of past imperial policy, present supranational supervision, and future independence (or membership in a confederation or federation) was bound to be interpreted in conflicting ways by all concerned: the United Nations hoped to improve colonial rule by its detailed supervision; the administering powers often hoped to continue their old colonial dominance under a new, more acceptable federal or confederal guise; and the trust territories in most cases desired neither a greatly improved foreign rule nor a union with their colonial masters in a federal venture. Therefore, the territories aimed at and obtained independent statehood.[27] However, the hesitation on the part of 90,000 Micronesians is, for the time being, an exception to this trend.

ALLIANCES [28]

The term *alliance* is very broad but is usually employed to describe a voluntary association of territorial communities primarily for the purpose of military defense of their common interests. The term *defense* is also very broad; even an aggressive alliance could be considered a defense of the expansionist coali-

---

[27] The former Italian colony, now an independent country, is the only case of a trust territory that had not been a mandate under the League of Nations. After World War II and Italy's defeat, Italian Somalia was detached from Italy as a colony but was given back to her as a trust territory for ten years (1950–1960), at the end of which period Italian Somalia was to be granted full independence. And it was.

[28] Compare Ivo D. Duchacek and Kenneth W. Thompson, *Conflict and Cooperation among Nations.* New York: Holt, Rinehart and Winston, Inc., 1960, p. 407.

tion. Of course, there is the traditional problem of distinguishing "offensive defense" and "defensive offense" from "pure aggression."

By concluding an alliance that in legal terms expresses limitations on, as well as commitment to, common policies and action, nation-states add precision to their community of interests and inform their rivals of the existence of their defensive compact. An alliance expresses and codifies a pre-existing community of interests. Without common interest an alliance is a scrap of paper. As Thucydides said, "Identity of interest is the surest of bonds whether between states or individuals."

Defensive alliances are as old as territorial communities. The older alliances usually represented only a verbal or written commitment to protect common interests or to pursue common policies through a common effort. Modern alliances have added some permanent machinery. They usually consist of a somewhat permanently working executive council, a deliberative assembly composed of foreign, defense, and economic ministers, a permanent secretariat with a permanent interallied staff, and in some cases, a unified high command (NATO and the Warsaw Pact) to which military contingents have been assigned in peacetime. Modern alliances have also added agencies in the social, intelligence, counterintelligence, and even cultural fields. Such complex alliances may be viewed—and are often described—as communities (the Atlantic Community or the Socialist Commonwealth) or confederations *sui generis*. Their other usual features are:

1. They are nonperpetual; alliance treaties usually provide for renewal about every twenty years.
2. The right of "secession" is guaranteed provided that due notice is given.
3. The principle of unanimity is explicitly or implicitly stated. Unanimity is to be achieved by negotiated compromise rather than by formal voting. An exception in the Organization of American States is noted later.
4. Most modern alliances claim that they are consonant with the goals of the United Nations and are authorized by the Charter, which (in Article 51) guarantees the right of individual and collective self-defense, which may be exercised only "until the Security Council has taken meas-

ures necessary to maintain international peace and security." On account of the disharmony between the Big Five these measures may never be taken. The reference to Article 51 in modern treaties is, therefore, only a verbal bow in the direction of the United Nations; in practice, alliances formed around one or more of the veto-holding Great Powers work (or do not work) independently of the United Nations Charter.

5.   Alliances are clearly directed against an external enemy. This is the reason for their existence. Some have been established to protect the member nations against *any* aggressor (but his identity seems often obvious, as in the case of NATO); others identify their enemies by name. In Europe the Communist alliances are directed "against Germany trying to resume her aggressive policy or any other State which directly or in any other form would be associated with Germany in a policy of aggression" (the Soviet-Bulgarian Alliance of March 18, 1948); in Asia, the Sino-Soviet Alliance mentions aggressive Japan and her allies instead of Germany.

The Organization of American States (Pact of Rio, September 2, 1947) is composed of twenty-one American republics. Canada (which was expected to join the United States Confederation of 1777) [29] was invited to join, but Canada declined the offer. Canada is, however, included in the area that the member nations agree to protect against an attack; an attack against any portion of the Western Hemisphere is considered to be an attack on all members. Concrete measures are to be adopted following a two-thirds vote by an assembly of foreign ministers (called the Organ of Consultation). The decision of the two-thirds majority is binding on all if it deals with economic matters, including economic sanctions against a violator of peace either from without or from within the treaty area. Military sanctions can be *recommended* by the same majority, but the decision is not binding.

[29] Article 11 of the Confederation states: "Canada acceding to this confederation, and joining in the measures of the United States, shall be admitted into, and entitled to all the advantages of this Union; but no other colony shall be admitted into the same, unless such admission be agreed to by nine States."

The Western Hemisphere association of states has moved a step beyond the prewar framework of alliances—it has established a common machinery: it has a permanent Council in Washington (composed of the ambassadors of member republics); the Pan-American Union services the organization as its Secretariat; and the decision-making assembly is its Organ of Consultation. Under the *Alliance for Progress,* organs promoting and organizing economic cooperation have been added.

The treaty is to "remain in force indefinitely" (Article 25) but guarantees a right of "secession" [30] and permits suspension of membership or expulsion of a member (Cuba, for instance).

The Organization of American States represents an interesting departure from the principle of unanimity typical of alliances. It provides for voting procedures in which a two-thirds majority may make binding decisions in some matters. Unlike the United Nations Charter, the Western Hemispheric one denies the only one Great Power that is a member any privileged position: there is no veto power. The principle is one republic, one vote. This illusion of a tight confederal structure should be qualified: first, the decision by a two-thirds majority can order member nations to apply economic sanctions but cannot order them to apply the use of military force; second, the United States, seemingly brought to the level of Guatemala or Honduras in voting rights, is reasonably confident that it will always be able to find one third of the voting republics by its side to prevent the organization from forcing it into any undesirable course of action. Even if a Latin-American unanimity minus one (the United States) were one day to manifest itself, it would hardly prove able to force the outvoted giant in the North to do anything against its will. We may assume that the Latin-American countries are aware of this, despite their occasional glorification of the democratic majoritarian principle in the Organization of American States.

NATO and *the Warsaw Pact* represent modern military

[30] Article 25: "This Treaty . . . may be denounced by any High Contracting Party by a notification in writing to the Pan-American Union." After two years such a notification ends the membership of such a High Contracting Party but preserves the treaty organization with respect to all the other member republics.

alliances endowed with complex and permanent machinery and built around the power and leadership of the two atomic superpowers. Both alliances are based, in principle, on Article 51 of the United Nations Charter, which authorizes collective self-defense.

The North Atlantic Treaty Organization, composed of fifteen nations,[31] was established on April 4, 1949. The core provision of the NATO Treaty reads as follows (Article 5):

> The Parties agree that an armed attack against one or more of them in Europe or North America shall be considered an attack against them all and consequently they agree that, if such an armed attack occurs, each of them, in exercise of the right of individual or collective self-defence recognized by Article 51 of the Charter of the United Nations, will assist the Party or Parties so attacked by taking forthwith, individually and in concert with the other Parties, such action as it deems necessary, including the use of armed force, to restore and maintain the security of the North Atlantic area. Any such armed attack and all measures taken as a result thereof shall immediately be reported to the Security Council. Such measures shall be terminated when the Security Council has taken the measures necessary to restore and maintain international peace and security.

An almost identical wording may be found in Article 4 of the Warsaw Pact, concluded on May 14, 1955:

> In the event of armed attack in Europe on one or more of the parties to the treaty by any State or group of States, each of the parties to the treaty, in the exercise of its rights to individual or collective self-defense in accordance with Article 51 of the Charter of the United Nations Organization, shall immediately, either individually or in agreement with other parties to the treaty, come to the assistance of the State or States attacked with all such means as it deems necessary, including armed force. The parties to the treaty shall immediately consult concerning the necessary measures to be taken by them jointly in order to restore and maintain international peace and security.

[31] United States, Canada, Iceland, Norway, United Kingdom, Netherlands, Denmark, Belgium, Luxembourg, Portugal, France, Italy, Greece, Turkey, and West Germany.

Measures taken on the basis of this article shall be reported to the Security Council in conformity with the provisions of the Charter of the United Nations Organization. These measures shall be discontinued immediately when the Security Council adopts the necessary measures to restore and maintain international peace and security.

The Warsaw Pact groups seven small Eastern European Communist states around the Soviet Union.

Both NATO and the Warsaw Pact are, therefore, highly asymmetrical. There are other similarities. Both alliances have added economic and cultural cooperation to their structures. The Communist Council for Mutual Economic Aid (CEMA or Comecon) was the counterpart to the Marshall Plan and its Western European ramifications. Both alliances have their permanent councils (NATO in Brussels and the Warsaw Pact in Warsaw), their permanent secretariats, regular meetings of their deliberative grand assemblies (attended by foreign, defense, and economic ministers in the case of NATO and by prime ministers and first secretaries of the party and their aides in the Communist case), and a unified command to which a composite military force has been assigned in peace time; the position of the superpowers in this context is nearly decisive in both cases. Both alliances are frequently referred to in confederal terms: the Atlantic *Community* and the Socialist *Commonwealth*.

In both cases the principle of unanimity, implying either the right of veto or the right of secession, prevails in theory. But in practice the weak members of both territorial associations have found it difficult, and in the Communist case impossible, to alter the leading power's general direction of the alliance.

Yet another similarity should be mentioned: both alliances experience an internal, mostly leadership crisis. The dominant positions of the United States and the Soviet Union in both alliance systems have come under increased criticism. The nations that are not superpowers resent the superpower's leadership of the alliance because it is deemed to be lacking in wisdom, foresight, and tact or to abound in the tendency to dictate to the allies and to assume too readily that what is good for the leading power is good for all the members of the alliance. Not infrequently, a superior power of the leading member is resented simply because it is superior.

The principle of national self-determination that has eroded polyethnic nation-states is bound to erode even more easily their alliances. And then there is the atomic problem and suspicions that go with it. When France decided to develop its own independent atomic deterrent, one of the reasons was its often-voiced suspicion that Washington might not consider Paris worth atomically dying for; the same doubt concerning Moscow's readiness to sacrifice the whole of the Soviet Union for Peking was one of the reasons for the development of the Chinese *force de frappe*. A similar suspicion is present in the small Eastern European states, but, unlike France, none (although scientifically and technically capable, like Poland, Czechoslovakia, or East Germany) has seriously considered such a financially and politically ruinous course of action. Also, the Soviet Union would simply not permit it.

There are also, of course, significant differences that result from geography (the proximity or distance of the leading power), the degree of asymmetry, and the democratic or authoritarian way of handling opposition or dissent within the alliance. The Warsaw Pact represents an extreme case of asymmetry: a group of seven dwarfs (Poland, Czechoslovakia, East Germany, Hungary, Rumania, Bulgaria, and Albania—the latter no more a member) are grouped around the mighty Russian giant. In the Socialist Commonwealth there is no counterpart to powerful Germany, the atomic powers France and Britain, and Italy. There is also an absence of the live-and-let-live tradition in the Communist hierarchical authoritarian context; the Soviet invasions of Hungary and Czechoslovakia demonstrated the difference in handling dissent in the Socialist Commonwealth. In NATO, France has never dreaded a punitive action by the United States when it has asserted its independent foreign and military policy.

THE COMMUNIST INTERNATIONALS

The *Comintern* (1919–1943) and the *Cominform* (1947–1956) represent ideological organizations with unusual territorial features. Both Communist organizations were composed, on the one hand, of Communist parties that had already captured the governments of their territorial communities, and, on the other hand, of parties that, in the opposition or in the underground, had been planning a seizure of their respective territorial authority.

When the Third Communist International (Comintern) was created in Soviet Russia by the Bolshevik leaders after World War I, it grouped all the left wings that had seceded from the world's social democratic parties (originally grouped in the Second Socialist International of 1889); the leader of the world organization from its beginning to its dissolution in 1943 was the Communist party of the Soviet Union, which at the same time was the government of a territorial state. The state was the party and the party was the state. It was a political association between a territorial state on the one hand and political parties fighting for the possession of territorial states on the other hand.

The Comintern was dissolved by Stalin in 1943 because its emphasis on proletarian internationalism had proved a hindrance to the Soviet mobilization of nationalist emotions in the European struggle against Nazi Germany.

The communiqué announcing the dissolution of the Comintern, signed by Stalin and the leaders of the member parties, said in part,

> Long before the war it had already become increasingly clear that to the extent that the internal as well as international situation of individual countries became more complicated, the solution of the problems of the labor movement in each individual country through the medium of some *international center would meet with insuperable obstacles. . . .* The deep difference in the historical roads of development of each country of the world, the diverse character and even contradiction in their social orders, the difference in the level and rate of their social and political development, and finally, the difference in the degree of consciousness and organization of the workers, conditioned also the various problems which face the working class of each individual country. [Italics added.]

The mixed ideological-territorial character of the Communist association re-emerged in the Cominform that was established in 1947 but was, in turn, liquidated by Khrushchev in 1956. Unlike the Comintern with its worldwide membership, the Cominform was a product and instrument of the Soviet Cold War in Europe. The Cominform consisted only of European Communist parties. In contrast with the Comintern, the new Communist association was dominantly an organization of *territorial* Communist communities. Members were the Communist parties-and-governments of Poland, Czechoslovakia, Bulgaria, Rumania, Hungary, Albania, and Yugoslavia (which was expelled in 1948). East Germany was never a member. In addition to these Eastern European Communist states, the Communist parties of France and Italy, then in the opposition and only hoping for a territorial conquest, were the founding members.

In the Cominform we may detect some of the features characteristic of alliances or confederations:

1. Common goals and ideology of Marxism-Leninism, even though later a profound dispute as to its exact interpretation and implementation deeply divided the Communist bloc.
2. The right of secession, or expulsion—which permitted Yugoslavia, originally against her will, to promote and manage its own way of communism with triumphant satisfaction.
3. The principle of unanimity, although clearly manipulated and enforced by the superior power of the Soviet party.
4. A common machinery, the Comintern or the Cominform, with its permanent revolutionary staff, regular meetings of the top executives (that is, party secretaries), its own journal, and international organizational links and couriers.
5. A hope—typical for confederation—that the Comintern and the Cominform were but the first steps to an integrated Soviet-led union of world Communism. Probably most people, both within and outside the Communist camp, have dreaded what the Russians have hoped for.

PUERTO RICO'S ASSOCIATION WITH THE UNITED STATES—A SPECIAL CASE

Some associations among territorial communities are almost impossible to classify: the "federal" association between imperial Ethiopia and Eritrea (an association that was recommended by the United Nations after World War II); the association of

West Germany with the western part of Berlin in the framework of the Soviet-American relations; the association of Switzerland with Liechtenstein; the association of Denmark with Greenland; the association of Monaco with France; the association of Andorra with Spain and France; the association of San Marino with Italy; and the association of Bhutan and Sikkim with India. (The sensitively situated Himalayan kingdom of Sikkim is recognized by a treaty with India as a self-governing and autonomous state. India, however, has full control over Sikkim's communications, foreign policy, and defense. Since 1962, on account of the Indian-Chinese tension, India has kept 25,000 soldiers in Sikkim, whose total population is 175,000—which means that one out of every eight persons is an Indian soldier; this became an issue in 1969, raised by the young king.)

The United States' relationship with Puerto Rico belongs to this undefinable category. The United States–Puerto Rico association has some ingredients to be found in alliances and in some confederations, such as the right of secession, recognized by both sides but, for the time being, claimed only by a minority of Puerto Ricans. On the other hand, the self-rule of Puerto Rico, which is not a member of the federal union of the fifty American states, is determined by an act of the United States Congress; the arrangement reminds us of imperialism (benevolent, to be sure) or, perhaps more accurately, of unitary decentralization, under which important autonomous powers have been delegated, yet, in principle, can always be revoked. This is theory. In practice, the scope of the Puerto Rican autonomy can only be extended but cannot be contracted or eliminated altogether. The real choice is among statehood in the American union, the present status, or full secession. Under the Federal Relations Act, the United States—Puerto Rican association means a common market and a common monetary system; the inhabitants of Puerto Rico are United States citizens (under the jurisdiction of the United States Constitution, bound by the decisions of the United States executive, legislative, and judiciary branches of government, subject to military service, and covered by different federal social and health benefits). Although subject to federal laws, the Puerto Ricans do not pay federal taxes, do not vote in federal elections (but they do participate, however symbolically, in the American parties' presidential conventions). Furthermore, certain Federal custom duties and excise taxes are paid back into the Treasury of the island.

Thus, Puerto Rico appears to us as a fully self-governing territorial unit in local affairs while enjoying great benefits from its association with the United States. However, to the present, the association itself with the United States has been beyond the island's political and legal controls. In summary, then,

> The people of Puerto Rico live under two governments, that of their own Commonwealth and that of the United States. The former they control through public officials of their own choosing. Over the latter, however, they exercise no direct control since they have no voting representation in Congress nor the right to vote in presidential elections. Is this dual relationship compatible with the notion that Puerto Rico is no longer a colony? The supporters of commonwealth status argue that it is, whereas the opponents of that status deny it.[32]

Many more cases of somewhat voluntary associations of states (associations that contain some or all of the ingredients of what make up a confederation, alliance, or functional association of territorial communities) could be added to our list and examined. However, we hope that it has been made sufficiently clear (in Chap. 5 and in the present one) that unitary systems that have been significantly decentralized and the territorial associations that have (forcibly or voluntarily) combined formerly independent units into relatively cohesive unions share what is common to all political systems: they defy neat classification and they resist categorization, especially if one is to examine not only their origins but also their subsequent working and evolution. Ever so often a decentralized unitary system shades off into a

---

[32] Henry Wells, "Puerto Rico's Association with the United States," paper presented at the Sixth World Congress of the International Political Science Association, Geneva, 1964, p. 6. Compare the inaugural statement by the governor of Puerto Rico, Luis A. Ferré, on January 2, 1969: "The political equality of statehood is necessary for safeguarding the rights of the people of Puerto Rico, an essential to their sense of dignity." This was in contrast with his predecessors, who had usually emphasized the economic benefits—including exemption from federal taxes—derived from commonwealth status.

federal system or a confederal system, and vice versa. This happens by constant oscillation between two extreme possibilities: complete territorial disintegration and atomization, a one pole of the continuum, and a complete unification and total integration at the other pole. For some authors, federalism represents an intermediary form between confederal association and a unitary system, borrowing from, and leaning to, one or the other under the pressure of constant environmental changes. Some tend to see federal process in just about everything that can be described as a combination of unity with diversity, be it the Soviet or the Canadian federation, a military alliance, a customs union, the Cominform, or a modern university. In his perceptive study of federalism, C. J. Hughes, Professor of Politics at the University of Leicester, criticizes what he calls the *Received Theory of Federalism* that usually proceeds from a provisional definition ("federalism is what I say it is"), which stands at the beginning of the book, through an examination of the empirical data in the light of that definition, to the end of the book and to the final assumption that "there is a real thing [called] federalism and it looks like that." Hughes then adds,

> We often treat federalism as a procrustean bed, lopping off or stretching empirical data which do not fit. . . . "What sort of concept is federalism? Is it a word or a thing?" . . . "How (if at all) can a particular definition of federalism be verified?" But these are cloudy matters, and it would be un-English to discuss them abstractly; in what follows I shall endeavour to keep as close to empirical data as possible." [33]

We, too, shall so endeavor in the following chapters on federalism.

[33] C. J. Hughes, "The Theory of Confederacies," a paper presented at the Sixth World Congress of the International Political Science Association, Geneva, September 1964, p. 2.

SEVEN
TEN YARDSTICKS
OF FEDERALISM

Nowhere before [1787] has so close a union been
combined with so much freedom (or autonomy) of
the component parts.

> ALEXIS DE TOCQUEVILLE (*Democracy
> in America*)

Federation appears to be on the group level what
association is on the interpersonal level. It unites
without destroying the selves that are uniting, and
is. . . . organized cooperation of groups as groups.

> CARL J. FRIEDRICH ("New Tendencies
> in Federal Theory and Practice")

A federal system is characterized by at least two
patterns of communities, one all-inclusive and the
other composed of several mutually exclusive sub-
communities. The *geographical* nature of the
community pattern and especially the location of the
boundaries among the sub-communities and around
the whole community are crucial to the federal
system.

> PETER H. MERKL ("Federalism and
> Social Structure")

There is no accepted theory of federalism. Nor is there an agreement as to what *federalism* is exactly. The term itself is unclear
and controversial. It is often used to describe a *process* of combining territorial communities that previously had not been
directly joined into a new unit of common interest, policy, and
action, or the opposite process of deconcentration of power (that
is, decentralization that endows territorial units with autonomous
sources of authority). In addition, *federalism* is also a term used
to describe the *result* or the tools of the federalizing process—a
constitutional federal system and its institutions.

It should be recognized, however, that the term *federalism*
is often also used in either *nonpolitical* or *nonterritorial* contexts.
At times, the federalizing process may even refer to ecumenism,
that is, to building or renewing unity among variants of a common creed or ideology. Examples of nonpolitical associations of
groups whose primary goals are services, production, or entertainment are federations of consumer or producer cooperatives,
chambers of commerce, veterans' posts, and sports, chess, and
stamp collectors' clubs. One might perhaps argue that the American League is a baseball confederation rather than an alliance.
Or is it a federation or a commonwealth? Other examples of nonpolitical federations are the commercial or industrial complexes
that have been created by association of previously independent
companies whose autonomy and identity have not been obliter-
ated but guaranteed in the merger; or the complexes that during
their successful growth and expansion have found it necessary
to decentralize and endow the new branches or sectors with
financial and administrative autonomy. Such a "federalizing"
process may be observed in both capitalist and communist economies; in both cases, flexibility and increased efficiency or service
are the evident goals.

Examples of federations engaged in political promotion
and defense of nonterritorial *functional* interests, usually reflecting diverse professional skills, are the American Federation of
Labor (AFL-CIO), the United Federation of Teachers, the
Trades Union Congress in Britain, the Swedish Federation of
Labor, the Federation of British Industries (FBI) in Britain, or
the Federation of German Industries (BDI) in West Germany.
In France and Italy, labor and other functional federations are
often so grouped as to represent extensions of political parties

into different professional fields. In France, *Confédération générale du travail* (CGT) is politically connected with the Communist party, *Confédération force ouvrière* (FO) with the Socialist party, and *Confédération française des travailleurs chrétiens* (CFTC) with the Catholic movement and Church. In Italy, *Confederazione generale italiana del lavoro* (CGIL) is under the influence of the Italian Communists, whereas *Confederazione italiana dei sindicati dei lavoratori* is Catholic-oriented.

We may also observe the use of federal terminology in political movements when the aim is to forge unity out of ideological, not territorial, diversity. In France, for instance, the Communists, socialists, radicals, and other leftist groups have formed a Federation of a Democratic and Socialist Left (*Fédération de la gauche démocratique et socialiste*). Although the Comintern and the Cominform, as discussed in Chapter 6, represented an ideological union of territorial parties, the first (1874) and the second (1889) Socialist Internationals represented associations of not only territorial groups but also different socialist ideologies. Their proletarian battle song, the *International,* seemed to express the hope that ultimately the proletarian federation may transform itself into one single international party with one uniform socialist creed.

The international anarchist movement that opposes any degree of centralism is composed of anarchist federations. Its congress held on August 31, 1968, at Carrara (Italy) was officially called "The Fifth International Congress of Anarchist Federations." It split asunder, however, between the supporters (mainly British and Swiss) of the leader of the French student revolts, Cohn-Bendit (who had denounced the delegates as bureaucrats), and the old-line anarchists (who were still awed by Bakunin, Proudhon, and other nineteenth-century revolutionary leaders). The final result of the anarchist congress was, appropriately, not a federation, but anarchy.

Churches often represent a combination of territorial and ecumenical "federalism." In Protestant churches, for instance, the parishes represent the basic territorial units that are combined into higher regional, national, and international federations. But in addition, different denominational Protestant groupings are federated in a World Council of Churches—a unity combined with both territorial *and* creed diversity. Even within the highly centralized Roman Catholic Church, dedicated to its dogmatic unity, some authors find federal institutions and habits; the territorial autonomy of the bishops and some orders within the tenets of a common faith is often very real in practice. At the 1964 Congress of the International Political Science Association in Geneva, one of the participating scholars presented a paper that analyzed the autonomy of the two hundred Benedictine abbeys in terms of federalism.[1]

ATTEMPTS AT DEFINING FEDERALISM

Federalism has now become one of those good echo words that evoke a positive response but that may mean all things to all men, like *democracy, socialism, progress, constitution, justice,* or *peace.* We see the term applied to almost any successful combination of unity with diversity, to almost any form of pluralism and cooperation within and among nations. In his book on federalism (1968),[2] Carl J. Friedrich describes *federalism* as a union of groups that may be nation-states or communities such as churches, trade unions, or political parties. Other authors (see, for example, the epigraph by Peter H. Merkl on p. 188) limit their definition of *federalism* to territorial communities. So do we in our study. By so narrowing our focus to the territorial distribution of political authority, we have not, however, rendered our task of defining *federalism* much easier. Nor have we facilitated our attempt at distinguishing federalism from a significantly decentralized unitary system or from loose or closely knit confederations, leagues, or alliances.

[1] Leo Moulin, *Le fédéralisme dans l'organisation politique des ordres religieux,* states in his summary: "Benedictine life is based fundamentally on the principle of abbatial autonomy. The pressure of circumstances has led to the groupings of abbeys. . . . At present about two hundred Benedictine abbeys are members of 15 Congregations, with very diverse regimes, but all with federal spirit. At the top, a summit rather than a central organization, a recently created (1893) Confederation strives to ensure a minimum of homogeneity and common observance for structures which life and history have made complex, moving, and diverse. It is not sure that it will succeed. The Benedictine soul lives in freely associated abbeys according to events in the past."

[2] Carl J. Friedrich, *Trends of Federalism in Theory and Practice.* New York: Praeger, 1968, p. 11.

When we read and ponder about the essential features of federalism that the specialists in the field offer, some of which have been quoted in the epigraphs introducing the present and the following chapters, we may note that despite some differences in emphasis and nuances in style or grammar, they all seem to contain the following two basic points:

First, in a federation the political authority is territorially divided between two autonomous sets of separate jurisdictions, one national and the other provincial, which both operate directly upon the people. Second, the existence of a single, indivisible yet composite federal nation is simultaneously asserted. A federal nation is, as it were, an unfinished nation. Constitutionally, it admits of the existence of several component territorial communities and their refusal to merge with the rest into one uniform whole. Neither of the two sets of governments is ready to abandon its sovereignty and yield fully to the other: uniformity is ruled out but so is secession. It is a conflict combined with a keen awareness of mutual dependence. Such an intrafederal conflict—"a brotherhood of tempered rivalry" (V. C. Wynne-Edwards)—is, therefore, similar to the conflicts among independent nation-states that are aware of their mutual dependence and some common interests despite their conflict. Morton Grodzins spoke of federalism as "antagonistic cooperation" [3] to indicate that groups can indeed engage in joint ventures on a regular basis even as they react to each other antagonistically. [4] A federal constitution may therefore be seen as a political compact that explicitly admits of the existence of conflicting interests among the component territorial communities and commits them all to seek accommodation without outvoting the minority and without the use of force. Or, in other words, a federal constitution expresses the core creed of democracy, pluralism, in territorial terms. It cannot and should not be ex-

[3] Morton Grodzins, *The American System: A New View of Government in the United States.* Skokie, Ill.: Rand McNally, 1966, p. 327.

[4] Moves and countermoves in a framework of an intrafederal conflict—or antagonistic cooperation—can probably be studied with the help of several insights of the games theory as "nonzero-sum games." Compare Thomas C. Shelling, *The Strategy of Conflict.* New York: Oxford, 1963, p. 83 ("Toward a Theory of Interdependent Decision" and other chapters).

pected to contain any precise guideline as to what exactly the mechanism and the solution of a conflict among communities might be if the consensus breaks down, neither side yields to the other, and a solution through mutual concession cannot be found. There is only an agreement to try to agree at a later date *again* (that is, there is a commitment to add, if possible, new federal bargains to the initial bargain). Federalism is by definition an unfinished business because many issues can be neither foreseen nor immediately solved; at the time of the initial bargain, some issues may not have yet crystallized and other issues may have already proven too controversial (too hot) to try to solve immediately. But this is the whole point and the political merit of a federal formula. It is based on a wise recognition that in politics many issues cannot be solved now or ever. With its seemingly precise and elaborate articles defining the way in which authority is divided between the two or more sets of different jurisdiction, a federal constitution is misleading: like any other political system it creates an impression of finality and accuracy in a context that leaves—and must leave—so many issues to future improvisations.

Western Europeans sometimes criticize the Americans for their impatience with problems that resist immediate and neat solution. "In European history the recognition of a problem has often defined a dilemma rather than pointed to an answer," wrote Henry A. Kissinger. In contrast, "Americans live in an environment uniquely suited to an engineering approach to policy making; as a result our society has been characterized by a conviction that any problem will yield if subjected to a sufficient dose of expertise." [5] A French sociologist, Michel Crozier, addressing an American audience, warned, "Beware of the temptation—difficult to resist—of the arrogance of rationality." Emphasizing psychological and emotional issues that resist social engineering, Crozier added that it was a kind of folly to assume that "a rational view of the world based on the inevitability of scientific progress can cope with a fragmented, culturally diverse society full of complex emotional problems." [6]

[5] Henry A. Kissinger, "Coalition Diplomacy in a Nuclear Age," *Foreign Affairs* (July 1964), p. 536.

[6] *The New York Times* (December 15, 1968), p. 11.

Although we may recognize some validity in the European evaluation of the American attitude toward international politics, it seems that the Founders in 1787 were either still very much European or quite unconcerned with the engineering or technical neatness of their approach to the then existing internal problems. Their federal Constitution, too, defined a dilemma rather than pointed to a final solution of conflicts and issues, the seriousness of which only a few tended then to underestimate.

One of the famous shorthand American definitions of *federalism* speaks of "an indestructible union of indestructible units,"[7] which seems on the one hand to separate a federal from a confederal system by ruling out secession and on the other to distinguish a federal from a unitary system by ruling out total elimination of provincial autonomy (a *theoretical* possibility in a unitary system). The result is a compromise between two territorial forces pulling in opposite directions: one toward national unity, which, if excessive, could suppress diversity and eliminate provincial autonomy, and the other toward diversity, which, if excessive, could dissolve the federal nation into its several constituent units.

On the basis of the previous discussion—and bearing in mind the dynamic and ever-changing scope and contents of any political system, including the federal system—a tentative working definition of *federalism* may now be suggested and subjected to critical examination and empirical testing: By a *federal system* we mean a constitutional division of power between one general government (that is to have authority over the entire national territory) and a series of subnational governments (that individually have their own independent authority over their own territories, whose sum total represents *almost* the whole national territory). Admittedly, the term *almost* in a definition is awkward, yet it seems unavoidable here because most federal governments extend their authority over an area wider than the one that the subnational governments administer. These are territories beyond the boundaries of the composite whole, such as colonies, federal territories, or strategic frontier areas (for instance, Himachal Pradesh, Manipur, and Tripura in India) or capital cities located in specially created districts as, for instance, New Delhi, Brasilia, Mexico City, or Washington, D.C.

[7] Texas v. White, 7 Wallace 700 (1869).

Our working definition, which will prove no less controversial than any other currently used is graphically expressed in
Figure 7–1. The model is not meant to represent any particular

Figure 7–1   A federal system

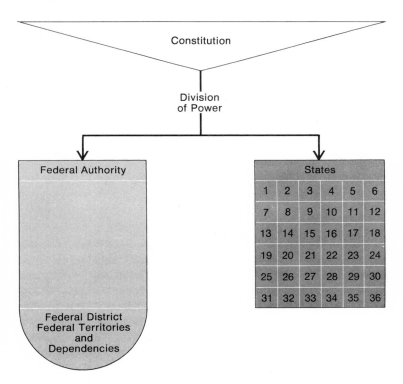

federal system. However, the thirty-six subdivisions could be
interpreted to mean the United States on November 1, 1864,
after admission of Nevada on the previous day. The semicircle
illustrating the direct federal control was to include Alaska in
three years (1867) and the Philippines and Hawaii in 1898.

We will submit our definition of *federal system* and the il-
lustrative model to several empirical tests by first analyzing the
wording of "federal" constitutional texts (Chaps. 7 and 8) and
then comparing the wording of "federal" constitutions with the
actual working of those constitutions (Chaps. 9 and 10).

Twenty-one out of some 130 existing nation-states are con-

Figure 7–2   Map of the federal systems of the world

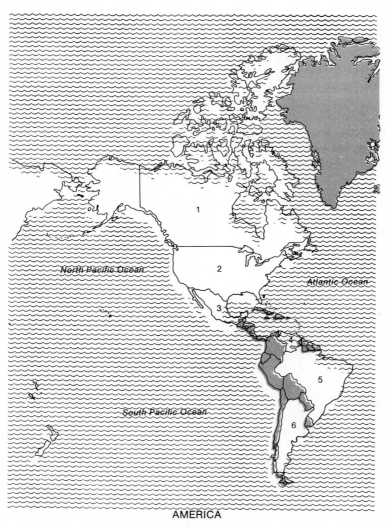

AMERICA

1 CANADA	3 MEXICO	5 BRAZIL
2 USA	4 VENEZUELA	6 ARGENTINA

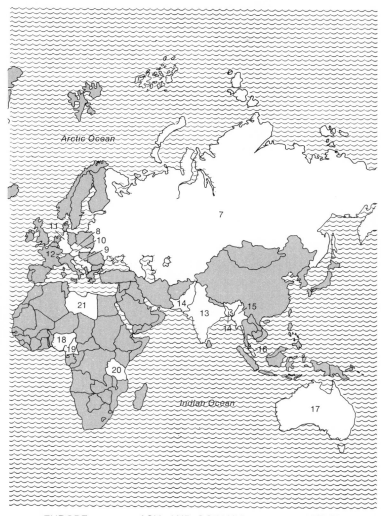

EUROPE	ASIA AND OCEANIA	AFRICA
7 USSR	13 INDIA	18 NIGERIA
8 CZECHOSLOVAKIA	14 PAKISTAN	19 CAMEROUN
9 YUGOSLAVIA	15 BURMA (?)	20 TANZANIA
10 AUSTRIA	16 MALAYSIA	21 LIBYA (?)
11 W. GERMANY	17 AUSTRALIA	
12 SWITZERLAND		

sidered or claim to be federal (see Fig. 7–2): in North America are Canada and the United States; in Latin America are Mexico, Argentina, Brazil, and Venezuela; in Europe are the Soviet Union, West Germany, Austria, Switzerland, Yugoslavia, and Czechoslovakia; in the Pacific and Asia are India, Pakistan, Burma, Australia, and Malaysia; and in Africa are Nigeria, Libya, Tanzania, and Cameroun. In some cases their claim to be federal may be confirmed; in other cases it may be questioned or denied. And some systems will prove impossible to classify.

Although the overwhelming majority of nation-states have adopted a unitary system of government that creates territorial autonomy by delegation of authority from the national center, in terms of square miles the twenty-one federal nations cover more than half of the land surface of our planet. Of the six largest nations of the world, only China (3.7 million square miles) is unitary (but its constitution guarantees its ethnic minorities a territorial autonomy). The other five claim to be federal: the USSR, over 8 million square miles; Canada 3.8 million; the United States, 3.6 million; Brazil, 3.2 million; and Australia, 2.9 million.

Some authors argue that there is a direct correlation between large size and the advisability of federalism, and they quote Thomas Jefferson in support of their argument: "Our country is too large to have all its affairs directed by a single government" (Thomas Jefferson to Gideon Granger in 1809). In his autobiography Jefferson also says, "Were not this country divided into States, that division must be made [by unitary decentralization] that each might do for itself what concerns itself directly, and what it can so much better do than a distant authority." The words of Thomas Jefferson are wise indeed but could be quoted, of course, also in support of unitary decentralization (that is, territorial distribution of authority by delegation from the central authority). In unitary systems, too, it may be argued, as Jefferson did in 1800, that the country is too large to have its provincial and local affairs directed by the national center. A recent study pointed to the fact that the American national government is only one territorial unit out of nearly 38,000 territorial units of self-rule (states, counties, municipalities, townships, and towns). If school and special districts are added to the number of territorial units, the national government is then only one territorial unit out of more than 90,000 units. It should be noted that only 50 out of the 38,000 territorial units reflect the American federalism; the other some 89,949 territorial units represent unitary decentralization by delegation. The fact of the unitary nature of state governments should be borne in mind when the study just quoted alarmingly concludes:

> The imagination boggles at the attempt to conceive of the United States as a democratic country operating at the national level by means of electoral leaders and competitive political parties and locally through a centralized bureaucracy, federally appointed and controlled, that would administer tasks now carried by 38 thousand territorial governments.[8]

Administrative efficiency, legislative and executive flexibility, and local initiative, participation, and responsibility justify decentralization in both unitary and federal systems, and they also represent important considerations in any federalizing process from "below," that is, when territorial communities bargain and agree to form a federal union. But in a federalizing process from "below" there are also other important goals to achieve. Federation is not an end in itself but a means to attain some or all of the following objectives:

1. Protection against external pressures, especially military dangers, can be achieved. We have already noted the aggregative effect of an external threat. Subversion by the imperialist tactics of "divide and rule" may often be neutralized by a *defensive* federal compact.

2. Benefits to all may be derived from bringing the diplomatic and military assets of member units into a common pool—benefits that may be translated into greater internal security and progress or, possibly, external expansion.

3. Economic advantages may accrue to all from planning, working, and exchanging products in a larger market and production area. In Africa, where economic progress is the number-one item on the continental agenda, plans for federal union have

---

[8] Robert A. Dahl, *Pluralist Democracy in the United States: Conflict and Consent*. Skokie, Ill.: Rand McNally, 1967, pp. 171–177.

often been marked by the desire to lure overseas investors who "tend to be more willing to invest in a large country (provided it appears to have a fair chance of political stability) than in a number of smaller countries." [9]

Economic considerations by themselves, however, are not sufficient to create a sufficient federal impetus; they result, at best, in customs unions or a common market. Other ingredients must be added to economic realities if, for instance, a common market is to "graduate" and become a confederal or federal system.

The federal impetus usually presupposes "mutual compatibility of main values, . . . expectation of economic, political and administrative gains, [and] unbroken links of social communication, both geographically between territories and sociologically between different social strata." [10] William H. Riker is right when he concludes that federalism "must be based on some deeper emotion than mere geographic contiguity with cultural diversity." [11] The leading cadres, if they wish to maintain national unity, can compensate for the centrifugal effects of noncontiguity, as a recent carefully documented study demonstrates. Its author, Richard L. Merritt, examines several examples of noncontiguous communities, ranging from ancient Greece and Georgian Anglo-America to present-day Pakistan, whose western and eastern provinces are separated by one thousand miles of unfriendly Indian territory, and the United States, whose forty-ninth state, Alaska, is separated from the national territory by Canada, whereas its fiftieth state, Hawaii, lies in the middle of the Pacific. Merritt's study of territorial noncontiguity concludes:

> Of the many types of discontinuities, territorial noncontiguity is only one. It may well be less important than ethnic, linguistic, religious, political or other discontinuities. West Berlin is perhaps the clearest example of this fact. Its ties of community are closer with the West German Federal Repub-

[9] Anthony Birch, "Approaches to the Study of Federalism," *Political Studies,* vol. 14, No. 1 (1966), 27.

[10] Karl W. Deutsch *et al., Political Community in the North Atlantic Area.* Princeton, N.J.: Princeton University Press, 1957, p. 58.

[11] William H. Riker, *Federalism: Origin, Operation, Significance.* Boston: Little, Brown, 1964, p. 35.

lic, more than one hundred miles away from the city limits, than with either neighboring East Berlin or the German Democratic Republic. In an age when cargo planes can airlift supplies to a beleaguered city . . . the fact of territorial contiguity is becoming still less important." [12]

On the basis of correlated data, obtained from a study of four major federal failures, Thomas M. Franck has identified as principal ingredients of the impetus for successful federation the transmission of ideological commitment from charismatic leaders to the people (*elite charisma*) or the transmission of broadly shared values (culminating in a federal value) from the people to the leaders (*popular charisma*). "The leaders, and their followers, must feel federal; there must be a positive political and ideological commitment to the primary goal of federation as an end in itself." [13]

4. The federal process is often also a means of preserving rather than building a new national unity out of many components. By timely concessions to, and constitutional recognition of, territorial communities and their desire for self-rule, a formerly unitary nation-state may be re-formed and its national unity saved. Only the future will tell us, for instance, whether the creation of additional states on a linguistic or religious basis in India after 1950 or the transformation of unitary Czechoslovakia into a federal state in 1968 were indeed timely measures and in the right direction and whether they have proved capable of channeling centrifugal or outrightly secessionist tendencies into a cooperative and constructive framework of a federal division of authority.

TESTING FEDERAL CONSTITUTIONS

Following are ten possible yardsticks of federalism in the form of ten questions to be directed at the national systems that are

[12] Richard L. Merritt, "Noncontiguity and Political Integration," paper presented at the 1966 Annual Meeting of the American Political Science Association, New York, pp. 18–19.

[13] Thomas C. Franck, *Why Federations Fail—An Inquiry into the Requisites for Successful Federalism*. New York: New York University Press, 1968, pp. 173–174.

considered to be or claim to be federal. These are further developed in this chapter and continue into the next chapter. Our yardsticks are primarily based on the United States Constitution because it is the most familiar to our readers. Also, the American system, whose federal nature has practically never been denied, has continuously existed the longest; it has acquired the reputation of a model.

Using American measuring rods, we are, however, far from suggesting that United States federalism should be considered the only "true" or "pure" one. Neither do we suggest that its birth and evolution are relevant for other countries that in the twentieth century may contemplate the adoption of a federal system. Some of the characteristics and aspects of United States federalism are so anchored in American soil that its experience and lessons can hardly be transplanted elsewhere. Furthermore, its record of preserving unity with diversity is much less impressive than some textbooks on American government would have one believe. Before proceeding farther, we should remind ourselves of some of the specific historical and local reasons for the success and crisis of the American federal system.

Unlike many other countries that have tried their hands at federalism in the present century, the thirteen original states had been aware of their collective identity and common interests before the adoption of the federal Constitution. They had indeed been a community before they became a federal nation. On the basis of a scholarly study of newspapers and pamphlet literature prior to 1776, a recent study demonstrates that the colonies had a remarkably congruent image of their country despite differences (whereas Massachusetts, for instance, was self-centered, Pennsylvania and New York had pluralistic outlooks, and the Southern colonies led in paying attention to the collective concept of common interest). "Moreover, they demonstrated their willingness to think of themselves as a single community without permitting the collective concept to overshadow the importance of individual colonies. It was this image of unity in diversity, essential to the American pattern of federalism that carried over into the Constitutional Convention of 1787." [14] Such an image of

---

[14] R. L. Merritt, *Perception of Unity and Diversity in Colonial America*. Geneva: International Political Science Association, 1964, p. 15.

unity is certainly not present in some of the modern federations, such as India, Burma, Nigeria, or Pakistan. As Valerie Earle says,

> where statehood in any but the most formal or legalistic sense scarcely exists, a discussion of federalism seems highly irrelevant and a federal system a venture beyond the reach of leaders who must struggle to stay in power and to begin to feed their people.[15]

There were other factors favoring the process of interlocking unity with diversity in the United States. While engaged in their federal experiment, the American states were able to remain relatively isolated from world tensions and wars and their corrosive or subversive domestic consequences. Today, none of the new and developing nations can enjoy the luxury of isolation that the young federation was able to maintain for so long. Also, there was no population explosion or pressure of excessive expectations on the meager resources. On the contrary, a dynamic immigrant population began to move into a rich and underpopulated continent as individual pioneers rather than as a mass anticipating social welfare from cradle to grave to be assured by governmental plan, funds and action. In a word, it was a different century, a different physical, political, and international environment—an era marked by individual and local self-reliance and self-discipline in empty spaces rather than the present-day ferment of excessive expectations in the midst of our overcrowded world.

The negative aspects of the American federal experience should be noted, too. The original federal formula recognized the identity and autonomy of the thirteen territorial communities and provided a framework for possible solutions of the conflicts of interests. It did not, however (and perhaps it could not), provide a machinery that could solve the more fundamental conflict between the two *regional* communities, one composed of Southern and the other Northern states. These two territorial communities, the North and the South, so differed in their eco-

---

[15] Valerie Earle, *Federalism: Infinite Variety in Theory and Practice.* Itasca, Ill.: F. E. Peacock, 1968, p. 212.

nomic interests and ways of life that, as some maintain, they had never actually formed a national community—they only hoped to form it perhaps at a later date.

"The great danger to our general government," rightly warned James Madison in 1787, "is the great southern and northern interest of the continent being opposed to each other. Look to the votes in Congress, and most of them stand divided by the geography of the country, not according to the size of the state." [16]

As noted before, the original thirteen states had been a community, fully aware of their common interest and collective identity with regard to England and the external world, but, as the tragic collision in 1860 indicates, the same thirteen states were not a community but two hostile subcommunities and potential nations when it came to the intrafederal, North-South issue. "If the cost of the Civil War in terms of casualties alone is calculated as part of the price of national unity," writes Henry Teune, "then perhaps the cost of national unity in the American experience is not one that many national leaders would be willing to pay." [17]

And then, of course, there is also the problem of cost in terms other than war casualties: for instance, the uneven economic and social development and the uneven progress in terms of civil rights, liberties, and education. Should diversity be promoted and protected as the highest value per se? William H. Riker, for instance, argues that throughout American history the main beneficiaries of federalism have been the Southern whites, who have been given the freedom to oppress blacks, first as slaves and later as a depressed caste. He concludes his book on federalism by a thought-provoking statement:

> If one approves the goals and values of the privileged minority, one should approve of federalism. Thus, if in the United States one approves of Southern white racists, then one should approve of American federalism. If, on the other

[16] Jonathan Elliot, *The Debates.* Philadelphia: Lippincott, 1888, Vol. I, pp. 465–466 (Yates minutes).

[17] Henry Teune, "The Future of Federalism: Federalism and Political Integration," in Earle, *Federalism,* p. 228.

hand, one disapproves of the values of the privileged minority, one should disapprove of federalism. Thus, if in the United States one disapproves of racism, one should disapprove of federalism.[18]

The United States federal Constitution (and all the others in existence) can be further criticized for its recognition of only some territorial or ethnic communities but not all. This is perhaps unavoidable because some territorial communities may emerge and assert their identity and interests long after the initial federal bargain. Today, for instance, the eighteenth-century American federal formula has still some relevance with reference to the identity and interests of New Hampshire and Rhode Island but has no relevance to the new dynamic, assertive, and potentially revolutionary or secessionist territorial communities that may either split some states or be regionally superimposed on several of them. We have here in mind such multistate regional communities or interest coalitions as the Eastern Seaboard, the Midwest, the Northwest, and the South, or, within the states, the big cities or new black or Latin communities with their own territorial identities (ghettos versus white suburbias) or their potentially broader territorial aspirations. The conflicting interests of these newer communities have necessarily become a subject of concern, recognition, and action on the part of the national government or the (unitary) state governments. In a manner characteristic of a unitary rather than a federal system, these new communities are being endowed by delegation with new autonomous powers, financial responsibility, and territorial self-rule. The school decentralization is a classic example of the new territorial dimensions of American politics —unitary decentralization—that is being added to the older and partly outdated federal formula.

Whatever the relevance of the American federal experience for other nations, a final note should be added: the rejection of a unitary system and the adoption of some variant of a federal formula is rarely a matter of free choice on the part of a handful

---

[18] William H. Riker, *Federalism: Origin—Operation—Significance.* Boston: Little, Brown, 1964, p. 155.

of constitutional lawyers gathered in an ivory-tower seminar on comparative constitutional law. There is often simply no practical alternative to the adoption of federalism—as we may assume, there really was no practical unitary alternative to the system as devised in Philadelphia in 1787. Before the Convention, James Madison wrote on April 8, 1787, to Edmund Randolph, Governor of Virginia: "I think, at the same time, that a consolidation of the states into one simple [unitary] republic is not less attainable than it would be inexpedient." Similarly, in many countries composed of different territorial, ethnic, tribal, lingual, racial, or religious communities, a unitary centralized system would cause such resentment and opposition as to jeopardize both the nation-building and the economic progress. Thus, the drafters of the Constitution may reluctantly favor the federal formula after having carefully weighed all the pros and cons of a unitary, centralized or decentralized, system, even though in theory they prefer a unitary system because it is less complex and less expensive and because it more directly leads to unity and progress. Of course, their choice may be wrong. There is really no reliable way of answering the question as to when the constitutional federal recognition and guarantee of diversity may ultimately contribute to a sense of satisfaction and unity or when, on the contrary, the federal formula may reinforce the sense of a separate territorial destiny, including the possibility of going it alone. Ever so often the road to territorial disintegration has been paved with best federal intentions.

In his *Democracy in America,* Alexis de Tocqueville called the American form of government "an incomplete national government" resting "in truth upon a wholly novel theory, which may be considered as a great discovery in modern political science." De Tocqueville stressed that, in contrast with confederations, the American federal government not only dictates but also executes its own laws and levies taxes not upon the states but upon each inhabitant. Deploring that "the human understanding more easily invents new things than new words," he concluded, "The new word which ought to express this novel thing does not yet exist." [19] James Madison himself referred to the proposed

---

[19] Alexis de Tocqueville, *Democracy in America.* New York: Vintage Books (Knopf and Random House), 1968, pp. 162–164.

constitution as one that "is, in strictness, neither a national [unitary] nor a federal constitution but a composition of both."[20]

Despite these and similar warnings concerning either the purity or applicability of American federalism as a universal model, our ten measuring rods, for purely practical reasons of comparison, will remain heavily based on the American federal theory, practice, and the Constitution—bearing in mind that, actually, the term *federal* never occurs in the text of the United States Constitution (*confederation* occurs only once in Article I, section 10, when states are prohibited "to enter into any confederation").

The ten yardsticks of federalism (the first four aim at measuring the reality and "indestructibility" of the union) that we will now use are:

1. Has the central authority exclusive control over diplomacy and defense as befits a nation-state in its relations *with other nation-states?*

2. Is the federal union constitutionally immune against dissolution by secession?

3. Is the exercise of the central authority as it reaches all citizens directly independent of the individual approval and resources of the component units?

4. Who has the ultimate control over amendments to the federal constitution?

5. Are the component units immune to elimination of their identity (antedating or postdating the union) and authority?

6. Is the collective sharing in federal rule making adequately secured by equal representation of unequal units in a bicameral system? What are the constitutional provisions for collective sharing in the executive and judiciary rule implementation?

7. Are there two independent sets of courts, one interpreting and adjudicating the federal laws and the other the state laws?

8. Is there a judicial authority in the central authority but standing above the central authority and the component units to determine their respective rights?

[20] Alexander Hamilton, James Madison, and John Jay, *The Federalist Papers.* New York: Mentor Books, 1961, p. 246.

9. Have the component units retained all the powers that the constitution has not given the central authority? And are these retained powers significant or marginal?
10. Is the territorial division of authority clear and unambiguous?

Even if we could answer all the preceding ten questions with unhesitant certainty by quoting appropriate articles or paragraphs of the twenty-one federal constitutions, there would still remain the second important test of federalism: that of comparing the constitutional text with actual practice, a subject to be discussed in our last two chapters.

YARDSTICK 1: EXCLUSIVE CONTROL OVER FOREIGN RELATIONS

Whether the end of a federal process is to create and maintain a new nation or to preserve an old one on a new (federal) basis, the emphasis is on making the federal nation-state a separate, sovereign, and identifiable unit vis-à-vis other nation-states. As with unitary states, a federal union's main purpose is to present itself on the international scene as possessing the power and the will to speak on behalf of its component units with one single legitimate voice; however, this purpose is in contradistinction to an alliance or a league of states. Unless the component units agree to this basic point, there is little likelihood that an alliance can transform itself into a federal nation; one of the reasons for the failure of the efforts in East Africa to combine Uganda, Tanzania, and Kenya into one federation was the insistence of the leaders of Uganda on retaining the right to conduct separate Ugandan foreign policy.

In a federation, then, it is the national (federal) government in whose hands lies the ultimate control over the major issues in foreign policy and the conduct of peaceful or violent international relations. (Chap. 9 will deal in some detail with the possible federal encroachments on state or provincial powers on account of the central government's supremacy in diplomacy and war powers.) The tasks of both the diplomatic service and the armed forces mirror the preoccupation, interests, and goals of the federal nation rather than those of the nation's territorial components. The United States Constitution, for instance, prescribes in Article 1, section 10, that

> no State shall enter into any Treaty, Alliance or Confederation.
> . . . No State shall, without the Consent of Congress, keep
> Troops, or Ships of War in time of Peace, enter into any
> Agreement or Compact with another State, or with a foreign
> Power, or engage in War, unless actually invaded, or in such
> imminent Danger as will not admit of delay.

Similarly, Switzerland in its 1848 Constitution gives the federal government "the sole right to declare war and conclude peace, and to make alliances and treaties, particularly customs and commercial treaties with foreign nations." The Swiss cantons can only exceptionally engage in minor direct diplomatic negotiations with neighboring nations (boundary and customs problems and so on).

Similar provisions for federal monopolies may be found in most federal constitutions; foreign affairs and defense are clearly placed in the list of exclusive, *nonshared* [21] federal powers in contradistinction to the state or concurrent lists. *In practice,* there seems to be no exception to this basic principle. In the *text* of a few constitutions that claim to be federal and not confederal, there are exceptions to this rule. The seemingly most important exception may be found in the Soviet Constitution of 1936 that was amended in 1944 to include the following provisions (Articles 18a and 18b):

> Each Union Republic has the right to enter into direct
> relations with foreign States and conclude agreements with
> foreign States and exchange representatives with them.
> Each Union Republic has its own Republican military
> formations.[22]

[21] In its Seventh Schedule, the Indian Constitution includes in its Union List (a list of powers given to the federal center) the usual provisions for diplomacy and defense, war and peace, treaties, the United Nations, pilgrimages outside India, piracies and crimes committed on the high seas or in the air, and offenses against international law. Yet, a few years ago, one of the Indian states (West Bengal) negotiated directly with the World Bank for a loan.

[22] All republican Constitutions were amended accordingly to include ministries of foreign affairs and defense in the list of the republican

By amending his own Constitution, Stalin transformed the Soviet federal union, on paper, into a *very loose* league of sixteen sovereign socialist republics. We say "a very loose league" because even the United States Confederation of 1781 refused to give its thirteen component states the right of direct diplomatic relations with foreign nations.[23]

On the part of Stalin, this represented a complete reversal of his attitude at the Twelfth Congress of the party in 1923, when he condemned confederal tendencies (mostly Ukrainian) in unmistakable terms:

> What becomes of the single union state if each republic retains its own People's Commissariat [Ministry] of Foreign Affairs? . . . We are creating not a confederation, but a federation of republics, a single union state, uniting military, foreign, trade and other affairs, a state which in no way diminishes the sovereignty of the individual republics. If the Union is to have a People's Commissariat of Foreign Affairs, a People's Commissariat of Foreign Trade, and so forth, and the republics constituting the Union are also to have all these Commissariats, it is obvious that it will be impossible for the Union as a whole to come before the outside world as a single state. One thing or the other: either we merge these apparatuses and face the external enemy as a single Union, or we do not merge them and create not a union state, but a conglomeration of republics, in which case every republic must have its own parallel apparatus.[24]

A. Y. Vyshinsky, who was later to become the Soviet prosecutor and foreign minister, accused the Ukrainians who wanted to preserve their own Ministry of Foreign Affairs of plans "to

---

governmental departments. Although several, but not all, republics established ministries of foreign affairs and appointed ministers to direct them, not a single republic has so far established a ministry of defense or have appointed a defense minister.

[23] Article 6: "No State without the consent of the United States in Congress assembled, shall send any embassy to, or receive any embassy from, or enter into any conference, agreement, alliance or treaty with any king, prince or state."

[24] J. V. Stalin, *Works,* Vol. V. Moscow: 1952–1955, pp. 341–344.

betray their people and the Union of its entirety" by preserving the legal possibility of contact with "their masters—the big imperialist powers and Poland." [25]

Stalin's reversal of his 1923 attitude in 1944 could be interpreted as a reflection of a changed situation inside the Soviet Union, which, after twenty-one years of federal life, was able to overcome its earlier centrifugal forces. Such an interpretation would be exaggerated in light of the fact that Stalin's 1944 "confederal" amendment has remained to the present day largely unimplemented in practice. The amendment—and this was probably its only purpose—allowed Stalin to ask a few months later at Yalta for sixteen votes in the United Nations General Assembly on behalf of the then sixteen union republics. Somewhat surprisingly he was finally satisfied when he obtained international recognition for the Soviet Ukraine and Soviet Byelorussia, whose separate national and diplomatic identities are expressed in their membership in the United Nations. We should note that this arrangement, which gives the Soviet Union three votes in the General Assembly, does not make sense at all: the Soviet Union as a confederation or a loose association of now fifteen socialist republics (see Fig. 7–3) [26] should have fifteen votes in the General Assembly or only one. As matters stand, the largest Soviet republic, the Russian Republic, is represented only through the Soviet federal government, as are the other Soviet republics of Estonia, Tadzhikistan, and Stalin's own Georgia. On the other hand, Soviet Ukraine and Soviet Byelorussia, which are members of the United Nations, have not been allowed to establish direct diplomatic relations with any other nation, not

---

[25] A. Y. Vyshinsky, *The Law of the Soviet State*. New York: Crowell-Collier-Macmillan, 1948, p. 264.

[26] The Soviet Constitution enumerates its fifteen major nationalities that constitute the component units of the Soviet Federal Union in the order of their respective numerical importance: the Russian Soviet Federal Socialist Republic (the RSFSR, extending from Leningrad and the Baltic Sea to Vladivostok and Alaska, is itself federated; the Russians constitute 50 percent of the total Soviet population), Ukraine, Byelorussia, Uzbek, Kazakh, Georgia, Azerbaijan, Lithuania, Moldavia, Latvia, Kirghiz, Armenia, Turkmenistan and Estonia. In addition, on the territories of the union republics may be found autonomous republics (ASSR), autonomous regions (AR) and national districts (NR).

Figure 7–3   Map of the federal divisions of the USSR

International Boundaries

Boundaries of Union Republics

Boundaries of Regions, Territories
and Autonomous Republics

Boundaries of National Areas

○ Capitals of Union Republics

1. ADIGEI AR
2. CHERKESS AR
3. KABARDIN ASSR
4. N. OSETIN ASSR
5. S. OSETIN AR
6. NAGORNO-KARABAKH AR

Union Republics
Other than RSFSR

Autonomous Republics
within RSFSR

even with neighboring socialist states such as Poland, Rumania, Bulgaria, or Czechoslovakia. When this curious deal was made at Yalta in 1945, the main argument of Stalin was more "sentimental" than constitutional (although he did point to the fact that the British Commonwealth at that time had more votes than the one vote of its leading member, the United Kingdom): he pleaded that Soviet Ukraine and Soviet Byelorussia be granted the right to United Nations membership because of their sacrifices in the United Nations common struggle against Nazism. In the Ukrainian capital of Kiev, a visitor can indeed find a Ukrainian foreign ministry housed in an office building of respectable proportions; he will have some difficulty in finding the ministries of foreign affairs in other republics. "The Georgian Foreign Ministry has its headquarters in a dilapidated structure in a dark corner of Tbilisi (1958) and consists only of a single reception chamber." [27]

Regardless of the degree of the Soviet implementation or nonimplementation of its "confederal" articles affecting foreign affairs and defense, there is, no doubt, some logic in the concept of federal decentralization, not only in domestic but also international affairs. In an interdependent world, one could indeed imagine that special cultural, economic,[28] and even political links that affect subnational units but that cross international boundaries may develop, especially between territorial communities that are contiguous yet separated by their respective nations' frontiers. The Swiss Constitution, as we have seen, permits minor links between cantons and neighboring nation-states; California and Mexico have a separate agreement concerning the importation of fruits and vegetables, and so forth. In Com-

---

[27] Vernon A. Aspaturian, "The Union Republics and Soviet Diplomacy: Concepts, Institutions and Practices," *The American Political Science Review,* Vol. 53, No. 2 (June 1959), 404. See also Aspaturian's fully documented and thoroughly researched book, *The Union Republics and Soviet Diplomacy.* Geneva: Librairie Droz, 1960.

[28] Reference was recently made to the existence of a Ukrainian Ministry of Foreign Trade that negotiated a new trade agreement with its Polish counterpart (*Nase Slovo* [Warsaw], May 5, 1968). In reality there is no Ministry of Foreign Trade, only Internal Trade, in Soviet Ukraine. The direct negotiation between a Ukrainian and a Polish ministry seems, however, a noteworthy novelty.

munist Yugoslavia (see Fig. 7–4) in the late 1960s a trend has developed to create special commissions for foreign affairs in all six federal republics (Bosnia and Herzegovina, Croatia, Macedonia, Montenegro, Serbia, and Slovenia) as well as for the two autonomous regions (Kosmet and Voivodina) for the

Figure 7–4   Map of the federal divisions of Yugoslavia

purpose of influencing the national Ministry of Foreign Affairs (located in Serbian Belgrade) to pursue foreign policies that would be "brought into line with [their] internal policies." [29] The argument heard in Yugoslavia is twofold: first, decentralization of foreign policy is only part of the general decentralization of communism; second, individual republics have some special problems with regard to their neighbors and have some

[29] *Politika* (Belgrade), October 19, 1966, reporting on a speech by the Moslem leader of the Communist party of Bosnia, Refik Hulic.

economic interests that may not call for an overall national commitment. This is further underlined by suspicion that foreign trade policy in particular was excessively determined by the interests as perceived by Serbia and its capital, Belgrade.[30] The republics of Croatia and Slovenia tend to translate their ancient links with their Catholic Western neighbors into favorable economic arrangements. On the other hand, the republic of Macedonia seeks additional protection against potential threats coming from neighboring Bulgaria and Greece, which both, at one time or other, voiced territorial claims with regard to Macedonia.

In the biethnic federal union of Canada, the French-English antagonism was bound also to affect the conduct of Canada's foreign policy that constitutionally and traditionally has been an exclusive prerogative of the government in Ottawa. On April 14, 1967, however, the Quebec Legislature set up a Ministry of Intergovernmental Affairs for the purpose of promoting the interests of French Canada not only with regard to the federal government in Ottawa but also in negotiations with foreign governments, which, at that stage, meant primarily France, to which a portion of the French-speaking elite in Canada feels more attuned than to Ottawa. The French Canadian "ministry of foreign affairs" resembles those of the Soviet republics or the commissions of the Yugoslav republics with one important difference: in the framework of a free and democratic society, the extraconstitutional assumption of diplomatic prerogatives may in practice be more meaningful than in either of the Communist party states.

A limited diplomatic initiative has been given to the component units of the German Federal Republic by Article 32, section 3, of the Constitution: "Insofar as the Länder have power to legislate, they may, with the consent of the Federal Government, conclude treaties with foreign states." This echoes the German confederal and imperial traditions. In Imperial

---

[30] *Borba* (Belgrade), January 28, 1968: "Of course, these new institutions (Commissions for Foreign Affairs) are in no way republican foreign ministries. However, there is no doubt that there is an increasing feeling that we need a more decisive course aimed at overcoming old practices in the pursuit of foreign policy, which thus far has been the exclusive prerogative of the central state organs [in Serbia]."

Germany, the twenty-three monarchies and three city-republics had the right of separate diplomatic relations with foreign states, and the monarchies that could afford it had their diplomatic representation abroad. Under the Weimar Republic, the central power reserved the right of final approval and ratification of the treaties that the Länder were constitutionally authorized to conclude with foreign states. Bavaria had direct diplomatic relations with the Vatican, and a French representative resided in Munich, Bavaria's capital.

Another form of possible influence of the territorial components on the federal conduct of foreign policy may be seen in the constitutional provisions that require the federal chamber (Senate) to approve presidential travels and sojourns abroad. This is so in all Latin-American federations and also in Malaysia. For instance, the Venezuelan Constitution provides in Article 189:

> The President, or whoever is acting in his stead, may not leave the national territory without authorization of the Senate or of the Delegated Committee. Likewise, he may not do so without such authorization within six months following the date on which he leaves office.[31]

The Malaysian federal Constitution contains the following provisions: "The Yang di Pertuan Agong [the Supreme Head of the Federation elected by the territorial hereditary rulers] . . . shall not without the consent of the Conference of Rulers be absent from the Federation for more than fifteen days."

Federal defense and war powers will be discussed fuller in Chapter 9. Here we may only note that in federal unions the traditional democratic right of the citizens to bear arms has its territorial counterpart: the right of the component units to be armed and not to be disarmed by the national government. "A well regulated Militia" in the United States Constitution (Second Amendment) and "Republican Military formations" in the Soviet Union (Article 18b, quoted previously) appear as adjuncts to or

---

[31] Similar wording may be found in the constitutions of Brazil (Article 66), Mexico (Articles 73 and 88), and Argentina (Article 83). The Latin-American objections to prolonged and costly absences of their presidents from the national territory can also be found in unitary constitutions, for instance, those of Chile, Colombia, and Ecuador.

parts of national armies maintained by the federal government.

In Switzerland, however, the Constitution specifically prohibits the national government from maintaining a standing army (Article 13). Only cantons can have permanent troops. The armed neutrality of Switzerland is based on cantonal armies, but the national government is responsible for the general organization of the armed forces, their strategic and tactical plans, and their command in both peacetime and wartime. In peacetime, the head of the Swiss military establishment is a civilian who is in charge of the military department and relies on the general staff composed of professional officers. In peacetime, no officer can have a rank higher than that of colonel. But if general mobilization is proclaimed, the national legislature (the Federal Assembly) promotes a colonel to the rank of general and makes him commander in chief. This was so during World War I and World War II. The appointment lapsed after the war.[32]

We may conclude here by stressing that the first yardstick of federalism—the exclusive control of diplomacy and national defense by the central government—does not and is not supposed to distinguish a federal from a unitary system; it is meant to draw the line between a federation and a league of states or an alliance in which the component units retain a decisive influence on common foreign policy and defense. This line, however, is very blurred when we consider the wording, although not the working, on the one hand of the American Articles of Confederation (which centralized the conduct of foreign policy) and on the other hand that of the Soviet Constitution (which decentralized the conduct of foreign policy). It could be said that up to a certain limit federal monopoly over foreign policy may be diluted by diplomatic autonomy of the component units. But what that limit is (that is, at what point a federal nation ceases to be one and becomes a loose association of several nations) will evidently remain controversial.

YARDSTICK 2: IMMUNITY AGAINST SECESSION

No nation-state is, or can be, immune against territorial secession. In some instances, constitutions clearly forbid it or proclaim or

[32] George Arthur Codding, Jr., *The Federal Government of Switzerland*. Boston: Houghton Mifflin, 1965, p. 142.

imply that the union is eternal [33] and therefore no territory can secede. Here, again, there are exceptions.

The United States Constitution does not contain any explicit interdiction of secession. Implicitly it may be argued that the Preamble's first sentence, which stresses a "more perfect Union," should be read in conjunction with the Articles of Confederation, which it amended and which had committed the thirteen states to a "perpetual union." In the first seventy years of the United States existence, there could be some doubt about the right of national self-determination of the federal components. The Civil War, however, "conclusively settled the question whether or not a state can constitutionally withdraw from the Union. In the words of the Supreme Court, ours is 'an indestructible union of indestructible states.' " [34]

The Soviet, Yugoslav, and Burmese Constitutions, on the other hand, contain provisions recognizing the right of territorial self-determination and secession. The Soviet Constitution reserves "the right freely to secede from the USSR" to every Union Republic (Article 17). All Union Republics have their boundaries contiguous to those of the Soviet Union, allegedly to be able to go it alone if they wish to do so without remaining an encircled island somewhere in the middle of the Soviet subcontinent. In reality, of course, the right of secession can be implemented only in the framework of socialism; that is, it cannot be exercised if it were to weaken the cause of communism and strengthen the cause of capitalism. As Stalin expressed it in 1920,

---

[33] Compare for instance the interdynastic federation of German states, following the loose German Confederation in 1871 (Bismarck's Constitution): "His Majesty, the King of Prussia on behalf of the Northern German Federation; His Majesty, the King of Bavaria; His Majesty, the King of Württemberg; His Royal Highness, the Grand-Duke of Baden; and His Royal Highness, the Grand-Duke of Hessen and of the Rhine— the latter for the section of the Grand-Duchy situated south of the river Main—conclude an *eternal* federation to protect the federal territory and the law of the land as well as to promote the welfare of the German people. This federation shall be known by the name of German Reich and shall have the following Constitution." (Italics added.)

[34] Edward S. Corwin and J. W. Peltason, *Understanding the Constitution,* 4th ed. New York: Holt, Rinehart and Winston, Inc., 1964, p. 93 (compare note 8 in this chapter).

Of course, the border regions of Russia, the nations and the tribes, which inhabit these regions . . . possess the inalienable right to secede from Russia . . . but the demand for secession . . . at the present stage of the revolution is a profoundly counterrevolutionary one.[35]

As the Soviet military invasion of Hungary in 1956 and the Soviet occupation of Czechoslovakia in 1968 demonstrated, even allied sovereign countries have no right to secede from the Soviet bloc if they occupy strategic geographic positions in the framework of the Warsaw Pact. It may actually be argued that one of the many reasons for the Soviet overreaction to both the Hungarian and the Czechoslovak desires for self-determination was the fear that secession by an ally might trigger secessionist tendencies within the western portions of the Soviet Union.

The right of secession is also subordinated to the cause of socialism in the Yugoslav Constitution, whose Basic Principles, Part I, read in part as follows:

The peoples of Yugoslavia, on the basis of the right of every people to self-determination, including the right of secession, . . . aware that the further consolidation of their brotherhood and unity is to their common interest, have united in a federal republic of free and equal peoples and nationalities and have founded a socialist federal community of working people, the Socialist Federal Republic of Yugoslavia. . . . The working people, and the peoples of Yugoslavia exercise their sovereign rights in the Federation when the Constitution determines this to be in the common interest and exercise all other relations in the socialist republics.

The Union of Burma [36] (see Fig. 7–5) guarantees "the right to secede from the Union in accordance with the conditions hereinafter prescribed" (Articles 201 and 202). The Constitution prescribes the procedure of orderly secession, including a plebiscite "for the purpose of ascertaining the will of the people of

---

[35] *Pravda* (Moscow, October 20, 1920).

[36] The ethnic composition of Burma is Burmese, 75 percent; Indians (nonterritorial), 9 percent; Karens, Chins, Shans, and Kachins (territorial ethnic groups), 7 percent; Chinese (nonterritorial), 5 percent; others (including Europeans), 4 percent.

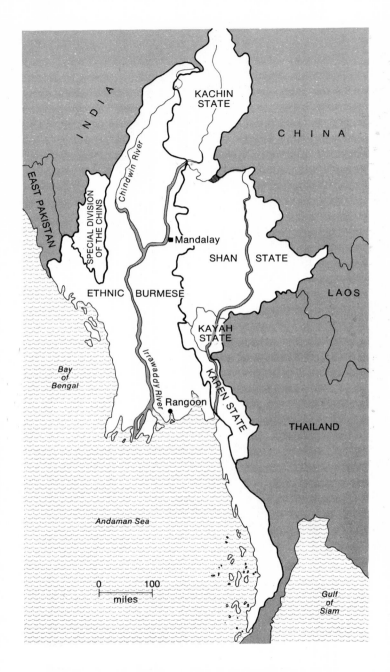

Figure 7–5 Map of the federal divisions of Burma

the State concerned." The right of secession was not to be exercised at all within ten years from the date of the proclamation of the federal Constitution, but apparently any time after 1957. The reason for this unusual provision was to give the federal idea in Burma a trial period of ten years. In practice, however, the constitutional and federal government in Burma was of very brief duration, if it started at all. A military dictatorship replaced constitutional democracy and attempts at tribal secessions by jungle warfare replaced the detailed provisions of the Constitution concerning the tribal and frontier areas.[37]

Quite understandably, in practice, no authority, federal or unitary, can be expected to view any territorial separatism with favor; [38] regardless of the nature of the constitution, the authority would yield to secessionism, gracefully or not, only under considerable pressure. In the case of the United Kingdom, as one author pointed out, "if Northern Ireland or Scotland, or perhaps even other elements, were to seek actively for secession, it seems most unlikely that the right would be challenged." [39]

This scholarly hypothesis became an explosive issue in 1969 in the wake of serious riots in Northern Ireland, which pitted the Catholic minority against the ruling majority in Belfast. On August 28, 1969, the prime minister of the Irish Republic, John Lynch, proposed a federal union between the Irish Republic and Northern Ireland as a solution of the crisis. Denouncing the 1921 partition between Belfast and the Republic as "unnatural and unjustifiable," Lynch envisioned the preservation of the Northern Ireland Parliament at Stormont and the republican parliament in Dublin as provincial legislatures; a new council was to serve as a federal parliament of the united Ireland. The invitation for secession from Britain and federation with the South

---

[37] The Constitution provides for a bicameral legislature. In its upper house, called the Chamber of Nationalities, the non-Burmese had a majority (seventy-two to fifty-three) composed as follows: Karens, twenty-five representatives; Shans, twenty-four; Kachins, twelve; Chin division, eight; and Karenni states, three.

[38] If the denial of the right of secession is assumed, may it be deemed to include the right of the territorial units not to be expelled against their will?

[39] William S. Livingston, "A Note on the Nature of Federalism," *Political Science Quarterly,* Vol. 67, No. 1 (March 1952), 92.

was promptly rejected by the then prime minister of Northern Ireland, James Chichester-Clark.

YARDSTICK 3: INDEPENDENT SPHERE OF CENTRAL AUTHORITY

In a federal system, powers are so divided "that the general and regional governments are each, within a sphere, co-ordinate and independent," [40] notes an English authority on the subject of federalism. Logically, an authority is not really divided unless its sectors can operate within their assigned sphere independently one from the other. If the central authority were politically and financially dependent in each of its moves upon the component units, we could define such an arrangement as an *alliance* or *confederation,* but we could not speak of an emergence of a federal nation and its government.

How can some of the constitutions whose drafters label them as federal pass this third test, which aims at differentiating a confederal from a federal system?

First, there is the issue of financial resources. Federal constitutions make the federal government independent of the constituent units by granting it the right to levy direct taxes and enforce the federal laws. This also implies that the rightful inhabitants of the federal state are federal citizens in *addition to* [41] or *instead of* [42] their local citizenship.

The federal government must be able to finance its operations, especially in view of the fact that it is, as we have indicated previously, in charge of international relations and defense; in modern times, the welfare functions have been added to the first two traditional ones. (More will be said about this in Chap. 8.)

A guarantee of the right and power of the provincial government to finance its operations cannot and must not tax the

[40] K. C. Wheare, *Federal Government.* New York: Oxford, 1964, p. 10.

[41] The United States Constitution states in Article IV, section 2: "The Citizens of each State shall be entitled to all Privileges and Immunities of Citizens in the several States."

[42] The Burmese Constitution states in Article 10: "There shall be but one citizenship throughout the Union; that is to say, there shall be no citizenship of the unit as distinct from the citizenship of the Union."

federal power out of existence. This was partly the issue in the famous case *McCulloch* v. *Maryland* in 1819, when a bank (a quasi-governmental institution incorporated by the United States and established in Baltimore) issued notes in violation of a Maryland law that required all banks to pay an annual tax of $15,000 or to pay a stamp tax on each bank note issued. The controversy was decided by the Supreme Court in favor of the federal government. In Chief Justice John Marshall's words:

> A goverment intrusted with such ample powers [to lay and collect taxes, regulate commerce, conduct war, etc.], on the due execution of which the happiness and prosperity of the nation so vitally depends, must also be intrusted with ample means for their execution. It can never be their interest, and cannot be presumed to have been their intention, to clog and embarrass its execution, by withholding the most appropriate means.[43]

Some echo of this early American rule protecting federal enterprises against tax voraciousness of component units in a federation may be found in modern federal constitutions that must also protect atomic and conventional power plants and other economic enterprises established and run by a welfare federal government [44] against the taxing powers of the states. The United States Constitution gave the Congress the power to lay and collect taxes, duties, imposts, and excises (Article I, section 8), but until 1913, in principle direct taxes were to be apportioned among the several states according to population. In 1913, the Sixteenth Amendment gave the Congress the right to impose income taxes "without apportionment among the several States, and without regard to any census or enumeration."

[43] McCulloch v. Maryland 4 Wheaton 316 (1819).

[44] The 1949 Constitution of Pakistan, for instance, prescribed (Article 113): "No Act of a Provincial Legislature shall impose or authorize the imposition of a tax upon the consumption or sale of electricity which is consumed by the Federal Government, and any Act of a Provincial Legislature imposing or authorizing the imposition of the tax on the sale of electricity shall secure the price of electricity sold to the Federal Government for the consumption by that Government shall be less by the amount of the tax than the price charged to other consumers of a substantial quantity of electricity."

Is the financial independence of the center impaired by an obligation of tax sharing, characteristic of modern federalism? In developing countries that have federal constitutions, sometimes special provisions create a common fund from which backward areas of the nation receive special grants-in-aid. According to the Indian Constitution, for instance, all revenues received and all loans raised by the central government form the Consolidated Fund of India (Article 266).[45] The Constitution also contains very detailed and specific provisions on how to divide some stamp duties of excise (Article 268 on "medicinal and toilet preparations") and how to channel back to the states some centrally levied and collected duties and taxes.[46] Similar provisions for sharing of duties or taxes may be found in the 1949 Constitution of Pakistan with respect to provincial mass media.[47]

Another form of dependence of the central authority on the territorial units may exist in purely political matters, especially in the provisions concerning the establishment and operation of the central authority. Here, again, if the central authority were dependent entirely on the whim and political mood of the component units, the federation would shade off into a league of states or alliances, whose common institution is usually an

---

[45] Article 273 of the Indian Constitution states, for instance: "There shall be charged on the Consolidated Fund of India in each year as grants-in-aid of the revenues of the State of Assam, Bihar, Orissa, and West Bengal, in lieu of assignment of any share of the net proceeds in each year of export duty on jute and jute products to those States, such sums as may be prescribed."

[46] Article 269 enumerates seven such categories of taxes, including taxes on railway fares and freights, sale or purchase of newspapers and advertisements published therein.

[47] Part VI, Article 131, section 1: "Notwithstanding anything in the Constitution it shall be competent to the Provincial Government to construct and use transmitters with respect to broadcasting in the Province:

"Provided that when a Provincial Government constructs and uses transmitters in the Province, it shall be entitled to a part of the net proceeds of the fees received by the federal government in respect of the use of any receiving apparatus in the Province, in such proportion as may be agreed, or, in default of agreement, as may be determined in accordance with the procedure prescribed in Article 129."

assembly of ambassadors appointed, instructed by, and entirely dependent on the component units.

Some authors argue that such a confederal dependence on the component units still exists in the United States, where not the federal government but the states determine qualifications for the exercise of the federal right to vote. It is true that constitutional amendments extending the right to vote regardless of race and sex as well as subsequent judicial interpretations limited the powers of the states to distort the right to participate in federal elections. It should be recalled that the founding fathers in Philadelphia assigned to the states the right to determine qualifications for voters because they could not agree then as to what these qualifications for free males with property should be. The Voting Rights Act of 1965 in particular was aimed at eliminating the Southern states' encroachment on the federal right to vote by imposing literacy tests for the purpose of keeping the black population from the polls. The Alabama literacy test, for instance, when given to thirty-six college seniors and college graduate students in California, demonstrated amply that an average citizen, white or black, could not possibly pass it without a single mistake—a sufficient reason for a local registrar to disqualify a prospective voter; the three highest scorers among the California students taking the Alabama literacy test answered sixteen questions out of sixty-eight incorrectly.[48]

[48] Until 1965, the Alabama Literacy Test consisted of sixty-eight questions, including these:

4. A United States senator elected at the general election in November takes office the following year on what date?
5. A President elected at the general election in November takes office the following year at what date?
9. Does enumeration affect the income tax levied on citizens in various states?
19. Who passes laws dealing with piracy?
30. Of the original 13 states, the one with the largest representation in the first Congress was _____.
58. On the impeachment of the chief justice of the Supreme Court of the United States, who tries the case?
64. If the two houses of Congress cannot agree on adjournment, who sets the time?

The reader may test his own voter qualifications.

Still another form of dependence of the central authority on local units may be seen in constitutional provisions for indirect elections of one of the two houses of the federal legislature. This was so in the United States until 1913, when the Seventeenth Amendment replaced the choice of senators by state legislature by direct popular election. In other federal systems such selection is still the practice. In Switzerland, for instance, the upper house of the Swiss federal assembly (the Council of States) is composed of two representatives from each canton; each canton determines the period of the representative's service, his salary (to be paid from the cantonal treasury), and the method of his selection (in most cases direct election, in other cases by cantonal legislatures). This indeed reminds us of a confederal assembly of ambassadors.

In West Germany, the members of the federal upper house are not elected nor do they serve a fixed term. (This was so also in Imperial and Weimar Germany.) They are members or officials of the cabinet in each of the twelve Länder. They vote on behalf of their territorial executive en bloc (3–5 votes, depending on the size of their land) and according to the instructions given by the respective Länder cabinet. The consent of the federal upper chamber is required for all matters involving the federal distribution of power and affecting the administration of federal laws by the Länder.[49]

In India, the members of the Council of State are "elected by the elected members of the Legislative Assembly of the State in accordance with the system of proportional representation by means of a single transferable vote." [50] In Venezuela each state elects two senators by universal and direct vote; the federal district (the capital city) also elects two senators, and a few additional senators represent the ethnic minorities. In addition,

---

[49] Peter H. Merkl, *Political Continuity and Change*. New York: Harper & Row, 1967, pp. 400–402. The author concludes that in the German type of federalism the Bundesrat "allows the Länder governments a degree of direct participation in all aspects of national politics, which no American state or Canadian province can boast."

[50] Article 80 speaks of election by the *elected* members because in India a small number of the members of the upper houses, both on the union and state levels, are not elected but appointed by the president or the state governor, respectively.

former duly elected presidents of the Republic become senators for life after having completed their term of office (Article 148). In the Communist federations, members of the upper house are elected by direct popular elections after being selected as candidates by the Communist party.

In conclusion, another type of potential dependence of the central authority on one of the component units should be mentioned. Is the seat of the national government separated from, or identified with, one particular territorial unit? Moscow, for instance, is the capital of both the Russian Republic and the Soviet Union; Bern is the capital of the canton and the Swiss federation; Belgrade is the capital of both Serbia and Yugoslavia. The capital of Canada, Ottawa, is a municipality of Ontario Province, situated on the Ottawa River, which separates English-speaking Ontario from the French-speaking Quebec. Four fifths of Ottawa's inhabitants speak English. The dominantly English atmosphere of Ottawa was bound to become an issue in the period when Canada aimed at a more truly bilingual and biethnic concept of the nation. The Royal Commission for Bilingualism and Biculturalism, reporting on its findings (June 17, 1969), warned that "in the first 100 years of confederation [*sic*!] no significant consideration has been given by either province [Ontario or Quebec] to the peculiar linguistic and cultural needs of the Ottawa area in its role as the capital of Canada." Other federations have established federal capitals as separate federal districts: New Delhi in India, Washington, D.C., in the United States, Mexico City in Mexico, Lagos in Nigeria. The Austrian federation, a very small country that has inherited the imperial size and glory of the capital of the former Hapsburg Empire, lists Vienna as one of its component units.[51] The federal district is usually small, one reason being that size could connote a territorial base for excessive federal power. The United States Constitution limits its capital district to ten miles (Article I, section 8, which gives the federal government exclusive legislation in the District and authority over forts, arsenals,

---

[51] The Austrian Constitution of 1920 states in Article 2: "Austria is a Federal State. The Federal State is composed of the autonomous Länder of Burgenland, Carinthia, Lower Austria, Upper Austria, Salzburg, Styria, Tyrol, and Vienna."

and dockyards purchased from the states). In Brazil, the decision to build Brasilia—"this collection of pyramids in the middle of nowhere," in Leslie Lipson's words—at such a huge cost when the country needed funds for seemingly more important tasks is a good example of the suspicions and fears in any association of territorial units that one of them may emerge more powerful than the others and dominate them. The recommendation made by the Brazilian professional geographers and urbanists who had taken into account such important factors as proper terrain, climate, adequate supply of water, fertility of neighboring soil, and attractive recreational areas was rejected by the majority of Brazilian state representatives. What was the reason? The geographers placed the future federal district too close to the economically powerful state of São Paulo, which threatens to be dominant even without having the capital district within its reach. A location much farther from São Paulo was finally selected and agreed upon.[52]

A similar problem of interstate jealousy and fears was encountered in Pakistan, whose original capital was the most important city of West Pakistan, Karachi. East Pakistan objected to such identification of a provincial with a federal capital— and won. A new capital is being built in the district of Rawalpindi. It is named Islamabad; it will be the seat of the executive branch of government (Article 211). A second capital,[53] Dacca, in East Pakistan, will be the seat of the national legislature— in Pakistani terms the Montesquieuan concept of the separation of legislative and executive power was stretched to mean a distance of a thousand miles.

[52] Preston E. James, *Latin America*. New York: Odyssey, 1959, pp. 567–568.

[53] The Constitution of federal Libya also provides for two capitals, Tripoli and Benghazi (Article 188). In Chapter I (2, 3), it further states, "Libya is a State having a hereditary monarchy, its form is federal and its system of government is representative. Its name is 'the United Kingdom of Libya.' The United Kingdom of Libya consists of the Provinces of Cyrenaica, Tripolitania and the Fezzan." The geographic problem of Libyan federalism, including the need for two capitals, is territorial noncontiguity of a special kind. According to the United Nations Commissioner in Libya (Report to the General Assembly, 1951), "the Libyan provinces are like islands in an ocean of sand, separated by hundreds of miles of desert wastes."

Another aspect of sensitivity as to the advantages that one component unit of a federation may derive from its identification with the federal power may be seen in the provision of the Malayan Constitution that forbids a fusion of the position of the supreme (federal) ruler with that of the local ruler—a somewhat tricky problem in an interdynastic federation in which the hereditary and mostly theocratic rulers are also territorial heads of the state church. The Constitution therefore forbids the supreme federal ruler to exercise his local political functions but permits him to continue his religious functions.[54] The Argentine Constitution of 1853 provided for the president of the republic to be also the mayor of the federal capital city.[55] The Venezuelan Constitution reflects another type of suspicion present in territorial associations: the fear that the states could try to limit the power of the federal government to its federal district without being capable of extending the national power over and into the component units. Article 11, which makes the city of Caracas the capital of Venezuela and "the permanent seat of the supreme branches of the National Power," adds that this should "not prevent the temporary exercise of the National Power in other places of the Republic." This may also happen during summer vacation or during a revolution.

The failure of federalism in the African state of Uganda may be, at least partly, attributed to the fact that Kampala, the capital city of the largest and richest kingdom of Uganda's five kingdoms, was chosen to be the federal capital; the king of Buganda, who remained the ruler of his kingdom, was made the president of Uganda. The symbolic and political identification of one powerful component unit with the collective federal power proved unbearable.

All the cases just mentioned seem to point to one common experience, or, more often, fear, that the federal power may so detach itself from its collective basis and identify with one particular segment of the nation that the result would be the

[54] Article 35: "The Yang di-Pertuan Agong shall not exercise his functions as Ruler of his State except those of Head of the Muslim religion."

[55] Article 86: "He is the immediate and local head of the Capital of the Nation."

domination of the whole by one of its parts. Prussia finally dominated Germany. Northern dominance was feared in the United States on the eve of 1861. On the other hand, it should be admitted that there is no country in the world, federal or unitary, that has not witnessed some resentment or jealousy of the capital city.

YARDSTICK 4: AMENDING THE FEDERAL CONSTITUTION

If the American model of federalism were viewed as the only pure one, the fourth yardstick may be expressed as a retention of veto over constitutional changes by a majority of, but not all, component units. According to many experts this is by far the most reliable yardstick of federalism when the *text* of constitutions is analyzed. If the ultimate control over constitutional changes is in the hands of *all* the component units, such a system, based on unanimity, seems not to have moved from an association of states to a new federal nation. A new supraterritorial identity, institutions, and power have not really been created if for any amendment the consent of every single component unit is required. If, on the other hand, only a vote of the central parliament is required (with or without a subsequent plebiscite), such a system, based on a national majoritarian principle, makes the amendatory process indistinguishable from that in a unitary system. This is so, for instance, in the Soviet case when a two-thirds majority in both houses of the central parliament is sufficient to adopt any type of amendment, including one that would transform the Soviet federation into a unitary state and eliminate all fifteen union republics altogether. Similarly, the Yugoslav federal Constitution can be amended without ratification by the component republics; a popular referendum is, however, required when two of the chambers composing the quinticameral Federal Assembly refuse to accept the motion to alter the Constitution as passed by the Federal Chamber and the Chamber of Nationalities.[56] Some constitutions distinguish between amendments that affect the federal distribution of power and those that

[56] The Yugoslav Federal Assembly is composed of a federal chamber whose members, elected by the republics and autonomous provinces, constitute a Chamber of Nationalities. The other four chambers are functional: (1) economic, (2) organizational-politic, (3) social welfare and health, (4) education and culture.

do not do so; only in the first case is the ratification by the component units required. The Indian and Pakistani Constitutions have such provisions.[57]

The problem with such a differentiation between federal and nonfederal amendments is that a constitutional change that does not seem to affect the federal division of powers may ultimately, in conjunction with environmental changes, affect it in a major way. By contrast, in the United States, all amendments, even if they do not affect the federal distribution of power, require ratification by three fourths of the states. One type of amendment cannot be passed and ratified by even forty-nine states out of fifty: the last sentence of the Amendatory Article 5 states that "no State, without its consent, shall be deprived of its equal Suffrage in the Senate." This is considered the basic point of the whole American federal bargain, as expressed in the Connecticut Compromise at Philadelphia in 1787. Some legal experts have, however, argued that the Amendatory Article could be amended and that its new version could eliminate the equal suffrage clause. In an abstract legal framework this may be so; in practice, it seems politically out of the question.

The four yardsticks discussed so far were intended to distinguish a federal nation-state from an association or confederation of sovereign states. Although these are helpful in discovering national variations of constitutional approaches to unity in diversity, they failed to provide us with a fully reliable criterion. In the following chapter we shall examine some other yardsticks of federalism, the purpose of which is to draw a line between a federal and a unitary constitutional system.

---

[57] Article 368 of the Indian Constitution prescribes approval by a majority of the total membership of both houses of Parliament (no less than two thirds of the members must be present and voting). If, however, the amendment is concerned with the election of the president, and representation of the state at the election, Union, State, and Concurrent Lists, high courts of states, union judiciary, union's powers and executive and judiciary powers of states, it must be also ratified by no less than one half of the states. Article 210 of the Pakistani Constitution of 1962 prescribes approval by two thirds of the total membership of the provincial assemblies in the case of an amendment that "would have the effect of altering the limits of a Province." Other amendments do not need ratification by the provinces. It is enough if two thirds of the total membership of the central legislature and the president approve it.

EIGHT
TERRITORIAL
SEPARATION
OF POWERS

Federalism is . . . a kind of division or separation
of power, but applied on a territorial basis.

> CARL J. FRIEDRICH (*Constitutional Gov-*
> *ernment and Democracy*)

Powers are divided between a general government
which in certain matters—for example, the making
of treaties and the coining of money—is independent
of the governments of the associated states, and, on
the other hand, state governments which in certain
matters are, in their turn, independent of the general
government. This involves, as a necessary consequence, that general and regional governments both
operate directly upon the people; each citizen is
subject to two governments.

> K. C. WHEARE (*Federal Government*)

A state with a federal income tax is no longer a
genuine federal state.

> KARL LOWENSTEIN ("Reflections on the
> Value of Constitutions in Our Revolution-
> ary Age")

The texts of federal constitutions recognize and pay due respect to two separate jurisdictions (national and state) and describe their respective spheres of action and responsibility. Their respective powers, however, are not and have not been meant to be equal. The national power is clearly favored. This is understandable because the purpose of the adopted federal structure is either to create one nation out of many or to preserve a nation by a timely recognition of its inner diversity.

On April 8, 1787, James Madison expressed his concept of the national primacy in a letter to Governor Edmund Randolph:

> I hold it a fundamental point, that an individual independence of the States is utterly irreconcilable with the idea of an aggregate sovereignty. . . . Let it be tried then whether any middle ground can be taken which will at once support a due supremacy of the national authority, and leave in force the local authorities so far as they can be *subordinately* useful. [Italics added.] [1]

Madison's middle ground has proven to be, not a perfect flat, but a gentle slope that has encouraged further sliding of power from the "subordinately" useful states to the national center—an interpretation that the wording of the Constitution has permitted but that its drafters found unwise, inexpedient, premature, or counterproductive to spell out or emphasize in detail. As we shall see, modern federal founders seem to be much more outspoken on the point of federal supremacy and undivided sovereignty. In another context we have already stressed that a federal system does not and cannot prescribe the exact means of resolving a conflict between the nation and its component parts when on a collision course. One or the other must have its way. Writing in his office, located on the grounds of the Jesuit university of Georgetown, Professor George Carey

---

[1] *The Writings of James Madison* (Hunt ed., 1901), II, 336–337. See also George Washington's letter to the Convention, September 17, 1787, in which he spoke of rights which the states must surrender to the central government as opposed to those which may be reserved to the states in order to secure the "greatest interest of every true American, the consolidation of our Union."

appropriately noted that the American founding fathers "could no more conceive of a political system with divided sovereignty than my good Jesuit friends could conceive of a world without God." [2]

The constitutional guarantee of the existence and autonomy of the component units seems to distinguish a federal from a unitary system in which the central authority has the right to create, extend, circumscribe, or altogether eliminate local self-rule. In a unitary system, units of significant territorial autonomy exist but may be viewed constitutionally as impermanent and destructible by a decision of the central authority. This contrasts with the permanent and indestructible components of a federation. This indestructibility and autonomy is, then, the fifth yardstick of federalism.

YARDSTICK 5: INDESTRUCTIBLE IDENTITY AND AUTONOMY

Like all the other preceding and following ones the fifth yardstick has to be qualified too. First, the very term *indestructible* is too absolute for the world of politics, where nothing can be deemed immune to change. Like men, political institutions are born; then they mature, prosper, live, become sick, and die a natural or a violent death. *Indestructibility* at best should be understood as a "relative eternity" or perhaps simply longevity.

Second, a unitary system in theory can, but in practice rarely does, eliminate units of local self-rule. The reason for the restraint is not a constitutional prohibition but politically wise respect for territorial pluralism or simply concern for greater administrative efficiency that overburdening of the national center would jeopardize. In a unitary system, Paris has no more intention to take over the administration of Marseille than Sacramento plans to capture the administration of Los Angeles. "Self-Government at the King's Command" [3] may sometimes be not less but more significant than under a federal constitution.

[2] *Federalism: Infinite Variety in Theory and Practice*. Itasca, Ill.: F. E. Peacock Publishers, 1968, p. 49.

[3] This is the title of a book by Albert B. White: *Self-Government at the King's Command: A Study on the Beginnings of English Democracy*. London: G. Allen, 1933.

Third, there are numerous unitary systems that promise local autonomy, leaving its scope and mechanism to future laws; many unitary constitutions not only guarantee the principle of local autonomy but describe its scope at some length and add specific provisions for autonomous legislative and executive organs, endowed with local taxing powers. These constitutions not only do not claim to be federal but stress their unitary character. In another context we have already mentioned some of such cases: the People's Republic of China, whose Constitution stresses its unitary nature but guarantees different levels of broad regional-ethnic autonomy; Italy's Constitution promises the establishment of regions, endowed with official autonomous organs (regional council, executive *giunta,* and its president), financial autonomy, taxing powers, and a share in national taxes. The unitary features,[4] on the other hand, are manifest in the provision that the central authority is to be represented in each region by a *commissario* with a veto power over local administration and with primary responsibility to the national capital. The regions are represented by senators on a proportional basis (one senator for every 200,000 inhabitants). We have also previously mentioned Czechoslovakia, which before 1968 asserted its unitary character but emphasized the equality and indestructibility of its two component peoples: "The Czechoslovak Socialist Republic is a unitary state of two fraternal nations, possessing equal rights, the Czechs and the Slovaks."

There are other cases of often undecipherable mixtures of unitary intentions with federal pretense or, on the contrary, federal intentions that dread the implications of full federalism and therefore the word itself. A good example is the first provisional Basic Law (*Loi Fondamentale*) of 1960 of the Congo, which replaced the former highly centralized Belgian colonial rule by relatively generous grants of power to the provinces. However, under the impact of a conflict between the Congolese federalists and unitarians the Constitution avoided the use of the adjectives "federal" or "unitary" in the description of its nature. The second Constitution (Luluabourg draft), which was ap-

---

[4] Article 5 of the 1947 Constitution proclaims that the Italian Republic, "which is one and indivisible, recognizes and promotes local autonomies."

proved by the Congolese electorate in 1964, appears more federal than the first one in both tone and content. The twenty-one component units of the Congolese state are listed by name. Their indestructibility seems certified. The capital, Kinshasa (Léopoldville), is the twenty-second unit. There are lists of powers given to be exercised by the national center, the provinces, and concurrently. Residual powers are to be kept by the provinces. All that sounds federal. Yet the term *federal,* which was part of the initial draft, had finally to be omitted. There were still many groups (trade unions in particular) that thought a unitary system combined with decentralization might preserve the unity of the Congo better than federalism, which may lead to tribal secessions and territorial disintegration.

The new Constitution of Uganda (1966) states in Article 74 that the central Parliament "shall have power to make laws for the peace, order, and good government of Uganda with respect to any matter"—a clearly unitary feature—but its Sixth Schedule enumerates some exclusive powers retained by the component kingdoms. Article 2 of the Constitution seems to make them "indestructible" by listing each of them by name: "Uganda shall consist of Kingdoms, Districts, and the Territory of Mbale. The kingdoms shall be the Kingdom of Ankole, the Kingdom of Buganda, the Kingdom of Bunyoro, and the Kingdom of Toro."

The above samples remind us strongly of what the French scholar Maurice Duverger once wrote about the resistance of political systems to be classified in neat, watertight categories: "As a matter of fact, there is no difference in kind, only in degree: decentralization is a mitigated federalism; and federalism is a very emphasized decentralization." [5]

Listing [6] of constituent units is usual and normal in constitutions that claim to be federal. The Constitution of the United

[5] Maurice Duverger, *Droit constitutionnel et institutions politiques.* Paris: Presses Universitaires, 1955, p. 74 (En fait, il n'y a aucune différence de nature mais seulement de degré: la décentralisation est un fédéralisme atténué; le fédéralisme—une décentralisation très poussée.)

[6] The following federal constitutions list their component units: Argentina, Australia, Austria, Brazil, Burma, Cameroun, Canada, West Germany, India, Libya, Mexico, Pakistan, Switzerland, USSR, Venezuela, and Yugoslavia.

States, however, failed to list the founding states, since their delegates were far from certain that all would accept their draft. For the same reason, the Preamble uses the formula "We the People" instead of enumerating the constituent units. The names of twelve of the original states (the thirteenth, Rhode Island, was not present) appear only at the end of the last article when the names of the delegates, starting with George Washington of Virginia, are listed, indicating the states they had represented in Philadelphia.[7]

If the people's awareness of being a separate territorial community is one of the criteria of federalism, does it matter at all if the territorial community issues from the federal system rather than precedes it? Not all federal systems represent a compact between territories aware of their personality and sovereignty; actually, very few have grown from "below," from an alliance and a confederation into a federal nation-state. Switzerland is a classical example of such a step-by-step growth of twenty-two cantons to a federal union, built around the original cluster of the first three allied cantons. Subsequently, however, even in the case of Switzerland, some further subdivisions, reflecting the interest of subcommunities, proved necessary: three of the cantons were divided into half-cantons. Unterwalden, one of the three constituting cantons, was divided in the fifteenth century into Obwalden and Nidwalden; the main reason was the difficulty of communication between the two major valleys constituting the territory. In 1597 Appenzell broke into two half-cantons on the religious issue (Outer Rhodes [Protestant] and Inner Rhodes [Catholic]). In 1833 the canton of Basel split into its urban and rural components, a result of rural resentment against the urban dominance. In addition, since World War II, a French-German lingual tension troubles the same canton. The French-speaking population (139,000) that lies in the mountainous northwestern corner of the canton (the old Bishopric of Basel, which was added to the exclusively

---

[7] Article VII "Done in Convention by the Unanimous Consent of the States present the Seventeenth Day of September in the Year of our Lord one thousand seven hundred and Eighty seven and of the Independence of the United States of America the Twelfth. In Witness whereof We have hereunto subscribed our Names."

German-speaking canton in 1815) complains about its being neglected by the German-speaking majority; the *Jurassiens* also ask for more influence on decisions concerning the watchmaking industry, a vital issue in that portion of Switzerland. Some Swiss consider the agitation of the *Jurassiens* as un-Swiss and contrary to the Swiss tradition of interethnic tolerance.[8]

The growth of the United States from the original league of thirteen colonies into a federal union of fifty states is another example of mixing territorial communities that had preceded the federal nation with the new ones (created, as it were, from "above"—that is, by transformation of federal territories into new states and by their admission into the union). Initially, some of the territories and states were perhaps as artificial as the *départements* established by Napoleon in France; but subsequently they too acquired a true territorial identity (the case of the two Dakotas was mentioned previously), based on their separate existence over a considerable span of time and buttressed by habit, tradition, local pride, and vested interest.

Need for adjustment to future territorial changes requires all federal systems to provide constitutional means not only for possible new territorial accessions but also for regrouping, division of existing units, and possible internal boundary changes.

In such constitutional provisions, the principle of indestructibility of component units seems to be satisfied by interdicting any change or extinction of territorial identity without the consent

[8] In 1968 the federal government sent a tank battalion to the Jura region to prevent the Jurassian separatists from seizing arms from federal installations whose protection seemed above the possibility of the cantonal police. At a meeting held in Délémont, the main center of the protest movement seeking to form the twenty-sixth half-canton, a statement was adopted that charged that the Swiss federal government had imitated the Russians in Czechoslovakia by issuing 40,000 rounds of live ammunition and quantities of hand and tear-gas grenades to a mechanized unit of the Swiss Army put at the disposal of the canton of Bern. In December 1968, when the Swiss Parliament was in the process of electing the President of the Swiss Federation for 1969, a group of longhaired demonstrators, wearing slacks and sweaters, disrupted the proceedings. They identified themselves as members of the Rams, the most radical group that advocates full independence or French annexation of the Jura area.

of the territorial units concerned; [9] federally speaking, a state or province may commit a territorial suicide voluntarily but cannot be halved, quartered, or otherwise slaughtered by anybody else.

But how does one classify the federal Constitution of India, which permits an easy creation of new states by the Central Parliament, requiring only that the opinion of the state legislatures concerned has been *expressed?* It is not clear whether the expression of opinion is really binding upon the central government. Conceivably, the state legislatures' expression of opinion could be overruled by the national Parliament.

When India emerged as an independent federal state, it was composed of nine fully autonomous states (labeled by the Constitution as Category A), eight somewhat less autonomous because they were more backward states (Category B), and ten minor states (Category C), which were to become federally administered territories (such as Delhi, Himachal Pradesh, Manipur, Tripura, and other strategically located areas). These divisions are constantly being altered, mostly in response to nationalistic linguism, expressed in the slogan "one language, one state." Finally, in the 1960s, the state of Punjab was divided on the religious issue between the Hindus and the noncaste religion of the Sikhs. By 1968 the Indian regroupment of its federal divisions resulted in sixteen States and eleven federal territories. The principle of linguistic nationalism imposed a substantial revision of territorial boundaries within India which had been drawn by the British [10] and then by the Indian nationalists for the sake of administrative efficiency but without much regard for local linguistic or cultural sensitivities.

The Mexican Constitution of 1917 permits the transforma-

[9] The United States Constitution provides in Article IV, section 3: "New States may be admitted by the Congress into this Union but no new State shall be formed or erected within the Jurisdiction of any other State; nor any State be formed by the Junction of two or more States, or Parts of States, without the Consent of the Legislatures of the States concerned as well as the Congress."

[10] Until 1947 the British administered some provinces on the Indian subcontinent directly while other territories, about 500 princely states, were administered indirectly.

tion of federal territories into states when they have a population of eighty thousand inhabitants and the resources necessary to provide for their political existence. When a state is to be carved out of an existing one, it must have a population of at least 120,000 inhabitants and must prove before the National Legislature that it has resources "necessary to provide for their political existence." A subsequent ratification by the states is necessary; a simple majority is required if the consent of the legislature of the state involved has been secured; a ratification by a two-thirds majority of the states is required when the state involved refuses to give its consent.

A federal system whose constitution permits an easy regrouping of existing units or creation of new ones, especially without the consent of the units concerned, has been sometimes referred to as *administrative federalism,* in contrast with a *federal bargain* which entails a voluntary grouping of existing sovereignties and identities into a new collective one while preserving the main features of the previous diversity. Administrative federalism reminds us of the creation of territorial units of self-rule in a unitary system because it, too, basically represents either an answer to local pressures or simply a rational delegation of power for the purpose of more effective administration.

A classic example of such administrative federalism—creation of indestructible units from "above"—is West Germany, where, of the previously existing Länder, only Bavaria and the two city-states Hamburg and Bremen coincide with previous units. Other Länder represent aggregates of former provinces, and two, Rhine-Palatinate and Baden-Württemberg, are entirely new. The Länder were carved out of German territory with a marked disregard for traditional internal boundaries. Thus, the Länder, with the exception of Bavaria, at first commanded little genuine attachment, but "the cake of custom by now has endowed the ten Länder structure with some kind of general recognition." [11]

Some authors tend to consider subsequent or simultaneous

[11] John H. Herz, "The Government of Germany," in G. M. Carter and J. H. Herz, *Major Foreign Powers.* New York: Harcourt, 1967, pp. 441–442.

creation of new units in a federation to be contrary to the theory of bargain and therefore not real federalism. This was the view of Lord Haldane,[12] who argued that the British North America Act of 1867 (the "Constitution" of Canada) was not a federal constitution because it had created a central government simultaneously with new provincial governments.

In Brazil only some units have preceded the federal nation; but even they, in Lipson's words, had to carve their place in the federal whole; "when the unity was prior to its parts, it is they which must seek to assert themselves." [13]

A special case is that of the Republic of South Africa, whose white minority originally experimented with federalism but finally decided for a unitary system. One of the reasons was to assure a more efficient control over the provincial and local governments, which are in an immediate contact with the black majority and other nonwhite groups. There are some leftovers of the original federal intentions. Until 1955, for instance, the unequal provinces had equal representation in the Senate. A new development with propagandized federal implications was the government's plan to create black areas with some degree of local autonomy under a strict white supervision. The first such area, Transkei, was created in 1963. Others have since been in process of being established (Ciskei and Ovamboland in South West Africa). The purpose does not seem to be federalism but a more manageable and acceptable control over the Bantu people. By lures of modest self-rule and careers connected with it the white minority hopes to promote ethnic and tribal antagonism among the Africans.

[12] *Attorney General for the Commonwealth of Australia* v. *Colonial Sugar Refining Company, Ltd.,* 1914.

[13] Leslie Lipson, "The Federal Principle and the Brazilian Reality," a paper presented at the Sixth World Congress of the International Political Science Association, Geneva, 1964, p. 2. By the end of the nineteenth century, three sectors of Brazil seemed to have acquired a considerable sense of identity: the states of the Northeast, Minas Gerais with the largest concentration of population, and the economically developed São Paulo. Some observers believe that São Paulo, if it had been geographically located near the borders of Brazil, could have developed secessionist tendencies, buttressed by constant complaints that this developed economy was heavily taxed to support underdeveloped parts of the country—the most usual complaint in all federations.

YARDSTICK 6: RESIDUAL AND SIGNIFICANT POWERS

The Tenth Amendment to the United States Constitution states, "The powers not delegated to the United States by the Constitution, nor prohibited by it to the States, are reserved to the States respectively, or to the people."

Some Americans too readily assume that this should be so if federalism is to be prevented from slipping down into an abyss of centralism. Yet, in the majority of federal systems today we find different constitutional provisions: powers given to the provinces are enumerated, the rest of the power being reserved by the central authority. This is so, for instance, in Canada, whose basic federal law was prepared in the period following the American Civil War. It was then generally believed that the residual powers of the American states were one of the main reasons for political confusion and civil war. Modern federal constitutions, like those of India, Pakistan, and Burma, contain long and detailed lists of powers reserved for the central authority (Union List), powers reserved for the component units (State List), and powers exercised by both elements (Concurrent List), with usually the provision that if the central authority chooses to exercise some of the concurrent powers it thus pre-empts the state powers.

More important than the location of residual powers in one or the other level of government is the requirement that in a true federation

> there must be some matter, if only one matter, which comes under the exclusive control, actual or potential, of the general government and something likewise under the regional government. If there were not, that would be the end of federalism.[14]

Here one question must be posed: Does it matter or not what kind of power is left to the exclusive domain of one or the other level of government? Territorial distribution of authority in a federal system has never been intended to be on a fifty-fifty basis; a federal system by definition favors the national power

[14] K. C. Wheare, *Federal Government.* New York: Oxford, 1964, p. 75.

by placing in its hands defense, war, and taxing powers. But if through a constitutional division of power, the federal center were to retain 99 percent of the power, leaving the territorial components with 1 percent, would it still be correct to speak of a federal system? If, on the other hand, the central authority were left with only some symbolic or ceremonial powers, it would not be a nation-state at all, only an alliance or a loose league. Evidently, here the old problem of quantitative measurement of political powers appears again. Is it indeed possible to quantify power so as to speak in terms of 99 percent to 1 percent? Furthermore, because power is only a means to an end, there arises the problem of also measuring the value of various ends that one or the other level of government may desire to attain. What seems provincially or locally vital may be viewed nationally as marginal, and vice versa.

The text of the Constitution of Uganda of 1966 offers a good illustration of the controversial nature of the concept of marginal or essential powers and values in any system that distributes authority territorially. The Constitution of Uganda denies the national Parliament power to alter the first four articles of the constituent kingdoms (Ankole, Buganda, Nuyoro, and Toro) and the first two articles of the territory of Busoga. The constitutions of the four kingdoms and of the territory are an integral part of the Ugandan Constitution. This seems to be a federal feature guaranteeing the indestructibility of the component units and their powers. The protected articles, however, deal only with the problems of royal succession, recognition of territorial kings, and the problem of regents. Article 75 describes the power of the legislatures of the component units, which, according to the Sixth Schedule, includes taxation as *prescribed by the central Parliament,* traditional and customary matters, and public holidays and festivals. The subordinate character of the component units is further emphasized by Article 76, which proclaims void any law enacted by the legislature of a kingdom if inconsistent with any law validly made by Parliament. The central Parliament is given power "to make laws on peace, order and good government of Uganda with *respect to any matter* [Italics added]." Assuming that the central Parliament will always at least abstain from including public holidays of any of the constituent kingdoms in "any matter" over which it can legislate, should we conclude that Uganda is a federation because at least one matter (for instance, an annual local fiesta) comes under the exclusive and independent control of the component units? Probably not. As Arthur W. Macmahon writes, "The matters entrusted to the constituent units (whether their powers are residual or delegated) must be substantial, and not merely trivial." [15]

YARDSTICK 7: BICAMERALISM AND EQUAL REPRESENTATION OF UNEQUAL STATES

Often viewed by Americans as an essential yardstick of federalism is the Connecticut Compromise, by which the American founders agreed on a proportional representation of unequal states in the lower house and an equal representation of unequal states (two senators per state) in the upper house (the Senate, a federal chamber to replace the British concept of a hereditary, aristocratic one). The United States bicameralism is a true and full one because both houses are equal in matters of legislation: no law can be enacted unless both houses agree on the same text. This is in contrast with many other bicameral systems in which the upper house often enjoys only a limited or suspensive veto over legislation. Furthermore, unlike the parliamentary system, the American lower house does not create the national executive branch (the cabinet). And the executive branch is not directly responsible to the lower house. The Senate's advice and consent to executive appointments and treaty making make the Senate, with its one hundred senators, actually a powerful body and a partner of the national executive; this is in contrast with parliamentary systems, where this role is exercised by the lower house.

Originally, the Senate could have been viewed as a guarantee and a channel for the decisive influence of the states on the shape and direction of the national policy. Because the practice of instructing senators disappeared more than a century ago and because their election has passed from the hands of the state legislatures to the hands of the people, it is debatable whether a senator still represents today his own state interests or, rather,

[15] Arthur W. Macmahon, *Federalism: Mature and Emergent.* New York: Russell and Russell, 1962, p. 4.

the multistate regional interests (the South, the Midwest, or the East), functional divisions (agriculture, cities), or his party. A similar observation can be made about the Australian Senate, created to safeguard and represent state interests, which has now "become a body in which divisions are along strict party lines." [16]

The principle of equal representation of unequal component units has been adopted by many federations. The Australian six unequal states are represented equally in the Senate; in Switzerland, too, forty-four councillors represent its twenty-two cantons (actually, Switzerland is divided into twenty-five units because three cantons have been subdivided into half-cantons, each represented by one councillor). The principle of equal representation is also present in all Latin-American constitutions as well as in the Communist federations. In federal Czechoslovakia now, the highest legislative organ is the Federal Assembly (composed of the House of the People and the House of the Nations). The House of the People is composed of 200 deputies, whereas the House of the Nations is composed of 150 members, half of whom are elected in Bohemia-Moravia and the other half in Slovakia. In the Soviet Union, each union republic is represented by twenty-five deputies in the Soviet of Nationalities, the federal chamber of the Supreme Soviet, the highest legislative organ (the other house is called the Soviet of the Union).

Furthermore, the Constitution provides that each of the fifteen union republics is represented by one deputy in the Presidium of the Supreme Soviet, the parliament in miniature that fulfills a dual role: to act as a permanent standing committee on behalf of the national legislature when that is not in session and to act as a collegial president, a ceremonial head of the Soviet Union. The Presidium is composed of one chairman, one secretary, fifteen members elected by the Soviet of the Union, and fifteen vice-chairmen representing the constituent units of the Soviet Union.

Soviet federalism is a multilayer one; its largest unit, the Russian Republic, for instance, is a federation itself. In addition, in the territories of some of the union republics, federal or not,

---

[16] Louise Overacker, *The Australian Party System*. New Haven, Conn.: Yale University Press, 1952, p. 328. The author also notes that the Australian Labour party antedates federalism; "it has become a national party even before Australia was a nation" (p. 30).

there are autonomous republics, autonomous regions, and national districts with the right of direct representation in the central legislature. Unequal autonomous republics are equally represented by eleven deputies each, autonomous regions by five deputies each, and national districts by one deputy each. The degree of direct representation in the national legislature is related to the degree of autonomy granted by the Constitution.

Similarly, in Yugoslavia, according to the 1968 revision of the Federal Constitution of 1963, the Chamber of Nationalities has 140 deputies delegated by six republics (20 delegates from each) and the two provinces (10 delegates from each). In Yugoslavia, too, we may speak of a two-layer federalism. Before 1947, at one point the British hoped to overcome the Hindu-Moslem problem by a three-layer federal formula that was to combine federal India and federal Pakistan into a federal or confederal union. It was one of the last-minute attempts to preserve the split of the Indian subcontinent into two hostile nations. Another similarly unsuccessful attempt was that of Holland, which in 1948 tried to bring together a federalized Indonesia and a unitary Holland into a federal or confederal association.

This sixth criterion of a federal structure needs, like all the other yardsticks, several qualifications:

1. Some systems that claim to be federal have not adopted the principle of equal representation of unequal units, but a compromise between size and equality. In India, for instance, the less populous states are favored, but not to the point of equality with the populous states. The allocation of seats in the Indian federal chamber, the Council of States, is determined by the Fourth Schedule.[17] The seats assigned ranged from a maximum of thirty-four for the most populous state of Uttar Pradesh to one for Nagaland; the federal capital of New Delhi is represented by three, and other federal territories by two or one.

---

[17] The Fourth Schedule of the Indian Constitution as amended provides for the following distribution of the 226 seats in the Council of States: Andhra Pradesh 18, Assam 7, Bihar 22, Gujarat 11, Haryana 5, Kerala 9, Madhya Pradesh 16, Madras 18, Maharashtra 1, Mysore 12, Orissa 10, Punjab 7, Rajasthan 10, Uttar Pradesh 34, West Bengal 16, Jammu and Kashmir 4, Nagaland 1. The federal capital and federal territories are represented in the Council of States as follows: Delhi 3, Himachal Pradesh 2, Manipur 1, Tripura 1, Pondicherry 1.

In the Nigerian federation, the Northern Region insisted on having equal representation: in the lower house it wanted representation equal to all the other provinces combined while in the upper house it agreed to the "Connecticut" equality. In the light of subsequent events and the Biafran secession, the exact weight is of only historical interest.[18]

In Canada the principle of equal representation of unequal units has been applied with ingenious modifications that reflect the very uneven population density of the vast territory of Canada. Provinces were divided into four groupings, each entitled to twenty-four senators;[19] within the third and fourth groupings, composed of several provinces, the provincial representation is roughly proportionate to the population. Newfoundland is in a separate category, with six senators. All 102 Canadian senators are appointed by the governor general in the Queen's name, that is, by the Canadian Cabinet.

[18] The distribution in the lower house was to be ninety-two deputies for the Northern Region and ninety-two for the rest, subdivided into forty-two for the Western Region and forty-two for the Southern Region, six for South Cameroons and two for the federal district of Lagos. In the Senate each region was to have twelve representatives and Lagos four. As we know, the numbers, however carefully established in the Constitution, are no substitute for national consensus. A Nigerian scholar writing on the subject in 1963 made the following comment: "The primary object in creating the Senate was to provide recognition of the legal equality of the regions. Undemocratic in its composition, with members undemocratically chosen and given a suspensive veto for only six months, the Senate was designed as an emasculated second chamber; it cannot [and it did not] allay the fear of a small region of a larger one in the popular chamber. A legislative chamber that finds itself in so unenviable a position in the legislative process may eventually come to consider itself merely a rubber stamp for the actions of the lower house." Eme Awa, *Federal Government in Nigeria.* Los Angeles: University of California Press, 1964, p. 133.

[19] The Canadian Constitution of 1867 (The British North America Acts as amended in 1915 and modified in 1949) contains the following provisions. Article 21: "The Senate shall . . . consist of One Hundred and Two Members, who shall be styled as Senators." Article 22 (the numbers in brackets indicate the number of senators assigned): "In relation to the Constitution of the Senate Canada shall be deemed to consist of Four Divisions: 1. Ontario [24]; 2. Quebec [24]; 3. The Maritime Provinces (Nova Scotia [10], New Brunswick [10], and Prince Edward Island [4]); 4. The Western Provinces of Manitoba [6], British Columbia [6], Saskatchewan [6], and Alberta [6]."

It should be mentioned that in contrast with the United States most federal systems have from their beginnings given legislative representation to federal territories and capitals. Argentina in 1853 placed the provinces, each represented by two legislators, on an equal footing with the federal capital, also represented by two legislators. The same is true of India, Nigeria, and other federations. In the United States only in 1961 did the Twenty-third Amendment extend to the District of Columbia the right to participate in the election of the President, but it did not extend the right of the District to be represented in the Senate.

2. Although bicameralism seems to be so intimately associated with federalism, there are two federations that have adopted a unicameral system. These are Pakistan and Cameroun, each composed of two units. In Cameroun the unicameral Federal Assembly is composed of forty members elected by the eastern and ten by the western portion of the country. In Pakistan the unequal western and eastern provinces elect an equal number of seventy-five representatives into their unicameral National Assembly.

In a federation composed of only two territorial units, bicameralism may indeed seem unnecessary because equal representation of unequal provinces should protect the components against the tyranny by the majority. There is one obvious drawback. The nation-states that are composed of only two territorial or ethnic communities, antagonistic yet searching for an adequate cooperative formula, cannot benefit from the variety of constantly shifting interterritorial coalitions; one group always faces the other as in a narrow corridor that does not allow any flexibility or side maneuvers. Either the common interest is discovered or the negative attitude of one group opposing the other implies a threat of a veto or secession.[20] This is so in biethnic

---

[20] In 1967 thirty-five Bengalis of East Pakistan were charged with plotting the secession of their province and accession to India. The Bengalis of East Pakistan often contend that they have been "colonized" by, not federalized with, West Pakistan, 1000 miles away across the vast expanse of India. They note that although they have nearly 60 percent of the nation's 105 million population and foreign earnings, they enjoy a markedly smaller share of political influence, position, and development.

Pakistan, biethnic Czechoslovakia, and this also plagues biethnic Belgium's search for a federal solution of its problems. The French-speaking Walloons, now in minority and, therefore, favoring a federal formula, proposed a solution to their interethnic tensions by requiring that each law be passed not only by a majority in the national parliament but also by a majority decision in both of Belgium's territorial communities (the Walloons and the Dutch-speaking Flemings). It is a version of a Connecticut compromise without the tempering influence that the greater number of component units in the United States represented.

3. The third qualification of the federal yardstick under discussion is the nature of bicameralism itself in a given system. By *bicameralism* we mean coequality not only of the legislative powers but also of the political powers of the two chambers of the central legislature. Yet, many federal systems that have adopted the British cabinet system of government make the prime minister and his Cabinet responsible to the lower house only. In the Commonwealth federations of Canada, Australia, India, Pakistan, and Malaysia (as well as those that have failed, such as Nigeria, Rhodesia, and Nyasaland), only the popularly elected, *nonfederal* lower house makes and unmakes cabinets. Furthermore, in a cabinet system, it is usually the lower house that also has the last word in legislative matters because the refusal of the upper house to go along may be overridden after a prescribed period of time. In India, for instance, a money bill can be delayed by the federal chamber for only two weeks; and it is the Speaker of the House who may determine which bill is a money bill. At best, the federal upper houses in British-inspired federal systems have a suspensive veto—a far cry from the awesome powers and prestige of the United States Senate.

Also, in West Germany, where the component units are represented by three to five delegates each, the federal upper house (Bundesrat) has only a suspensive veto on many subjects of legislation except in matters affecting the federal distribution of power, where its veto power is absolute and annuls the measure. In theory it was assumed that the number of bills potentially subject to the absolute veto would be small. In practice it was not so, partly because of the Bundesrat's insistence that it can veto a whole bill when a portion of it is subject to absolute veto.

The lower house (Bundestag), however, performs the decisive political role of a national cabinet maker.

The initial concentration of the federal founding fathers on bicameralism was in accordance with the then accepted concept of the primary importance of parliaments as rule makers; this was to be the central fountain of all decisions to be implemented by the executive branch and interpreted by the judiciary. The fact, however, is that the legislative rule-making monopoly has been replaced now almost everywhere by the rule-making activities of both the executive and the judicial branches of the government. In the modern era some of the most important rules have been made either by executive orders or by judicial creative interpretation of the existing laws and the constitution. The question should then be asked whether and how the principle of equal representation of unequal component units could be reflected in the executive branch and in the judicial branch. In the Soviet Union, for instance, new laws provide for a representation of Soviet nationalities on the Council of Ministers (law of May 10, 1957) and on the Supreme Court (law of February 13, 1957). In the interim Tanzanian Constitution, we find the provision that the prime minister of Zanzibar "shall be the Vice-President of the United Republic appointed for that purpose, and he shall be styled the President of Zanzibar" (Article 53).[21]

In conclusion, it is necessary to point to the inevitable physical difficulty of any attempt to have a federal structure faithfully mirrored at the top of the political pyramid where the decision-making body tends to be less numerous than the number

---

[21] Article 54 adds: "Executive power with respect to all matters in and for Zanzibar other than Union matters is vested in the Executive for Zanzibar. Legislative power with respect to all matters in and for Zanzibar other than Union matters is vested in the Legislature for Zanzibar." These provisions, the aim of which was to combine a full recognition of Zanzibar's identity with the assertion of its future integrated destiny, did not work too well in practice. Since April 26, 1964, when following a bloody revolution in Zanzibar the merger of the island and the mainland nation of Tanganyika was proclaimed, centrifugal tendencies prevented a full implementation of the federal bargain as expressed in the interim Constitution. In an interview, granted on the Union Day in 1968 at Dar es Salaam, Zanzibar's ruler and Tanzania's Vice-President, Sheik Abeid Amani Karume, asked that further federal integration with the mainland be stopped.

of groups it desires to represent. In federations composed of a small number of units, the cabinet may succeed in reflecting the component units on a roughly proportional basis. In Australia all of its six states are usually represented in the national Cabinet. In Canada somewhat more rigid rules are followed: every province has at least one member. Quebec has four members (one must be English-speaking and one each must be from Montreal and the city of Quebec); the province of Ontario gets five members (one is always from Toronto); several ministerial posts are assigned to sections of the country according to their economic interests (agriculture to the prairies, fisheries to the Maritime Provinces). The result is a guarantee of federal representativeness, not necessarily of competence.[22] In Switzerland the seven members of the Swiss Cabinet (Federal Council) are composed of five Germans (two of whom come from Bern and Zurich), two Frenchmen (one from the largest French canton of Vaud), and one Italian (from Ticino). In Tanzania, as we have seen, the Constitution provides for the president to be always from Tanganyika and the vice-president from Zanzibar. But how can a cabinet faithfully reflect the component units in federations composed of more than six to ten states?

When we consider the executive in terms of real concentration of power, even a federation composed of two units (like Pakistan, Cameroun, or Czechoslovakia), of six units (like Australia or Yugoslavia), of fifteen units (like the Soviet Union), or of seventeen units (like India) has a serious problem because what finally matters is the power held in the hands of one man, a president, a prime minister, or a party chairman. How can one "federalize" the body and soul of a single man? What is left besides the constitutional checks and balances is an extraconstitutional hope that the chief executive will have a "federal" personality capable of tolerance and justice to all the component units and generally immune against any particular subnational pull, be it his birthplace (South, East, or West in the United States), religion (Moslem in India, Hindu in Pakistan), lan-

---

[22] Alexander Brady, *Democracy in the Dominions.* Toronto: University of Toronto Press, 1958, p. 83. Compare also William S. Livingston in Valerie Earle (ed.), *Federalism: Infinite Variety in Theory and Practice.* Itasca, Ill.: F. E. Peacock Publishers, 1968, p. 112.

guage (French in Canada), color of skin (Chinese in brown-race Malaysia), or ethnic origin (a Ukrainian in the Soviet Union or a Croatian in Yugoslavia).

The composition of other federal institutions poses problems similar to those of a national legislature and a chief executive because bureaucrats, managers, and judges not only interpret or adjudicate federal rules but also partly create them. Should, for instance, the principle of equal representation of unequal units be applied to the civil service, managers of the national economy, and federal judgeships, or would that mean a change of a federal system to a confederal one? Should the federal principle, for instance, be so applied as to have the Supreme Court in the United States composed of fifty judges, in India of seventeen and in the Soviet Union of fifteen, corresponding to the "indestructible" units of the federation? As there is no provision for such federalization of the judiciary, it is legally possible, though not politically wise, that in the United States all the Supreme Court justices be from Massachusetts, in India from the Hindi-speaking North, and in the USSR from Russia. Or should there always be two sets of administration, that of economy and welfare and that of courts, one set federal and the other serving the interests and expressing the authority of territorial units?

YARDSTICK 8: TWO SETS OF COURTS

Two sets of courts may seem a minor criterion, but some find it important. Commenting on the nationally controlled judicial system in Venezuela, one author writes, "In 1945 the states surrendered their last major power when they ratified a constitutional amendment which conferred upon the national government exclusive control of the judicial system." [23] Herman Finer lists the absence of a dual federal-provincial judicial system as one of the reasons for which the Soviet Union does not qualify as a federation. He lists eight criteria of federalism: (1) control over the amendments; (2) assignment of powers to the center as compared with the residue left to the states; (3) special representation, and veto and deadlock powers preserved by the compo-

[23] M. C. Needler (ed.), *Political Systems of Latin America*. Princeton, N.J.: Van Nostrand, 1964, p. 255.

nent units in the upper chamber; (4) existence of a court that stands above the Union and the territorial units; (5) independent financial resources; (6) exclusive control of foreign relations by the Union; (7) independent party organization in the several units; and (8) existence of two independent sets of courts, one for the Union, the other for the units. On all these eight counts, Herman Finer argues, the Soviet Union fails to pass the test of federalism.[24]

Actually, only a few federations—the United States and, with modifications, Mexico and Brazil—have developed two parallel networks of courts: federal courts to adjudicate national laws and provincial courts to adjudicate local laws. The United States, for instance, has established a complete judicial hierarchy on both the federal and the state levels. In the federal-court structure there are, in ascending order, district courts, circuit courts of appeal, and at the top of the federal judicial pyramid the Supreme Court. In each state another judicial pyramid of state courts culminates with the state supreme court. The two systems, however, are not "federally fully separate"; not only is the federal Supreme Court the highest court of appeal from both networks but the two systems actually interlock by a degree of *concurrent* jurisdiction, shared by both the federal and the state courts. Only some matters are reserved for the exclusive jurisdiction of the state courts. Some other matters are under the exclusive jurisdiction of the federal courts, such as crimes and offenses against the United States; prize, patent, copyright, and some bankruptcy cases; civil cases of admiralty and maritime jurisdiction; cases to which a state is a party; and cases involving foreign ambassadors.

In all the other federal systems we find different variants of a single integrated court system, usually provincial or state courts, topped by a federal highest court of appeal. For special cases, sometimes a federal court is added to the system. For instance, in Canada, in addition to the Supreme Court, there is a special federal court of exchequer and admiralty. In Switzerland the "organization of the judiciary, legal procedures and the administration of justice remain in the cantons" (Article 64A);

[24] Herman Finer, *Theory and Practice of Modern Government.* New York: Holt, Rinehart and Winston, Inc., 1949, p. 820.

the cantonal courts adjudicate both federal and cantonal laws. A Federal Tribunal stands above the whole system as a court of appeal over the cantonal courts and as a court of original jurisdiction in some federal matters. West Germany, too, has a single integrated system of state courts with a Federal Supreme Court at the top. The state courts and their procedures are, however, regulated and made uniform by federal codes. In Communist federations each of the component territorial units (union republics and their subdivisions in the Soviet Union; republics in federal Yugoslavia) has its judicial system that is topped by the republican supreme court, which, in turn is topped by the federal supreme court.[25] They adjudicate uniform Soviet codes. The Soviet network of procurators that play such a decisive role in all criminal proceedings is, on the other hand, rigidly centralized under the supervision of the powerful federal office of prosecutor general. In the British Commonwealth federations the constitution permits the establishment of a dual (federal and state) judicial system, but only the state system is in actual operation. This is so, for instance, in Pakistan, India, and Australia. The Indian Constitution (Article 247) authorizes Parliament to establish "any additional courts for the better administration of federal laws," but it has chosen not to do so.[26] There are only state courts supervised by India's federal Supreme Court. A similar situation has developed in Australia, whose constitution (Article 73) provides that the federal supreme court (the High Court of Australia) shall "hear appeals . . . from all judgments of any other federal court . . . or any other court of any State"; yet the Australian Parliament has so far not established a complete federal judicial hierarchy but has mostly employed the state

[25] Article 102 of the Soviet Constitution: "In the USSR justice is administered by the Supreme Court of the USSR, the Supreme Courts of the Union Republics, the Courts of the Territories, Autonomous Republics, Autonomous Regions and Areas, the special Courts of the USSR, established by the Supreme Soviet of the USSR, and the People's Courts." Article 104 charges the Soviet Supreme Court with the supervision of the judicial activities of all the judicial bodies of the USSR. The different territorial courts are elected for five years by the corresponding soviets except the district people's courts, which are elected directly by the citizens of such districts or cities.

[26] Ani Chandra Banerjee and Krishna Lal Chatterji, *A Survey of the Indian Constitution*. Calcutta: A. Mukherjee & Co., 1957, p. x.

courts for federal purposes.[27] In Canada the provinces have established, as the Constitution permits, their own judicial systems, and they regulate their procedure in civil matters. The central government, however, appoints and pays all the judges, regulates the procedure in criminal matters, and has conferred upon provincial courts jurisdiction in most matters of national law. The whole system, again, is topped by a supreme court that has an appellate jurisdiction in civil and criminal matters from the provincial courts.

In Africa we often find two sets of courts, modern and native African, in both federal and unitary systems. They do not reflect the territorial division of judicial authority in the constitutional sense but represent a parallel existence of two entirely different legal systems and traditions: the modern one as enacted by national legislatures, and the traditional tribal customary law. In Nigeria, for instance, the native courts "provide the forum for almost all cases involving the family law of Nigerians, and it is difficult to see how their word in this field of civil law can be discharged by the professional courts as satisfactorily, as conveniently, or as cheaply." [28]

If a fully developed parallel federal and state court system were a decisive yardstick of federalism, only the United States (and, with some qualification, Mexico and Brazil) could pass the test.

YARDSTICK 9: THE SUPREME COURT

In all systems, federal as well as unitary, there is a need for an impartial agency that can ascertain the meaning of the nation's supreme law, the constitution, and that, in light of its findings, can determine the compatibility of any given law or official act, national or local, with the constitution. This may lead and has led to a broad concept of the judicial review, the right of the courts to annul or confirm the validity of laws passed by national or

[27] Geoffrey Sawer, "Judicial Power under the Constitution," in M. Else-Mitchel (ed.), *Essays on the Australian Constitution.* Sydney: The Law Book Co., of Australasia Pty Ltd., 1961, p. 71.

[28] E. A. Keay and S. S. Richardson, *The Native and Customary Courts of Nigeria.* Lagos: African University Press, 1966, p. vii.

local legislatures. Because the American practice of judicial review, as exercised by the Supreme Court, has been in modern times characterized by the Court's support of civil rights and liberties, many unitary and federal constitutions, in one form or another, have now imitated the American theory and practice to some extent. Constitutional courts in unitary France, federal Germany, Communist Yugoslavia, and Moslem Pakistan represent brave attempts to transplant the American institution of judicial review from its native American soil to areas somewhat less hospitable to the power of the judges to decide issues that often are political and social in nature, although presented in legalistic garb. As yet, in no country is there a real counterpart to the awesome power of the United States Supreme Court. Especially in Europe, there is some doubt concerning the wisdom of placing a few judges above the people and its elected representatives when it comes to the interpretation of the nation's fundamental law that expresses political and social theory of the founders.

In a federal system there seems to be an even more acute need for an impartial agency, because the interpretation of the meaning of the constitution includes also the delicate original political agreement between territorial communities from which the whole federal system had issued. In its role of protector and interpreter of the federal compact and arbitrator of possible disputes about the division of power between two jurisdictional spheres, such an agency should be, ideally, independent of both the federal and the provincial governments and should stand sublimely above both.

Only Switzerland seems to be near the ideal. Not judges, but only the sovereign people of Switzerland can question the validity of federal laws (the courts may question the validity of cantonal laws): either 30,000 voters or eight cantons can challenge any law passed by the federal legislature and so either confirm its constitutional validity or annul it. A simple majority of voters decides the issue in a legislative referendum; the majority of cantons is not required. This is in contrast with a formal amendment of the Swiss Constitution, which also requires, in addition to the majority of voters in a constitutional referendum, approval by the majority of voters in the majority of the cantons.

Until 1949 Canada had another form of impartial constitutional agency, independent of both the national and the provincial governments; it was the Judiciary Committee of the Privy Council (composed mostly of the law lords of the British House of Lords), located in the British Empire's original center, London. This is no longer so, and Canada's Supreme Court has now become the only final court of appeal in the Dominion.

With the exception of the Soviet Union, in all the other federal systems (including Communist Yugoslavia) a judicial agency has the role of interpreter of the original federal consensus and, therefore, is arbitrator in potential jurisdictional disputes between the federal and provincial governments. In most cases it is the additional function of the highest federal court of appeal; in West Germany, however, a special constitutional court was established. In contrast with most German courts, its members are elected by Parliament; half is elected by the federal chamber, the Bundesrat, and half by a special committee of electors, reflecting the proportional strength of political parties in the popularly elected chamber, the Bundestag.[29]

In the Soviet Union, not the Supreme Court, but the permanent standing committee of the national legislature (the Presidium of the Supreme Soviet) is given the power to interpret the laws of the USSR (Article 49, section c), which may imply arbitrating jurisdictional disputes between the federation and its components.

Such an agency, whether it is the highest court of appeal, a special constitutional court as in West Germany, or a presidium of the national legislature as in the Soviet Union, is not, and clearly cannot be viewed as, independent of one or the other party involved in a potential jurisdictional dispute; these agencies are, as a rule, created and can be dismissed (by impeachment) by the national government with the concurrence of the national legislature. "The result has been," as is noted by K. C. Wheare, "that Supreme Courts or their equivalent have been accused from time to time of undue partiality to the general government"[30]—their creator.

It is possible that the national (federal) selection of the

[29] John H. Herz, "Germany," in Carter and Herz, *Major Foreign Powers,* pp. 449–450.

[30] Wheare, *Federal Government,* p. 59.

judiciary for the role of supreme arbitrator may not be ideal. But what is the alternative—except perhaps the legislative and constitutional referenda that Switzerland has had. The judiciary may indeed be assumed to be more impartial than any other institution. One should not, for instance, too readily assume that the supreme court created by the national government will necessarily prove partial to it. In Canada the judicial interpretation of the federal Constitution finally resulted in curbing rather than extending the powers of the national government in relation to the provinces. Before the contrary happened in the United States the difficulties that, in the period of the New Deal, President Roosevelt experienced with the Supreme Court amply demonstrated that judges, although appointed federally, may prove quite partial to states' rights because of their political and social philosophy. In conclusion, let us add that even the highest court of all is only composed of men—and men, including the Supreme Court justices, have their political and social preferences.

YARDSTICK 10: CLEAR DIVISION OF POWER

A constitutional division of power between the center and the component territorial units is a central point in most definitions of federalism and also in our graphic model of a federal system. When we study constitutional texts we discover, however, that the dividing line between the central and the provincial powers is neither clear nor neat. There are deliberate and some unwitting overlaps in the territorial division of power, just as the separation of executive, legislative, and judicial powers has never been intended nor proved possible to be absolute. Five principal overlaps that blur the critical line between central and provincial powers (extraconstitutional overlaps will be discussed in Chaps. 9 and 10) may be noted:

1. The federal monopoly in the field of foreign policy and defense and its implications
2. The emergency provisions (related to 1)
3. The concurrent power
4. The elastic or coefficient clauses (related to 3)
5. The lack of verbal precision, partly deliberate and partly unwitting, which may be found in all federal constitutions

The federal monopoly in foreign policy and defense, and its implications

The federal monopoly in foreign policy and defense spills over easily into the seemingly exclusive domain of provincial powers. This is actually a genetic feature of all federations because the fundamental reason for most federations is to create a nation vis-à-vis other nations, which means a nation with a unified foreign policy and a unified concept of collective defense, based on a unified defense establishment.

Federal constitutions, therefore, logically place the power to conduct foreign policy in the hands of the national government, in most cases specifically within the hands of the executive branch, that is, in the hands of the president, the prime minister, the secretary or minister for foreign affairs, or the diplomatic service. The legislative branch has the power to modify or reject international treaties, influence the executive branch by the legislative power over the purse, and prod or curb the executive branch by different means of parliamentary controls, ranging from resolutions or laws (the United States Neutrality Act, for instance) to debates, questions, and votes of confidence in cabinet systems. Whatever the share of the legislative branch may be, it is the national government that has the primary constitutional right to make friends and enemies abroad.

The problem of a possible spillover of the federal power into the provincial sphere lies, first, in the subject matter of the treaties contracted by the national government and foreign countries and, second, in the subsequent need to pass the legislation necessary to bring these treaties into effect. If the component units of a federal union have the right to prevent international treaties or their implementation, the national government cannot be effective on the international scene and may therefore fail in protecting or promoting the collective interest of the composite whole. If, on the other hand, the component units have no practical choice but to bow to international treaties or the implementing legislation, the so-called exclusive powers of the component units may become concurrent at best or nil at worst. Here, again, we observe how federal constitutions point to a dilemma rather than to an unequivocal solution.

The danger of federal encroachments on provincial exclusive powers is greater today than before World War I. International relations in our time are increasingly concerned with social and economic matters in addition to the traditional diplomatic and military affairs. Protection of human rights, education, control over drug traffic and international criminal links, protection of wildlife and fisheries, and labor conditions have become subjects of modern international treaties.[31] When such treaties are contracted by the federal government and then implemented by national legislation, they invade the sphere of what has traditionally been considered the exclusive welfare and police powers of provincial and state governments.

Modern federal constitutions express with bluntness the unavoidable federal supremacy that results from the national government's foreign policy powers. The Indian Constitution (Article 253), for instance, states very clearly that the national Parliament "has power to make any law for the whole or any part of the territory of India for implementing any treaty, agreement or convention with any other country or countries or any decision made at any international conference, association, or other body." Some may see in such a provision a realistic expression of the present-day overriding concern for transnational cooperation and interdependence. Others may see in it another indication of a fatal decline of the federal division of powers. In Malaysia the federal Parliament can also make laws with respect to matters on the State List when implementing an international treaty; the only restriction on the federal dominance is that such an international treaty must not deal with any Moslem custom or law.

The United States Constitution (Article VI) seems to differentiate between federal laws and international treaties as supreme laws of the land: "This Constitution, and the Laws of the United States which shall be made in Pursuance thereof, and all Treaties made, or which shall be made, under the Authority of the United States, shall be the supreme Law of the Land." Is

---

[31] This was an issue when Canada in 1935 ratified two international conventions adopted by the International Labour Organization concerning working conditions and weekly rest in industrial enterprises. These treaties affected property and civil rights within the provinces of Canada.

the term "Treaties made under the *Authority* of the United States" more permissive than laws made in "Pursuance" of the Constitution? Some authors believe so; others defend the opposite view. The contrast between the wording of the United States Constitution, on the one hand, and that of the Indian and other modern constitutions on the other, is obvious: the latter are direct and blunt, whereas the United States Constitution may seem hesitant or unclear. In practice, however, the United States Supreme Court has consistently tended to solve the federal dilemma with reference to international treaties in favor of the national center. As early as 1796 the Supreme Court clearly sided with the national government:

> A treaty cannot be the *supreme law of the land,* that is, of all the United States, if any act of a State legislature can stand in its way. . . . It is a declared will of the *people* of the *United States* that every treaty made by the authority of the United States shall be superior to the Constitution and laws of any individual state; and their will alone is to decide. . . . If a law of a state, contrary to a treaty is not void, . . . the will of *a small part* of the United States may control or defeat the will of the *whole.*[32]

Another famous judicial siding with the national government as being "more supreme" in matters of treaty making than in that of federal law making concerned a seemingly marginal issue of migratory birds that, on their way through Missouri to Canada and back, were viewed by trigger-happy Missourians as a welcome addition to their diet—as well as a clear case of the exclusive power of a state to regulate all wildlife within its territory, whatever the wildlife's origins. In 1917 a congressional statute was passed to protect the birds; it implemented an agreement between the United States Federal government and Great Britain on behalf of Canada. However, the state of Missouri brought suit against the federal warden Mr. Holland (*Missouri v. Holland*), that is, against the Federal government; Missouri's main argument was that the Federal government cannot take away by an international treaty that which had been reserved to

---

[32] Ware v. Hylton, 3 Dall., 199.

the states by the Constitution. Justice Holmes' ruling established an important precedent in favor of the Federal power:

> We do not mean to imply that there are no qualifications to the treaty making power but they must be ascertained in a different way. It is obvious that there may be matters of sharpest exigency for the national well being [apparently, such as a good relationship with Canada and Britain] that an act of Congress could not deal with but what a treaty followed by such an act could. . . . The only question is whether it is forbidden by some invisible radiation from the general terms of the Tenth Amendment. We must consider what this country has become in deciding what that Amendment has reserved. . . . We see nothing in the Constitution that compels the Government to sit by while a food supply is cut off and the protectors of our forest and crops are destroyed.[33]

All that has just been said on the subject of the conduct of foreign policy by federal governments applies also and even more emphatically to the federal power to make war in defense of national interests. Defense is often seen as continuation of diplomacy by violent means. War calls even more than a peacetime foreign policy for a unified and highly centralized policy—the very opposite of the pluralistic concept of federalism.

All federal constitutions assign the war powers to the national government, permitting the component units to defend themselves only under extremely exceptional circumstances. In the national government, the primary responsibility to prepare for, wage, and end war is that of the executive branch, especially the president or the prime minister as commander in chief of the armed forces. The power of the executive branch is only somewhat curbed by a frequent constitutional requirement that the right to declare war be reserved to the national legislature. The record shows that often this reservation may be a sheer formality because the executive branch may have created the very conditions that will force the legislature to declare war or have committed the armed forces and the prestige of the nation in such a way that the national legislature has no choice

---

[33] Missouri v. Holland, 252 U.S. 416 (1920).

other than to make the appropriate declaration of war and to fund financially the executive branch's prior decision.

In federal constitutions a special problem arises in connection with the composition of the armed forces that is unknown to unitary constitutions; it is a question whether, consistently with the requirement of a necessarily unified and highly centralized war effort, there should be only one national military establishment or whether, in accordance with the federal concept of power separation, the component units should have their own military formations instead of or in addition to the national armed forces (this was mentioned in Chap. 7). The absolute majority of federal constitutions provides for one unified national force. Only Switzerland, the United States, and, with qualifications, the Soviet Union and Yugoslavia seem to provide otherwise. The Swiss army is organized on a cantonal basis (its units are formed from one and the same canton), but the federal supervision, control, regulation, strategic planning, and financing are decisive. The Constitution does not allow the maintenance of a permanent standing national army. In the United States the Constitution provides for "military federalism"; there are state militias under the command of state governors and the national army under the command of the President. It is, constitutionally, a dual system, yet, in fact, the National Defense Act of 1916 transformed the members of the state militias, now renamed the National Guard, into members of the National Guard of the United States and thus into a reserve component of the national army, under the command of the President and in the service of the nation. The change of the name from "*state* militia" to "*national* guard" eloquently confirms that the military symbol of the states' independence has passed to the nation.

In the Soviet Union, the 1944 amendment, mentioned previously, endowed all the constituent units of the Soviet federal union with the right to have their own military formations (Article 18b). Therefore, on paper there is also a dual military system in the Soviet Union: there is the Soviet Army and also, according to the Constitution, the Ukrainian, Byelorussian, and other union republican militias. In his speech to the Supreme Soviet, Molotov mentioned that Latvian, Lithuanian, Estonian, Georgian, Armenian, Azerbaidzhan, and Kazakh national formations had already been established, but since 1945 nobody has ever heard of or noticed their existence. (The federal encroachments on the state powers implied in the federal power to prepare for war in peacetime and to liquidate its unitary and centralizing effects after its conclusion will be discussed in the framework of extraconstitutional overlaps in Chap. 10.)

The emergency provisions

The emergency provisions in connection with the defense of the federal nation-state against external and internal enemies represent the second major avenue through which the federal authority is encouraged or authorized to cross the federal-state Rubicon and to curb temporarily or totally eliminate local autonomy in the name of the survival and the security of the federal collective whole. We cannot imagine federal constitutions without such provisions, but with them the question necessarily arises how real is the tenth yardstick of federalism, a clear division of federal and local powers. The determination of the existence and gravity of an external or internal threat to the federal way of life is in the hands of the central executive; his power is usually limited by a requirement that the central legislature has subsequently to approve a proclamation of emergency or martial law within a determined period of time. In practice, this is a lesser impediment to the federal executive than it seems, especially in the federations where the bicameral parliament is tilted to the advantage of the popular lower chamber (in a cabinet system) or where the dominant party in the executive and legislative center is tempted to use federal power to curb state-based opposition parties. Furthermore, there is the well-known problem of *objective* measurement of the seriousness or imminence of an external or internal danger to peace and security. Even if we rule out an evil intent on the part of the central authority—which, in practice, we cannot do—there remains, as the familiar controversy on the subject of the freedom of expression and its permissible curbs has taught us, an honest disagreement as to whether the federal intervention was indeed warranted by a "clear and present," "imminent and grave," nebulous and distant or wrongly perceived danger. The Indian Constitution, for instance, authorizes the central government to supersede a state government and assume to itself all the executive and legislative powers of the state government concerned when a state of emergency is proclaimed.[34] Portions of the Indian Constitution that deal with the federal division of powers may be suspended (Article 356).[35] Although in principle the emergency powers are granted for a limited period of time (they are supposed to "cease to operate at the expiration of two months unless before the expiration of that period it has been approved by resolutions of both Houses of Parliament"— Article 352, section 2c), a recent experience shows that suspension of civil rights and preventive detention may last as long as six years. In 1962, after the start of border hostilities with Communist China, the emergency measures were issued and were kept in all India until 1967, when the Home Minister Y. B. Chavan informed the Parliament that the emergency would remain in effect indefinitely but that the arbitrary powers of the central government would be used only in certain border areas, such as Jammu and Kashmir, Nagaland and the Mizo Hills in the state of Assam. The Constitution,[35] which unmistakably au-

[34] Article 352 of the Indian Constitution: "If the President is satisfied that a grave emergency exists whereby the security of India or of any part of the territory thereof is threatened whether by war or external aggression or internal disturbance, he may, by Proclamation, make a declaration to that effect. . . . A proclamation of Emergency . . . may be made before the actual occurrence of war or of any such aggression or disturbance if the President is satisfied that there is imminent danger thereof." Article 353: "While the Proclamation of Emergency is in operation then . . . the executive power of the Union shall extend to the giving of directions to any State as to the manner in which the executive power thereof is to be exercised; the power of Parliament to make laws with respect to any matter shall include power to make laws conferring powers . . . as respects that matter, notwithstanding that it is one which is not enumerated on the Union List."

[35] Article 356: "If the President, on receipt from the Governor of the State or otherwise, is satisfied that a situation has arisen in which the government of the State cannot be carried on in accordance with the provisions of this Constitution, the President may by proclamation assume to himself all or any functions of the Government of the State . . . declare that the powers of the Legislature of the State shall be exercisable by the authority of [national] Parliament, make such incidental and consequential provisions as appear to the President to be necessary or desirable . . . including provisions for suspending in whole or in part the operation of any provisions of this Constitution relating to any body or authority in the State.

thorizes the central authority to take over a state government that is found incapable of satisfactory performance has also been invoked quite frequently by the ruling Congress party, which seemed to be quite ready to use the federal powers against the extreme left or the extreme right, both insignificant forces on the national level but enjoying mass support in some states. Thus, New Delhi several times dismissed the left-oriented coalition Cabinet in the state of Kerala. In Orissa, West Bengal, and Haryana, the state governments were dismissed and replaced by a federal rule when local parties proved unable to form a coalition cabinet.

From clear cases of national emergencies, caused by an external attack or by an internal insurrection, we have now moved into a twilight zone in which federal intervention in the affairs of the component states may be justified simply because the "republican" institutions are threatened, the political situation seems unstable, financial administration is irresponsible,[36] or—which is the most permissive clause—to ensure that federal laws are faithfully executed locally. The Indian Constitution, for instance, gives the federal government the power to issue administrative directives to the states as may be necessary to "ensure compliance with the laws made by Parliament" (Article 256) and to guarantee that "the executive power of every State shall be so exercised as not to impede or prejudice the exercise of the executive power of the Union" (Article 257, section 1). Furthermore, the federal center is represented in each of the seventeen Indian states by a federally appointed governor who, according to the Constitution, is supposed to be only a ceremonial figurehead under normal conditions, the real power being in the hands of state chief-ministers (that is, prime ministers and their cabinets). An amendment (Article 258A) passed in 1957 transformed the seventeen governors into powerful extensions of New Delhi in the seventeen states. It reads as follows:

> Notwithstanding anything in this Constitution the Governor of a State may, with the consent of the Government of

---

[36] Article 360 permits similar superseding of the state authority by the central authority when "the President is satisfied that a situation has arisen whereby the financial stability or credit of India or of any part of the territory thereof is threatened."

India, entrust either conditionally or unconditionally to that Government or to its officers functions in relation to any matter to which the executive power of the State extends.

The federal overlap in India appears so predominant that a close-range scholar-observer of the Indian theory and practice, S. A. H. Haqqi of the Aligarh Muslim University, concluded that

"notwithstanding [a] formidable testimony to the federal character of the constitution,[37] one cannot, on a closer scrutiny, help agreeing with those who hold that the Indian Union is not a true federation, an indestructible Union of indestructible States but a unitary state with subsidiary federal features. . . . The Indian Constitution vests in the Union Government such formidable powers that, not only in times of war or during an emergency but even in times of peace, it can, if it so wishes, superintend, direct and control the activities of the State Governments." [38]

Latin-American federations may be similarly characterized as "unitary states with only subsidiary federal features" on account of the constitutionally legalized and frequently used practice of federal intervention. The Argentine Constitution (Article 6) gives the federal government the right "to intervene in the territory of a Province in order to guarantee the republican form of government or to repel foreign invasion, and at the request of the constituted authorities, to support or to re-establish them, should they have been deposed by sedition or invasion from another province." The Mexican Constitution authorizes the national government to see that democratic governments prevail in the states and that the Constitution and federal laws are executed by the state officers. Similar constitutional authorizations and practice characterize the federal states of Brazil and Venezuela. The Constitution of the latter provides (Article 241),

---

[37] Passing successfully most of our ten criteria tests, notably all except numbers 5 and 10.

[38] S. A. H. Haqqi, "Federalism, Single Dominant Party and the Problem of Linguistic Autonomy in India," paper presented at the Sixth World Congress of the International Political Science Association, Geneva, 1964, pp. 2–3.

"In case . . . of grave circumstances that affect economic and social life, the President may restrict or suspend the constitutional guarantees, or some of them."

In Canada the Constitution authorizes the central government to veto or disallow provincial bills (a power rarely used) and to appoint provincial lieutenant governors and provincial judges. In the Soviet Union, the Presidium of the Supreme Soviet as well as the Soviet Council of Ministers may annul the decisions of the Council of Ministers in each of its fifteen constituent union republics; the Procurator of the Soviet Union appoints the procurators in all fifteen union republics—not a minor federal power in a police state.

In Switzerland it is in the competence of the central legislature (Federal Assembly) to guarantee the constitutions and the territory of the cantons and in consequence of this guarantee to intervene as well as to take measures for the internal security of Switzerland and for the maintenance of peace and order. The executive branch (Federal Council) is empowered to examine the laws and ordinances of the cantons that are required to be submitted for its approval and is empowered to supervise the branches of cantonal administration that are placed under executive control.[39]

In contrast with the just-mentioned, sometimes detailed, often sweeping general authorization for federal intervention, the provisions of the United States Constitution appear laconic and dispersed in several articles. Each state is guaranteed a republican form of government and federal protection against invasion and "on Application of the Legislature or of the Executive (when the Legislature cannot be convened) against domestic Violence" (Article IV)—which, of course, may take the form of intervention; another article makes the Federal executive responsible for a faithful execution of the laws (Article II, Section 3); and Article I provides for "calling for the Militia [now the National Guard] to execute the laws of the Union, suppress Insurrections and repel Invasions." In combination with the defense powers of the President as commander in chief,

---

[39] The cantons may, for instance, enact measures necessary for the repression of abuses of the liberty of the press but must submit them to the Federal Council for approval (Article 55).

the provisions just mentioned represent a potentially wide open door for federal interference because the request of the state authorities for action is not necessary when the issue is local resistance to federal laws or is a serious threat to internal peace in the United States. In 1842, President Tyler was ready to send troops to Rhode Island to protect one of the two governments, each of which claimed to be the legitimate one. In 1960, President Eisenhower sent law-enforcing troops to Little Rock, Arkansas, to enforce a court order for school desegregation. "The action at Little Rock affected the balance of forces in the Federal system because it proved that in an eventual confrontation between the national government and the state on the question of civil rights, the state must comply." [40]

The concurrent power

The third type of a deliberate constitutional overlap between federal and state powers is the provisions for sharing or reciprocal delegation of powers, often in the form of a Concurrent List that we find in modern constitutions and that represent, as it were, a bridge for a two-way traffic between the otherwise exclusive shores of federal and state powers. The concurrent lists usually contain a clause that makes the federal law prevail over the provincial law when the federal authority chooses to legislate on any matter in the Concurrent List. Their lengths vary greatly from very brief (Canada) to very long (India).

Article 254 of the Indian Constitution expresses this principle as follows:

> If any provision of a law made by the Legislature of a State is repugnant . . . to any provision of an existing law with respect to one of the matters enumerated in the Concurrent List, then . . . the law made by Parliament . . . shall prevail and the law made by the Legislature of such State shall, to the extent of the repugnancy, be void.

However, the Constitution provides that in an exceptional case, when the President of India consents, the conflict between a state and a federal law may be resolved in favor of the state law,

[40] Harry Lazer, *The American Political System in Transition.* New York: Crowell, 1967, p. 79.

despite the repugnancy. The Indian Concurrent List contains forty-seven items, starting with some portions of the criminal law and procedure, family law, contracts, and bankruptcy and trust and ending with price controls, social security, trade unions, newspapers, electricity, boilers, prevention of cruelty to animals, and vagrancy.

A related constitutional overlap between federal powers and state powers may be seen in the reciprocal delegation of authority and in federal-state subdivisions of one shared power so that a portion of it is given to the federal government while another part of the same matter is kept in the hands of the local authorities. Examples are the shared federal and state controls over the National Guard in the United States, controls over banking, trade, and railroads in Australia, and control over family law or alcoholic beverages in Switzerland. Delegation of the execution of federal laws to local units is a frequent feature in many federations. In Switzerland, for instance, a federal penal code, as noted previously, is adjudicated by cantonal courts; their organization and procedures also remain cantonal. Laws as to the organization of the Swiss army are enacted by the federal legislature, but the execution of the military laws is cantonal (Article 20). The same is true with regard to the modern welfare provisions of the Swiss Constitution (the utilization of water power, the welfare of the people, the economic security of the Swiss citizens, the regulation of banks, measures to prevent economic crises and to relieve unemployment); [41] the Constitution requires that cantons be consulted before the enactment of federal regulations and that "as a rule, the execution of the federal regulations be entrusted to the cantons."

Such a formula of federal concurrence of otherwise divided powers is also clearly present in the German tradition and practice of federalism. It seems to translate the Montesquieuan constitutional separation of executive and legislative powers into territorial terms, leaving the bulk of the legislative power to the federal center while transferring administrative and judicial powers largely to the states, with the exception of foreign affairs, defense, and the mail. Peter H. Merkl appropriately calls such a type of territorial distribution of authority *executive-legislative*

---

[41] Article 24A, Article 31A, Article 31C, Article 31D.

federalism [42] and points to the continuity of the concept and practice under the Imperial Constitution of 1871, the Weimar Constitution, and the present Basic Law of West Germany. Under the current Constitution, even the collection of federal revenues is delegated to the Länder administration. Because the federal government has not established its own field agencies, the Länder administer the rules, initiated by the federal cabinet and enacted by the federal parliament, with their own local agencies, personnel, and funds. Such a practice, dating back to the empire, entails minimum interference in the long-established administrative structures and practices of the member units; for the average German citizen, the establishment of the federal union "brought about no changes in the government officials with whom he had to deal." [43] One of the consequences of federal-legislative federalism is a brake on the growth of the federal administrative apparatus. Today the total federal administrative personnel represents only 9 percent of the West German total (in the Weimar Republic it was 13.1 percent), whereas the Länder and local administrative personnel account for 91 percent (in the Weimar Republic it was 86.9 percent).[44] The German variant of federalism differs substantially from the American concept because, as Arnold Brecht described it, it provides for "horizontal" division of powers in contrast with the "vertical" division in the United States.[45]

Concurrent lists as well as constitutional provisions for cooperation, mutual dependence, and reciprocal delegation or sharing of powers between federal and state governments are

[42] Peter H. Merkl, "Executive-Legislative Federalism in West Germany," *The American Political Science Review,* Vol. 53, No. 3 (1959), 732–741. See also Peter H. Merkl, *Political Continuity and Change.* New York: Harper & Row, 1967, p. 401.

[43] Karl H. Cerny, "Federalism in the West German Republic," in Earle, *Federalism: Infinite Variety in Theory and Practice,* p. 145.

[44] Merkl, "Executive-Legislative Federalism," p. 734.

[45] Arnold Brecht, *Federalism and Regionalism in Germany: The Division of Prussia.* New York: Oxford, 1945, chap. 6. Compare George Carey, "Federalism: Historic Questions and Contemporary Meanings—A Defense of Political Processes," in Earle, *Federalism,* p. 49: "Federalism can be defined as a division of powers between the State and national governments, a *vertical* distribution of powers, as distinct from a *horizontal* distribution embodied in the doctrine of separation of powers."

viewed by some observers as logical, inevitable, and desirable but are deplored by others as possibly contrary to, or at least harmful for, federalism. In defense of concurrent lists and provisions for delegation of authority, it may be also said that sometimes such provisions represent a transitional solution on the part of the founding fathers who are not and cannot be certain which powers would be best delegated to the central authority and which to local governments. This is certainly reflected in both the first and second constitutions of Pakistan (Article 143).

> Notwithstanding anything in this Constitution, the President may, with the consent of a Provincial Government, entrust either conditionally or unconditionally to that Government, or to any officer or authority of that Government, functions in relation to any matter to which the executive authority of the Republic extends.

We should add that some analysts condemn the concurrent jurisdiction in federal systems because it may add "yet another series of disputes about jurisdiction to the already formidable list of possible conflicts which are inevitable in even the simplest federal system." [46]

In our view, the existence of concurrent powers of concurrent lists is simply another reflection of the fundamental impossibility and also the undesirability of dividing political powers neatly or permanently.

The elastic or coefficient clauses

The fourth possible channel for federal executive and legislative infiltration of the states is known in the United States as the "necessary and proper," "elastic," or "coefficient" clause. This is the last, eighteenth grant of exclusive powers to the federal center (Article I, section 8), which in addition to the previous seventeen specific grants of power authorizes the Congress "to make all laws which shall be necessary and proper in carrying out the foregoing" seventeen Federal powers. The problem evidently is who interprets—and with what bias—the meaning of the two crucial but controversial adjectives *necessary*

---

[46] Wheare, *Federal Government*, p. 77.

and *proper.* In 1819 in the famous case of *McCulloch* v. *Maryland,* Chief Justice Marshall interpreted these words as meaning "useful and convenient" rather than "absolutely indispensable." Even this ruling did not and could not eliminate further disagreements about the real meaning of not only "necessary and proper" but also "useful and convenient" or "absolutely indispensable."

The lack of verbal precision in all federal constitutions

Finally, we should mention a problem that underscores all the previously discussed overlaps: the lack of verbal precision in the constitutional description of the territorial distribution of authority. However finely chiseled a constitutional text may be, the federal needle seems always to have a sufficiently big eye for the unitary camel to go through. There are several reasons for it. One is basically semantic: the significance of terms tends to change in time and space. The legal language is only somewhat more accurate than that of the poets; if this were not so, the profession of law through centuries would not have been so profitable. The lack of verbal precision in federal constitutions also reflects the difficulty of quantifying political power. What are central and national matters as distinct from peripheral or provincial matters proves quite resistant to an exact specification and a neat division into watertight compartments of separate jurisdiction. Finally, the lack of verbal precision may sometimes also be deliberate; some founders simply wish to conceal a unitary hope in a federal wrapping.

CONTROVERSIAL RESULTS OF TESTING

Any yardsticks chosen to test federalism are necessarily of unequal weight and, therefore, different relevance. Independence of the national center on the component territorial communities in rule making seems to us more important than a constitutional guarantee of two separate, federal and provincial, sets of courts; dependence on the component units for amending the constitutional division of powers seems more essential than equal representation of unequal units in the federal chamber (or the other way around?); and a neat and precise division of authority strikes us as more fundamental than such questions as where the federal capital is located or where the residual powers are kept. Even if we assign a very approximate greater or lesser weight to our ten yardsticks we still cannot convincingly demonstrate that the absence of a very important criterion can be compensated for by five or six criteria of the less-important categories. Taking the example of West German federalism, what is, in final analysis, more important: (1) the federal supervision of local administration and adjudication of federal laws, federal regulation of the selection and training of civil servants and judges, federal prescription of uniform administrative and judicial procedure throughout all the Länder, and the federal power of defense, foreign policy, mail, and railroads, or (2) the dependence of the federal upper chamber (Bundesrat) on the component units that determine both their delegations and their votes, the local administration and adjudication of federal rules, and even the local collection of federal taxes? [47]

Having now applied our ten yardsticks of federalism, we should be reasonably close to an acceptable answer to the question what constitutes real federalism—*but we are not.* Yet we feel justified in flexing our definitional muscles, as it were, because the exercise has at least acquainted us with the infinite variety of the federal theme in different times and in different national environments and has warned us against a possible ethnocentric tendency to equate the American experience with "true" federalism. Our tests, we believe, further demonstrate that many federal constitutions deliberately, and sometimes unwittingly, tend to transmute the definitional boundary between unitary, federal, and confederal systems into a sieve that permits mutual interpenetration. Hybrid rather than pure-bred systems are the result, and we refer, therefore, to many systems as "federal with unitary features," "pseudofederal," "quasi-federal," or, on the contrary, "unitary systems with federal features, tendencies, or dynamics." There are unitary constitutions that emphasize that they are not federal and that yet guarantee the identity, future, rights, and territorial self-rule

---

[47] Peter H. Merkl, "Executive-Legislative Federalism," p. 736, calls the role of the Bundesrat pivotal and traces its peculiar character back to the *Confederal* Congress consisting of the instructed representatives of the princes. See also his *Political Continuity and Change,* p. 401.

of various communities. On the other hand, all federal constitutions, as we have seen, authorize some degree of central interference in the domestic affairs of the component units by various implicit or explicit grants of emergency or potential powers. These range from the "elastic clause" and the federal right to preserve a republican or democratic form of government in each state to the implied tendency toward centralization that may result from the federal monopoly to make war, engage in international politics, and promote the general welfare. Many modern federal constitutions, as we have seen, have also deliberately bridged the "great divide" by authorizing or encouraging mutual dependence and reciprocal delegation of authority between the national and subnational governments.

In our two concluding chapters we shall now turn our attention away from the institutional and constitutional criteria of federalism to the extraconstitutional causes of contraction or expansion of the central power. We are guided here by the wise admonition of William S. Livingston:

> We are too prone to say that federal constitutions must contain a certain five or eight or ten characteristics and that all constitutions lacking any of these are not federal. Such a set of criteria ignores the fundamental fact that institutions are not the same things in different social and cultural contexts. . . . The essence of federalism lies not in the institutional or constitutional structure but in the society itself. Federal government is a device by which the federal qualities of society are articulated and protected.[48]

[48] William S. Livingston, "A Note on the Nature of Federalism," *Political Science Quarterly,* Vol. 67, No. 1 (March 1952), 81–95.

NINE
FEDERAL ASYMMETRY
AND POLYETHNIC UNIONS

It is scarcely conceivable that all parties to the
federal bargain at all times and in all places seek the
same things, in the same proportions, for the same
reasons. . . . At best the federal compact can only
be a formalized transaction of a moment in the
history of a particular community.

> RUFUS DAVIS ("The 'Federal Principle'
> Reconsidered")

To consider problems of federation . . . apart from
[the] fundamental fact of the uneven distribution of
interdependence and power would invite the delusion
of omnipotence.

> KARL W. DEUTSCH (*National and Social
> Communication*)

There is no greater pitfall for federal nations than to
take consensus for granted. . . . Only blind men
could expect a consensus to be lasting if the national
flag or the national image is merely the reflection of
one part of the nation, if the sum of values to be
protected is not defined so as to include the language
or the cultural heritage of some very large and
tightly knit minority, if the identity to be arrived at
is shattered by a color bar.

> PIERRE ELLIOTT TRUDEAU (*Federalism
> and the French Canada*)

Our initial illustration of a federal system (Fig. 7–1) in contrast with the unitary system placed an emphasis on the constitutional division of power between one central government and a series of subnational governments that, on the basis of a guaranteed principle of territorial autonomy and exclusive powers, administers the component units of the federation. In light of our previous testing of federalism by the ten yardsticks, our model is in obvious need of refinement and correction. Several links that connect the two spheres of separate and seemingly exclusive jurisdictions must now be added to illustrate the *constitutional* overlaps. They are shown in Figure 9–1 by seven numbered lines:

1. The "elastic clause."
2. Constitutional authorization for federal supervision of local execution of national laws.
3. The right to insure the republican or democratic form of government.
4. Emergency powers in case of invasion or insurrection.
5. War and foreign policy powers.
6. Concurrent powers.
7. Dependence of the central authority on the state governments, in such things as state control of national elections, control over the upper chamber, and local administration of national programs. Dependence of the central authority on the components also includes the possibility of blackmail, implied in the constitutional grant of the right of secession.

This correction of our model of federalism, although perhaps useful, is not sufficient. We must try now to add the often decisive dimensions of *extraconstitutional* reality; the model is to reflect not only the wording but also the actual working of a federal constitution.

First, there is the problem of federal asymmetry and polyethnicity. The component units that the constitution views as somewhat equal for the purpose of government are now to be marked on our model as being highly different in size and population, possessing different economic and political powers, and manifesting unequal interest in the way in which the federal system is supposed to operate. This problem of asym-

Figure 9–1   New model of a federal system

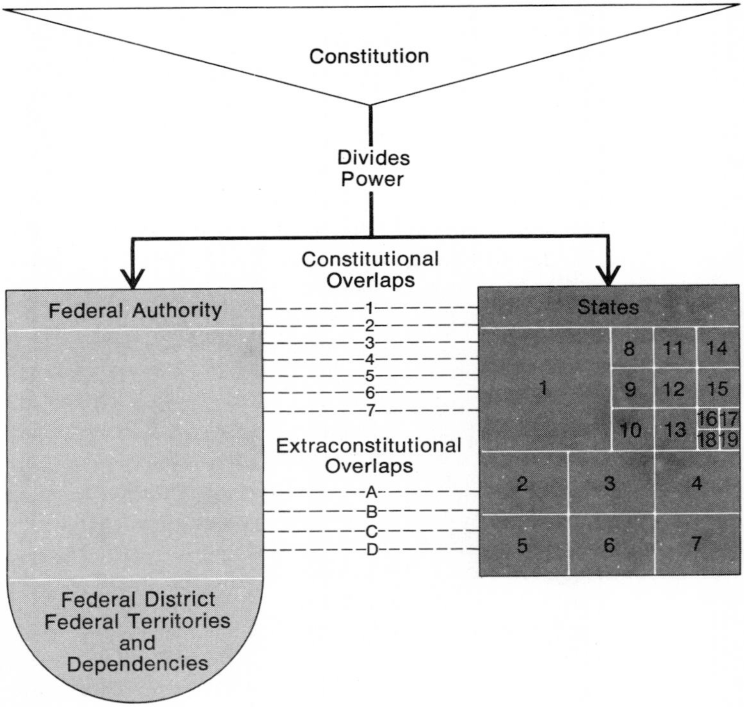

metry may sometimes lead either to intrafederal hegemony or to explosion, especially if such asymmetry is compounded by linguistic, ethnic, racial, or religious differences coinciding with territorial subdivisions. These differences are often exploited by external interference.

Although our initial model of federalism presented all units as being constitutionally of equal size, the corrected model suggests inequality of power and interest (see the square indicating the territorial divisions). Furthermore, our model will now also indicate a series of extraconstitutional links between the center and the component units; they blur the division between the two jurisdictions. These links represent environmental changes that the drafters did not and perhaps could not foresee and take into account. They are marked on our model by lettered lines:

A. Economic and social imperatives such as economic planning, technological innovation (atomic energy, computers, and other costly projects calling for national financing and controls), social welfare programs, and the growth of large national organizations that cut across the territorial divisions, such as manufacturing corporations, insurance companies, banks, labor and farm organizations, and mass media. They all challenge the intrafederal boundaries ("the worst inanities," as Morton Grodzins called the boundaries of the American states) that had been drawn in earlier eras and that cannot be justified on any grounds of rational efficiency.

B. Population shifts, especially the growth of big cities, the emergence of new regional territorial communities regardless of state boundaries, or emergence of new territorial communities within the existing state boundaries.

C. External pressures (threats and opportunities) that result in further extension of the federal powers.

D. Political culture and political parties whose orientation, structure, and changing leaders may have a profound impact on the reality of federalism.

Our new model of federalism, like the initial one, marks the federal authority as extending its power over more than the total area of the component units to indicate the federal control over the national capital, colonies, and territories. Our model is static; it cannot, of course, express the constant *changes* in the relationship between the federal and state powers, especially the dynamic growth of the central power in relation to the subnational units; neither can it depict the new forms of localism and the resistance to the unitary and centralizing tendencies observed in all systems.

The lines marked *A* through *D* that on our model connect the federal and state authorities illustrate the impact of extraconstitutional factors on the working of a federal system. It may be argued that neither the lines illustrating the constitutional overlaps nor the lines depicting the extraconstitutional ones should be presented by such thin threads. Consistent with actuality, they should perhaps be marked by very thick lines, indicating two-lane bridges permitting a constant two-way traffic.

DISPARITY OF POWER INGREDIENTS

There is no federal system in the world in which all the component units are even approximately equal in size, population, political power, administrative skills, wealth, economic development, climatic conditions, predominance of either urban or rural interests, social structure, traditions, or relative geographic location (for instance, near to, or far from, sources of potential external dangers). As a result, they necessarily vary in their attachment to the federal nation and in their readiness to contribute to or abide by different federal programs. Their insistence on the scope of territorial autonomy necessarily differs, too.

All the twenty-one federations that have been examined in our study offer such an image of profound contrast on every possible level. Let us consider, for instance, the disparity of power—and interest in and support of the federal nation—between Russia and Armenia, Estonia, or the Uzbek Republic in the Soviet Union; between the most populous (Hindu and Hindi-speaking) state of Uttar Pradesh and the microstate of the largely Christianized Naga people in the Indian Federation; West Pakistan (oriented toward the Middle East, with which it largely shares a way of life and economy) and East Pakistan (so clearly anchored in the monsoon and rice-cultivating area of Southeast Asia); or the large Catholic state of Bavaria and the two city-states of Hamburg and Bremen in West Germany. In Switzerland two populous cantons of Zurich and Bern have almost one third of the 196 seats in the federal legislature, whereas the seven cantons of Uri, Schwyz, Unterwalden, Glarus, Zug, Appenzell, and Schaffhausen have between them only 14 seats. In the Canadian House of Commons two provinces, Ontario and Quebec, have 160 members out of the total of 265. In Australia the two most populous states, South Wales and Victoria, have 80 representatives out of 124. The disparity in size, wealth, and power in Latin-American federations is usually cited as the main reason for their unitary centralism instead of the constitutional federal pledge. For instance, in Argentina (composed now of twenty-two provinces, the federal capital, and the federal territories), the federal capital of Buenos Aires contains one third (33.58 percent) of the total population. Before the city was separated from its province, the province itself contained two thirds of the Argentine population and about three fourths of the total wealth. A similar disparity characterizes federal Venezuela (composed of twenty states, federal district and federal territories) where the state of Bolívar (26.09 percent of the country's total surface) contains only 2.84 percent of the Venezuelan population. In Mexico [1] the federal capital contains more inhabitants than any of the component twenty-nine states. In Brazil, which is composed of twenty-two states and the federal capital of Brasilia, some of the states cannot be considered administratively and economically viable. Only six states are fairly advanced (São Paulo, Minas Gerais, Rio Grande do Sul, and Guanabara, which includes Rio de Janeiro, Paraná, and Santa Catarina); the other states are or have become backward (for instance, Baía and Pernambuco, which were prosperous at the time of the boom of the sugar economy). But even in the category of the fairly advanced states there are abysmal disparities. The state of São Paulo and its capital of the same name contain the largest concentration of industry in South America; the state's population (13 million) represents 18 percent of the total population of Brazil.

An extreme disparity in the level of industrial development, size, and population also characterizes the United States federation. It is not necessary to elaborate on the contrast between Alaska (with its 245,000 inhabitants) and New York State (with over 16 million), or Wyoming (with 330,000) and California (with nearly 16 million). The fifty-two senatorial votes that may determine a federal chamber's action can be, theo-

---

[1] Henry Kantor in his study of Latin-American federalisms (in Valerie Earle (ed.), *Federalism: Infinite Variety in Theory and Practice.* Itasca, Ill.: F. E. Peacock Publishers, 1968, p. 198) argues that in Mexico localism and regionalism tended to separate the various groups so much that an integrated state could not function. According to Kantor this in large part led to the loss of half the country to the United States, namely Texas, New Mexico, Arizona, and California.

retically, so drawn as to represent twenty-six states whose combined population would be under 30 million (29,747,000), that is, a bare 16.05 percent of the total population of the United States. Other possible or actual consequences of federal asymmetry are illustrated in most college textbooks on American government. One frequent example is the comparison between a senator from the state of New York who usually represents around 3 million votes (Robert F. Kennedy in 1964: 3,728,864) and a senator from Nevada who may represent only 65,000 votes (Howard B. Cannon in 1964: 66,907). Asymmetric federalism (and they all are) violates the principle of equality of franchise (one man, one vote) which requires that everyone's vote should have the same weight and value. It is sacrificed for the sake of the federal principle of equal representation of unequally populated territorial units. In the Presidential (Electoral) College, made up of 538 electors (each state having as many electors as it has seats in both houses of the Congress), a presidential candidate can be elected President if he were to win the electoral votes of only the twelve most populous industrial states, regardless of the way in which the vote of the remaining thirty-eight states were cast. In (wild) theory, if the twelve states were politically to gang up against the less-populated thirty-eight states, they could become, as it were, an imperial oligarchy in the Federal union of fifty states.

The component units may perceive the objective facts of disparity of power, present in all federations, either correctly or incorrectly. They may underestimate such disparity with confidence or overestimate it with exaggerated suspicion. As we know, situations defined as real are real in their consequences; even a grossly erroneous perception of asymmetry of power in a federal union may produce dissatisfaction and resistance to the federal way of life. In his study on symmetric and asymmetric federations, Charles D. Tarlton speaks of a "secession potential" [2] present in such situations. His study presents an interesting theoretical construct of symmetric federations in which the

[2] Charles D. Tarlton, "Symmetry and Asymmetry as Elements of Federalism: A Theoretical Speculation," *Journal of Politics,* 27 (1965), 870.

component territorial units share in *interests* and *concerns* common to the federal system as a whole. They are, in fact, "miniature reflections of the important aspects of the whole federal system." [3] The opposite asymmetrical model expresses the extent to which the component units do not share in these common features.[4] This is another approach to the study of the reasons for which some federations fail to be established or, when established, dissolve again into their components. A recent study on the subject of federal failures argues that what was essential, and also lacking, in the four federations that have failed (the Malaysian federation with Singapore, the Caribbean federation, the East African federation of Uganda, Tanganyika, and Kenya, and the Rhodesia-Nyasaland federation) was

> commitment to the primary political, ideal of federation itself, and charismatic leaders or events to generate such commitment—the absence of a positive political or ideological commitment to the primary goal of federation as an end in itself. . . . Where what is wanted is not a new nation but a pragmatic solution of certain problems of trade and marketing, population movement, defense or foreign policy, some other solution different from classic federalism may be more realistic and so, more successful.[5]

Perception of federal asymmetry in power ingredients may influence the orientations of the component units toward the desirability of composing one federal nation in two directions:

First, a prosperous, advanced, and powerful component unit may find the benefits derived from the federal association not commensurate with its contributions. In particular it may resent being taxed without a proportionate share in policy making and so, in fact, forced to contribute to the advancement of its poor (or lazy) relatives in the union. Underpopulated and oil-rich Sumatra, for instance, displayed such a resentment against poor and overpopulated Java, the dynamic center

[3] Tarlton, "Symmetry and Asymmetry," p. 868.
[4] Tarlton, "Symmetry and Asymmetry," p. 861.
[5] Thomas M. Franck, *Why Federations Fail*. New York: New York University Press, 1968, pp. 197–198.

of Indonesian nationalism and the politically dominant unit in the originally federated United States of Indonesia. At other times, such a fear against excessive contribution to the federal funds may dissolve a federation before it has been given a chance to prove its worth. This was the case of the Mali Federation in Africa, established in 1959 by agreement between two former French colonies, Senegal and Sudan. Unlike Indonesia, whose initial federalization was imposed from without by Holland, Mali's federal concept seemed to have native roots and support. There were no explosive racial issues, and yet the federation was dissolved after one year. The leaders of relatively prosperous and conservative Senegal staged a coup, and the collapse of the Mali federation followed. Poor, landlocked, and more left-oriented Sudan assumed the name Mali; Senegal retained its original name and went it alone.

The plan for the federation of former British colonies in the Caribbean failed for very similar reasons. The original intent was to combine the two large islands, Jamaica and Trinidad (the two islands account for 80 percent of the total population of the West Indies), with the Leeward Islands (Saint Kitts, Nevis, Montserrat, and Antigua), the Windward Islands (Dominica, Saint Lucia, Saint Vincent, and Grenada), and Barbados. The central issue was Jamaica's reluctance to share its superior assets with the other islands; in Jamaica the per capita income is almost twice as high as on the other islands. The original constitutional plan provided for forty-five members of the federal Parliament, out of which only seventeen would come from Jamaica; this indeed could be viewed by Jamaica as taxation without commensurate representation, especially when at one point all the other islands suggested retroactive federal taxes. On the other hand, Jamaica's effort to wield political power in proportion to its contribution led to a fear that the Caribbean federation would become simply Jamaica writ large. There were other complicating factors: a relative lack of West Indian identity in contrast with the insular identities of the component units; tension between the Negroes and the East Indians who, especially on Trinidad, dreaded a black-dominated federal structure; some linguistic problems that opposed the educated classes, who used English as a lingua franca, to the majorities on different islands who spoke different Creole dialects or French patois in Dominica and St. Lucia.[6] As noted previously, in 1967 the process of further atomization prevented even a federation of the microscopic island of Anguilla with Saint Kitts and Nevis.

Long-established federations are not free of similar tensions between their more prosperous (and, therefore, more contributing) parts and the rest. The two largest states of the Australian federation (New South Wales and Victoria) resent what they consider a disparity between the federal benefits received and the taxes collected from their residents. In Yugoslavia, the two republics Croatia and Slovenia, which, in the paradoxical colonial way, benefited in economic and technological development, from their former status as provinces in the Austro-Hungarian Empire, complain that they have become excessively the main subsidizers of the other, underdeveloped, republics, mainly Macedonia, whose present economic and technical underdevelopment at least partly reflects its former status as a neglected province of the decaying Ottoman empire.

The second adverse effect of federal asymmetry is the rise of suspicion or fear, justified or not, on the part of the weaker members that one particular unit, on account of its power or skill, may acquire a position of overwhelming dominance—a problem already mentioned in connection with a potential Pan-Jamaican orientation of the Caribbean federation.

In all associations or groups, a leading element may, or perhaps, must, as Robert Michels maintains, arise. In his thesis on the inevitability of leadership in any organization, as a result of specialization, division of roles, and need for coordination, Michels describes the equally inevitable tendency to oligarchy. Leaders who have sincerely and honestly conceived of their roles as servants of collective interests tend to organize themselves at the top and to consolidate their leading positions to the point that they may have enough power to detach themselves from their dependence on, and service to, the collective whole, and develop their own interests, including that of self-perpetuation. "It is Organization," wrote Michels, "which gives the dominion of the elected over the electors, of the mandatories

---

[6] Amitai Etzioni, "The West Indian Federation: A Constitution against Reality," paper presented at the Sixth World Congress of the International Political Science Association, Geneva, 1964, pp. 14–15.

over the mandators, of the delegates over the delegators. Who says Organization, says Oligarchy." [7]

Much of what Michels had to say about oligarchic tendencies and reality in political parties applies to many federal systems. Faced with the Prussian hegemony in the German federation, many a German state might have paraphrased Michels: "Who says Federation, says dominion of one over the others." Heinrich von Treitschke declared Imperial Germany the very opposite of federalism. No member of a federal system can rule out the possibility that one leading element, be it a state or a coalition of states, may emerge and distort the principle of equality into that of a master-servant relationship. This may be the restult of environmental changes such as uneven economic development, population shifts, new technology, or dynamic leadership and political skill in one of the component units. Hegemony in a federation, which is the very opposite of the federal principle, may be a fact, may be half-fact and half-fiction, or may be a matter of wrong perception altogether. In either case it will lead to strain and in some cases to explosion. In United States history the Southern insurrection against the political and economic leadership of the North is one tragic example.

In the case of the original German federation, the power asymmetry led to the curious situation that Prussia favored federalism as a guarantee of its potential hegemony while dreading a unitary formula that could have absorbed Prussia into an all-German unity. It was for this reason that liberal forces tended to favor unitary rather than federal Germany. In the German context, federalism did not mean pluralism and democracy but meant Prussian hegemony. As Arnold Brecht noted in his study *Federalism and Regionalism in Germany,* the very size of Prussia was disproportionate to the scattered remainders of small principalities, for neither of which there is any analogy in the history of American federalism.

The fear of the weaker units that the association with one powerful component unit would transform a federation into an imperial structure (in which the powerful unit might, in fact, subject the rest to its domination) was necessarily present in all

---

[7] Robert Michels, *Political Parties.* New York: Dover, 1959, p. 401.

the situations noted previously in Chapter 6, in which a former colonial power tried to associate its former colonial dependencies in a new confederal or federal venture. The experience with colonial domination was too fresh in the new countries to dissipate the fear that the European powers aimed at preserving their economic, political, and cultural domination of Africa and Asia under a new formula. Such a mistrust characterized not only the African and Asian opposition to new links with Europe but also some intra-European plans to federalize what had been imperial. The Czechs, Slovaks, Slovenes, and Croatians did not trust a last-minute Habsburg plan to federalize the Austro-Hungarian Empire; nor did the Irish trust the British when the Act of the Union in 1801 was to establish some British-Irish federation. The Act of the Union provided for Irish representation in the British Parliament, while the Parliament on College Green in Dublin was to cease to function. In the House of Commons, Ireland was to have one hundred members, two for each county and for the cities of Dublin and Cork, one each for thirty-one other cities, and one for the University of Dublin. In the House of Lords, Ireland was to have twenty-eight temporal lords elected for life by the Irish lords and to have four spiritual lords. The British colonial behavior in Ireland as well as the ingrained British attitudes toward the Irish and the Irish reaction to both finally made secession, not federation, inevitable.[8]

The fear that the federation would be tilted to the advantage of one of its component units differs from but is related to another type of federal asymmetry, that of an excessive growth of the federal center. This has already been mentioned in connection with the problem of federal capital cities. In many federations, the federal city is not only the seat of federal power but also the center of mass media, publishing, economic and financial powers, and national cultural institutions (for example, Moscow, Buenos Aires, Caracas, or Mexico City). It is also this concentration of federal and all the other attributes that has made

---

[8] Richard Ned Lebow, *White Britain and Black Ireland: A Case Study of Colonial Perception,* doctoral dissertation, The City University of New York, 1968, analyzes the mutual mistrust and inimical stereotypes that prevented a federal solution of the English-Irish relationship in the nineteenth century.

these federations, in addition to their party systems, so clearly top-heavy. This was also the case when Berlin was a capital of federated Germany. Noting Berlin's growth in the Bismarckian empire, Peter H. Merkl pointed to the consequences of the massive movement of people into the growing metropolis; the inhabitants

> would find employment with the national government or with central offices of Big Business, or the interest groups of the new age, with banking and credit institutions, with transport or other services of the national economy, or with manufacturers of books and periodicals and the entertainment industry.[9]

There is a set of factors that can accentuate a federal asymmetry or that can create a new one juxtaposed to the initial one. These factors are the movement of population to the capital city because of its cultural, economic, and political attractiveness (a phenomenon present in all federations except the United States, where Washington, D.C., attracts only political professionals and civil servants) or the shift of population from one state to another or, within states, from the rural areas to the urban areas. This will be discussed in more detail in Chapter 10.

LINGUISTIC AND ETHNIC DIFFERENCES

If linguistic, ethnic, racial, or religious differences either coincide with the intraterritorial boundaries or, on the contrary, overlap and are not federally recognized, an explosive dimension is added to the tensions caused by the disparities in power and attachment to the federal system. A good example is the resentment of the French Canadians, mostly but not exclusively concentrated in the province of Quebec (French Canadians constitute about 30 percent of the Canadian population; four fifths of their total number live in Quebec; they are relatively scattered, with only a small concentration in New Brunswick, where the French Canadians represent about 39 percent of the local population). French Canadians object not only to the economic and linguistic domination by English Canadians but also

[9] Peter H. Merkl, *Political Continuity and Change.* New York: Harper & Row, 1967, p. 392.

to the international political orientation of the country toward Britain and the Commonwealth. Both in 1914 and in 1939 the French province of Quebec strongly opposed the conscription and Canada's participation in the two world wars. Both wars were considered to be dominated by the non-Canadian interests of Britain. The participation and fate of France did not alter the French Canadian opposition to these wars because, strangely enough, the conservative and Catholic French Canadians did not admire the French Third Republic. The image of royal France, as it was before 1789, was actually more popular in French Canada than the Republic led by the anticlerical Radical Socialist party. This has been profoundly altered by the orientation of France under the traditionalist and devoutly Catholic de Gaulle. But whatever the attitude toward France in Europe, the concept of France in America was bound to be reasserted in the present era of vibrant nationalism everywhere. A good example of the new Canadian effort to tone down the English orientation was the adoption of a new Canadian national flag. The old one expressed a Canadian variant of the British Union Jack, composed of three superimposed crosses of Saint George (England), Saint Andrews (Scotland), and Saint Patrick (Ireland). Now a red maple leaf is supposed to provide the French and the English Canadians with one common Canadian symbol. (The former and the present Canadian flags are reproduced in Fig. 9–2.)

In 1967 the Canadian Broadcasting Corporation also carried a stirring rendition of a new bilingual [10] version of the Canadian national anthem. This was suggested by a biethnic enthusiast, Mrs. Jo Ouellet of Quebec. The anthem was sung by a choir from an Ottawa high school, and a joint Senate-Commons committee listened to the performance. The reaction was sympathetic, but the bilingual version was not adopted officially.

As the Prime Minister of Canada, quoted in this chapter's epigraph, warned, there is no greater pitfall in polyethnic federations than to take consensus for granted.

Resentment against the English orientation of biethnic

---

[10] The stanza of alternating French and English words begins "O Canada! Our home—notre pays/ La feuille d'érable, one flag from sea to sea."

Figure 9–2   The new and old Canadian flag

New

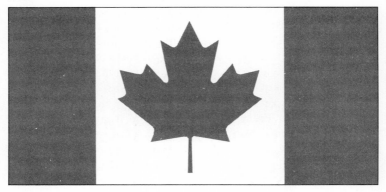

Old

Canada has now acquired even secessionist ingredients. The links with France are being strengthened. The Royal Commission Report on Canada (1965) took note of the French Canadian rediscovery of the cultural and potentially political and economic link with a worldwide French community. It has a reassuring effect and brings them promise of valuable cultural enrichment; in this way French Canadians are becoming more conscious of being a part of a much larger cultural world.[11]

---

[11] *A Preliminary Report of the Royal Commission on Bilingualism and Biculturalism,* 1965, p. 114.

The Royal Commission did not elaborate on the *political* implication of the Canadian membership in the worldwide French community; General de Gaulle, uninvited, volunteered to do so when he attempted to electrify the French Canadians by his famous exhortation at the time of the World Exposition in Montreal in 1967: "Vive le Québec libre!"

It should be noted that, as a consequence of Canada's active and liberal immigration policy, a new group of Canadians, who are of neither English nor French origin, seems to be emerging as a political force. They are immigrants of mostly German, Italian, Scandinavian, Greek, and Eastern European origins. By 1970 these new Canadians comprised more than 27 percent of the population of twenty million, thus closely approaching in number the French Canadians, who represent roughly one third of the total.

No polyethnic federation (as a matter of fact, no federation at all) can be considered immune from external pressures or lures directed at the territorial communities that for ethnic, linguistic, racial, or religious reasons feel dissatisfied, in one way or another, with their status and life within the federal state. Another polyethnic federation with a potentiality of interethnic tensions is the Soviet Union. We may assume that the fourteen Soviet Union republics suspect the superior power of the mighty and enormous Russian Republic, the dominant component unit with its one hundred million inhabitants and a territory extending from Finland in Northern Europe to islands in the Bering Sea. These component republics would have reason to suspect the Russian Republic even if the Soviet Union were ethnically more homogeneous; the giant-dwarf relationship between Russia and the rest of the union republics is too evident to overlook its implication. But, as the USSR is a polyethnic union, the fourteen non-Russian republics, composing the other half of the population, tend to view the Soviet Union as a political as well as an ethnic extension of Russia.

The ethnic Russian domination of the Soviet federal scene is obvious and can be statistically demonstrated. The percentage of the Great Russians in the party and its leading organs has been consistently much greater than the Great Russian percentage of the total Soviet population; in the Russian context, any suggestion of the federal principle of equal representation of unequal units within the party would probably lead to prosecution for high treason. The statistics show that in 1926 the Great Russians accounted for 53 percent of the Soviet population but made up 72 percent of the party membership. In 1962, when the first ethnic breakdown of the party in decades was published, Great Russians constituted 55 percent of the population and accounted for 64 percent of the party members. The disparity between Great Russians and all the other members of the Soviet Union is even more obvious when the ethnic composition of the party's leading organs is considered. Under Stalin the politburo had two Georgians (Stalin and Beria), one Armenian (Mikoyan), but no Ukrainian, no Central Asian Moslem, and no Byelorussian, showing a clear dominance of the politburo by the Great Russians and Caucasians at the expense of all the other nationalities.[12]

In other polyethnic federations there have also been complaints concerning the ethnic underrepresentation on the part of the Croatians and Slovenes because of the dominance of the Serbs in Yugoslovia and on the part of the Dravidian South with respect to the Hindi-speaking overpopulated North. The preceding analysis has already indicated the importance of emotional factors as well as wrong and unjustified perceptions. In the matter of ethnic or linguistic egoism, more often than not the suspicions of minorities are justified.

New nations in Africa and Asia seem particularly plagued by such suspicions. Usually the authority of the postliberation national government is fragile; the sense of national community, federal or not, is in its infancy. A federalizing process, by definition, requires some sacrifices of central power and many compromises with local autonomy. Such sacrifices or compromises are usually difficult for the leaders to accept.[13] But in our age of assertive nationalism and demands for increased par-

[12] V. V. Aspaturian, "The Soviet Union," Roy C. Macridis and Robert E. Ward (eds.), in *Modern Political Systems*. Englewood Cliffs, N.J.: Prentice-Hall, 1963, pp. 500–502. Also V. V. Aspaturian, *The Union Republics and Soviet Diplomacy*. Geneva: Librairie Droz, 1960, p. 155.

[13] Joseph S. Nye, Jr., "Functionalism and Federalism in East Africa," paper presented at the Sixth World Congress of the International Political Science Association, Geneva, 1964, p. 12.

ticipation in politics, wealth, and cultural achievements, even long-established nations, as we have noted, suffer from the pull of centrifugal lingual or ethnic forces. Persons living in linguistically homogeneous nation-states are usually unfamiliar with one of the most explosive issues in multilingual communities: the right to express one's own ethnic or territorial identity in one's own language in communicating with the authorities, the right to an education in one's own separate but equal schools, and the right to be addressed in one's own tongue by the government, mass media, cultural institutions, posters, and traffic signs. Wherever there exists a multilingual problem of significant dimension (there may be a controversy as to what constitutes a significant dimension because 100 percent ethnic or linguistic homogeneity is really nowhere in existence), the new as well as the old nations, all beset by these problems today, have used different devices to solve them. Usually one national language understandable and acceptable to all is adopted so that the elites and the masses can communicate for the purpose of building a new society and a new state or of modernizing both; at the same time, the right of minorities to preserve their identity and language and to develop them further is also guaranteed. Here, again, we detect the formula of, and the main argument for, a federal solution: a combination of linguistic unity with linguistic diversity. In practice it means that internal boundaries in a federation are made to coincide with the ethnic, tribal, or linguistic ones. This is then a *polyethnic* federalism, as adopted by India, Burma, the Soviet Union, Yugoslavia, Czechoslovakia (since 1968), but only partly by Switzerland and Canada, in contrast with somewhat *monoethnic* federations such as the United States, Australia, Latin-American federations, West Germany, or Austria.

As to African federations, it is perhaps too early to say whether tribal-territorial loyalties will ultimately lead to further atomization of the African continent or permit their recognition under some variants of a federal formula. The example of Nigeria is not encouraging on this point. The transformation of quasi-federal structures in Uganda, Libya, and Cameroun into authoritarian centralized units further challenges the initial hopes for federal solutions. In the Congo (Kinshasa), tribal political power has never ceased to press for a structural change that would make the provinces coincide with tribal boundaries. In 1962 (August 5), *The New York Times* published the following report filed in Kinshasa:

> Observers view [the reassertion of tribal political power and its demand for new provinces] as essentially federalist and traditionalist and thus anti-nationalist and against the mainstream of Pan-African political development. It marks, in effect, the failure of the late Patrice Lumumba and his nationalist movement to make any deep inroads into the traditional alignment in the Congo.

MULTINATIONAL FEDERATIONS

In the Soviet Union, as noted previously, the internal federal boundaries divide the country into fifteen union republics, each dominantly inhabited by a different ethnic and lingual group and each endowed with territorial autonomy and equal representation by twenty-five deputies each in the Supreme Soviet. In addition, ethnic subdivisions within each of the fifteen union republics are also endowed with territorial autonomy and direct representation (eleven for autonomous republics, five for autonomous regions, and one for ethnic districts) in the upper chamber of the Supreme Soviet. The descending order of representation reflects also the descending degree of local autonomy.

The Socialist Federal Republic of Yugoslavia is divided into six socialist republics, namely, Bosnia-Herzegovina, Slovenia, Croatia, Macedonia, Montenegro, and Serbia, which contains the autonomous provinces of Vojvodina and Kosovo-Metohija (inhabited by the Albanian-speaking minority). In the Yugoslav Chamber of Nationalities, each republic is represented by ten members and each province by five members. Slovenia, Croatia, Macedonia, Vojvodina, and Kosovo-Metohija represent distinct ethnic groups. Bosnia and Montenegro represent federal subdivisions of the Serbian ethnic group. It seems that in the case of Yugoslavia the federal formula was also used for the purpose of breaking the previous Serbian supremacy that has been often viewed by the non-Serbian groups as a threat to their interests.

India is today composed of seventeen states (see Fig. 9–3), the majority of which are based on linguistic boundaries (and in two cases on religious ones), a situation contrary to the origi-

Figure 9–3   Map of the federal divisions of India

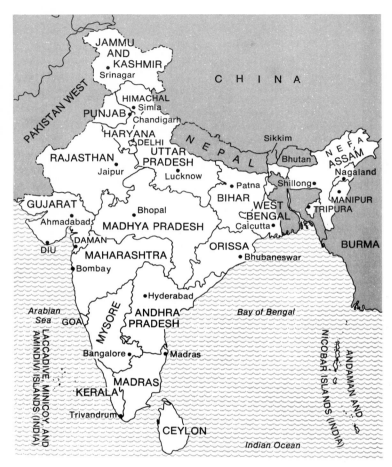

nal intention of India's two founding fathers, Nehru and Gandhi. The process may not have ended. The Indian political leaders, elated over the bloodless victory achieved by a united Indian effort against the British, were to experience a series of severe blows directed against their cherished ideas of a united and secular India. The first major shock was the Moslem insistence on secession. Pakistan and the never-ending dispute over Kashmir were the results. Secularism and modernization then began to weaken the unifying concept of the Hindu religion, another cement of Indian unity (after the main one, the British Raj, was gone).

In 1953 the reorganization of the Indian federation on the linguistic line began. Following the fast-unto-death of the Telugu congressman Potti Sriramulu, the 33 million Telugu-speaking Indians were allowed to establish their territorial unit, Andhra State, in 1953. Frank Moraes, the editor of the *India Times,* later wrote, "It is always easy to be wise after the event, but looking back on developments since India's independence, we can see that Nehru's major mistake was to yield to the creation of Andhra State on linguistic grounds." [14] In 1960, the state of Bombay had to be divided between its Gujarati- and Marathi-speaking portions. In 1962 a mixture of religion, tribalism, and geographic isolationism led to the creation of the sixteenth state, Nagaland, whose inhabitants are to a large extent Christianized. Nagaland is located in an eccentric geographic position in the far eastern corner of India. Many Naga groups openly manifest secessionist tendencies. In 1966, on the basis of agitation by the adherents of the Sikh religion (an anticaste offshoot of Hinduism) and a fast by their leader, Fateh Singh, the state of Punjab was divided into Punjabi Subha for the Sikhs and Haryana for the Hindus; the two new states are in dispute over the capital city, the famous Chandigarh, the "organic city" designed by the world-famous architect Le Corbusier. The divisive tendencies within India may be further demonstrated by the results of the plebiscite in the former Portuguese colony of Goa, annexed by Indian troops in December 1961. The partly Catholicized people of Goa were asked to determine whether they would like to merge with the neighboring state of Maharashtra or to remain separate as a federal territory. Through a strange coalition between the highest Hindu caste and the Roman Catholics, the plebiscite held in January 1962 refused the merger.

To complicate the complex Indian matters further, there exist separatist movements motivated by a strange combination of class and territorial interests rather than by lingual, ethnic, or religious considerations. For instance, in 1969 the southern state of Andhra, created in 1953 in the name of lingual unity, was

[14] Frank Moraes, "Succession and Division in India," *Foreign Affairs* (July 1961), p. 640.

about to split into two because its northwestern corner, the Telangana region (once the heart of the former kingdom of Hyderabad), asked for separate statehood, contending that since the time of independence it had been discriminated against and exploited by Andhra's wealthier coastal belt. Similar separate-statehood movements have appeared in other economically depressed areas (for instance, the Saurashtra region in the state of Gujarat, the Chattisgarh area in Madhya State, the eastern districts in Uttar Pradesh, tribal areas of Bihar, and the hill districts of Bengal). The separatists seem to hope that their more direct relations with the federal center in Delhi will bring relief to their territorial plight quicker than through the intermediary of the existing states, dominated by the wealthier region. Separatism in the depressed regions of India provides an ironic postscript to the history of colonialism: it occurs in the areas formerly run by native princely rulers and therefore now backward in contrast to the areas that were directly run as colonies by the British.

Some authors consider the Indian concession to territorial linguism a useful concession that may save the Indian nation, because the validity of the Indian nation is really not at stake. The cause of centrifugalism "is not a local revolt against the idea of the nation as a whole but against the idea of particular formation of the local unit." [15] This may be so in some cases; other authors point to the seriousness of the Dravidian regionalism in the South and its secessionist aims.

The Union of Burma, under military dictatorship, can hardly be discussed in relation to federalism. However, it should be noted that the federal idea, as expressed in Burma's first Constitution, was somewhat peculiar. On the one hand, it granted its component non-Burmese nationalities the right of secession (to be exercised only after ten years of common experience); on the other hand, it did not provide for state legislatures in the component units of the federation. It guaranteed the non-Burmese a majority of representatives in the upper house of the central parliament. Thus Burmese federalism combined the confederal feature of the right of secession with the communal representation, basically a unitary feature.

[15] Franck, *Why Federations Fail*, p. 191.

OFFICIAL LANGUAGE AS A FEDERAL PROBLEM

Polyethnic federalism, a federal distribution of authority corresponding to the territorial-ethnic boundaries, cannot quite escape the problem of designating one or several languages to serve as a federal lingua franca, the official language to be used in the national army, parliament, the administration, the courts, official publications (texts of laws), official signboards, communications among the component units, and communications by the minorities that cannot be given the right to communicate with authorities in their own idiom because of their numerical insignificance.

Three ways of solving the issue of a national language in a polyethnic federation that institutionalizes lingual and ethnic diversity have been applied:

1. Only one language, native or foreign, has been selected as official in the federal center and in communications among the units. In the Soviet Union the predominance of the Russian language is a self-evident extraconstitutional fact, despite the constitutional pledge of equality for all the other fourteen major languages. In federal Nigeria and semifederal Uganda, English was selected as the only official language, probably with a hope that one of the native languages may in due time replace it.

2. Two official languages have been adopted on equal footing. English and French are the official languages in Canada and also in Cameroun, which was created by a merger of a former English trust territory with a French one.

3. Several languages have been adopted in a somewhat explicit hierarchical order. One or more languages are proclaimed official in the central authority, and others in the component units; and still others may serve as auxiliary. This is so with important variations in federal Yugoslavia, Burma, Pakistan, India, and Switzerland.

The Yugoslav federal Constitution proclaims the languages of the peoples of Yugoslavia and their different scripts equal (Article 42) but stipulates that in the army "commands, military drill and administration shall be in the Serbo-Croatian language." Evidently, no slight to the Slovene, Macedonian, or Albanian languages has been intended, but concern for practicality has induced the drafters to stress simultaneously *equality and preference* for the Serbo-Croatian language spoken by the majority (the Serbo-Croatian language is written in the Cyrillic script by the Serbians and in the Latin alphabet by the Croatians). Laws are made public in four languages.

The Burmese Federation, which, in the Constitution, recognizes and guarantees the existence, languages, and the right of secession of its four major minorities (Karens, Kachins, Shans, and Chins) used the English language as an auxiliary official language in the period of transition from dependence to independent statehood. The Constitution of the Burmese Federation was so printed that on each page the official Burmese text faced the official English text.

Pakistan has proclaimed the dominant language of its eastern province, Bengali, and the lingua franca of its western province, Urdu, to be the official languages of the federation.[16] But the Constitution (Article 215) adds that the article "shall not be construed as preventing the use of any other language and, in particular, the English language may be used for official and other purposes until arrangements for its replacement are made." The Constitution has fixed the year of 1972 as a date on which a presidential commission is to examine the replacement of the English language for official purposes. In July 1969, however, the military regime of Pakistan announced that without any further examination of the problem English was to be eliminated as an official language within six years. The downgrading of English and the new emphasis on Urdu and Bengali were part of an effort to make the government more acceptable to the people as well as to eradicate illiteracy (at that time only 20 percent of the Pakistani population was literate). Simultaneously, Bengali-speaking East Pakistan proposed to replace the federal system and constitution of 1965 by a new, very loose association of two fully autonomous states. The leading East Pakistani political party, Awami League, accused West Pakistan of treating the

[16] Five main languages are spoken in Pakistan: Bengali (54.6 percent), Punjabi (28.4 percent), Urdu (7.2 percent), Pushto (7.1 percent) and Sindhi (5.8 percent). Urdu is the lingua franca of most Moslems in both India and Pakistan. Urdu as well as Punjabi use the Persian script, while Bengali, the language of the eastern province, employs a script derived from Sanskrit.

eastern province as "a colony and a market," not as an equal partner in a federal union.

The adoption of two languages in Pakistan was not without difficulties. The creators of Pakistan wanted only one official language, the Moslem lingua franca of the Indian subcontinent, Urdu. The founder of Pakistan, Jinnah, discussing the Bengali demand for linguistic equality, originally refused to yield and uttered words that perhaps apply also to many other countries that are unable to settle on one language only: "Let me make it very clear to you that the State Language of Pakistan is going to be Urdu and no other language. . . . Without one State Language, no nation can remain tied up solidly together and function." [17]

India's linguistic problems are even more complex than those of Pakistan. The Census of 1951 recorded a total of 845 languages or dialects. This includes 720 Indian languages or dialects, each spoken by less than 100,000 persons. The Indian Constitution (Eighth Schedule) has recognized thirteen spoken major languages and one scholarly language (Sanskrit) as official. These thirteen languages are not minor tribal idioms spoken in some remote valleys of the Himalayas. They are used by millions of people. These major lingual groups have their own literature, periodicals, and broadcasts; they are mutually unintelligible, many using different, mutually unrecognizable scripts and numerals.[18] The southern Dravidian language Telugu, for instance, which became the basis for the creation of the state of Andhra, is spoken by as many people as there are Spaniards in Spain. The problem of communication among and within component units of the Indian federation is indeed staggering. In Bombay the newscast every evening is in six languages, including two mountain tribal ones and English. A one-rupee Indian banknote shows its value in seven different languages and seven different scripts, including the Latin alphabet for English. A hundred-rupee banknote has its value expressed in all official languages.

[17] *Quaid-i-Azam Speaks.* Karachi: official publication, n.d., p. 133.

[18] The Punjabi language, a variation of Hindi, is written in two different scripts by the Sikhs in the Punjabi State and by the Hindus in Haryana. The Sikhs use the Gumurkhi script and the Hindus use the Devanagari script.

The thirteen official languages are, in addition, divided into mutually intolerant groupings, the North and the South. The northern languages are mostly Aryan and are in their roots related to Sanskrit, the language of the Hindu holy scriptures, a "Latin" of sorts in South Asia. The languages of the South are totally unrelated in origin and syntax to the Aryan ones; they belong to the Dravidian family. Table 9–1 contains the names of major languages in India, the states in which they are dominantly spoken, the number and percentage of people using them, and the circulation figures of periodicals printed in these languages.

The Indian Constitution proclaimed Hindi in Devanagari script to be the official *federal* language (that is, in the federal administration, the parliament, the judiciary, and official publications). For a period of fifteen years (that is, until 1965) English was also to be used by the federal center; in 1965 Hindi was to replace the language of India's former colonial master.

Even the northern Hindi-enthusiasts do not claim that the federal official language, Hindi, based on spoken Hindustani and enriched by terms from classical Sanskrit, is understood and used by the majority. They claim that 46 percent of the Indian population uses it. This claim has been challenged. If Punjabi is treated as a separate language (the Sikhs write it in a different script—Gurmukhi) and if Hindustani as used in Bihar and Rajasthan are considered distinct from Hindi, the percentage of Indians speaking Hindi falls below 30 percent.

When, after fifteen years of promotion of Hindi [19] stipulated by the Constitution, the time came to replace Hindi by English, it could not be done. Extraconstitutional facts of life prevented the constitutional pledge from being executed. There were, as it could perhaps be expected, opposition and bloody riots in the

---

[19] The Indian Constitution states in Article 351: "It shall be the duty of the Union to promote the spread of the Hindi language, to develop it so that it may serve as a medium of expression for all the elements of the composite culture of India and to secure its enrichment by assimilating without interfering with its genius, the forms, styles and expression used in Hindustani and in other languages specified in the Eighth Schedule, and by drawing, wherever necessary or desirable, for its vocabulary, primarily on Sanskrit and secondarily on other languages."

Table 9–1 Official Indian languages

Language	State	Number Speaking (in millions)	Percent Speaking	Newspaper Circulation (in thousands)
Aryan group in the north				
English	Used in and by the Center			3997
Hindi [1]	Bihar Madhya Pradesh Rajasthan Uttar Pradesh	150	46.3	3553
Punjabi [1]	Haryana Punjabi Subha			153
Marathi	Maharashtra	27	8.3	1054
Bengali	West Bengal	26	7.8	923
Gujarati	Gujarat	17	5.0	1159
Oriya	Orissa	14	4.1	99
Assamese	Assam	5	1.5	53
Kashmiri	Kashmir	0.005		?
Sanskrit	Used by scholars	0.001		7
Dravidian group in the south				
Telugu	Andhra	33	10.2	663
Tamil	Madras	29	8.2	2125
Kannada	Mysore	19	4.5	470
Malayalam	Kerala	14	4.1	801
Urdu [1]	Spoken by Moslems, related to Hindustani, written in the Persian script			1047

Source: Based on Government publications *India: A Reference Annual, 1959* and *Annual Report of the Registrar of Newspapers for India,* 1960.

[1] Hindi, Punjabi, and Urdu are closely related to Hindustani, the lingua franca of the North. Hindi, the official language, is a purified form of spoken Hindustani.

South that reflected a preference for the English language to Hindi; as seen by the Dravidian South, the new language Hindi, rooted in the Aryan North, was not an all-India language but merely a language of one of its segments, another minority, after all. And that segment was further suspected of promoting its language for the purpose of linguistic-political-economic domination of the South by the North. And there were nationalist riots in the North because the retention of English, as desired by the South, meant a continuation of the official use of the language of the former colonial ruler. Students at the Delhi and Lucknow Universities threatened people with "dire consequences" if they failed to remove all English signboards within twenty-four hours.[20]

A subsequent compromise solution, expressed in the *Official Language Bill* (1967) failed to calm down either side. The bill provided for the continued use of English as an "associate" language for the official purposes of the central authority, until its discontinuance is approved by the legislatures in the states where Hindi is not the official local language and is also ratified separately by each house of Parliament. An editorial in the Delhi semiofficial paper *The Statesman* (December 2, 1967) explained:

> The provisions of the Bill fully take into account their [non-Hindi states] fears that the switchover to Hindi at the Center may result in subordinating, if not eliminating, their position and importance in politics and administration at the Center; allaying these fears has always been regarded as the minimum price to be paid for maintaining national unity in the context of the forced pace of change-over to Hindi as the Union official language.

Also in 1967 the Indian Parliament introduced a simultaneous translation system of every English speech into Hindi and every Hindi speech into English. Every seat in the Indian Parlia-

---

[20] The Indian national anthem, a song composed by the Bengali poet and Nobel Prize winner Rabindranath Tagore and sung for the first time in 1911, carefully enumerates the component units of the Indian Union—a "poetic federalism" of sorts. In the poet's own translation into English, as published in 1919 under the title "Morning Star of India," the first stanza reads as follows: "Thou art the ruler of the minds of all people, dispenser of India's destiny. Thy name rouses the hearts of the Punjab, Sind, Gujrat and Maratha, of the Dravid and Orissa and Bengal. . . . Victory, victory, victory to thee." It was adopted as the national anthem of the Indian Union on January 24, 1950.

ment is fitted with a headphone and a language-selector switch. It has been admitted that

> never since the enactment of the Constitution in 1947 did all the members of Lok Sabha [House of the People] know both Hindi and English and therefore whatever happened to be the floor language in the House at any time, there were always some members who, not being bilingual, could not follow the proceedings of the House.[21]

The modern technology seemed to have solved the problem of the members of Parliament who knew either Hindi or English, but the technology did not help those who spoke neither language but spoke only their own regional language. The Constitution (Article 120) actually permits "any member who cannot adequately express himself in Hindi or in English to address the House in his mother tongue." Neither the Constitution nor technology provides for such a member of Parliament any facility to understand what is being said on the floor in Hindi or in English.

The issue of one or two official languages in any polyethnic state is admittedly both highly emotional and highly practical. It is no wonder that controversy on this point has often absorbed the passionate interest and energy of a developing nation more than any other aspect of nation building and modernization. Whatever the solution is, there is bound to be some resentment. If a native language is adopted and if it happens to be that of one group, whether a majority or a minority, all the other ethnic-linguistic groups are bound to suffer some adverse consequences, the most obvious being the need for all the other linguistic groups to learn a second language in order to compete with the dominant group for access to the political, administrative, and economic power structure. If, on the other hand, a foreign language is chosen that minority groups actually prefer to a native one, other problems necessarily arise. One of these problems is psychological. Nations like India, Pakistan, Nigeria, Congo, Uganda, or Cameroun, which at long last succeeded in

[21] *Journal of Constitutional and Parliamentary Studies,* Vol. 2, No. 1 (New Delhi, January–March 1968), 85.

liberating themselves from foreign rule, economy, and culture, have to express their new and exuberant nationalism in a *foreign* language which, in addition, is that of their former masters. They may then sing their new national anthems, write and cite their new constitutions, and damn their former oppressors in English or in French. Necessarily, borrowing the former master's language or institutions occasionally exposes the leaders of the new nations to domestic criticism that in this way they continue the old dependence on the master, in a new subtle, cultural, "neocolonial" way. To borrow or not to borrow may become an explosive issue in many countries. The Dean of Law at the University of Zambia, Oxford-educated K. Bentsi Enchill, dealt with this issue at a conference on "The Next Twenty Years in African Research, 1969–1989." His paper on "Problems in the Construction of Viable Constitutional Structures in Africa" included the following:

> Conditioned as we are by our education and upbringing to think institutionally in terms of French or British [constitutional] arrangements, my call is for the comprehensive and eclectic scrutiny of foreign expedients and a hard objective look at the realities of our domestic situation and the provenances of our traditional laws and customs. Only so can we begin to do some independent thinking. Independent thinking, however, does not exclude deliberate borrowing and adaptation. We in Africa have no need to apologize to anyone if in our mature judgment we decide to borrow institutional arrangements from this or that foreign system. Everybody borrows and copies. . . . We shall not cease to be different from the people from whom we may decide to borrow some institution or other—not even when we purport to adopt their language!

Another problem is the addition of a lingual gap to what already separates the English- or French-speaking intelligentsia, on one hand, from the masses, on the other hand. This gap of mutual *incomprehension* in the literal sense of the word is bound to be exploited by the new half-educated and half-modernized elites who have received education in local vernaculars and who may add the promotion of lingual parochialism to their opposition against the foreign-speaking national center. It is a fact that a mass struggle against illiteracy raises the prestige and political value of local vernaculars and thus also increases the tendency on the part of local politicians to base their careers and their opposition to the federal center on lingual territorial patriotism.

Furthermore, in the era of mass education all nation-states experience a dearth of teaching personnel in all fields. In poly-ethnic federations that retain English or French as their official or auxiliary language, the problem often is how to produce enough people quickly enough who can read and write at least in their own local idiom. Even a successful struggle against mass illiteracy cannot be asked or expected to produce accomplished linguists.[22] This was, of course, quite different under the colonial rule, when only a few selected natives were given the opportunity to study in London or Paris and return to their country speaking, writing, thinking, and even perhaps dreaming in English or French (it was said that Nehru did dream in English). So equipped they could either participate in or effectively subvert the colonial rule.

There are, however, also powerful arguments for the retention of the former master's language. In some cases former masters' languages have, as noted, at least temporarily prevailed. First, there remain the still important economic and cultural links with the former "mother-country," especially within the Commonwealth and within French-oriented Africa. These links represent invigorating injections into what could otherwise become a dying language, detached from its roots. Second, in some situations, however paradoxical this may sound, a foreign language may appear more acceptable because it is more neutral than any of the native languages. Furthermore, the English language is nearly a universal idiom in international politics, commerce, and technology that not only the educated elites in India, Pakistan, Nigeria, Ceylon, or Burma but also those of Russia, China, Japan, and even de Gaulle's France consider

[22] The Indian states, the majority of which are based on linguistic territorial communities, use a trilingual formula in the conduct of their interstate business: the native official language of the State, English, and Hindi or any other official language of India. Trilinguism seems a stiff requirement indeed, especially in a developing country.

eminently useful to master. Some Indian writers expressed also the hope that English, in due course, may be "Indianized" as English and Spanish were "Americanized." The parallel between immigrants and their linguistic imports and ancient communities adopting a new language does not seem valid.

Another argument for the retention of English or French is frequently the cost that translating all documents and university textbooks and scientific manuals involves. If the new national language is of great lyrical beauty but is underdeveloped in terms of modern science, nuclear physics, and space exploration, a translation of Einstein's theory of relativity or of Norbert Wiener's *Cybernetics* may require inventing many new words or involve borrowing heavily from English or French so as to render the translation unintelligible except to those who know English or French already.

Switzerland, our last example of multilingual federation, represents another federal solution of the coexistence of three world languages and one local one. According to the Constitution (Article 116) the *national* languages of Switzerland are German, French, Italian, and Romanche; the *official* languages are only German, French, and Italian. The difference between a national and an official language is important: a citizen may communicate with his government in any of the three official languages; members of the national legislature may discuss issues and laws in any of them; their equal use is guaranteed in the pleading of cases before the Federal Tribunal. Also, all three languages must be represented on the Swiss high court. The fourth language, Romanche, which is perhaps derived from the Latin of the Roman legions in the Alps and which is spoken mostly in the southeastern canton of Grisons, has been given constitutional recognition without having been made compulsory on the federal level.

Out of twenty-two Swiss cantons, eighteen are unilingual, three are bilingual, and one is trilingual. The Swiss citizens rarely speak more than two languages. The French-speaking citizens are less likely to learn German or Italian than the German- and Italian-speaking citizens to learn French.[23] It has been some-

---

[23] George A. Codding, Jr., *The Federal Government of Switzer-land*. Boston: Houghton Mifflin, 1961, p. 8.

times argued that the geographic proximity of France and Italy bolster the vitality of the French-speaking Swiss (20.2 percent) and the Italian-speaking Swiss (4.1 percent) against what otherwise would be the crushing power of the German language (spoken by 74.4 percent of the Swiss citizens). The nonintegration of the Romanche group (1 percent) since the time of the Roman Empire indicates that an ethnic and linguistic group does not need a geographic proximity or a related group to persist as a separate entity for centuries. This is what makes the issue of language so important and explosive.

A recent study on multilingualism as a source of tension and conflict within political systems offers additional useful insights into the problem. It finds, first, that multilingualism is a lesser problem in primitive agrarian societies than in societies that are industrial or are in the process of modernization. In such societies official recognition of one or more languages significantly affects careers in and services provided by public institutions, including nationalized industries. Multilingualism is also a source of serious conflict "when members of different language groups are under unequal pressures to learn the languages of the others" and "when the direction and/or intensity of pressures to learn the language of the other group and groups is changing." [24] Although the study was primarily focused on European problems (Switzerland, Czechoslovakia, Alsace-Lorraine, and North Schleswig), evidently these observations apply to the non-European situations just referred to.

In developing countries the process of social mobilization increases the volume of all demands addressed to the authorities and widens the scope of politics and political participation; but the same process necessarily also increases the importance of the language through which people are to communicate with their leaders. "Other things assumed equal," says Karl W. Deutsch,

the stage of rapid social mobilization may be expected, therefore, to promote the consolidation of states whose peoples

[24] Walter B. Simon, "A Comparative Study of the Problem of Multi-Lingualism," paper presented at the 1967 Meeting of the Canadian Society of Sociologists and Anthropologists, Ottawa. Published in *Mens en Maatschappij*. Amsterdam, 1968, p. 101.

already share the same language . . . while the same process may tend to strain or destroy the unity of states whose population is already divided into several groups with different languages or cultures or basic ways of life.[25]

[25] Karl W. Deutsch, "Social Mobilization and Political Development," *American Political Science Review* (September 1961), p. 501.

TEN
FEDERAL
MARBLE CAKES

A constitution, to contain an accurate detail of all
the subdivisions of which its great powers will admit,
and of all the means by which they may be carried
into execution, would partake of the prolixity of a
legal code, and could scarcely be embraced by the
human mind. . . . It would have been an unwise
attempt to provide, by immutable rules, for exigencies
which, if foreseen at all, must have been seen dimly,
and which can best be provided as they occur.

> JOHN MARSHALL (*McCulloch* v. *Mary-*
> *land*)

Virtually, all the great driving forces in modern
society combine in a centralist direction. The political
urge for equality of rights and greater equality of
treatment; the extension of the market, increased
standardization of products and the growing
uniformity of taste; the quest for social security and
economic stability; the tensions of military prepared-
ness and the technology of warfare . . . such
conditions do not harmonize with separated powers
and scattered jurisdictions.

> LESLIE LIPSON (*The Great Issues of*
> *Politics*)

Today all national systems—federal and unitary, mature and developing, democratic or totalitarian, socialist or not—initiate, implement, and supervise central economic plans and programs of social welfare, education, and health. Some of the reasons for the universal adoption of the theory and practice of a modern service state may be traced back to the theories of Karl Marx and Vladimir I. Lenin, to Lords Keynes and Beveridge, or to Mussolini and Hitler. In addition to (or instead of) any economic theory, the rise of national welfare states may be simply ascribed to the pragmatic imperatives of modern science and technology and the resulting need to think and plan in rationally larger territorial aggregates, to the modernization fever of the developing nations, and to the universal tide of rising expectations of social security, free education, and cultural benefits from cradle to grave. Federalism—conceived in an era of free economy, maximum private initiative and local responsibility, and a concomitantly minimal role of government in the economic and social fields—has had to adapt itself to the profound environmental changes of the twentieth century. These changes, according to some people, may spell the end of federalism: "Federalism thrived as long as free economy thrived." [1]

In the present context of an almost universal acceptance of the role of the national government as economic planner and often owner of the means of production, job provider, and social engineer, national governments endow themselves with formidable tax revenues to be able to initiate, finance, organize, direct, establish, and own projects that are well beyond the financial and technological means of the territorial communities or private concerns. Examples in many countries include atomic or conventional hydroelectric plants (for instance, in the case of the Tennessee Valley Authority the Valley proved a more important factor than the eighteenth-century territorial divisions), development of supersonic transportation, nationwide welfare and health programs, nationwide drives against poverty and illiteracy. Such a commitment to planning and welfare necessarily results in a

---

[1] Karl Lowenstein in A. Zurcher (ed.), *Constitutions and Constitutional Trends since World War II*. New York: New York University Press, 1951, p. 210.

formidable increase in the number and power of national administrators.[2] Economic planning and social programs further increase the national government's influence in such fields as foreign and interstate commerce; fiscal, monetary, and credit policies; control over consumption by means of price and credit controls; labor conditions and production standards, often including all-national guidelines for entering and remaining in certain careers and professions. The purpose of many of these measures is to prevent economic crises or the erosion of national progress and welfare by local neglect, backwardness, or incapacity.

In countries where the means of production have been largely or totally collectivized, we sometimes find proposals for "federalization" of the collective ownership of the means of production. This is a characteristic concept of the Christian Socialists in Western and Eastern Europe, some Fabians in England, and other non-Marxian Socialists, who all dread the political authoritarian consequences of economic centralism, that is, national ownership and control of economy that may result in an awesome concentration of all powers in the hands of a very few in the national center. The term *federalization* of collectivized economy should be understood as meaning, first, that the ownership and control of the means of production have been transferred from private hands to public authorities and, second, that the ownership and management are not in the hands of one single central authority but have been decentralized. Territorial autonomous units, such as municipalities, provinces, and regions, or functional groups, such as agricultural or industrial cooperatives, own and manage these units of production.

THE WELFARE STATE AND INTERLOCKED FEDERALISM

In developing countries where resources and manpower must be rapidly mobilized for the purpose of national modernization as

---

[2] When in 1939 the Hatch Act was passed in the United States to prohibit political campaign activities of federal employees, one of the aims was to prevent the federal government from building a political support for itself on the basis of the activities (and loyalty) of the federal civil servants.

well as for the purpose of nation building, the decline of local autonomy in general is often viewed as a precondition for national development. In a study concerned with the changing nature of the relationship of local communities (villages) to the national state, a modern state was characterized as a depository of industrial technology dedicated to an effort to obliterate the divergence between the political goals of the state and those of the village, and by a gradual appropriation of the village's political power by the national center. This is in contrast with a premodern state in which the village claimed the power that legitimately belonged to the nation-state; in the modern state the national center "claims the power that traditionally has belonged to the village." [3] In federal unions there is a third governmental level, the state, between the national center and village or town. This additional level has often been assailed as particularly inappropriate to developing nations, as a "luxury" because the federal formula so often results in authority conflicts between the state and national authorities. Myron Weiner observes that such conflicts may stymie much of the developmental program in an underdeveloped country intent upon central planning for economic and social progress. This warning, based on a study of economic planning in India, applies to all developing countries.

It is mainly the size, complexity, and cost of modern economic and social tasks that in so many cases prove to be far beyond the financial, technical, and administrative capacities of the component territorial units. There just may not be sufficient resources to fund and ensure a desirable quality of two sets of governments—national and provincial—with the concomitant danger of possible duplication or conflicts. A federal system is a structurally complex as well as an expensive system; the expense is not meant here only in terms of appropriations and mobilization of resources and available skills but also in terms of uneven economic, social, and educational development from province to province. Of course, no system in the world is or can be immune to wasteful duplication of governmental activities and equally wasteful jurisdictional conflicts. But these wastes in a federal system seem inevitable. In his analysis of the reasons

[3] Harumi Befu, "The Political Relation of the Village to the State," *World Politics* (July 1967), p. 617.

for which American federalism remains decentralized in theory as well as in practice, Morton Grodzins lists four major causes: *history* (the existence of the states predating the union); *creed* (the traditional belief in the vitality and usefulness of local government); local *pride;* and, significantly, the sheer *wealth* of the nation that

> allows all groups, including state and local governments, to partake of the central government's largesse, supplies room for experimentation and even waste, and makes unnecessary the tight organization of political power that must follow when the support of one program necessarily means the deprivation of another.[4]

Professor K. C. Wheare noted that the leaders of the South Africa finally rejected federalism for economic reasons. Franz Neumann points to "the financial inadequacy or political unwillingness of the smaller units to respond satisfactorily to serious economic troubles," and, on this basis, concludes that the "unrestrained adulation of federalism seems all the more unwarranted." [5]

The problem with this argument is that no system, federal or unitary, can really operate efficiently without some degree of decentralization (by delegation in unitary or imperial systems) and without some effort to mobilize local initiative and responsibility. There is as yet no convincing proof that a federal system is measurably much more expensive than a unitary decentralization.

The explicit and long Constitution of the United States of Mexico incorporates the problem of adequate local resources into its list of conditions for creating new states out of the existing ones; it must be proven, for instance, before the Mexican national Congress that a section or sections seeking to be made a state shall have a population of at least 120,000 inhabitants and "the resources necessary to provide for their political existence" (Article 73, section 3). Parenthetically, it may be observed that

---

[4] Morton Grodzins, "The Federal System," in The American Assembly, *Goals for Americans*. Englewood Cliffs, N.J.: Prentice-Hall, 1960, pp. 265–282.

[5] Franz Neumann, "Federalism and Freedom: A Critique," in A. W. Macmahon (ed.), *Federalism: Mature and Emergent*. New York: Russell and Russell, 1962, p. 55.

the Mexican Constitution imposes more stringent conditions on the birth of new administrative units within the national territory than does the United Nations with regard to new sovereign states and their membership in the world organization. A United Nations member, the Maldive Islands, with its 95,000 inhabitants, would not pass the Mexican test; Iceland would just barely qualify.

The financial inadequacy of state or provincial governments led to several fiscal and economic remedies that some authors consider violations of the federal principle of division of powers, although the remedies were useful and perhaps inevitable. The remedies range from federal grants-in-aid of local social, health, or educational projects, with or without federal supervisory strings or review strings attached, a guaranteed share in national income tax revenues, local tax credits against the federal tax, and so on. In his attack on "American Militarism: What Is It Doing to Us?" (*Look* Magazine, August 12, 1969), Eric Sevareid reported that allegedly "no one in Washington even *knows* how many Federal programs involving aid to states and cities now exist. Dr. Arthur Burns, the President's Counsellor, thinks it is around six hundred. United Press International, which conducted its own study, estimates it to be at least one thousand."

In 1967 two representatives, Charles E. Goodell from New York and Melvin R. Laird from Wisconsin (Secretary of Defense in the Nixon Administration of 1969) proposed two separate bills aiming at strengthening the federal system by states' revenue sharing. Laird's proposal, for instance, provided for returning to the states a straight 5 percent of the federal personal income tax with no strings attached, with an optional provision that 5 percent of the sum allocated to each state be used for improving state administrative machinery. In addition, the Laird bill was to provide for a federal income tax credit for state and local taxes paid by individuals. To support his legislative proposal (H.R. 5450), Laird inserted into the Congressional Record a report of a special study of the Republican Coordinating Committee [6] dealing with the problem of federal-state fiscal relations.

[6] The report, entitled "The Restoration of Federalism in America," was issued by the coordinating committee, whose members were President Dwight D. Eisenhower, Barry Goldwater, Richard M. Nixon, Thomas E. Dewey, Alf M. Landon, Everett M. Dirksen, and others.

It opened with an attack on President Johnson's statement made in March 1967 to a meeting of state governors in which he said, "What we are living through together are the birth pangs of a fundamentally new process in the American government—a new kind of Federalism—Federal-State interaction never contemplated by the Founding Fathers."

The general thrust of the report that denounced the excessive flow of power from cities and states to Washington and that recommended the reversal of the trend became an important part of the Republican party platform during the presidential election of 1968. Candidate Richard Nixon pledged a new federal-state tax-sharing formula instead of the complicated and unsatisfactory grants-in-aid formula if his party were to win in November. The following summer (August 13, 1969) President Nixon sent his proposal of a new welfare and fund-sharing program to Congress. He proposed that "a set amount of Federal revenues [initially, in 1971, $.5 billion to reach successively $5 billion by 1975] be returned to the states to be used as the states and their local governments see fit—without Federal strings." There was little criticism of the decentralizing features of the program ("The momentum for Federal expansion has passed its peak; a process of decentralization is setting in"). In an editorial called "Toward New Federalism" (August 10, 1969), *The New York Times* commented on the whole positively:

> The Nixon concept of "creative federalism" . . . represents a White House recognition that the problems of poverty and racial deprivation and poisoned environment now plaguing the cities are national in their impact. But it also reflects the President's conviction, strongly enunciated in the campaign, that more of the administrative and planning obligation for deciding how each community ought to deal with them should be decentralized.

Criticism was mostly directed against the inadequate amount of money to be shared (ultimately 1 percent of the nation's taxable income); this seemed to be in contrast with the opening paragraph of the presidential message, which denounced the rise of the central government everywhere in the world and stressed that "in the United States, revenues of the Federal Government have increased 90-fold in 36 years." Another criticism concerned the inadequate provisions for giving a larger share of revenues to poor states with a narrow tax base and to the ailing core cities, overpopulated by masses with very low earnings.

What President Nixon called "creative" federalism, meaning decentralization and stronger local responsibility, what President Johnson praised as "a new Federal-State interaction never contemplated by the Founding Fathers," meaning a stronger influence of federal standards on local prejudice or neglect, and what the Supreme Court approvingly called "cooperative federalism" [7] is a phenomenon in all federal states. There are, of course, variations. In most cases these favor the national center, in other cases (as in the United States) they are moderately in favor of the territorial components. However, everywhere it basically means a new form of federal-state-district-municipal sharing in revenues and administration of national programs, a clear case of a territorial concurrence rather than a division of power, with focus on particular goals to be achieved by common action. Rivalries between cities, states, and the federal center still exist, but there is close partnership with reference to the problems that neither of the three levels of government can solve alone.

[7] The Federal Aid to Families with Dependent Children (AFDC), a welfare program designed to give financial aid to children deprived of parental support, was called by Chief Justice Earl Warren, writing for the United States Supreme Court (*Smith* v. *King,* June 17, 1968), a program "based on a scheme of cooperative federalism." He described it as "financed largely by the Federal government on a matching fund basis, and is administered by the states. States are not required to participate in the program, but those which desire to take advantage of the substantial Federal funds available for distribution to needy children are required to submit an AFDC plan for the approval of the Secretary of Health, Education, and Welfare. . . . The plan must conform with several requirements of the Social Security Act and with rules and regulations promulgated by HEW . . . [which] clearly require the participating states to furnish aid to families with children who have a parent absent from the home, if such families are in other respects eligible." The issue of interlocked federalism reached the Supreme Court because of a regulation, adopted by the state of Alabama, that tried to cut off aid from children in families without a father if their mother was alleged to live in sexual intimacy with another man. The case was taken up by the American Civil Liberties Union on behalf of an Alabaman mother with four children. The Supreme Court ruled against Alabama by a 9–0 decision and so approved the concept of welfare cooperative federalism.

Such a federalism is called "cooperative," "shared," "interlocked," "intertwined," "creative," "interdependent," or simply "marble cake." This last is the often quoted formula coined by Morton Grodzins in his study "The Federal System" (p. 265):

> The American form of government is often, but erroneously, symbolized by a three-layer cake—federal-state-local government. A far more accurate image is the rainbow or marble cake, characterized by an inseparable mingling of differently colored ingredients, the colors appearing in vertical and diagonal strands and unexpected whirls. As colors are mixed in the marble cake, so functions are mixed in the American federal system.

Economic and political realities force federations to be "pragmatic rather than dogmatic in their application of the federal idea," writes R. L. Watts, who has analyzed interdependent federalism in the federal systems of the Commonwealth. He adds:

> Invariably in the area of economic policy [the founders of the federations and their successors] have found it impossible to divide the functions of general and regional governments into two isolated compartments and have been forced to recognize the interdependence of governments. Generally, as a result of the placing of major fiscal instruments for economic policy in central hands, the regional governments have become heavily dependent upon the former for their financial resources. At the same time, however, the central governments tended to be heavily dependent for the implementation of national economic and social programmes upon autonomous regional ministries and legislatures directly responsible to their electorates. This situation of mutual dependence of each level of government upon the other has characteristically produced a proliferation of institutions and arrangements for consultation and cooperation between governments in a wide variety of economic fields.[8]

---

[8] R. L. Watts, "Recent Trends in Federal Economic Policy and Finance in the Commonwealth," paper presented at the Sixth World Congress of the International Political Science Association, Geneva, 1964, p. 22.

In many modern federations the concept of interlocked federalism has already been institutionalized. The Constitution of Venezuela (Article 137), for instance, empowers Congress to grant, by a vote of two thirds of the members of each house, "specific matters of national competence to the States or Municipalities, in order to promote administrative decentralization." In other federations permanent superagencies for common federal-state or federal-municipal planning or review have been established. In India, such a planning agency is composed of the premiers and Cabinet ministers of both the federal and all the state governments. It is called the National Development Council; it corresponds to the National Economic Council in Pakistan and the National Finance and Land Council in Malaysia. A study of the Indian federal scene confirms that, in practice, the central authority is almost completely dependent on the states for the administration of social-action programs.[9] This qualifies what has been so often said about the Indian federal system as being, according to the Constitution, a unitary system with only subsidiary federal features.

As to the periodic review of the use of federal grants, shared taxes or loans, numerous grant, loan and fiscal, federal-state commissions or councils have been established or provided for in modern federal constitutions. Some people view such commissions and councils as threats to the federal concept, whereas others consider them the inevitable expression of modern federalism. It has been rightly pointed out time and again that the central government that has the unpleasant duty of levying and collecting taxes cannot be expected to abstain from review and interference when it sees the territorial units spending the federal funds unwisely. When "the central government comes to the states—not the states to the nation—bearing gifts," [10] there is always a danger that such a federal support of local autonomy may result not only in interaction and "interdependent federal-

---

[9] Paul Appleby, *Public Administration in India—Report of Survey.* New Delhi: Manager of Publications, 1953, p. 3.

[10] Charles Aikin, "The Structure of Power in Federal Nations," paper presented at the Sixth World Congress of the International Political Science Association, Geneva, 1964, p. 1.

ism," but also in an outright dependence of the recipient government on the federal giver. This could result in a deadly atrophy of territorial pluralism. The sum total of these different technological, economic, social, organizational, and fiscal factors, as discussed before, has been marked on our model of federal reality (Fig. 9–1) as *A, economic and social imperatives.* They are closely connected with the second extraconstitutional link between the central and provincial governments, *B, population shifts.* In response to new economic opportunities or challenges, populations have been on a constant move within federal unions, paying little attention to intrafederal territorial delineations. Such migration and new settlements have altered the realities on which the initial federal bargain was based; territorially these changes manifest themselves mostly in the appearance of new regional and other territorial communities and in the growth of big cities that often need a new form of municipal decentralization or intramural "federalism."

Regions and cities

Reflecting the development of new forms of transportation, resources, and job opportunities, the emerging new multiprovincial or multistate regional communities have been superimposed on the preexisting territorial communities that the federal constitutions had originally recognized and sanctioned.

New problems and new tasks call for the common concern and action of several states, but not the whole nation. The boundaries drawn in the preindustrial era are simply disregarded. Regionalism adds a new, often fully institutionalized layer between the federal and state governments; a good example is the New York Port Authority, which combines the interests of New York and New Jersey in the smooth operation of the port, bridges, and tunnels. Multistate agreements on a common fight against air and water pollution result from a multistate recognition that the pollutants have shown a marked indifference to the federal concepts and state loyalties of the founding fathers. The federal legislation that makes regional planning a condition for receiving federal grants, as well as the Model Cities Act (Title II) that offers incentives for regional cooperation in the drawing of a plan, may also be quoted as examples of a regional layer being superimposed on the American federal structure by extraconstitutional developments.

Other examples of regionalism are the zonal councils in India that group the Indian states into five zones (North, Center, South, East, and West). Their councils "discuss and make recommendations to the Centre with regard to matters of common interest in the field of economic and social planning, border disputes, linguistic minorities, inter-state transport, etc." [11]

In the Soviet Union there also seems to be a plan, mentioned in Chapter 2, partly spelled out by Khrushchev in the late 1950s, to group Central-Asiatic, Caucasian, and other republics into new rational federations within the Soviet federation; the new boundaries were to correspond to new economic realities rather than to the old linguistic-ethnic divisions whose significance has also been decreased by population shifts. For instance, the Kazakh Union Republic, once predominantly inhabited by the Kazakhs, is now in the process of losing its ethnic Central-Asian character in favor of the Great Russians, soon to constitute the majority in the republic. A similar "Russification" by immigration threatens the ethnic character of some of the Baltic republics. The undeniably rational features of the Soviet territorial reform have clashed with the reality of strong ethnic-linguistic emotionalism and so far have prevented its implementation.

And then in all modern or modernizing federations there is the dramatic growth of powerful urban centers vulnerable to all types of social ills and their explosive consequences. In 1968 the Ninth Annual Report of the Advisory Commission on Intergovernmental Relations discussed the relationship of the local, state, and federal units of government in the United States. The opening, quite alarming, paragraph said:

> In 1967, the American political system—and in turn, Federalism and the Federal system—was on trial as never before in the nation's history with the sole exception of the Civil War. The major crisis threatening the political system and, indeed, the whole fabric of American society, was in the nation's cities. The crisis was characterized by serious rioting,

[11] Norman D. Palmer, *The Indian Political System*. Boston: Houghton Mifflin, 1961, p. 142.

the breakdown of law and order, and, in a number of areas, the disappearance of any meaningful sense of community among the residents of blighted neighborhoods.[12]

The report concluded that the inability of all levels of government to prevent the deterioration of urban life raises the prospect of pervasive federal dominance in the name of security, that is, a possible sacrifice of political diversity, including territorial pluralism, for the sake of national peace and progress. A recent book on federalism noted in this connection that indeed American cities may burn to the ground and may be desolated and that "urban man [would] cease to be recognizable as man" [13] if the inhabitants of the cities cannot come soon to recognize, whatever their vantage point, a community of interests and purposes. In a somewhat lighter tone, the *New Yorker* magazine illustrated the problem by the cartoon in Figure 10–1.

Modern cities spill over to the neighboring areas not only with their social problems but also with their inhabitants, by urbanization and the growth of suburbs. As a result of the expansion of both the physical and the "problem" substance of big cities, municipalities tend to bypass the intermediary federal level, the state governments. They do so partly on account of the financial and administrative weakness of many a state government, and partly because of a conflict between the often entrenched rural interests of the state government and the consumer, labor, youth, ethnic, or racial interests of the city and suburban city dwellers.[14] They enter into agreements or "alliances" with the national government directed against the alleged neglect or incapacity of the state government. Evidently, such agreements do not create but follow or reflect the new fact of regional juxtaposition to the former constitutional division of territorial authority. These new territorial patterns of interests,

[12] In order to justify the parallel between the Civil War and the 1967/1968 crises of federalism, a member of the staff of the Advisory Commission, Eugene R. Elkins, told *The New York Times* (January 31, 1968) that in the 1860s "it was a matter of some states pulling out of the Union" whereas in the 1960s "it's a matter of the Federal system going down the drain altogether."

[13] Valerie Earle (ed.), *Federalism: Infinite Variety in Theory and Practice*. Itasca, Ill.: F. E. Peacock Publishers, 1968, p. 85.

[14] Peter H. Merkl, *Political Continuity and Change*. New York: Harper & Row, 1967, p. 11.

**Figure 10–1   Cartoon illustrating the problem
of recognizing a community of interests and purposes**

"Attention, middle class. Attention, middle
class. You have been given twenty-four
hours to get out of town"

Source: Drawing by Chon Day; © 1968 The New Yorker Magazine, Inc.

as was noted by Peter H. Merkl, pay no respect to existing regional boundaries of a federal country. Many a great metropolis grew up next to a state line, spilling over into a neighboring state and, perhaps, appropriating a large portion of it as its economic hinterland. Legions of commuters might work in the city, using services and facilities in the one state, yet living and paying taxes in the other. Some states might not have any notable urban center, and their economies may be under the sway of outside centers.[15]

A good example of the federal consequences of the growth

[15] Merkl, *Political Community and Change,* p. 393.

of modern cities is the movement in the Swiss canton of Basel which, in the past, had to be divided into two half-cantons, Basel Town and Basel Country. Their interests and way of life differed than so diametrically that one canton could not contain them both; it had to be subdivided according to the Swiss flexible formula. Yet now when the urban Basel has so encroached on the rural Basel, there is a demand for reunification in one canton in order to avoid duplication of services and simplify the problems of taxation. The whole canton has become, in fact, the city of Basel and its suburbs.

EXTERNAL PRESSURES

War, world economic crises, economic or military threats or offers of aid, menacing political changes within the neighboring countries all usually cause or reinforce not only national unity but also centralizing and unitary tendencies in all systems, including the federal system (they are marked as *C, external pressures,* on our model of federalism [Fig. 9–1]).

When a federation has to wage a war (defensive or offensive), the federal war powers undergo a rapid inflation. It is usually necessary to mobilize the whole economic, social, and political life of the nation to make the collective war effort effective. In World War I the United States Congress, for instance, authorized the President (that is, the *National* Legislature authorized the national Executive) to exercise quasi-dictatorial powers over the national economy. The Food and Fuel Control Act of August 10, 1917, provided for the following:

> *Section 1*   That by reason of the existence of a state of war, it is essential to the national security and defense, for the successful prosecution of the war, and for the support and maintenance of the Army and Navy, to assure an adequate supply and equitable distribution, and to facilitate the movement of foods, feeds, fuel including fuel oil and natural gas, and fertilizer and fertilizer ingredients, tools, utensils, implements, machinery, and equipment required for the actual production of foods, feeds, and fuel, hereafter in this Act called necessaries; to prevent, locally or generally, scarcity, monopolization, hoarding, injurious speculation, manipulations, and private controls, affecting such supply, distribution, and move-

ment; and to establish and maintain governmental control of such necessaries during the war. For such purposes the instrumentalities, means, methods, powers, authorities, duties, obligations, and prohibitions hereinafter set forth are created, established, conferred, and prescribed. The President is authorized to make such regulations and to issue such orders as are essential effectively to carry out the provisions of this Act.

Section 12   That whenever the President shall find it necessary to secure an adequate supply of necessaries for the support of the Army or the maintenance of the Navy, or for any other public use connected with the common defense, he is authorized to requisition and take over, for use or operation by the Government, any factory, packing house, oil pipe line, mine, or other plant, or any part thereof, in or through which any necessaries are or may be manufactured, produced, prepared or mined, and to operate the same. . . .

Section 25   That the President of the United States shall be, and he is hereby, authorized and empowered, whenever and wherever in his judgment necessary for the efficient prosecution of the war to fix the price of coal and coke, wherever and whenever sold, either by producer or dealer, to establish rules for the regulation of and to regulate the method of production, sale, shipment, distribution, apportionment, or storage thereof among dealers and consumers, domestic or foreign: said authority and power may be exercised by him in each case through the agency of the Federal Trade Commission during the war or for such part of said time as in his judgment may be necessary.

A similar legislative authorization, shifting the domain of state powers and private enterprise to the federal center, had to be enacted by all the other federations participating in World War I and then in World War II. The danger of Japanese expansion in the Pacific scared the Australian Commonwealth into the National Security Act of 1939, which gave the national government the power to deal with any matter that could affect Australia's participation in the war. This included wheat requisition, rent control, public safety and order, taking over of the states' administration of income tax collection, and prohibition of all advertising in wartime. We have noted in Chapter 8 how long and extensive the powers of the central authority in India had become as a consequence of the Indo-Chinese border war in 1960. Understandably, the Soviet federation in World War II became 100 percent more totalitarian than in peacetime, if such doubling of something already total is logically possible.

Even federations that do not participate in war and that remain neutral cannot escape the war imperatives. A classic example is Switzerland, which in both world wars mobilized its armed forces for the purpose of protection of her neutrality, and the national legislature (the Federal Assembly) authorized the national executive (the Federal Council) "to take measures necessary to maintain the security, independence and neutrality of Switzerland, to safeguard the credit and economic interests of the country and to secure its supply of food" (August 30, 1939).

The problem for federal systems is that the increased power acquired by the national center in war tends to linger on long after war has ended. In principle, the war emergency power should end when the war ends; international and domestic aftermaths of the war crisis, postwar shortages, disruption of international commerce, and objective organizational problems connected with the disbandment of wartime agencies delay or prevent the national government from restoring the federal division of powers to the prewar situation. To the objective international, economic, and organizational factors we should add the long-observed tendency of any organization, including a federal national government, to keep the power once acquired. The case of neutral Switzerland, which did not participate in any war in the twentieth century, is eloquent: as a result of world wars and their economic and social aftermaths, the scope of the national government's authority and activity has vastly increased; as a result the federal jurisdiction has grown at the expense of the cantons, whose powers, in turn, seemed to have grown at the expense of the individual.

The problem of federal war powers that are so vast while the war is waged and that tend to remain partly so after the war has ended has still another dimension: the prewar crisis. Evidently, no war, but especially a modern one, can be improvised. Defense of a country must be prepared for many decades: army, navy, and air force raised, trained, and equipped; alliances maintained; military research and intelligence organized; counter-intelligence put into operation; propaganda machinery established; and sizable military, technical, and administrative personnel, as required by the military complex, hired—in a word, preparing for war may permit substantial national encroachments on the reserved police powers of the territorial components. Long before the federal nation's participation in war, the central government may feel obliged, and be so authorized, to mobilize economic resources, education, and manpower and so orient the whole economic and social life of the country toward defense. A besieged fortress has never been considered to be a place that abounds with freedom and diversity. Federalism cannot be expected particularly to thrive when a society is or believes itself to be besieged.

Changes and crises in the modern international environment have also lent new meaning to the federal diplomatic and treaty-making powers. The United States federal monopoly in foreign policy was weaker at the time of the American isolation from the world (that is, from European politics) and in the age of laissez faire than it is today. Today the United States is a superpower with commitments all over the world. Also today many international treaties (as noted in Chap. 9) are bound to deal with economic and social matters that in federal systems have been traditionally and constitutionally considered to concern either the police powers of the component units or private initiative.

In developing countries another impact of the international system on the actual working of federations may be noted: because developing countries that have adopted a federal system, for instance, India, Nigeria, or Brazil, are in need of foreign aid, technical assistance, or credits, the central government also in connection with its foreign treaty and foreign commerce powers becomes the logical recipient, administrator, and distributor of foreign supports. In order to make a federation attractive for foreign investment and worthy of foreign aid and credit, the central government must for practical reasons appear as a source of decisive power and, therefore, as a reliable guarantor of efficient distribution and administration of foreign aid. Furthermore, again for practical reasons, foreign donors or creditors cannot be expected to deal separately with each component unit of a federation without running several serious risks, as, for instance, local inefficiency or embezzlement, erosion of the national development plan by narrow-minded petty localism, or, in some cases, suspicion on the part of the national government that direct contacts between local authority and foreign governments may bolster local subversive and secessionist tendencies. (There are occasional but rare exceptions to this practice, which we have already noted in Chap. 9; some states of India and some provinces of Nigeria were able to engage in an independent search for foreign aid.) The combination of all the just-mentioned factors seems to warrant a general conclusion that preparing for, waging, and liquidating the aftermath of wars, reacting to world economic crises and depression, and responding to international tensions represent another series of extraconstitutional impulses that reinforce centralizing unitary tendencies within federations.

Finally, one special problem that may emerge in polyethnic federations, reacting to international environment, should be mentioned. We have said earlier that external threats usually enhance national unity as well as unitary tendencies in federations. This should be qualified when external pressures are not directed at the federation as a whole but at some of its component units. Interference in the domestic affairs of a federation often takes the form of foreign support of secession. This, in turn, may cause the national government to reassert its powers with reference to the external danger and its internal subversive counterpart. Few federations are in the relatively happy situation of Switzerland and Austria, whose neutral status is recognized both by their neighbors and by the great powers. It should be noted that the internal balance of polyethnic Switzerland may appear more fragile than that of monoethnic Austria.

Switzerland is composed of three ethnic groups whose relatives outside the Swiss borders (Germany, France, Italy, and Austria) have engaged in long and bloody wars for centuries. Often but erroneously the Swiss interethnic federalism is quoted as an example of a federal remedy for peace among nations. However, one wonders. It took Switzerland over 600 quite turbulent years to create, as it were, a supraethnic federal nation. Only one hundred years ago Switzerland nearly split asunder in a civil war caused by antagonism between the Catholic minority (42.1 percent) and the Protestant majority (57 percent). The final and undeniable success was due to many factors, some of which were internal but extraconstitutional while others were dominantly international. The Swiss unity has initially been helped by geography, especially in the earlier eras when the Alps seemed inaccessible and unassailable. Another contributing factor was the fact that the religious and party affiliations did not coincide with the ethnic-linguistic boundaries. Another extra-constitutional factor was the pressure of the neighboring great powers that needed a buffer state between them; the federal system partly mirrored the balance of power around Switzerland. The final factor, sealing all the others, was the adoption of a policy of neutrality, an imperative requirement for a German-French-Italian federation located between Germany, France, Italy, and Austria. The policy of armed neutrality is, then, the cement of the Swiss unity:

> The Swiss admit that neutrality is one of the requirements of their domestic equilibrium. . . . A foreigner who observes from the outside the peaceful and prosperous country does not always grasp the effort required to insure its stability, to smooth the inevitable tensions which crop up in a multilingual country, and compensate for the attraction exerted by various [German, French, and Italian] cultures to which Switzerland belongs without being the homeland of those cultures.[16]

PARTIES AND FEDERALISM

Political parties are sometimes called great centralizers or de-centralizers of a federal system. Their number, internal structure, ideology, leaders' commitment to pluralism or unitary centralism, and actions are evidently related to the actual working of federalism. This relationship is, however, very complex. It is not a clearly causal one. Political parties not only shape but also reflect the constitutional and institutional framework and the political habits and traditions of a given society.

The first question that may be usefully asked concerns the relation between the *number* of political parties and the federal

---

[16] Jacques Freymond, "European Neutrals and the Atlantic Community," in Francis O. Wilcox and H. Field Haviland, Jr. (eds.), *The Atlantic Community: Progress and Prospects.* New York: Praeger, 1963, p. 86.

system. There are some federations in which only one party stands as guarantor of national and ideological unity; and there are some federations where there are as many political parties as there are territorial components to guarantee diversity. And then there are federations where the existence of two or more parties is not visibly related to federalism except—and this is essential—that they guarantee conditions of pluralism and democracy without which territorial pluralism and territorial autonomy cannot exist.

If in a single-party system the dominant party is monolithic, that is, totalitarian or authoritarian, and internally not federated, such a party cannot permit its monopolistic power to be in any real sense decentralized, divided, distributed, or diluted. The one-party monopoly puts in grave doubt the reality of federalism in countries such as the Soviet Union, Latin-American federations, Burma, Pakistan, Libya, Cameroun, Yugoslavia, and Czechoslovakia.

There may, however, be a system in which for decades the national center has been in the hands of one single dominant party that permits other parties to exist and to compete freely although they do not seem to have a genuine chance to accede to national power. Nationally, they seem in permanent opposition, whereas provincially they may be successful and may occasionally control provincial governments. India is an example of such a *competitive one-party system*. The Congress party has been in power for more than two decades. There are several reasons for its continued electoral success. The aura of its pre-liberation and liberation record, the charisma of its first two leaders, Gandhi and Nehru, and a relatively thorough all-national party organization have all combined to ensure the Congress party of a continuing dominance in Delhi. However, the party's position in some states has been successfully challenged by left-wing, right-wing, and Hindu traditionalist parties, by the separatist Dravidian movement in the South, and by secessionism in Nagaland. The Congress party has not resorted to a totalitarian method of suppression of all political competition, and, although occasionally adopting stern measures against secessionism, the party has remained relatively tolerant of dissent. It is, however, obvious, that the unchallengeable, near monopolistic position of the Congress party in Indian politics has reinforced the unitary tendencies in the Indian constitutional system. "The absence of a strong and well-organized opposition capable of offering an effective challenge to the Congress has been responsible for terrible centralization of power in India and has tended to reduce the States, in some respects at least, to the status of glorified and magnified municipalities." [17]

Since the 1960s many observers have, however, pointed to the emergence of new leaders and political professionals in India who are primarily oriented toward, or interested in, the defense of state and local interests, often in conjunction with local linguistic loyalties and goals to be asserted against the national leadership of the party in New Delhi. It is at least conceivable, even though still controversial, that the Indian Constitution, whose unitary features seem to be so obvious (as the preceding chapter has shown), may become a framework for federal practices *within* the dominant party, due to the increasing bargaining and blackmailing powers of the prime ministers of the component states of the Indian Union (they are called chief ministers in the Indian Constitution). These prime ministers, whose powers very roughly parallel those of American governors, are all members of the ruling Congress, yet they all have become primarily anchored in the politics of their states and tend to promote their states' interests against their own party in the federal center. In another connection we have already pointed to the dependence of the Indian federal center on the states for implementation of social and economic federal programs.[18]

Federalizing a single-party system into territorial parties poses some interesting theoretical as well as practical problems. Some authors actually argue that, by definition, a classic political party negates the federal idea of power dispersion, because political parties are deemed to aim primarily at aggregating and welding different elements of territorial and functional interests and power into one phalanx, committed to a common goal and action under one leadership. Political centralism, whether exer-

---

[17] S. A. H. Haqqi, "Federalism, Singe Dominant Party, and the Problem of Linguistic Autonomy in India," a paper presented at the Sixth World Congress of the International Political Science Association, Geneva, 1964, p. 7.

[18] See note 9 in this chap.

cised by a party or a government, necessarily abhors what federalism glorifies and institutionalizes, that is, dispersion of authority. A federalist party then seems logically impossible because a party truly committed to federalism must cease to be one party and transform itself into a federation of state parties.[19]

But if a totalitarian party dissolved into component territorial or ethnic parties, would we still refer to such a situation as federalism? Would the territorial oligarchies (which would suppress any dissent and any political competition within their domains) be still able to combine unity with federal diversity, that is, competition with, and opposition to, the union center? Or would the centrifugal forces of territorial self-determination dissolve the union into a loose league of territorial oligarchies? We may only speculate whether Lenin might have had anticipated a federal union of national communist dictatorships, founded on common class interests and belief in Marxism, when he dreamed about an ultimate Proletarian Federation of the World. Hypothetically and highly speculatively, the Soviet Union could transform itself into a federation or confederation of territorial dictatorships when and if the monolithic Soviet Communist party, following a change of its Politburo's heart, transformed itself into an internally federated party, that is, into a union of truly self-governing territorial Communist parties.

In his paper on controversial problems in research on Soviet federalism, Wiktor Suchecki from the Warsaw University objects to the frequent equation sign placed between federalism and democracy: "Federalism is not tantamount to democracy, just as decentralization need not be equivalent to democracy, or centralization imply the opposite." [20] In his subsequent argu-

---

[19] This was the argument of Pierre Duclos in his paper "L'état et le fédéralisme" presented at the Sixth World Congress of the International Political Science Association in Geneva, 1964: "A federalist party is a negation of federalism since every party has a goal to have a unified program, method of conquest of power and a unified following which it prevents from deviating." ("Un parti fédéraliste est la négation même du fédéralisme tout parti ayant pour objectif ramener à l'unitarisme d'un programme, et d'une tactique de conquête de pouvoir, tous ceux qui seraient tentés de s'en écarter.")

[20] Wiktor Suchecki, "Controversial Problems in Research on Soviet Federalism," paper presented at the 1964 Congress of the International Political Science Association, Geneva, p. 19.

ments, the Polish scholar relates federalism, centralism, and decentralization to the *goals* they are supposed to serve. In this kind of treatment, centralization or decentralization is either praised or condemned, depending on the historical era and results achieved. Centralism of the bourgeois states, for instance, may be viewed as more progressive than medieval decentralization and

> the centralism of the Bolsheviks . . . a better guarantee of progress in the Russian revolution than the decentralization advocated by the Social Revolutionaries or Anarchists. On the other hand the decentralization tendencies noted in the Soviet federal state over the past few years seem to favor democracy much more than the centralism of the Stalin period.[21]

These value judgments of centralization or decentralization as means to some other ends are interesting but do not quite answer the question as to the compatibility or incompatibility of federalism with one single totalitarian party system.

Another variant of oligarchic federation, yet tilted to the advantage of the component units, was "feudal federalism," as experienced by Brazil after 1889 when the revolution replaced monarchy by a federal republic. It was not a step toward democratic territorial pluralism. Statewide oligarchies solidified their own authority in the states while accepting the principle of alternating the control of the national presidency among themselves. The governors controlled the election of their states' representatives, who were to function more like diplomatic envoys and transmitters of their states' wishes than as legislators in the nation's center. "They were in the capital to give their support to the national president who in turn gave his support to the governors of the States." [22] When local oligarchs are combined in a limited give-and-take pluralism in the national center, is it federalism?

The problem of territorial parties (that is, a system of as many parties as there are territorial subdivisions in a federal union) should be also examined in the context of multinational

---

[21] Suchecki, "Controversial Problems," p. 20.
[22] Harry Kantor, "Latin American Federalism: Aspiration and Futility," in Earle, *Federalism,* p. 194.

unions. When the boundaries of popular support and organization coincide geographically with internal territorial *and* ethnic boundaries, such parties are or may become, for all practical purposes, the political arms of territorial communities that may, as potential nations, press for secession. In India, the separatist party of the Dravidian South, DMK (*Dravida Munnerta Kazhagam*), achieved a spectacular victory in the southern state of Madras in 1967, when in coalition with some minor parties it was able to capture 138 out of 234 seats in the State Assembly. On the national level, of course, the DMK obtained only 3.69 percent of the total national vote as opposed to 39.57 percent obtained by the Congress party. In African federations many political parties represent highly centralized and internally autocratic modern versions of former traditional tribal territories and organizations. Such territorial-ethnic parties may erode the federal union and transform it into a loose association of independent territorial states at best, or into a fratricidal battlefield at worst. The second tragic alternative has been that of the territorial-tribal parties in Nigeria. (The danger of secession has been often exaggerated by military or autocratic leaders to justify their methods of suppression of political liberties and political parties in general.)

It should be emphasized at this point that the danger of territorial ethnic parties promoting mutually exclusive ethnic interests is not limited to federations. National unity may be threatened by new or revived separatism in any system; secession can happen in the best of unitary families. In another connection we have noted, for instance, that the unitary British polyethnic structure will perform well so long as the Scots and the Welsh continue to vote for the British Conservative Labour, and Liberal parties and not for the territorial-ethnic Scottish and Welsh nationalistic parties. The same applies to biethnic but unitary Belgium, whose system has for a long time depended on the Walloons and Flemings voting as Socialists, Liberals, or Catholics rather than as members of their respective territorial ethnic communities. The Belgian experience also confirms the fact that minorities tend to view federalism as their constitutional protection, so long as they are minorities. The Flemings favored Belgian federalism while numerically inferior. Now, when the French-speaking Walloons are in the minority, they seem to prefer some biethnic variant of a federal formula. In Ceylon, a Tamil federal party advocates federalism in its opposition to the numerical, political, and economic domination of the country by the Sinhalese. In the United States, only the future will tell whether the black vote will force upon the unitary system of the state governments some variant of biethnic intrastate and intracity federalism.

Turning our attention now to the federal systems in which we observe a meaningful distribution of power and a free competition between territorial units and the national center, we cannot help noticing that these are all two-party or multiparty systems: the United States, Canada, Australia, West Germany, Austria, and Switzerland.

However, it would be wrong to explain the working of federalism by the existence of several competing parties that are not directly related to the federal territorial subdivisions. What seems to be a more accurate explanation is simply that the conditions that permit the existence and competition between different parties permit also a meaningful territorial competition—in a word, democracy is a condition for federalism, whereas a totalitarian system excludes autonomy of all political groups, including the territorial ones. Federalism is incompatible with any type of system that means an unrestrained rule, whether by a majority or a minority, that excludes any dilution of power and makes the authority unresponsive to the wishes of all minorities, including the territorial ones. As Leslie Lipson put it, "Not all democracies have federal governments. But all genuine cases of federalism are found in democratic states." [23]

Some further qualifications are necessary with reference to the correlation between federalism, democracy, and several competing political parties. A federal system does not guarantee that a competitive party system in the central authority will be necessarily duplicated on the provincial level. In India, for instance, a competitive one-party system exists in the federal cen-

[23] Leslie Lipson, "The Federal Principle and the Brazilian Reality," paper presented at the 1964 Congress of the International Political Science Association, Geneva, p. 1. Compare Robert A. Dahl's statement in his *Modern Political Analysis* (Englewood Cliffs, N.J.: Prentice-Hall, 1963), p. 37: "Whether 'federal' or 'unitary' in legal theory, modern democracies tend to be 'federal'—*i.e.,* pluralistic in actual practice."

ter while a two-party or multiparty system prevails in many of the Indian states. In the United States, on the contrary, there is a two-party competitive system in the federal center while many states have either a competitive one-party rule (in the South) or a three- or more party system in the states or cities (the Democratic, Republican, and Liberal parties in New York, for instance). In Canada we find the duplication of the federal two-party system only in Ontario and the Maritime Provinces. In other Canadian provinces, minor parties often become dominant with little correlation to their lack of importance on the federal level (such as the French-oriented parties in Quebec, the Social Credit party in Saskatchewan, or the New Democratic party in a few provinces). In Australia there are three major parties (Labour, Liberal, and Country) that triangularly compete in the states but that form a two-party system on the national level because the Liberal and the Country parties have formed a bipartisan national coalition to compete with the Labour party.

Furthermore, a multiparty system does not mean that all the parties competing within its framework are equally dedicated to the idea of the territorial division of power. Here, again, the problem of federal asymmetry returns. In many a federal system we may note the existence and opposition of fascist or Communist parties whose dedication to democracy and federalism is doubtful. Even in democratic Australia, the Labour party occasionally expresses a negative attitude toward the federal system in light of some of the decisions of the Supreme Court, which keeps on interpreting the federal Constitution as forbidding a collectivization of industries whose activities extend over several component units of the Australian federation.

Finally, we should note that even if all parties in a competitive system profess their attachment to the federal concept, their commitment to federalism may change. Many a party that in the opposition appears as a passionate defender of the federal faith may adopt a somewhat lukewarm attitude toward the dilution of central power as soon as it succeeds in capturing it. Furthermore, within the party, whatever its members' and supporters' commitment to federalism or unitarianism, there may emerge a charismatic leader of exceptional talent and skill whose personal bias against, or in favor of, a territorial dispersion of power may give a new orientation to the party and to the political system. The tendency to identify with the collective whole or its part may be a result of the leader's life experience or his education abroad in a unitary or federal environment that may have marked an intellectual or native colonial administrator for life. One could, for instance, speculate whether the Congolese elites educated in Belgium, were or were not affected by the French-Flemish problem of the former colonial master, in contrast with the elites in French, English, Spanish, or Portuguese Africa. Some further influences could be the leader's administrative training, his economic activities (businessmen's struggle against intraterritorial trade barriers, for instance), or his ethnic or racial origin (experience with a first-class or third-class citizen's status). Thus a federal system may be presided over by a "unitary personality" (John F. Kennedy in the United States?) and a unitary system may be presided over by a "federal personality" or—a more frequent case—a promoter of one local interest against all the others. The action of any party leader "is as much the result of environment as it is the manifestation of a personality structure." [24] When in the Soviet context the "federal" personality of Lenin is contrasted with the "unitary" personality of Stalin, Isaac Deutscher and other scholars tend to explain the contrast by the minority (Georgian) origins of Stalin, who knew better than the Great Russian Lenin how much the non-Russian nationalities hated the Petrograd and Moscow overlords. The contrast between "federalist" Lenin and "centralist" Stalin was stressed by W. Suchecki:

> Extreme centralism, the concentration of power within the hands of a narrow group, the slighting, and, in some case, the brutal trampling underfoot, of the rights of the nationalities of the Soviet State during Stalin's reign, contributed to the warping of the Lenin idea of federation and of his view on the national question in the USSR.[25]

THE CONSTITUTION AND THE PARTIES

Because the main purpose of political parties is to gain control of public authority—and the goal of interest groups is to influ-

[24] Franz L. Neumann, "Approaches to the Study of Political Power," *The Political Science Quarterly,* Vol. 65, No. 2 (June 1950), 162.
[25] W. Suchecki, "Controversial Problems," p. 3.

ence it—both political parties and interest groups have to adapt themselves to the rules, means, and loopholes of the constitutional system unless they are determined to subvert or destroy the system and to replace it by one that would be more to their liking. The parties may be seen as mirrors (occasionally, quite curved ones) of the constitution and the institutions created by it. However, here again we should warn against any suggestion of simple or straight causality. The problem is that the mirror itself has been created by the political parties and is now manipulated by them.

In the American federal context, Morton Grodzins identified six major influences of the constitutional system on the working of the two major political parties:

1. The states have important responsibilities for conducting the election of the President and Vice-President, primarily by choosing the electors.

2. The power of state parties is further strengthened by the institution of the Electoral College in combination with the party conventions where the state party bosses play the decisive role of king-makers.

3. Congress is elected through the states. House districts are apportioned among the states on the basis of population. In the Senate, each state is represented by two senators.

4. Members of Congress are constitutionally forbidden to hold any other governmental office; this prevents them from becoming federal administrators and thus, so to speak, from being nationalized and "delocalized." The party representatives in the Congress remain highly sensitive to pressures from below and rather unsensitive to pressures from above—they serve as transmitting agents for communications from local constituencies to the federal government.

5. A further element in the decentralization [is] the fixed and staggered terms of the President and members of Congress.

6. And, finally, there is the difficulty in altering the decentralization features of the American system in view of the constitutionally prescribed extraordinary majorities in Congress and the states.[26]

[26] Morton Grodzins in *The American System*. Skokie, Ill.: Rand McNally, 1966, pp. 277–278.

The existence of the states as separate largely self-sustaining power centers is considered by some authors as the most important explanation of the federal nature of the American political parties. David B. Truman stresses three fundamental consequences of the states' existence on the parties' structure, nature, and operation:

1. They represent channels for the claims of local socio-economic groups.
2. As self-contained units of power they invite a use of them by interests that are territorial only in a tactical sense on the part of groups whose scope of interest is not local but national.
3. They provide for competing nuclei of decentralized intra-party conflict.

Suggesting that territorial interests may be a matter of political expedience and tactics rather than principle, David B. Truman adds,

> The basic political fact of federalism is that it creates separate, self-sustaining centers of power, privilege and profit which may be sought and defended as desirable in themselves, as means of leverage upon elements in the political structure above and below and as bases from which individuals may move to places of greater influence and prestige in and out of government.[27]

The American parties are so loosely organized as to merit a confederal rather than a federal label; only at the time of presidential elections do they transform themselves into temporarily closely knit federations endowed with a national program and a national leadership. After the elections, only occasionally one or both parties press for centralized national action, using all the constitutional loopholes for this purpose. At other times in spirit and action the parties remain the great decentralizers. Some authors argue that they, rather than the Constitution, seem to make American federalism work as it does. William H. Riker

---

[27] David B. Truman, "Federalism and the Party System," in Arthur W. Macmahon (ed.), *Federalism: Mature and Emergent.* New York: Russell and Russell, 1962, p. 123.

finds that the nature of political parties represents *the* single most important explanation of the working of any federal system:

> The federal relationship is centralized according to the degree to which the parties organized to operate the central goverment control the parties organized to operate the constituent [state or provincial] governments. This amounts to the assertion that the proximate cause of variations in the degree of centralization (or peripheralization) in the constitutional structure of a federalism is the variation in degree of party centralization. . . . The variations in partisanship are causally related to variations in federalism.[28]

In his analysis of the American parties, Morton Grodzins goes so far as to call them "antiparties" because, like the antiparticles with respect to particles in atomic physics, the American political parties manifest qualities directly opposite to the "classic" parties whose aim it is to weld different segments of power into a unified whole.

In conclusion, it should be re-emphasized that the constitutional and institutional framework, even if deemed very important, is only one of the many realities that the parties and their leaders take into account when determining policies and when deciding on action. Even in the democracies where the respect for the written constitution is very high, parties may choose to adapt their policies and actions to extraconstitutional pressures, as discussed previously: the economic and social imperatives, new technology, shifts of the population, growth of new territorial communities, or international facts of life. As a result, the parties may try to circumvent the constitution, to adapt it to the new situation by creative reinterpretation, to respond to extraconstitutional challenges and problems extraconstitutionally, or to alter the constitutional framework altogether by formal amendment.

The explanation of the working of a particular federal system by the nature of the political parties and their leaders begs, on the other hand, another question: if it is not the constitution that determines the federal nature of the parties and if it is the

---

[28] William H. Riker, *Federalism: Origin, Operation, Significance.* Boston: Little, Brown, 1964, p. 129.

parties that endow the constitution with federal or unitary contents, then what is it that makes the parties behave in a federal or unitary fashion in the first place?

We seem to detect a complex circular movement of three (mutually reinforcing or mutually eroding) factors: (1) *the constitution;* (2) *the parties,* and (3) a rather nebulous concept of habits and traditions that we tentatively call *political culture.* Diagrammatically, the triangular movement may be perhaps expressed as in Figure 10–2.

Figure 10–2   Circular movement of three mutually reinforcing or eroding factors in a federal system

FEDERAL POLITICAL CULTURE

The term *federal culture,* as a variant of *civic culture,*[29] is used here to describe a set of orientations toward the federal political system and attitudes toward the role of self (in the federal case, the component units as well as the individuals) in the system. The definition is borrowed and adapted to our needs from the Almond-Verba study of orientations and attitudes toward politics in the United States, Germany, Mexico (all three federal

[29] Gabriel A. Almond and Sidney Verba, *The Civic Culture.* Boston: Little, Brown, 1965, p. 12.

systems in the constitutional sense), Italy (with a constitutional promise of regional federalism), and Britain (with federal practice in a unitary framework). Although the Almond-Verba study does not deal with federalism as such, some of its findings have partial relevance to our analysis because they detect and describe political attitudes at a local territorial level. In particular, the authors ask the fundamental question as to what people have in mind when they say, for instance, that ordinary man ought to play some part in his territorial community. It was found, for instance, that the interest in participation in local government bodies is about as strong in federal United States as it is in unitary England, but much weaker in federal Germany and federal Mexico, and very weak in unitary Italy.[30] The findings of participatory interest on the lowest local level is not indicative of the reality of interest and participation on the intermediary level, that is, the provincial or state government, in between the local and national government. Franz L. Neumann writes, "The smallest territorial unit—the municipality—is potentially the most responsive to the will and interests of the people and, consequently, local self-government must be considered the indispensable cornerstone of a modern large-scale democracy." Neumann also adds warningly, "But is it possible to assert that the federal structure maximizes local self-government and that, in a unitary state, we therefore find a shrinkage of local powers?" [31]

Our previous discussion has already indicated how meaningful and broad may be the local autonomy—and participation —in unitary systems that create the units of territorial self-rule by delegation, usually irrevocable, from "above."

In our context the term *federal culture* should be understood also in the context of constant changes and the interlocking links [32] that caused Morton Grodzins to refer to federalism as a rainbow or marble cake.

---

[30] Almond and Verba, *The Civic Culture,* pp. 128–129.

[31] Franz L. Neumann, "Federalism and Freedom: A Critique," in Macmahon, *Federalism,* p. 51.

[32] Compare Ivanko Srnić in his paper on Yugoslav federalism (*Les caractéristiques et l'expérience du fédéralisme en Yougoslavie*) presented at the 1964 Congress of the International Political Science Association in Geneva: "A federation is not a single coexistence of the federal union and its component units. In the framework of a federation all the

Attitudes toward, as well as institutional forms of, a federal system slowly change under the impact of (1) charismatic leaders and political movements; (2) interests vested in the continuation or alteration of given orientations; (3) new economic, social, and international realities; (4) the decline of legislative assemblies as rule initiators and rule makers and the shift of rule initiation and rule making toward the national executive and national bureaucracy (the federal nature of a political system is usually more clearly expressed in the legislature, especially its federal upper chamber, than in the national executive); and (5) functional interests organized on a national, nonfederal basis.

Different interest groups whose activities and organization cut across internal federal boundaries may alter the originally federal habits and attitudes more significantly than even the most antifederal political parties. Examples of such interest groups are labor and farm organizations, manufacturing corporations, banks, insurance companies, mass media, and transportation concerns.[33]

We do not have as yet any reliable data that would permit us to assert that there is a measurable thing called a *federal* or a *unitary* political culture that may be either expressed or suppressed by a given political system. We may only tentatively argue, for instance, that a local, provincial, or regional habit (if discovered and proven) of looking for guidance to the national capital and not questioning its directives constitutes prima facie evidence of a unitary rather than a federal political tradition, irrespective of what the system may be constitutionally. An Indian observer-scholar noted that in India "there is a general tendency to look to New Delhi and the Congress party high com-

---

constituent communities establish different and varied forms of interaction, coordination, cooperation, understanding and mutual tolerance with the community in its broad sense and among themselves."

[33] Samuel Huntington noted the parallel between the growth of the power of a national executive vis-à-vis Congress and the concomitant expansion of the responsibilities and size of the national administration, on the one hand, and the growth of large nongovernmental national organizations, such as unions, corporations, and mass media. "Congressional Responses to the Twentieth Century," in The American Assembly (ed.), *The Congress and America's Future,* Englewood Cliffs, N.J.: Prentice-Hall, 1965, p. 16.

mand for decision in all matters, governmental and organizational, from interstate wrangles, state trading in food grains, formation and composition of state cabinets to the scramble for power all over the country." [34]

In Latin America, according to several authors, federalism has not taken roots because it is basically a foreign import from the North into a unitary political culture, dominantly shaped by a tradition of centralizing uniformity as represented by the Catholic Church, Roman law, and the unitary political culture exported from Spain and Portugal into Latin America.

On the other hand, in politics, the tendency or habit of thinking primarily in terms of local (territorial) initiative and responsibility, observable in the English-speaking countries, may perhaps present prima facie evidence of a "federal political culture" in the sense of intensive interest and participation in local government. In unitary Britain one could actually speak of a federal political culture in light of the keen awareness and assertion of territorial identity and territorial interests in Northern Ireland, Scotland, Wales, the Isle of Man, and the Channel Islands. The vigor of participation in local subdivisions of England is also high.

The presence of a federal political culture was expressed in poetical rather than political terms by Walt Whitman in his succinct "federal" admonishment, contained in *Leaves of Grass*:

> To the States or any of them or any city of the States,
> *Resist much, obey little,*
> Once unquestioning obedience, once fully enslaved,
> Once fully enslaved, no nation, state, city, of this earth, ever
> afterward resumes its liberty.[35]

In political terms, as noted previously, Morton Grodzins (p. 314) spoke of the American traditional belief in the vitality and usefulness of local government, "federal *creed*." William

---

[34] S. A. H. Haqqi, "Federalism, Single Dominant Party and the Problem of Linguistic Autonomy in India," paper presented at the 1964 World Congress of the International Political Science Association, Geneva.

[35] Walt Whitman, *Complete Prose and Selected Prose and Letters*, edited by Emory Holloway. London: Nonesuch, and New York: Random House, 1939, p. 10.

S. Livingston succinctly warns that the essence of federalism "lies not in the institutional or constitutional structure but in the society itself. Federal government is a device by which the *federal qualities* of the society are articulated and protected."[36] Thomas M. Franck (see Chap. 9) speaks of *"federal feeling"* and *"federal popular charisma"* and David B. Truman of *"social factors"*: "In a federal system decentralization and lack of cohesion in the party system are based on the structural fact of federalism, but . . . the degree to which these become the dominant characteristics of the distribution of power within the political parties is a function of a variety of other governmental and *social factors* which are independent of the federal structure or are merely supportive of its tendencies. [Italics added.]"[37]

Analysts of the Australian federal scene seem to agree that the federal "political culture" antedated the formal constitutional arrangement. The states had their political identity before they collectively formed a nation-state. Major interest groups in Australia were organized on a state basis before they formed their national superstructure. Their interest in perpetuating their state-based existence, defended by a large body of personnel and their state-oriented vested interests, makes the Australian territorial dispersion of power more meaningful than the differences in outlook and interests between the states as states would otherwise make it.[38] The outstanding feature of the three national parties —Labour, Liberal, and Country party—is their subnational rather than national basis for their operations, such as disbursement of funds, electoral management, and endorsement of candidates; it is from the subnational territorial centers that both state and federal politics are dominantly influenced.[39]

The concept as well as a proof of a federal or unitary polit-

---

[36] William S. Livingston, "A Note on the Nature of Federalism," *Political Science Quarterly,* 62 (1952), 85. (Italics added.)

[37] Truman, "Federalism and the Party System," p. 133.

[38] Aaron Wildawsky, "Party Discipline under Federalism: Implications of Australian Experience," *Social Research,* 28 (Winter 1961), 442. 442.

[39] Rufus Davis, "The Federal Principle Reconsidered," *Australian Journal of Politics and History* (May 1965), pp. 223–244. Louise Overacker spoke of the national Labour party antedating federalism (see Chap. 8, note 16).

ical culture requires more research than the previous sweeping generalizations reflect. Like captains of old, we seem to have a map of federalism that has several areas relatively well chartered, such as federal constitutions, federal parties, and the history of federalism, but that contains some quite unexplored areas, including a blank that we have tentatively called *federal political culture* (other analyses use such general terms as *federal creed, social factors, federal qualities of the society,* or *federal charisma*). Perhaps at this stage we could simply call the unchartered blank *Hic sunt leones foederales.* However labeled, the federal or unitary culture—in particular either the territorial or functional tendencies in subnational politics—should be considered an important though not yet fully explored part of any study of extraconstitutional aspects of federalism.

CONCLUSION
A WORLD SAFE
FOR DIVERSITY?

To use the word "federalism" to classify . . . not
fully constitutional states . . . is like trying to
classify cows by the number of petals. It is not useful.
> C. J. Hughes ("The Theory of Confed-
> eracies")

Modern man is oppressed by the sense of heavy
organization and distant controls; he longs to resolve
things into comprehensible and manageable portions.
> Arthur W. Macmahon (*Federalism:
> Mature and Emergent*)

If there is a political revolution going on throughout
the world, it is what might be called the participation
explosion. . . . the belief that the ordinary man is
belief that the ordinary man is politically relevant—
that he ought to be an involved participant in the
politically relevant—that he ought to be an involved
participant in the political system—is widespread.
. . . what the mode of participation will be is uncertain.
> Gabriel A. Almond and Sidney Verba
> (*Civic Culture*)

Our study of the territorial dimensions of politics has been primarily, although not exclusively, concerned with conflict, competition, and cooperation among territorial communities within nation-states (mostly federal). Their values and goals, conflicting on one level of contact, have not precluded permanent and routinized cooperation on another level; thus diversity could often be successfully, though never easily, combined with relative unity.

Absolute unity mocks at diversity and absolute diversity denies unity; "to be fruitful, the two ideas must find their limit to one another." [1] Unity without uniformity and diversity without anarchy are not novel themes. They are millennia old. They belong to the only too familiar set of pairs of desirable yet conflicting goals or values that may prove mutually destructive if either pushes too hard, that is, if one or the other is aimed at or achieved in an absolute or near-absolute sense. The list of such pairs of desirable opposites is long. Besides unity and diversity, it includes freedom and justice, majority rule and minority rights, order and liberty, ecumenism and localism, freedom and equality, national security and social progress, and collective welfare and individual rights. All of them, to use Madison's terms, search for a middle ground that would permit mutual accommodation and flexible shifting of mutual boundaries in response to changes in the environment and in man's priorities.

The preceding chapters have pointed to the great driving forces that, for different reasons, in both developed and developing societies combine into modern centralizing (antifederal) processes. To speed up economic progress, to eliminate territorially uneven social and economic development, and to ensure national security, it seems imperative to provide for centralization of economic and political powers on which a nationally unified policy and action may be based. Such centralizing tendencies in federal systems have complicated our task of differentiating with any degree of precision a federal from a unitary system. The extraconstitutional internal and external pressures

---

[1] We have—federally—paraphrased Albert Camus, who wrote in *The Rebel:* "Absolute freedom mocks at justice and absolute justice denies freedom. To be fruitful, the two ideas must find their limit to one another."

seem to conspire to make the federal decentralization fade by "imperceptible graduations" [2] (or sometimes proceed by dramatic leaps and bounds) into unitary centralism with or without subsidiary federal features. Such centralizing trends within federal systems are often dreaded because they may be (and probably rightly so) interpreted as threats to all pluralism—political and ideological as well as territorial. On the international level, centralizing trends are feared when they represent unification by imperial forces against the wishes of the communities concerned. In contrast, international unification is often glorified as a welcome transfer of the federal formula from the domestic to the world scene, if based on voluntary consent of the participants and clearly aimed at combining unity with preservation of national diversity. Many authors today see in it a means of securin peace and of reducing tensions and conflicts among nation-states. In such a hopeful context common markets, regional confederations, and even alliances are sometimes seen (not quite accurately) as perhaps the first right steps in the right direction leading to an ultimate United States of the World. In his *Locksley Hall,* Alfred Tennyson wrote,

> Till the war drum throbbed no longer and the battle flags were furled
> In the Parliament of Man, the Federation of the world.

Similarly a French poet, Victor Hugo, presiding over the second peace congress in Paris (1849), spoke of the possibility of a universal peace based on "the union of all nations by a common bond, the gospel as a supreme law, arbitration taking the place of war." In a poetical vein he saw a confederation of sorts between "these two agglomerations, the United States of America and the United States of Europe, facing each other and stretching out their hands across the seas in close cooperation." He assumed then that technical innovations, notably railroads, would speed up the process. "What do we need?" he asked; and he

---

[2] C. J. Hughes in his "Theory of Confederacies," a paper presented at the Sixth World Congress of the International Political Science Association, Geneva, 1964, pp. 5–6 wrote: "As against unitary *fully constitutional* government federalism just shades off. . . . The difficulty concerning definition corresponds to a difficulty within the thing itself."

answered, "To love each other." [3] A more down-to-earth expression of a hope of solving international conflicts by a federal remedy was voiced in 1968 by a Greek premier, George Papadopoulos, who, on behalf of his military dictatorship, suggested in an interview with a Turkish newspaper, *Milliyet* (June 24, 1968), a Greek-Turkish federation: "If I had magic powers I would immediately lead our peoples toward a Greek-Turkish federation." Neither he nor anyone else seems, however, to have acquired such magic powers for the purpose of a federal peace among nations.

Before poets or prosaic military dictators carry our federal dreams too far, it should be also noted that most of the existing supranational unions derive their relative cohesion from their collective reaction to external pressures. They are basically defensive communities directed *against* other similar supranational blocs or particular nations and can hardly be explained in terms of any other positive factor: the Arab League against Israel, the African unity against the whites, Western Europe against the Soviet Union's and the United States' possible hegemony, and the Atlantic Community against the Communist Commonwealth.

So far the common fear of disastrous consequences of the splitting of the atom has tended only further to "atomize," not unite, mankind.

The increasing number of microstates whose viability and identity are often rightly in doubt is indicative of the strength of their desire, at least in former colonial areas, to go it alone, no matter what, rather than, federally, to go it with others.

Those who occasionally indulge in daydreaming about regional or world federalism without a pre-existing positive consensus tend also to forget that a federal system is not, and cannot be, by itself a guarantee of peace among the component units; even when there is an initial consensus, it may fade away or be eroded later. The failure of the American federation in 1860 should serve as a warning against an excessive reliance on a federal formula as a guarantee of interterritorial peace and cooperation. What has been so integrated may disintegrate in blood, as the case of Biafra and other secessions has shown.

[3] Quoted in Hans Kohn, *The Twentieth Century*. New York: Crowell-Collier-Macmillan, pp. 5–6.

It would now be quite tempting to imitate Cassandra and on the one hand forecast on the international scene a trend toward further atomization in the name of national self-determination and on the other hand record within the national scene the decline of territorial and other pluralism and the rise of centralism with possible authoritarian tendencies.

Such a Cassandra-like posture, although perhaps correct in a short run, does not seem to be quite warranted in the long run. On the international scene ecumenism and national parochialism are still in search of some middle ground. Simultaneously with the trend toward atomization in former colonial areas we observe attempts to build higher unions out of many nations in the developed portions of the world. Admittedly, with the partial exception of Western European unification, the federal or confederal efforts on the international scene have nowhere scored any spectacular success. Political relations among nations and men change with a tempo only too familiar to geologists.

On the national scene, on which our study has primarily focused, the undeniable trend toward unitary centralism has been challenged by new and dynamic forces in both democratic and authoritarian frameworks. This challenge to excessive centralism comes from two opposite directions. The first challenge comes from "above." There is a search on the part of central authorities for a greater efficiency, flexibility, responsibility, and initiative on the local level. The willingness of the central authorities to finance and closely cooperate with the units of territorial self-rule is not a result of any federal sentimentality or ideology but is a very pragmatic concern for a more effective use of common funds for the purpose of promoting equal economic and social progress in all parts of the land. Paradoxically, uniformity needs diversity to be effective. Decentralization means an increased reliance of the central authorities on local familiarity with local possibilities and limitations and on local pride in participation and responsibility. The latter is expected to result not only in useful local innovative initiatives, consistent with the overall national objectives, but also in interterritorial competition for better performance and better services. This seems to be particularly attractive to bureaucratic socialist states which, having eliminated private competition in the economic field and so also some of its healthy ingredients, look now for a possible substitute for competition within a collectivized economic system. As may be seen, federal decentralization has rarely been a matter of ideological preference or free choice but has been that of pragmatic considerations or necessity.

The second challenge comes from "below." There are either territorial or other interests that in a political system press for institutional recognition of their right for self-expression, dignity, and self-rule. Some are of older vintage; the United States Constitution, for instance, recognized only the old territorial components whose origins and justification date back to the eighteenth and nineteenth centuries; they have no significant roots in the last two decades of the twentieth century. But other new communities have emerged; these are neither recognized nor guaranteed by the federal system. Some of them may not have existed at all at the time of the initial federal bargain; others may not have had any territorial dimension but may have acquired it later. They can be satisfied only by a new federal arrangement or by a unitary delegation of authority that, in many instances, would resemble federalism because the grant of territorial self-rule would be treated by all concerned as practically, though perhaps not constitutionally, irrevocable or unamendable. In the United States, as previously noted, new regional communities that combine the economic, social, transportation, and other interests of several states into one have been superimposed on the eighteenth- and nineteenth-century territorial divisions; and within the states the cities, their suburban areas, and the municipal subdivisions (white towns, black towns, rich towns, and Spanish towns) represent often more assertive territorial communities and more meaningful objects of loyalty, pride, participation, responsibility, and action than the traditional subdivision of the federal union.[4] Speaking in particular of American black towns, W. H. Ferry described their aim to participate in the American system on new terms:

> The issue is the creation of a new kind of coexistence [shall we say here, "federation"?] between blacktown and

[4] The Institute of Policy Studies in Washington, D.C. has experimented with theories and models of neighborhood corporations. The greatest value of the neighborhood corporations is said to be their role as instruments on one hand for accepting political obligations and on the other hand for enhancing political participation.

whitetown since what blacktown wants most whitetown cannot confer. Blacktown wants independence and the authority to run its own affairs. It wants to recover its manhood, its self-love, and develop its ability to conduct a self-reliant community.[5]

The existence and vigor of forces that press for new ways and means of both participation and decentralization may, and most probably will, affect what otherwise may have appeared as an inevitable drive toward unitary centralism everywhere. Although welcome as a healthy reaction against excessive centralism, the dangers of secession or even anarchy should always be recognized. But whatever the dangers inherent in any form of dynamic politics, the deconcentration of power as well as the participation in both local and general policy making can be expected to remain an integral part of the contemporary scene. In his study of federalism Arthur W. Macmahon (see the epigraph at the beginning of this chapter) speaks of modern man's longing to resolve things into manageable portions. In the name of group as well as individual autonomy men protest against big government, mammoth unions, excessively large universities, impersonal giant places of work, vast impersonal cities in which "the individual is confronted by uncontrollable dimensions in comparison with which he is a small particle. All he can do is to fall in step like a marching soldier or a worker on the endless belt. . . . He can act, but the sense of independence, significance has gone." [6] Certainly one part of the worldwide protest against the "establishment" is the desire to recapture the sense of indi-

[5] W. H. Ferry, "The Case for a New Federalism," *Saturday Review* (June 15, 1968). Similar to many other ethnic movements advocating decentralization and autonomy, a portion of the black militant movement expresses its ultimate goals, as noted previously, in territorial and secessionist terms. For instance, upon his return to the United States from a self-imposed exile (1961–1969) in Cuba and China, Robert Franklin Williams, a black nationalist leader, was referred to by his lawyer (*The New York Times,* September 12, 1969) as the "future President of New Africa" to be created out of Alabama, Mississippi, Louisiana, Georgia, and South Carolina.

[6] Erich Fromm, *Escape from Freedom.* New York: Holt, Rinehart and Winston, Inc., 1941, pp. 131–132.

vidual and group identity and independence. There seems to be a broadly felt need and demand for deconcentration of institutional and impersonal power as well as for more effective individual and group participation in and influence on the exercise of local and national power. This is why federalism—as a territorial dimension of democracy—remains so much a part of the contemporary scene, even though its classical and constitutional forms appear obsolete and not readily adaptable to the new problems.

How to make political institutions responsive to the will of groups and individuals (that is, how to ensure democracy) is a very old problem. But two dimensions have been added to it today. The first dimension is only indirectly connected with the problem of territorial distribution of authority: it is the desire to make the institutional environment (the political system, place of work, and school) respond *rapidly* to group demands. This is probably in tune with the general tempo of our present life and with the concomitant rise of impatient expectations. A mood different from what underscored the earlier, somewhat leisurely experiments in democracy and federalism characterizes the present era.

The second new dimension of an old problem is more directly connected with the issue of federalism: it is the demand that political institutions be responsive not only to the will of the majority (which is understood unless one favors a rule by minority) but also and *simultaneously* to the wishes of important groups that do not constitute (nor expect to be) a majority. These are *minorities* in the broadest meaning of the word; they include not only the classic minorities (ethnic, racial, linguistic, or religious), but also the students, the intellectuals, the aged, and—in the framework of our present analysis—all types of territorial communities. A right to veto, which would give a minority an absolute protection, would make the political system inoperative; it would actually dissolve the system. A rule by majority, if absolute and unrestrained by minority rights, would prevent any division of power, territorially or otherwise. We do not expect to find an easy solution for this old and difficult problem; some persons advocate new federalism, others advocate participatory democracy, confrontation politics, anarchy, or elitist dictatorship. However, we should recognize that a search for a better solution has been made more pressing by the two dimensions of the present ferment: (1) impatience (the desire for, if not the right to, quick results) and (2) simultaneity (the demand for, if not the right to, a simultaneous responsiveness of political and other institutions to both the majority and the minorities). Both demands form the background of what we have called the territorial dimension of politics.

"The time has come," writes Herbert J. Gans, author of *The Levittowners* and *People and Plans,* "to create a pluralistic democracy," one that would not do away with majority rule, but would assure minorities of attaining their most important demands, even when numerically outvoted. He then adds:

> Outvoted minorities can also achieve greater political power by the alteration of existing political boundaries and powers so that they could even become majorities in their own bailiwicks. Current proposals for decentralization and community control are boundary-altering proposals with just this political consequence. . . . But the concept of redrawing boundaries ought to be applied more broadly, since many existing political subdivisions are anachronistic. For example, it is difficult to justify the existence of many of the states as political units today, and it might be useful to think about creating smaller and more homogeneous units in highly urbanized parts of the country, perhaps of county size, particularly in order to reduce the number of outvoted minorities [Norman Mailer has suggested just that in proposing statehood for New York City.] [7]

The pragmatic, organizational, and material aspects of new demands for decentralization are eminently important. But there are also important emotional, psychological, and spiritual intangibles, such as the previously mentioned search for group dignity or territorial pride. Dealing with the Boer War in 1899, the British coined the slogan "Good government is no substitute for self-government." A Filipino leader expressed the same idea with reference to the United States in a somewhat more colloquial

[7] Herbert J. Gans, "We Won't End the Urban Crisis until We End Majority Rule," *The New York Times Magazine* (August 3, 1969), p. 28.

fashion: "Better a government run like hell by Filipinos, than one run like heaven by foreigners." Today the theme of these quotations has been expressed by many others in many other places. Statements of the need for and right of territorial autonomy (or community control) do not promise or imply that, according to the usual yardsticks, the quality of the group's own government will necessarily and immediately be better than the former alien rule. In fact, it may temporarily prove worse—more corrupt and less efficient. "It will be a mess," an Algerian nationalist once told a French newspaperman, "but it will be our own." A performance measurable in economic, social, and administrative statistics is really not the point. This is expected to come later, in due course. The demand for territorial autonomy seeks satisfaction of emotional and psychological needs of alienated groups first. One expression of the right of communities to be what they want and to live as they want was succinctly expressed by a representative of an American blacktown: "Leave us alone." The subnational "Leave us alone" seems, however, to be combined with a national "Let us in" (that is, "Let us, as a group, participate in all the major decisions affecting our interdependent world, since even the most alienated group is not nor thinks itself to be an island"). The simultaneity of the "leave us alone" and "let us in" characterizes much of the modern ferment in all countries, whether voiced by the territorial or ethnic groups or by students and intellectuals.

Is this, perhaps, a new federal formula? Unlike the classic formula of the federal process that was aimed at building a union from several autonomous units, the new formula is dominantly concerned with the demand for concessions to the new group interests, which then, endowed with autonomy, responsibility, and dignity, may compose the union on a new basis —or, of course, decompose it. Unlike the delegation of authority in unitary systems, characterized by its revocability, the new territorial decentralization seems to imply quasi-federal guarantees against present or future centralism. As *capitalism* and *socialism* mean today something quite different from what they had meant at the time of Queen Victoria and Karl Marx, so does *federalism;* the term seems to be acquiring a different meaning from what Madison, Bismarck, and Lenin had meant by *federalism.* Perhaps a new word should be coined for the new combination of decentralization and autonomy on the subnational levels with participation on the national level. Some may agree today with the observation made by Alexis de Tocqueville, who, studying the American experiment with constitutional federalism, 170 years ago concluded, "The human understanding more easily invents new things than new words."

SELECTED BIBLIOGRAPHY

This list of suggested readings is divided into two parts. The first part contains titles of comparative studies of federalism, to which a few related books on nationalism are added. General works on comparative federalism are relatively few in number. It may be noted, for instance, that two of the widely used recent readers on comparative politics (Eckstein-Apter and Macridis-Brown) do not contain any single article on the subject of federalism.

The second part contains selected single-country studies. Evidently, each of the hundreds of books dealing with the political systems of the United States, the Soviet Union, India, Switzerland, Germany, Canada, Australia, and other countries that claim to be federal will have some reference to the causes, forms, and effects of the territorial distribution of authority and may be consulted for this reason. Our list suggests the titles deemed directly useful to students preparing studies that compare two or more federal systems.

Comparative Studies of Federalism

Aiyar, S. P. *Federalism and Social Change*. New York: Asia Publishing House, 1961.

Akzin, Benjamin. *States and Nations*. Garden City, N.Y.: Doubleday, Anchor Books, 1966.

Birch, A. H. *Federalism: Finance and Social Legislation in Canada, Australia, and the United States*. New York: Oxford University Press, 1955.

Bowie, Robert T., and Carl J. Friedrich (eds.). *Studies in Federalism*. Boston: Little, Brown, 1954.

Carter, Gwendolen M. (ed.). *National Unity and Regionalism in Eight African States*. Ithaca, N.Y.: Cornell University Press, 1966.

Currie, David P. *Federalism and the New Nations of Africa*. Chicago: University of Chicago Press, 1964.

Curtis, Michael. *Western European Integration*. New York: Harper & Row, 1965.

Earle, Valerie (ed.). *Federalism: Infinite Variety in Theory and Practice.* Itasca, Ill.: F. E. Peacock Publishers, Inc., 1968.

Emerson, Rupert. *From Empire to Nation.* Cambridge, Mass.: Harvard University Press, 1960.

Franck, Thomas (ed.). *Why Federations Fail: An Inquiry into the Requisites for Successful Federalism.* New York: New York University Press, 1968.

Friedrich, Carl J. *Constitutional Government and Democracy: Theory and Practice in Europe and America,* 4th ed. Waltham, Mass.: Blaisdell, 1968.

———. *Trends of Federalism in Theory and Practice.* New York: Praeger, 1968.

Glaser, K., and D. S. Collier. *Western Integration and the Future of Eastern Europe.* Chicago: Regnery, 1964.

Haas, Ernst B. *Consensus Formation in the Council of Europe.* Berkeley, Calif.: University of California Press, 1960.

———. *The Uniting of Europe: Political, Social, and Economic Forces, 1950–1957.* London: Stevens, 1958.

Haines, C. Grove (ed.). *European Integration.* Baltimore: The Johns Hopkins Press, 1957.

Hallstein, Walter. *United Europe: Challenge and Opportunity.* Cambridge, Mass.: Harvard University Press, 1962.

Hay, Peter. *Federalism and Supranational Organizations: Patterns for New Legal Structures.* Urbana, Ill.: University of Illinois Press, 1966.

Hayes, Carlton J. H. *Historical Evolution of Modern Nationalism.* New York: Crowell-Collier-Macmillan, 1937.

Hicks, W. K., *et al. Federalism and Economic Growth in Underdeveloped Countries.* London: G. Allen, 1961.

Hughes, Christopher. *Confederacies.* Leicester: Leicester University Press, 1963.

Institute for Studies in Federalism. *Essays in Federalism.* Claremont, Calif.: Claremont College, 1963.

Kitzinger, Uwe W. *The Politics and Economics of European Integration: Britain, Europe, and the United States.* New York: Praeger, 1963.

Kohn, Hans. *Nationalism: Its Meaning and History.* Princeton, N.J.: Van Nostrand, 1965.

Livingston, William S. *Federalism and Constitutional Change.* New York: Oxford University Press, 1956.

——— (ed.). *Federalism in the Commonwealth.* London: Cassell, 1963.

Macmahon, Arthur W. *Federalism: Mature and Emergent.* New York: Russell and Russell, 1962.

McWhinney, Edward. *Comparative Federalism: States' Rights and National Power.* Toronto: University of Toronto Press, 1962.

————. *Federal Constitution-Making for a Multinational World.* Leyden: Sitjhoff, 1966.

Merkl, Peter H. *Political Continuity and Change.* New York: Harper & Row, 1967.

Miller, J. D. B. *The Commonwealth in the World.* London: Duckworth, 1958.

Morley, Felix. *Freedom and Federalism.* Chicago: Regnery, 1959.

Mumford, Lewis. *The City in History.* New York: Harcourt, 1961.

Robson, William A. *The Development of Local Government.* London: G. Allen, 1948.

———— (ed.) *Great Cities of the World: Their Government, Politics, and Planning.* London: G. Allen, 1954.

Schlesinger, Rudolf. *Federalism in Central and Eastern Europe.* London: Routledge, 1945.

Servan-Schreiber, J. J. *The American Challenge.* New York: Atheneum, 1968.

Snyder, Louis L. *The Imperialism Reader: Documents and Readings on Modern Expansionism.* Princeton, N.J.: Van Nostrand, 1962.

Stokes, William. "The Centralized Federal Republics of Latin America," in Institute for Studies in Federalism (ed.), *Essays in Federalism.* Claremont, Calif.: Claremont College, 1963.

Wheare, K. C. *Federal Government.* New York: Oxford University Press, Galaxy Books, 1964.

————. *The Constitutional Structure of the Commonwealth.* Oxford: Clarendon Press, 1960.

Wildawsky, Aaron (ed.). *American Federalism in Perspective.* Boston: Little, Brown, 1967.

Zolberg, Aristide R. *Creating Political Order: The Party States of West Africa.* Skokie, Ill.: Rand McNally, 1966.

Single-Country Studies

Adams, Thomas W., and Alvin J. Cottrell. *Cyprus between East and West.* Baltimore: The Johns Hopkins Press, 1967.

Ambedkar, B. R. *Pakistan; Or, The Partition of India,* 3d ed. London: Thacker, 1946.

The American Assembly. *The Forty-Eight States,* New York: Columbia University Press, 1955.

Amlund, Curtis A. *Federalism in the Southern Confederacy.* Washington, D.C.: Public Affairs Press, 1966.

Appleby, Paul. *Public Administration in India.* Delhi: Manager of Publication, 1953.

Armstrong, John A. *Ukrainian Nationalism, 1939–1945.* New York: Columbia University Press, 1955.

Aspaturian, Vernon V. *The Union Republics and Soviet Diplomacy.* Geneva: Librairie Droz, 1960.

Awa, Eme O. *Federal Government in Nigeria.* Berkeley, Calif.: University of California Press, 1964.

Awolowo, Obafemi. *Thoughts on the Nigerian Constitution.* Ibadan: Oxford University Press, 1966.

Barghoorn, Frederick C. *Politics in the USSR.* Boston: Little, Brown, 1966.

Bennet, Walter H. *American Theories of Federalism.* University, Ala.: University of Alabama Press, 1966.

Brackman, Arnold. *Southeast Asia's Second Front: The Power Struggle in the Malay Archipelago.* New York: Praeger, 1966.

Brecht, Arnold. *Federalism and Regionalism in Germany.* New York: Oxford University Press, 1945.

Carter Gwendolen M., Thomas G. Karis, and Newell M. Stultz. *South Africa's Transkei: The Politics of Domestic Colonialism.* Evanston, Ill.: Northwestern University Press, 1967.

Codding, George A. *The Federal Government of Switzerland.* Boston: Houghton Mifflin, 1961.

Coleman, James. *Nigeria: Background to Nationalism.* Berkeley, Calif.: University of California Press, 1965.

Crépeau, P. A. *Future of Canadian Federalism.* Toronto: Toronto University Press, 1965.

Despres, Leo A. *Cultural Pluralism and Nationalist Politics in British Guiana.* Skokie, Ill.: Rand McNally, 1967.

Elazar, Daniel J. *American Federalism: A View from the States.* New York: Crowell, 1966.

————, Bruce R. Carroll, Lester E. Levine, and Douglas St. Angelo. *Cooperation and Conflict: A Reader in American Federalism.* Itasca, Ill.: F. E. Peacock Publishers, Inc., 1969.

Ezera, Kalu. *Constitutional Development in Nigeria.* New York: Cambridge University Press, 1960.

Foltz, William J. *From French West Africa to the Mali Federation.* New Haven, Conn.: Yale University Press, 1965.

Friedrich, Carl J. *Puerto Rico—Middle Road to Freedom.* New York: Holt, Rinehart and Winston, Inc. 1959.

Goldwin, Robert A. (ed.). *A Nation of States: Essays on the American Federal System.* Skokie, Ill.: Rand McNally, 1961.

Gopal, Ram. *Indian Muslims: A Political History (1858–1947).* London: Asia Publishing House, 1959.

Graves, W. Brooke. *American Intergovernmental Relations: The*

Origins, Historical Development, and Current State. New York: Scribner, 1964.

Greenwood, Gordon. *The Future of Australian Federalism.* Melbourne: Melbourne University Press, 1946.

Grodzins, Morton. *The American System: A New View of Government in the United States.* Skokie, Ill.: Rand McNally, 1966.

Hanham, H. J. *Scottish Nationalism.* Cambridge, Mass.: Harvard University Press, 1969.

Hanna, Willard. *The Formation of Malaysia: New Factor in World Politics.* New York: American Universities Field Staff, 1964.

―――. *The Separation of Singapore from Malaysia.* New York: American Universities Field Staff, 1965.

―――. *Sequel to Colonialism: The 1957–60 Foundations for Malaysia.* New York: American Universities Field Staff, 1965.

Harrison, Selig S. *India: The Most Dangerous Decades.* Princeton, N.J.: Princeton University Press, 1960.

Hughes, Christopher. *The Federal Constitution of Switzerland.* New York: Oxford University Press, 1954.

Hunter, Sir William W. *The Indian Musalmans.* Calcutta: Comrade Publishers, 1945.

James, Herman G. *The Constitutional System of Brazil.* Washington, D.C.: Carnegie Institution, 1921.

Kahin, George McT. *Nationalism and Revolution in Indonesia.* Ithaca, N.Y.: Cornell University Press, 1952.

Khaliquzzaman, Choudhry. *Pathway to Pakistan.* Lahore: Longmans Pakistan Branch, 1961.

Kolarz, Walter. *The Peoples of the Soviet Far East.* New York: Praeger, 1955.

―――. *Russia and Her Colonies.* New York: Praeger, 1955.

Kyriakides, Stanley. *Cyprus: Constitutionalism and Crisis Government.* Philadelphia: University of Pennsylvania Press, 1969.

Lazer, Harry. *The American Political System in Transition.* New York: Crowell, 1967.

Lowenthal, David. *The West Indies Federation.* New York: Columbia University Press, 1961.

Lower, A. R. M., *et al. Evolving Canadian Federalism.* Durham, N.C.: Duke University Press, 1958.

Menon, V. P. *The Integration of the Indian States.* New York: Crowell-Collier-Macmillan, 1956.

Miller, J. D. B. *Australian Government and Politics.* London: Duckworth, 1954.

Moon, Sir Penderel. *Divide and Quit.* London: Chatto and Windus, 1961.

Mordecai, Sir John. *Federation of the West Indies.* Evanston, Ill.: Northwestern University Press, 1969.

Osborne, Milton. *Singapore and Malaysia.* Ithaca, N.Y.: Cornell University Data Paper No. 53, 1964.

Palmer, Norman D. *The Indian Political System.* Boston: Houghton Mifflin, 1961.

Pye, Lucian W. *Politics, Personality, and Nation Building: Burma's Search for Identity.* New Haven, Conn.: Yale University Press, 1962.

Pylee, M. V. *Constitutional Government in India.* Bombay: Asia Publishing House, 1961.

Rothberg, Robert I. *The Rise of Nationalism in Central Africa: The Making of Malawi and Zambia, 1873–1964.* Cambridge, Mass.: Harvard University Press, 1965

Rowe, L. S. *The Federal System of the Argentine Republic.* Washington, D.C.: Carnegie Institution, 1921.

Schlesinger, Rudolf (ed.). *The Nationalities Problem and Soviet Administration: Selected Readings on the Development of Soviet Nationalities Policies.* London: Routledge, 1956.

Sen, Sachin. *The Birth of Pakistan.* Calcutta: General Printers and Publishers, 1955.

Shiller, Arthur A. *The Formation of Federal Indonesia.* The Hague: Van Hoeve, 1955.

Sklar, Richard. *Nigerian Political Parties.* Princeton, N.J.: Princeton University Press, 1967.

Stolberg, Winston V. *The Federal Convention and the Formation of the Union of the American States.* New York: Liberal Arts Press, 1958.

Tilman, Robert O., and Taylor Cole (eds.). *The Nigerian Political Scene.* Durham, N.C.: Duke University Press, 1962.

Trager, Frank N. *Building a Welfare State in Burma.* New York: Institute of Pacific Relations, 1958.

Trudeau, Pierre Eliott. *Federalism and the French Canadians.* New York: St. Martin's, 1968.

Van Doren, Carl. *The Great Rehearsal.* New York: Viking, 1948.

Warner, Sam Bass (ed.). *Planning for a Nation of Cities.* Cambridge, Mass.: The M.I.T. Press, 1966.

Weinberg, S. *An Outline of the Constitutional Law of the Federation of Rhodesia and Nyasaland.* Salisbury, Rhodesia: Federal Government, 1959.

Weiner, Myron. *Party Politics in India: The Development of a Multi-Party System.* Princeton, N.J.: Princeton University Press, 1957.

Welensky, Sir Ronald. *4000 Days.* London: Collins, 1964.

Wells, Roger H. *German Cities*. Princeton, N.J.: Princeton University Press, 1932.

—————. *The States in West German Federalism*. New York: Bookman Associates, 1961.

Wheeler, Geoffrey. *Racial Problems in Soviet Muslim Asia*. New York: Oxford University Press, 1960.

INDEX